GCSE Sociology:
Social Life

Dave Longmate and Grahame Coates

Hodder & Stoughton

A MEMBER OF THE HODDER HEADLINE GROUP

Every effort has been made to trace copyright holders of material reproduced
in this book. Any rights omitted from the acknowledgements here or in the text
will be added for subsequent printings following notice to the publisher.

For the reproduction of copyright materials, the publisher would like to thank the following.

Blackwell Publishers for reproduction of Thinking Sociologically by (1990) Zagmunt Baumen; the University of
Edinburgh for extracts from CES Briefing No. 19 by Linda Croxford; The Independent Newspaper for the articles
'Parents are no longer a family's great dictator', 31st July 2000, by Cherry Norton, 'Register to vote and naff up your
ballots' by Clare Garner, 17th February 1997, and 'Nearly 20 country pubs are being forced out of business every
month' by Chris Grey, 31st July 2001; the Big Issue in the North article on page 311; Sage Publications for The
Exclusive Society by J. Young, Pelgrove Publishers for Gender and Power in the Workplace by Harriet Bradley; Eugenie
Bryan for permission to reproduce her article 'With so many of Britain's Older Jamaicans . . .' from The Guardian on
page 33.

Thanks to Polly for typing; and to Sue, Kate, Tom, Polly and Rosie for help and encouragement and allowing me the
time. Thanks to Paul Lawrence and Jen Welbourn for reading sections of the manuscript and offering invaluable
comments.

Cover Illustration by Stewart Larkin

Photographs appear courtesy of Photofusion, p47; The Press Association, p127, p209; Corbis, p127; Hulton Getty,
p236; and Hodder and Stoughton.

Orders: please contact Bookpoint Ltd, 130 Milton Park, Abingdon, Oxon OX14 4SB.
Telephone (44) 10235 400454, Fax: (44) 01235 400454. Lines are open from 9.00–6.00, Monday to Saturday, with a
24 hour message answering service. E-mail address: orders@bookpoint.co.uk

British Library cataloguing in Publication Data
A catalogue record for this title is available from The British Library

ISBN 0 340 781513

Typeset by Wyvern 21 Ltd, Bristol
Printed in Great Britain for Hodder & Stoughton Educational, a division of Hodder
Headline PLC, 338 Euston Road, London NW1 3BH by Bath Press Ltd.

Contents

What is Sociology?

Being Connected

This book is about sociology. It is a basic introductory book and so you would expect to find some sort of definition at the start. This is not as easy as it seems. If you look in most dictionaries or textbooks you will find a definition something like this:

Sociology is the study of the structure and functioning of human society. (Chambers)

or

Sociology is the science of the development and nature and laws of human society. (Concise Oxford Dictionary).

While these definitions are true they don't really tell us very much. In fact it is quite difficult to give a definition of sociology that tells you what the subject is and what it is that sociologists do in a sentence or two. So the aim of this part of the book is to give you an idea of the way that sociologists think, and what they think about, when they are being sociologists. This particular way of thinking has been called **the sociological imagination**, and as well as explaining what this means this chapter will give you a chance to develop your own sociological imagination.

Here is a question for you to think about:

How many people are required for you to be able to read this book?

Take five minutes and write a list. In case you're thinking that it won't take long to write your name, and possibly ours, here are some extra questions to get you going.

- Where did you get the book?
- Where are you reading it?
- Who taught you to read?
- Is there a light?

Ok, so back to your list. When you have finished, carry on with the chapter.

Reading is often something we do on our own. We don't usually think of it as a social activity. But when you start to think about how many people are required in order for you to sit and read a book the list is potentially endless. Here are some of the people you might have considered:

- Us, the authors
- Your teachers
- The publishers

- The printers
- The shop or library that supplied the book
- The people who work for the electricity company
- The people who made the chair you are sitting in

So far so good, but we can make a list a bit more complicated. For example, if you are reading this in a classroom, and the book has been provided by your school or college, then you are dependent on the actions and decisions of a wide variety of other individuals. These might include:

- The teacher who chose this book for your course
- The staff who decided that it was all right to spend money on sociology books
- The people who provided the cash by paying taxes or course fees

So in the relatively simple act of reading a book you are connected to, in fact dependent on, many other individuals and groups. Your act of reading can be seen as depending on the actions and decisions of many people. Your teacher might have chosen a different textbook, your school or college might have been short of money for new books, our publishers might have chosen not to publish this particular textbook, sociology might not have been on your curriculum.

By now you are possibly beginning to get the idea of what sociology is about. But before we go any further try two more exercises.

Firstly, how many people are you dependent on when you turn on the light?

Secondly, how many people do you depend on in order to make your daily journey to school or college?

In each case try to include people from other countries and also from the past in your lists.

From these exercises you will have seen how even in the most simple activities that we all take for granted we are caught up in networks of other people. These networks are made up of individuals who depend upon each other in various ways. Just as you depend on your teacher for a lesson to take place so your teacher needs students. Likewise for the lesson to take place both you and your teacher require the presence of many others in the present and in the past – like your teacher's teachers, the people who built the school or college, or those who wrote the syllabus. It is the way we are all interconnected that forms part of the subject matter of sociology.

When we use our sociological imaginations we can look at people around us in such a way as to see the interconnections and how society is made up of these kinds of interconnection. But doing sociology is not just about examining the way we are all dependent on each other in various ways.

Belonging to groups

Sociology is also about how we are all members of different social groups, and how belonging to one group or another can affect our lives in different ways. For example being a woman in a society dominated by men can limit our chances of getting to the top of most organisations, while being a man can make this easier. This may be because girls are brought up to see their futures in different ways to boys, although this may be changing as you will see, for example, in the chapter on education. It may also be possible that people act differently towards us according to whether or not we are male or female. So people in positions of authority in large organisations may look at a female applicant for a job and see someone who is likely to take time off to have children or look after her children and therefore be less likely to appoint her than a man.

Belonging to a social group then can affect how we see ourselves and how other people see us and both of these can affect how our life works out.

All of us belong to some very large groups. The most important ones, and the ones that will appear in every chapter of this book in some form or another, are based on:

- **GENDER**
- **CLASS**
- **ETHNICITY**
- **AGE**

For example the authors of this book (and many others in your school or college library) are middle-aged, middle class, white males. Both of us have enjoyed advantages in our society because of our membership of these groups, and also perhaps some disadvantages.

Try to think of at least one way in which

a) Being male
b) Being white
c) Being middle class
d) Being middle-aged

might give us an advantage over someone who is not a member of one of those groups. You have had one example above so try to think of another way in which men have an advantage over women in society.

When you have done that try to think of a situation in which being a middle-aged, middle class white male might be a positive disadvantage.

Here are just a few examples you might have thought of:

a) Being male can give us an advantage if we want to train as a plumber. Many people, including some women, do not see this as an appropriate job for a woman.
b) Being white means that we are much less likely to suffer racist abuse than if we are Asian or Afro-Caribbean.
c) Being middle class means that we are more likely to have a job that offers us career opportunities than someone who is working class.
d) Being middle-aged means that quite often people will take our opinions more seriously than those of teenagers or the very old.

Of course there are situations where these characteristics are a disadvantage. For instance if I wanted to give up my job to stay at home and do the housework I might find that some people take a dim view of my decision and let me know about it.

Being a member of a particular group can affect our lives in many different ways because of how we see ourselves, and how others see us. We might have a greater chance of becoming rich or poor; we might have more chances of living to a ripe old age or of dying fairly young; we might have a better chance of going to university or more chance of leaving school at 16 with no qualifications; we might have a high chance of being employed or unemployed; we might have more chance of bringing up children alone; we might have more chance of being stopped and searched by the police or of obtaining an expensive lawyer to fight our case.

For sociologists some of the most important groups we might belong to are those we have already mentioned – those based on Gender, Class, Age, Ethnicity. Throughout the rest of the book we will be looking at a variety of ways in which memberships of these particular groups can affect how we see ourselves and how other people treat us and what the consequences are for us and for others.

But these are not the only groups we might belong to: religion might have important consequences for our lives living in Northern Ireland; being a criminal can obviously affect us, as can being a single parent or an immigrant or a pupil at a private school. Some of these groups might be ones we have actively chosen to belong to, some might be groups that other people put us into. We could decide to join a group of eco-warriors but because we do we might find that people treat us as some sort of deviant. We may see ourselves as honest upstanding citizens but find that some people treat us differently to others because of the part of town we live in.

Thinking like a sociologist

If we want to do sociology we have to learn to think like a sociologist. Thinking like a sociologist has two important parts:

First, it involves seeing the various ways in which we are all dependent to a greater or lesser extent on other people. If what others do changes what we do might have to change. For example a textile worker in Huddersfield might have to retrain and find another job if she is made redundant because clothes are being produced more cheaply abroad, and then imported to the UK.

Secondly we are all members of a variety of social groups. Our membership of these groups can affect not only how we see ourselves but also how other people see us and treat us. Both of these factors can affect the way in which our lives turn out. If our textile worker above is an Asian woman born in Britain she may find she has to cope with different expectations as to what is an appropriate role for a woman in 21st–century Britain from various individuals or groups in her local community.

Social structure

One of the remarkable things about human societies is that they look pretty much the same today as they did yesterday. The same sorts of patterns repeat themselves. For example in the UK schools, colleges and universities teach young people and adults; hospitals treat the sick; cinemas, clubs, pubs, and theatres provide entertainment; TV, radio and newspapers inform and entertain; factories produce all manner of goods and shops of all sizes put these goods on sale. Within all these organisations people carry out their duties. Bosses give out instructions and workers carry out their tasks; teachers and lecturers set work and their students dutifully carry it out (well maybe not, but more of that later in the book); bands, DJs and other entertainers rehearse, and the audience pays to see them perform. This kind of regularity extends to other areas of society too. People meet, fall in love, maybe get married, move in together and maybe bring up children. Some people can't find work and have to live on benefits. Young people may well rebel against the wishes of their parents.

In short anyone looking at society would see regular patterns of human conduct across whole areas of social life. There is a sort of orderliness in society. You can think of society as being a bit like a building: in this room the children are brought up, in that room they learn things, in another room people work, in another they enjoy some recreation, in yet another they are looked after if they are ill and so on. Of course society isn't a building, this is only a way of thinking about the fact that what we do in society has a pattern to it and that each part of society is related in some way to all the other parts. In other words most of the time social life is pretty orderly. The regular patterns of social life – going to school, going to work, catching the bus, going out with our friends – don't usually break down unless there is some sort of enormous change, like that caused by a natural disaster or a social upheaval like a revolution.

The idea of social structure is not just important because it emphasises the way in which societies are orderly. This idea can also help us to think about how our lives are affected by whereabouts in society we find ourselves, or our position in the social structure. According to where we are in the social structure some things will be made easier, some things more difficult for us. For example you may have seen those troupes of acrobats who construct human pyramids. While the person at the top is free to perform various gymnastic feats and to dazzle us with their skill, the individuals at the bottom do not have the same amount of freedom, they have to concentrate on keeping the structure stable and so their freedom of movement is quite limited. (And of course they wouldn't get paid if they started doing their own thing.)

Figure 1 The structure of Russian society in 1900.

Look at the picture on page 5 which shows the various layers of Russian society in 1900. What kind of point about the relative power and freedom of those at the top and the bottom of society was the author making?

Whatever your diagram looks like it is quite likely that the people you've put at the top have more of something you think is important, like money, power, or freedom, and those at the bottom have less of it or are stuck in situations they can't do much about like living on low pay or low pensions, having to be told what to do, or having to deal with some sort of unfair treatment like racism or sexism. If we go back to our idea of society as a building then you can see how those at the top have a better view and can see further than those at the bottom. Society probably seems a better place to be to those with a pleasant view than to those at the bottom, seeing others go by them on their way to the top floor and watching the litter and the drunks roll around the street.

Figure 2 Our society can be thought of as a building.

So the idea of **social structure** is an important one in sociology. It is a **way of thinking** about societies that helps us to see how societies are orderly places, how our position in society affects what we can and cannot do. It even helps us to see how our position in society can affect how we think about the world around us. (Remember how the world looks different to someone in a penthouse than to someone living in the basement of the same building.) The idea of social structure is useful in another way too. This is because it helps us to think about how what we do is governed by social rules, and how these rules make an orderly society possible. The rules that govern our actions vary from situation to situation. To understand this idea we'll have to look at the idea of social roles.

Roles

EXERCISE

Here are a number of situations for you to think about, and then a number of questions for you to answer.

a) You are at home watching TV with your parents.

b) You are out for the night with a group of friends.

c) You are at work (you have a Saturday job in a shoe shop).

Questions

i) Do you behave in the same way in situations (a) (b) and (c)?

ii) Do you use the same language in (a) (b) and (c)?

iii) In situation (c) do you speak to your work colleagues in the same way as you speak to customers? Do you speak to your boss in the same way you speak to your colleagues?

Chances are that the answer for most readers is no to all the questions. The next question of course is why? Why do we change how we act according to who we are with and where we are? Think about the situations outlined above and see if you can come up with an answer.

You've probably answered the question with phrases like 'you act according to who you're with', 'you can relax more with your friends,' and 'they expect you to act in a certain way.' It is this last answer that is the key to understanding the sociological concept of roles.

A **social role** refers to the expected patterns of behaviour associated with a position in society.

For example, in situation (c) above the customers in the shoe shop would expect you to be polite, serve them efficiently and to know what you are doing, whereas your colleagues wouldn't expect you to call them 'sir' or 'madam', they wouldn't expect you to approach them and ask if you could help in any way each time they came into the shop, nor would they expect a farewell like 'have a nice day' or 'missing you already' on leaving.

For sociologists we all play social roles almost all the time. Roles are like parts in a play or film – we act out our part according to the rules of the situation. So we know what is expected of us as pupil or teacher, as daughter or son, as bank manager or customer, as interviewer or candidate for a job. Most of the time we do this automatically, we slip into the role without thinking. If you've been out with your friends joking or swearing, you find it quite easy to adapt your behaviour when you go home – you moderate your language, tell different jokes and discuss the physical attitudes of celebrities on TV in a different way. (Of course if you don't you can expect some sort of retribution, but that process and how we learn the rules is the subject of the next section on culture and socialisation.)

Roles and role conflict

We all have a number of roles to play in society and much of the time these roles might complement each other. As a father I might feel that it is expected of me to provide for my family. Getting and keeping a job that provides me with an income therefore fits quite well with my role as father. However on occasions we can find ourselves in situations where the expectations of one role conflict with another. A working mother may experience guilt at having to leave her children with a childminder in order to go out to work. A police officer called out to a disturbance in the street might find that it is her younger brother who is the cause of the trouble. Does she act in accordance with her role as police officer and arrest him or according to her role as elder sister? Role conflict refers to a situation where the demands or expectations of one role clash with those of another.

Role models

Sociologists use the term role model to describe someone who we look up to and whose behaviour or actions we might copy. In our early years our parent(s) might be our role model(s). We model our behaviour on them and we want to be like them. Later in life we might adopt other role models. These might be people we see a lot in the mass media: pop stars, actors, TV personalities, or sports stars for example. Sometimes our role models can find their own behaviour criticised because they are in the limelight and in a position to influence our behaviour and attitude and they are behaving in an unacceptable fashion.

Think about who your role models are, or who they have been in the past. Have they always acted in socially acceptable ways?

Can you think of individuals whose actions have been criticised because they are role models?

Roles and structure

One way of thinking about society is to see it as having a social structure that is made up of different institutions that are themselves made up of collections of social roles.

The word '**institutions**' when used by sociologists means those parts of society which seem to be permanent, like the family, the education system, work or religion. For some people institutions are the main parts of the social structure. Each institution is made up of a collection of roles with a set of expected behaviours for each. Schools are obviously an important part of the institution 'education' in Britain. Within each school you will probably find the following roles:

- Head Teacher
- Deputy Head
- Head of Department of Humanities
- Teacher in Charge of Sociology
- Class Teacher
- Pupil
- Cook
- Cleaner

Culture and socialisation – How we learn to be us

Up to now we have looked at society as a whole. We've seen that an easy way of looking at society is to see it as a structure of institutions that are made up of roles which carry with them certain expectations as to how we should act. This next section is concerned with the ways in which we learn what kinds of behaviour are appropriate for who we are. First of all there are some terms that you will need to know.

When sociologists talk about the **culture** of a society they mean the whole way of life of that society. (This is different from the way that we may use the term in everyday life to refer to particular kinds of cultural music or literature, say the paintings of Picasso, the music of Bach and the writings of Thomas Hardy. In sociology the definition of culture is much broader than that.) For sociologists culture is made up of **Norms** and **Values** as well as the different kinds of knowledge that people have, the skills they possess and the kinds of material goods that exist in society.

Norms are the rules governing everyday behaviour. They are the expectations about how we should act, like eating with a knife and fork, getting along with our colleagues at work, or obeying the laws of the land.

Values in sociology refer to the general ideas about what is good and bad or right or wrong. In our society, for example, we place a high value on individualism, competition and material goods. These are seen as being good things. We are encouraged to 'stand on our own two feet', to 'make the most of ourselves' in competition with others. We will know when we've made it because we'll have the big house and the big car.

Socialisation: Sociologists use this term to refer to the process by which we learn the rules of our culture.

Socialisation is an important idea (or concept) in sociology because it refers to the way in which we learn how to be a fully fledged member of the society that we are born into. For sociologists when we are born we do not know any of the rules of society, **we have to learn them**. How we turn out to be depends on the society in which we are born. Had I been born in China I would have grown up speaking a different language, eating different food with different implements and probably thinking differently as well. Unlike animals, human behaviour, at least as far as sociologists are concerned, is not based on instinct – it is learned.

As far as we know the worker bees in a hive do not have to learn their patterns of behaviour, these are determined. If you like, the worker bees grow up pre-programmed to behave in certain ways. It is not like that for people, according to sociologists. We have to learn how to behave. We might have certain biological drives, like the need for warmth and shelter, for food, or for reproduction, but how we meet those drives is not determined by our genes, but by the rules of the society in which we live.

What evidence is there for the sociological point of view? There are many examples of children who have received very little socialisation at all. Such children are unable to take part in society in any sort of meaningful way, at least not until they have been socialised to some degree. These extreme examples of neglect show us how important socialisation is for us to develop as fully rounded human beings able to take our place in society. Look at the extract below which illustrates this point:

9

In 1938 a girl of more than five years of age was found locked up in a room on a lonely farm in America. She had been incarcerated in this room from babyhood because she was illegitimate. When she was finally discovered and removed from the room she could not walk or talk and was in very poor physical shape. After two years in an institution 'Anna' could at least walk, feed herself, and understand simple commands, but still she did not speak. She was taken to a private home for retarded children where she made much more progress. By 1941 'Anna' had acquired firm habits of personal cleanliness and her feeding habits were normal, except that she only used a spoon. The most striking thing of all was that she had finally begun to speak and could construct a few complete sentences. 'Anna' died in August 1942.

The absence of adequate social relationships in Anna's early life had resulted in a creature that was hardly recognisable as a human being.

Adapted from Human Societies, Geoffrey Hurd (1973) Routledge and Kegan Paul

We have to be socialised so that we can act in society. We need to learn the rules of our culture so that we can interact with others in a meaningful way. How does this happen? Sometimes we are simply taught like, for example, the way our parent(s) might teach us how to eat with a knife and fork and to say please and thank you. Sometimes the process is more indirect. To understand this we need to understand something about the process of social control.

Social control refers to the various ways in which individuals and groups persuade others to conform to their rules.

Think about when you were quite young. How did your parent(s) or other adults get you to behave in the way they thought was right?

You've probably thought of times when you were grounded for doing something wrong. Maybe you had your pocket money stopped or were sent to your room. Perhaps you were smacked. These are all forms of social control. By imposing negative sanctions, like punishments, our parents let us know when we had broken the rules. If we think more about this process, though, we can probably remember times when we were rewarded for doing something right. We may have been praised for doing well at school, or allowed to stay up late to see something on TV if we behaved ourselves, or maybe bought a present for passing exams. Sanctions can be positive as well as negative. Social control is not just about being punished for doing wrong but it is also about being rewarded for appropriate behaviour.

However the process of social control can be even more indirect than this. Popularity amongst our friends or work mates can be seen as a form of social control, just as unpopularity can. If we are not popular we may change how we act in order to fit in better, that is to say to conform to the rules of a particular group. Popularity can be seen as a positive sanction, unpopularity as a negative sanction. Similarly the image of men and women on TV and in magazines and newspapers can be seen as a form of social control. If we see ourselves reflected in these images we probably feel ok, if we don't see ourselves reflected in the mass media we may want to change the way we look in order to fit in. We may want to lose weight or become fitter or change the clothes we wear, for example. Role models are important in this aspect of socialisation. If we look up at someone we see on TV we may model our behaviour, our looks or our attitude on what they do, how they look or what they think.

Sociologists refer to the individuals or groups who try to get us to conform to their rules as **Agents of Social Control**. Some people in society have jobs that are based upon the idea of making sure that we conform to a particular set of norms. For example it is the role of the police force, the courts, the prison service and occasionally the armed forces to get us to conform to the laws of the land or to enforce sanctions if we don't. When the rules are written down, as is the case with the laws of a country, and the sanctions for breaking a rule are also written down, we can describe this as formal social control. The police, therefore, are formal agents of social control.

Much of the time though social control happens in a much more informal fashion. Unless we live in a very unusual household the rules of family life are not written down, and the sanctions for breaking them can vary quite a lot. Sociologists refer to the kind of social control that takes place within the family as **Informal Social Control** and to the family as an informal agent of social control.

Socialisation is a process which goes on throughout our lives. We are socialised by our families, when we get to school by our teachers and by our friends. When we get a job we are socialised not only by our work mates but we are also subject to the rules of the organisation we work for. We are socialised when we watch TV or read a magazine or listen to a CD. If we belong to a religious organisation we are also socialised by the beliefs of that organisation which tell us about right and wrong, good and bad.

Think about the following questions:

i) At work how might we be subject to formal social control?

ii) At school when are we subject to informal social control and when is it informal?

iii) If we are a member of an organised religion, are we subject to formal or informal social control?

At work there are usually formal rules about timekeeping, maybe there is a dress code, and maybe there is a correct way to address our customers, for example. If we break these rules we are subject to formal social control – we may lose an hour's pay or even get the sack. At school we are subject to formal sanctions if we break the school rules – detention, suspension or even expulsion, but at the same time we are subject to the informal control of our peers. If we are a practising Catholic, for example, we could see the act of confession as an example of formal social control and the approval or disapproval of the fellow members of our congregation as informal.

Sociologists refer to those who break the norms of society or of a particular group as deviants. A deviant is someone who breaks the norms of his or her group. You can read more about deviance and social control in Chapter 4.

From what we have said so far it might well appear that we are brainwashed or pre-programmed by society. The emphasis on the way in which we are socialised into the norms and values of society might make us think that we have little or no choice about what we do. But if we think about this for a moment we know that this is not the case. We may be like our parents or our sisters and brothers, but we are not exactly the same as them. Some of this may be because we are different biologically or psychologically, but we are different sociologically too. All of our socialisation is not the same. We have different groups of friends, we maybe go to different schools or colleges, we watch different things on TV, we perhaps take more notice of particular relatives. In other words we may be exposed to different sets of norms and values than other members of our family during our socialisation.

In the same way we are not necessarily all socialised into a single culture. While there may be certain elements of British culture that are the same, in British society there are also a number of **subcultures**. A subculture is a smaller set of norms and values within a large culture. So in our society there are different subcultures associated with different ethnic groups, or different regions, or different classes, for example. There are also different subcultures associated with groups of young people like Goths or Punks.

While we grow up we are exposed to a variety of social influences. As well as this socialisation is not just something that happens to us, it is also something that we are doing to others.

Think about the ways in which you have influenced your parent(s) since you were born. How do young people socialise their parents?

Socialisation then is not a one-way process. While we are being socialised we are socialising others. As human beings we can also make up our own minds about the world around us. We can decide we like what we see or we may not like it and do something to change some aspect of the social world. This could be something fairly small like not liking the kind of music they play at our local club and persuading the owners to put on something that we do like, or it could be on a much larger scale like taking part in road protests or demonstrations to have Third World debt removed.

The real significance of the idea of socialisation for sociologists is that we learn to be how we are, and so it follows that we can learn to be different. In other words societies do not have to be the way that they are. Things can be different.

We said earlier in this chapter that one of the remarkable things about societies is that they stay much the same in some important ways. Strangely enough the other remarkable thing about societies is that they change. 100 years ago women did not have the vote, there were no Goths

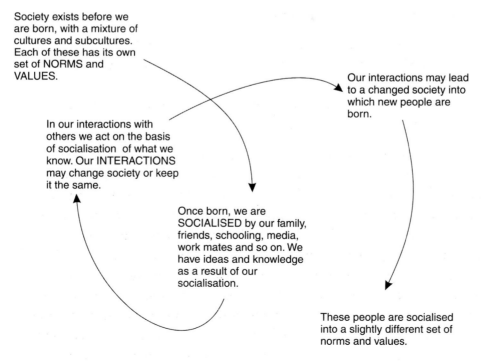

Society exists before we are born, with a mixture of cultures and subcultures. Each of these has its own set of NORMS and VALUES.

In our interactions with others we act on the basis of socialisation of what we know. Our INTERACTIONS may change society or keep it the same.

Once born, we are SOCIALISED by our family, friends, schooling, media, work mates and so on. We have ideas and knowledge as a result of our socialisation.

Our interactions may lead to a changed society into which new people are born.

These people are socialised into a slightly different set of norms and values.

Figure 3 The process of socialisation.

or Punks, and no one knew what the Internet was. If we were just puppets controlled by society this kind of change would not be possible. Society stays the same if we behave in exactly the same way as the generation before us. If we don't then we create a slightly different society, or even a very different society. We are born into a society and into a particular culture that exists before us. But in our interactions with others we can change the society into which we are born, perhaps a little, perhaps a lot. Perhaps the best way to think about the relationship between society and ourselves is as shown in the diagram on page 12.

Culture, socialisation and identity

Who am I? This is a question that we might ask ourselves from time to time. Think back to our discussion of roles earlier: which is the real me? The person out with my mates? The daughter or son? The sociology student? The shop assistant? For sociologists the idea of identity has become important for a number of reasons.

First of all, the way I think of myself can affect how I act in society. For example if I see myself as a keen student of sociology, as a budding sociologist, this will affect my attitude to the subject, to my homework, course work and exams. If I see myself first and foremost as an athlete, I may make sacrifices in order to achieve some success in athletics.

However, my identity is not simply determined by how I think of myself. I may see myself as a keen student but my teachers may have other ideas. They may see me as someone who asks awkward questions just for the sake of it, and I may find myself being treated not as a keen student, but as something of a nuisance. I may well begin to find this identity quite appealing and live up to it. I may become a nuisance, and revel in this identity. (See Chapter 3 for a discussion of the consequences of labeling in education).

We could say that our identity has two important parts:

- Those that we choose ourselves – e.g. we may decide that we are a Goth or Punk and dress and act accordingly, listening to the music, reading the literature and mixing with fellow Goths or Punks.
- Those that are chosen for us – e.g. if I live in the 'wrong part of town' I may find that people treat me differently because of where I live.

The idea of identity is quite a complex one in sociology. In this chapter, and throughout the rest of the book, we refer to four variables many times – Class, Gender, Age, Ethnicity. These too can be, and often are, significant aspects of our identity. For example, think of a young woman growing up on a council estate in the North East of England with a young child and no partner. How is she likely to see herself, and how will others see her? If she sees herself first and foremost as a working class person this may affect her views on politics; if she sees herself first and foremost as a woman, this may also have consequences for her sense of identity – she may find herself drawn more to women's groups than working class groups. If she happens to be Afro-Caribbean she may find that this is the most important aspect of her identity. At different times it may be all, or any one of these. Other people will have different expectations of her based on what they see first – a working class person, a woman (who is also a single parent), a black woman, a young woman.

So our identity is a complicated issue. What is more, ideas about identity are not limited to the four variables we have mentioned. We can also see ourselves, and be seen by others, in terms of our sexuality e.g. whether we are gay or straight. We may be seen as 'normal' or as a 'deviant', we may see ourselves as part of a social movement or as a 'clubber' or a 'raver.'

The last important point about identity for sociologists is that our identities come about in social interaction. Just as we can pick up ideas about how other people see us from the way they react to us, so we can use our knowledge of society and its rules to construct an identity. For example if we go to an interview for a job that we particularly want we know how we should act, so we can 'put on' the identity of a young and dynamic employee.

- What is your identity? Who are you?
- What aspects of your identity have you chosen?
- What aspects have been chosen for you?

Throughout the rest of this book the subject of identity will appear in different ways.

Doing sociology

So far we've looked at how to think like a sociologist and at some of the terms and ideas that we might use when doing that. This next section is about what sociologists do when they are doing sociology.

Describing, defining, and measuring

Part of doing sociology is simply about describing society or certain aspects of a society. We may be interested in knowing how well girls and boys are doing at school since the National Curriculum was introduced in 1988. One way of doing that is to find out how many 16-year-old boys got five GCSEs at grade A–C and how many 16-year-old girls got the same. This gives us a basic description of the levels of education amongst 16year olds. What we are doing here, really, is measuring the educational success rates of 16-year-old boys and girls – how much success do boys have, how much success do girls have?

If we wanted to describe the poverty levels in the UK today we would have to do basically the same thing. We would need to find out how many people live in the UK so that we could say what proportion of the population are living in poverty. This would give us a measure of poverty. However before we could say how many people were living in poverty, we would have to define it. (Just as in the example above we actually defined educational success as having five GCSEs at grade C or above.)

Part of doing sociology, and a very important part, is this business of defining what we are talking about. To measure poverty, to say how many people are poor, we have to say what we mean by that, we have to have some way of saying this person is poor, that person isn't. As you will see in the chapter on poverty this is not necessarily an easy task. Many of the disagreements in sociology come from exactly this problem of defining what we are talking about so that we can measure it.

Try this:

Define what you mean by:

➡ JOB SATISFACTION
➡ WORKING CLASS
➡ POVERTY

Now compare your definition with someone else's. Do you agree? Does everyone in the class agree?

Coming up with definitions is a tricky business. Not all sociologists will define class or poverty or job satisfaction in the same way (as you will see throughout the rest of the book). How much poverty we find, for example, may well be the result of how we define it.

The important point for the moment is that if sociologists want to be able to describe society this will involve measuring some aspects of society. To measure something we have to define it.

Explanations, theories and evidence

Sociology wouldn't be very interesting and it wouldn't tell us very much if it just stopped at description. What we usually want to know is '**Why**'? Why are things the way they are? Why are girls doing slightly better than boys at GCSE and A Level? Why are there poor people? Why do men on average still get paid more than women?

What sociology also offers us is a range of explanations for questions like those above. Sociologists won't just describe the way that society is, they will try to explain why it is that way. In order to do this they will come up with theories.

The best way to think about a theory is that it is a story that tries to explain something. For example, we could explain why some boys aren't doing as well in education in terms of the disappearance of many of the jobs that men used to do, like mining or shipbuilding, and the lack of new ones to take their place. Because there aren't any jobs that boys see as 'men's jobs', they don't try to get qualifications at school. That would be an example of a simple theory (a simple story) to explain the achievement rates of some boys in education.

However, having a theory isn't enough. We want to know whether it is right or wrong. Sociologists not only come up with theories but they will also gather evidence to find out whether their theories are right or wrong. We might carry out an investigation on a group of boys to find out if the lack of traditional male jobs actually affects the way that they think about school and qualifications. The evidence we get might suggest that it isn't because of the change in jobs available but that for teenage boys it is particularly important to be seen as 'cool' and 'macho' and so to impress their mates at school they mess about. This kind of evidence would not support our theory but might make us change our original ideas and think of a new theory.

An important aspect of doing sociology then is to:

➡ gather evidence
➡ test theories which explain aspects of social life.

Doing research, gathering evidence or collecting data

How do sociologists gather the evidence to test out their ideas about how society works?

What follows is a general introduction to sociological research methods. You will find more detail throughout the rest of the book, but particularly in the coursework interlude.

There are basically two ways in which sociologists can gather evidence or collect data:

1   They can collect the data themselves. Data collected by sociologists is called **primary data**.
2   They can use data that has already been collected by someone else. This kind of data is called **secondary data**.

When sociologists collect their own data they generally use one or both of the following methods:

- **Surveys**
- **Observation**

There are other ways of obtaining information about society which will be dealt with else, where in the book but when it comes to collecting their own data sociologists have two main methods:

i)   They can ask people questions and record their answers.
ii)   They can observe what people do and record their observations.

You have probably come across the first way of collecting data – surveys.

To many of us the sociologist is someone who, armed with a questionnaire, spends their time conducting surveys and asking questions. It is perfectly sensible that we should have this idea about how sociologists collect their data. After all, people can speak and if you want to know someone's views on politics or how many GCSEs they have or how many times they have been married, the simplest and quickest way to find out is to ask them.

Asking questions can be done in a number of ways. We can write some questions out on a sheet of paper with some answer boxes for our respondents to tick (these are called closed questions) and then let our respondents fill in the form for us. This way we can have a large number of people filling in our questionnaire at the same time. This makes this way of collecting information quick and easy for us. Using this kind of **questionnaire** also means that we can post them out to people all around the country or all around the world if we want to. We could even put the questionnaire on the Internet.

We may, however, want to be present when our respondents give their answers. In other words we want to **interview** them rather than have them fill in a questionnaire. There are various reasons why we might want to do this. First we might want to be able to make sure that they understand the questions that we are asking, and we can only really do this face to face. Second we might want to ask open ended questions where we have not provided a set of boxes to be ticked. This could be so that we get more chance to find out how our respondents actually think about an issue. For example if we want to find out about the effects of unemployment on individuals, we might obtain more detailed information if we ask questions like 'How did losing your job affect your family life?' and letting our respondents answer how they want to rather than providing a set of possible set of answers for them. By asking questions in this way we might obtain answers that we had not thought of, and we can also follow up our respondents answers with more questions. In this way we can really find out how the person thinks. Of course if we are present at the interview we can also be sure that the person answering the questions is the right person. There is always a risk with questionnaires that someone else fills the form in. Not only that, when we are interviewing we can also get a better idea if people are telling the truth because we can see them and their reactions to our questions. We can also see their surroundings and how they act with others which can also give us more detail for our research.

However, there may be situations where we feel that asking questions is not appropriate. This may be because we feel that people might not give us honest answers to our questions. It may be because we don't actually know what questions we should ask. It may also be because we would rather see and hear what people actually do and say rather than ask them questions. In these situations we might prefer to observe.

Sociologists use **observation** in a variety of ways. First we can observe in order to count. For example we might want to find out if boys misbehave in class more than girls do. To do this we could draw up a chart with a list of the various forms of naughtiness we think might happen and then tick the appropriate boxes as we see misbehaviour by boys or girls.

More often though sociologists do not use observation for counting, but for finding out about a particular way of life, or some aspect of social life in great detail. Sociologists tend to use observation to find out how life is lived. Observing a group of people over a long period of time can give us a great deal of insight into their way of life. We can begin to understand what it feels like to live in a particular way. We can see how society looks from the point of view of a particular group.

In order to get these kinds of insight sociologists observe in one of three different ways. We can just observe a group of people from the outside. For example to find out about what teachers think about their jobs we could watch and listen to the way they act and how they talk in the staffroom. We might get a better insight into teaching as a job, though, if we could actually become a teacher for a while. This joining a social group to find out about them is known as **participant observation**. In this way we would gradually learn about all aspects of the job, including, for example, how the parents of our pupils react to us. If, however, the rest of the staff in our school or college knew that we were doing research they might not act in their normal fashion, they might put on an act (think about what happens when there is an inspector in the class), so we might decide not to let anyone know we are really an undercover sociologist. We might decide to do **covert participant observation**. In this way we can be sure that people around us are acting normally.

A particular advantage of joining in with a group is that as we get to understand how people think, and how they see the world around them, we can get a better idea of what questions to ask because we have some idea of what is important to them.

EXERCISE

● Think about the following situations. In which ones do you think asking questions would be appropriate? In which do you think some sort of observation would give you better information?

i Finding out about the lifestyle of a group of travellers.

ii Finding out about the political opinions of pupils doing A levels at a local FE college.

iii Finding out about what makes certain groups of pupils rebel against school.

iv Finding out what kinds of people go to festivals in the summer.

v Finding out whether or not the introduction of tuition fees has had an effect on the number of individuals intending to go to university.

Discuss the reasons for your answers. There are no specifically correct answers to this exercise

Why study sociology?

In this introductory chapter we've tried to show you what sociologists do and how sociologists think. But at this point you're entitled to ask – 'but what will I get out of studying sociology?' – a perfectly reasonable question.

Firstly you will gain an insight into the workings of the society in which you live, for example, you'd know about the variety of family types, about what goes on in education, about changes in the ways we work, about the political system, all of which may help you to become a better informed citizen when you leave school or college.

Secondly doing sociology may teach you to think in different ways. Not only might you look at society in a different way, using your own sociological imagination, but by the end of your course you will be used to the idea that explanations need evidence. If nothing else sociology will get you into the habit of looking for evidence to support your ideas.

Thirdly, and this is a reason that might make more sense when you have read the rest of the book, sociology can help you act in an informed way.

Doing sociology can help us all to understand the ways in which the shape of our social lives is pushed and pulled by a variety of social factors. It shows us the ways in which we are all linked together and it can help us to understand not only the lives of others but also our own. This may give us greater insight and understanding of the social world in that we can begin to see why people do and say the things they do. As an eminent sociologist has put it:

'The great service sociology is well prepared to render to human life and human cohabitation is the promotion of mutual understanding and tolerance as a paramount condition of shared freedom.'

(Zygmunt Bauman (1990): Thinking sociologically, Basil Blackwell, Oxford)

In other words doing sociology is a particularly important way of increasing our understanding and understanding is an important condition for tolerance. The more we understand and tolerate difference the more free we all become.

The Family

2

Time Scale

1945   The end of the Second World War

1957   The publication of *Family and Kinship in East London* by Young and Willmott. There was much interest in the later 1950s and early 1960s in seeing whether the extended family was still strong in Britain.

1961   There were 91 births per 1000 women in this year

1964   The publication of *The Captive Wife* by Hannah Gavron. Note the title.

1969   The Divorce Reform Act was passed.

1970   The number of first marriages per year peaked – and has fallen ever since.

1971   Fewer than one in ten live births in Britain were outside marriage.

1972   The average age of first marriage was 24 for men, 22 for women.

1973   The number of divorces rose above 100,000 per year.

1974   Publication of *The Symmetrical Family* by Young and Willmott, who suggest that adult relationships within the family are evolving towards equality and sharing.

1975   Publication of *Housewife* and *The Sociology of Housework* by Ann Oakley, who points to the lack of equality between men and women in the family.

1993   Publication of *Rising Crime and the Dismembered Family* by Norman Dennis, who attacks those sociologists who argue that the family is only changing, not declining.

1997   The average age at first marriage had risen to 29 for a man, 27 for a woman.

1997   Over two-fifths of marriages were remarriages.

1998   Almost four out of ten live births in Britain were outside marriage.

1998   There were 59 live births per 1000 women in this year.

Introduction

You do not need to be a student of sociology to have come across or used the word 'family'. People talk about 'family holidays', the 'family home', a 'death in the family', or a 'family man'. We have all heard people say that their family is important to them or that they are fed up with their family. Politicians sometimes try to increase their own popularity by praising 'family life' or promising to defend 'family values'. Public houses try to attract customers with notices proclaiming that they are 'family friendly'. Cinemas advertise films as 'good family entertainment'. Churches invite people to 'family worship'. Almost everybody would say that they belong to a family or have belonged to a family at some time during their life.

Family is a popular, powerful and occasionally controversial idea in our society. We see images of the family as we go about our everyday life – shopping, watching television, going to church, reading the newspapers. Different people may, however, think about the family in different ways. There are different opinions about what the family is and what it should be. Perhaps this is not surprising. Discussion amongst even a small group of friends is likely to uncover differences, sometimes startling, in the pattern of experience people have as members of families.

Consider the following statements, each of which suggests a family situation. Note particularly the different relatives who are mentioned and the different kinds of relationship which are suggested.

i) An elderly widow living in sheltered housing, whose married daughter is in Australia. She says: 'Families were real families when I was young. Close, you know. It's not like that today. My daughter sends a Christmas card each year, but never writes.'

ii) A 22-year-old woman with a toddler says: 'I don't want anything to do with my ex. He got six months for burglary after making me pregnant. I don't want my Darren growing up like him. My mam and dad and his mam and dad have been great. Darren has a rubbish dad but two brilliant granddads.'

iii) A British Bangladeshi teenager says: 'Sometimes it's awkward having granddad and grandma living in our house – they moan about my music. But most of the time I like it. They tell me really interesting stuff about how they used to live.'

iv) A young wife says: 'We're both very busy although I'm working only part time until our daughter starts school. But we try to spend time together as a family.'

v) A teenager says: 'My mum was right to get divorced – my dad used to swear at her and hit her. I used to be frightened. My stepdad is OK. Mam is a lot happier now.'

vi) A 30-year-old lesbian with a six-year-old daughter says: 'Some of the other mothers at school are still a bit puzzled and I think they worry that Natalie doesn't ever see any men. It's silly really. Just because my partner and I don't fancy men doesn't mean we don't mix with them.'

Things have changed

In the 1950s a passer-by would have assumed, probably correctly, that any mother pushing a pram was married – and married to her first husband. The vast majority of children growing up at that time would have lived with the same pair of married parents until they left home. A few lone parents and cohabiting couples with children could be found but they were not seen as 'proper' families. 'Getting into trouble' and 'living in sin' were two of the more polite phrases which were used to indicate public disapproval of pregnancy and living arrangements outside marriage. A couple married until death did them part was the basis of the dominant, typical, normal form of the family.

At the beginning of the 21st century a passer-by should not assume that a mother pushing a pram down the street is married to her first husband. Today, some of us live as lone parents or as cohabiting couples with children and most of us know unmarried adults bringing up children and children being brought up by an unmarried adult or adults. Few of us see this as remarkable or peculiar. We refer to lone parent families and cohabiting couple families. Different from the traditional or conventional family formed by a married couple we see them as families and as an everyday part of the way we live. Sociologists recognise this and recognise also that reconstituted families have become more common in our society when they refer to the increasing diversity of family forms; and also when they ask whether it is still realistic to talk about 'the typical British family'.

Great Britain	**Percentages**			
	1971	1981	1991-92	1998-99
Lone mothers				
Single	1	2	6	9
Widowed	2	2	1	1
Divorced	2	4	6	8
Separated	2	2	4	5
All lone mothers	7	11	18	23
Lone fathers	1	2	1	2
Cohabiting couples	92	87	81	75
	100	100	100	100

Families headed by lone parents as a percentage of all families with dependent children.
From Social Trends

Figure 4 How families have changed.

EXERCISE

Study the table and answer the following questions:

1   Which type of family was the most common in 1998–99?
2   a) Which type of lone mother was less common in 1998 than in 1971?
     b) How do you explain this?
3   For which type of family has the increase in the percentage between 1971 and 1998–99 been the most striking?

Married couple families

Marriage is seen by many as an appropriate basis on which to build family life. We are encouraged to hold this belief by those who speak on behalf of the major religions and governments. To the religious, marriage is the morally correct or 'god given' way of bringing men and women together to have and raise children. Governments tend to see married couple families as presenting fewer problems.

Marriage in early adulthood lasting until one of the couple dies, with parenthood following marriage seems no longer to be the rule. Even someone who 'believes in' marriage and becomes part of a married couple family may live in another form of the family at some time in his or her life. He or she may cohabit with a partner before a first or, following a divorce, a second marriage. He or she may become for a time the head of a lone parent family after a divorce. He or she may remarry and create a reconstituted family. The term 'married couple family' covers many different family circumstances. Some couples will be married for the first time. Some will have been married, divorced, and then remarried one or more times. One child may have simply a mother, father, brother or sister – the cereal packet family. Another child may have a large collection of step relatives, ex-step relatives, half brothers or sisters. Reconstituted families can become very complicated.

DIVIDED LOYALTIES

By the year 2010 there will be more step families than birth families in the UK. 40% remarriages involve live-in children. The number of children in step families has more than tripled from three quarters of a million in 1991 to 2.5 million today.

'Step parents often compare themselves with immigrants who have been plonked down in a strange country to face an unfamiliar language and culture,' says an expert. Researchers followed the lives of 1000 women aged between 16 and 40 who had a baby in 1991. They found that 4 in 10 of the couples who had their first child together but also lived with children from previous relationships were not together 21 months after the birth – compared with only 5% of families in which everyone was related to each other. Other figures show that 40% of remarriages end in divorce within four years.

Adapted from an article by Debbie Humphry in *The Guardian*, Wednesday 13 September 2000

EXERCISE

Read the article and answer the following questions:

i)   What might a step-parent think that they have in common with an immigrant? Is it a useful image? Are there any obvious differences in the situations of step-parents and immigrants?

ii)   In what ways might relationships and life in a family with only birth children be different from relationships and life in a step family from the standpoint a) of the adults; b) of the children.

Families without marriage

There is no shortage of articles in newspapers about lone parent families. Sometimes these articles are sympathetic – referring to the difficulties faced by lone parents, for example. Often, however, the articles suggest or imply that the rise in lone parenthood indicates that the family in Britain today is in crisis and that moral standards have declined. Whether this perspective is convincing or not will depend on the image of the lone parent presented in the article. If it leads the reader to believe that the typical lone parent is a 15-year-old girl who became pregnant after a boozy night out, the reader might conclude that standards of parenting, of personal responsibility and morality have declined. Such a conclusion would be less convincing if the lone parent suggested as typical is a woman in her 30s or 40s who had lived in a steady relationship ended by divorce, separation or death. There are different routes into lone parenthood and the circumstances of one lone parent family can be very different from those of another. From the standpoint of the child the second parent may be dead, living somewhere else or unknown. He or she may have no relationship with the child, may reluctantly provide some financial support, or may be very active in the upbringing of the child. Be cautious when making generalisations.

As there are different routes into lone parenthood so the significance of cohabitation for a couple depends very much on their attitudes and circumstances. One couple, with or without a child, may be living together to test their mutual commitment, 'to see how it works out', to learn to live together. They may have established a 'trial marriage'. Another couple may be cohabiting as an alternative to marriage. They may feel that marriage is just a 'bit of paper' which would add nothing to their personal relationship. Another couple may be gay or lesbian, prohibited by the law as it stands, from affirming through marriage their commitment to a stable relationship. As the article below suggests, the prospect of two men being responsible for the upbringing of a child remains highly controversial.

STORM OVER BABY TWINS' TWO DADS

A huge row erupted last night over the case of the new born twins with two gay fathers and a mother. Opinion was split over the twins – born to a surrogate mum from eggs fertilised by one of the self made millionaires.

Family and Youth Concern said: 'It's thoroughly bad news. The children won't have a natural environment'.

Families Need Fathers said: 'Children need a role model of each sex to know what the world is about.' But gay group Stonewall said: 'It's about having a stable environment. Gay parents don't bring up gay children – it doesn't happen like that.'

Adapted from an article by Lorraine Fisher in *The Mirror*, Monday 13 December 1999

EXERCISE

Read the article and answer the following questions:

i)   Is there a 'natural' environment for bringing up children?
ii) If there is what is it?
iii) Explain either why you think the environment you have mentioned is natural, or why you do not think we should refer to a natural environment in this context.

Many people, you included, may hold very strong beliefs about marriage and the family. It is worth pointing out therefore that when thinking as a sociologist you must try to hold these beliefs 'at arm's length'. It is not acceptable for you, the sociologist, to think or to say, 'of course it is better for a child to be brought up in this kind of family rather than that kind of family,' just because people around you say it, or because of your religious beliefs or because it is politically correct. As a sociologist you will want the answer to several questions before judging the suitability of different kinds of family for bringing up children. Have any studies been done comparing the situation and treatment of the children in the different kinds of family? What differences, if any, have been found in the ways the children from the different kinds of family relate to adults, in school achievements or in rates of anti-social or delinquent behaviour? What do adults who were raised in the different kinds of family say about their childhood? If, when you read the article, questions like these came into your mind and you wondered, 'What is your evidence for saying that?' you are already thinking sociologically.

One life, several kinds of family

If you were to question a cross section of the British public about their family situation, some would be lone parents, some would be in once-married couple families, and some in reconstituted families. This would give you evidence of the diversity already described. If you were able to ask the same people the same questions five years later a similar range of families would be mentioned. You would find, however, that the family situation of many individuals had changed. Someone who, five years ago, was a lone parent is now married. One married women is now, following a divorce, a lone parent and another has become, through divorce and remarriage, a member of a reconstituted family. Your research would have shown that many people live, at different times in their lives, either by choice or circumstance, in several different family structures. Just as politicians and economists have been insisting during the last 20 years that no one should expect a 'job for life', sociologists can perhaps suggest that today it is unrealistic for anyone to expect a 'one family structure' for life.

1 IN 4 TRY AND FAIL TO LIVE TOGETHER

Almost 1 in 4 young adults has had a failed live-in relationship, the first official study of its kind revealed. Some 9% of men and 6% of women aged 25–34 said that they had two or more such relationships.

The research, included for the first time in the government's 'General Household Survey', has until now been regarded by population experts as the 'missing link' in the ability to map patterns of stability of modern relationships.

There are an estimated 3 million people cohabiting at any one time.

Fewer than half of marriages now involve couples who have not been living together.

Adapted from an article by David Brundle in *The Guardian* Thursday 2 December, 1999.

EXERCISE

Read the article and answer the following questions:

i)   What evidence is there in the article that cohabitation has become a more significant feature of adult life in society today?

ii) What word is now commonly used to refer to these relationships and to the status of those in the relationships? Note the way in which the word suggests that the relationship is based on quality.

Divorce in the 1950s

Imagine the situation of a wife in the 1950s in a marriage which she no longer finds satisfactory. She considers the possibility of divorce. The first question she might ask is whether she has legal grounds for a divorce. Can she prove that her husband has committed adultery, deserted or been cruel to her? A second issue may be the economics of divorce. Could she afford the court costs and, in the longer term, could she support herself and any children after a divorce? A wife in the 1950s, particularly with children still at home, was probably a house-wife with no income of her own. She might have few relevant job qualifications, no recent job experience and, in any case, adequately paid jobs for women might be scarce. Achieving a rea-sonable standard of living, even with some maintenance from her ex-husband, may look an almost impossible task. A third issue might be the disruption of personal relationships which could follow a divorce. As a wife a woman had some sort of security within a set of relation-ships. Would her relatives, neighbours, friends fall out with her? Without their support would she begin to see herself as a failure and feel guilty that, for example, she had let her children down or been selfish? It is not difficult to understand why a wife might reach the conclusion that divorce involved too many problems and risks and that it would be safer to put up with an unsatisfactory marriage. You might usefully consider whether a husband in an unsatisfactory marriage would have reached similar conclusions.

Changes

Much has changed since the 1950s. Until just over thirty years ago British divorce law more or less reflected the traditional Christian belief that marriage should be for life. Divorce should be granted only in exceptional situations – when one spouse had offended or sinned against the marriage sufficiently seriously. This approach was already being challenged in the 1950s by those who focussed on personal satisfaction and fulfilment within marriage. If a couple failed to achieve this the marriage had no point and might even create tensions which could damage those involved. The law as it then was – which limited the availability of divorce and forced people to remain in unhappy marriages – appeared from this viewpoint to be cruel and out of touch with reality. In 1969 a majority of Members of Parliament agreed and the law was changed to allow people a greater chance of escaping from marriages which were not working. Furthermore, the legal procedures were made less intimidating and less costly.

The woman in the 'cereal packet family' of the 1950s had been essentially a dependent: dependent as a non-earning housewife on her breadwinner husband for material support; dependent as a wife on her husband for social status so far as any life beyond her family was concerned; dependent as a wife and mother on her husband and children for some sense of personal satisfaction and fulfilment.

During the last fifty years a larger proportion of women have become part of the waged, salaried, self-employed workforce. With the trend towards later marriage and child bearing, women now have more time to gain experience and qualifications useful for paid employment. Many maintain some level of participation in the workforce during marriage and whilst caring for their children. Being employed or being confident of securing employment can soften the impact or reduce the risks of a divorce. Employment offers both a chance of an adequate – if reduced – standard of living outside an unwanted marriage and a network of friends and workmates willing to provide support.

Such support is important. A person needs to feel that he or she is doing the right thing! It is difficult to feel this unless at least some of those around him or her are expressing approval. 'Well, you've made your bed, now lie on it', embodies a sentiment which was quite widespread in the 1950s. Putting up with unhappiness in marriage was part of being a good wife. People expected others to live with it, just as they had done. Demanding better risked the disapproval of others. Divorce could threaten ties with neighbours, relatives and friends.

Since the 1950s opinions have changed. Divorce is respectable. Most people no longer see divorced men and women as having done something wrong. People do not have to justify their divorce to others in order to become acceptable to them. That marriages go wrong and people get divorced is a fact of life. Today we are perhaps more likely to think someone odd for enduring an unhappy marriage.

Divorce today

Imagine a wife today in a marriage which she no longer finds satisfactory. She considers the possibility of divorce. Now, as 50 years ago, it will create difficulties, require adjustments and cause pain. At the same time there is a less restrictive law, a better basis for her economic survival after the divorce and more supportive public opinion. Divorce has become a more practical proposition for more people.

Why divorce?

People do not divorce just because they can. There would be no divorces if every married person was happy with their marriage. Explaining why divorce is a more practical proposition for those who no longer wish to remain married is not the same as explaining why they no longer wish to remain married. Any consideration of trends in the divorce rate must then be concerned with the features of life in society which might lead to discontent in marital and family relationships. Has building a successful marriage become more difficult in recent years?

A simple point is that we live for longer today. 'Til death us do part' can mean 40 years. During this time the married couple have to steer the relationship successfully through many different situations: they will be parents of young children; parents of teenagers; a couple whose children have left home; a couple who have retired from paid work; a couple one or both of whom is/are frail or poorly. Coping with the changing needs of others in the family and with the different circumstances in which the family finds itself over the years at the same time as satisfying one's own changing needs may be difficult. Further, much of the reality of a long, married life may not have been anticipated when the couple first got together. It is easy to imagine someone thinking at some point in their marriage both, 'This is not what I signed up for, not what I want', and 'I have enough years left to make it worthwhile for me to get out and try again.'

Sociologists have often drawn attention to the ways in which people 'expect more' from their life today. 'You only live once, you know' seems to imply an entitlement to whatever is available – because you are not given another chance. In modern Britain there is a lot available; much to want. TV, magazine, newspaper images of nice houses and cars, beautiful and successful people, sexual bliss, stylish living are the backdrop against which we live our lives. Of course we understand that much of it is 'not real life' but it is nonetheless a constant invitation to us to hope – or even to expect – that things could be better for us. Perhaps, if only in a small way, this makes us less tolerant of unsatisfactory situations and less able to deal with problems.

There has also in recent times been a greater emphasis within our culture on individual rights and on choice. As consumers we are told by advertisers that there are products to buy which are wonderfully suited to our particular requirements. As citizens we are told by politicians that we are entitled to expect the education system or the health service, for example, to offer high quality provision. We are encouraged to 'shop around', to insist on 'value for money' and not to tolerate poor service. Is it unrealistic to suspect that our approach to marriage and the family life built on it has been influenced by this way of thinking? Perhaps divorcing a spouse can be likened to exercising our consumer right to return faulty goods.

THE NEW DIVORCE

Who divorces and why? An analysis of three surveys of adult lives discovered that the deprived are more divorce prone, as are those who have cohabited more than once before marriage, those who have embarked on relationships at a young age, those who have experienced parental divorce and those who have 'low emotional wellbeing.'

Meanwhile, academics are examining how married couples living in the least advantaged areas make their relationships flourish, against the odds. Part of the answer appears to be in strong networks of family and friends, and a willingness to ask for support.

Two other influences may also play a part in the 21st century divorce. One is time. Increasingly both partners are stretched by their jobs. Absence makes the heart grow fonder but not if the reunions are fraught and fleeting. A second factor is the inflated value of perfection; perfect wedding, perfect baby, why not order up the perfect marriage too?

Adapted from an article by Yvonne Roberts in *The Guardian*, Monday 25th September 2000

SOME FACTS

- During the 1950s a majority of those requesting a divorce were men.
- In 1997, seven out of ten decrees were granted to women,
- More than half of the decrees granted to women in 1997 were for unreasonable behaviour

From Social Trends

EXERCISE

Look at the facts and answer the following questions:

i) How do you explain the change indicated by the first two facts?

ii) Can any conclusion be drawn from the third fact about the relationships within marriage today?

Reading and writing about divorce: a warning

Few articles you have read or documentaries you have watched were neutral in the way they treated divorce and its impact on married and family life during the last 50 years. How often have you seen headlines like, 'Divorce rate up again', 'Record number escape unhappy marriages'; 'Prime Minister claims credit'? Journalists have interests and agendas. They select 'facts' to present a version of what is happening that fits in with their paper's standpoint.

Ask yourself what you say when someone tells you that they have just been divorced. Do you feel sad, happy or confused? Do you say, 'I am sorry' – perhaps thinking of the unhappiness which the people involved must have suffered or of the pain and problems which the divorce will cause? Or, do you say, 'Good for you, well done' – perhaps thinking of the good sense, courage or energy which has helped the person to get out of an unhappy marriage to start a new life? Both are reasonable responses, each suggesting a different kind of feeling about divorce. Having such feelings is part of living a social life. From childhood we see and hear about what goes on in society and try to make some sort of sense of it. Some things we do not approve of, some things we do. When thinking sociologically it is important to be aware of any such feelings so that you can prevent them from bringing a bias into your treatment of a subject.

We can find out about the present in detail. Life today seems to be and is very complicated. When looking back at the past, even the fairly recent past, things can seem more simple and straightforward. Being distant from it, we cannot see the detail. Some information is more readily accessible than other information. It is easy, for example, to find figures for the number of divorces which took place 25, 50 or 100 years ago. Divorces are granted by judges. Divorce statistics are part of the official records. If you have only the divorce statistics to look at the past appears as a time when marriages were less likely to end in divorce – a golden age of the family. Not as accessible to you is the kind of information which might challenge that conclusion. You will not find in Social Trends statistics showing how many wives or husbands were utterly fed up with or hated their spouses and who would have divorced them had it been practically possible.

It is important always to recognise that your conclusions may be biased by some potentially vital information being unobtainable. Never worry if you find yourself saying – at the end of a piece of coursework, perhaps – that it is difficult to be sure about the conclusion because you suspect that there is information which might have been significant but which you have not been able to obtain.

Births outside marriage

No trend has been greeted with more prediction of doom for the family. A high divorce rate can at least be seen as compatible with the ideal of marriage and the family, particularly when linked with remarriage. An increase in births outside marriage, on the other hand, seems to suggest that more people are seriously questioning whether marriage is the best basis for their family life. 'Outside marriage' can, of course, cover several situations. Some babies are registered by both parents who give the same address, some by both parents giving different addresses; some by the mother only. The term 'outside marriage' by itself tells us little about a baby's situation.

Why are there more births outside marriage today? Because fewer people want or feel they ought to be married before having children. Marriage today can be seen as an option rather than a pressing obligation. A majority choose this option – marriage remains popular. Some do not. It was not always like this. Until the last 30 years almost everybody saw having children as an important part of their life and saw marriage as the only proper basis on which to have children. It was 'when you have children . . .' not 'if you have children' and 'when you get married,' not 'if you get married'. People found it almost impossible to imagine a respectable and fulfilling life outside this pattern. The pressure on a couple from relatives, friends, the church and even employers to get married was considerable. Children born outside marriage were 'bastards' – hardly a description or status which a caring parent would want for her child.

[handwritten margin note: Marriage can now been seen as an option rather than a pressing obligation]

'MY BABY WAS RIPPED AWAY AS I BREAST FED HER I WAS HYSTERICAL'.

FOR 30 YEARS, THOUSANDS OF TEENAGE GIRLS IN BRITAIN WHO GOT PREGNANT HAD THEIR BABIES FORCIBLY TAKEN AWAY FOR ADOPTION

Pat is one of the thousands of British mothers forced to give up their children between the mid 1940s and mid 1970s. She was only 15 in 1961 when she became pregnant. 'I was so innocent, for eight and a half months I thought I had a tummy bug. When the doctor told me I was pregnant, I asked how the baby was going to come out of my belly button'.

Her father sent her to an unmarried mother's home run by the Church of England. 'We were treated like criminals. I looked after my daughter for nine weeks but the pressure was relentless. We were told we were incompetent and that we had no choice. We were told we were entitled to no financial or material help at all, so how could we bring up a baby? We were warned that if unsupported mothers left the home they would be arrested as a moral danger to themselves and others and our babies would be taken away. The day they came to take Elaine away two women held my arms and forced me down and the third ripped my daughter from my breast.'

There are more than 750,000 women in Britain with stories like Pat's according to new research by the Natural Parent's Support Group. The group believes that adoption agencies repeatedly lied to mothers about the benefits available to them, making them believe that adoption was the only option. A range of alternatives was in fact open to young mothers, including national assistance, welfare support and housing benefits.

Adapted from an article by Amelia Hill in *The Observer*, 9 July 2000

Having read the article, try to work out what attitudes those who took the babies must have had towards the young women who got pregnant for them to believe that their actions were justified.

Were there alternatives to marriage for young women, most of whom had few qualifications and job prospects? They would gain economically from marriage since in the 1950s men earned considerably more than women. Effective contraception usually depended on the goodwill and competence of the male. The pill had not yet given women control of their own fertility. Regular sex was much safer within a marriage. Once married the young woman could focus on the career for which she had been prepared and from which she would gain social approval and a sense of fulfilment: she would be a wife and be able to think of becoming a mother.

What disadvantages could she have set against this? She would have been giving up her independence. But of what value was such independence in a society which discriminated against her and offered her few opportunities outside marriage and family life?

The situation today

Today attitudes are different, though when making generalisations you should be cautious and try to avoid oversimplifying the situation. At a person to person level there is acceptance of lone parents who can expect support from relatives, friends and neighbours. People might not see lone parenthood as ideal but it happens, and few reject those in that situation. So far as public debate is concerned, however, sections of the media, some politicians and even some sociologists have, during the last ten years, persistently attempted to turn the public against lone parents by accusing them of scrounging benefits, jumping queues for council flats, and bringing up layabouts. Such attacks have made it difficult for lone parents to feel positive about themselves and have also helped to create an atmosphere in which it has become acceptable for those who design and administer welfare benefits to take a harsh or mean approach to claimants in this situation.

Nonetheless young women today can perhaps feel more in charge of their own lives. They are generally in a stronger economic position than 50 years ago; better qualified and with a range of job or career opportunities available. The pill and more openness about and understanding of sexual matters has given women more choice in the way they organise their sex lives. Independence becomes more possible. Independence can also look desirable. Marriage and partnerships seem less likely to last; changes in the economic and occupational structures have made many men less reliable providers; the greater willingness of individual women to talk about and report male violence and of police, journalists and opinion formers to take it more seriously has highlighted the potential danger to women and children of close, private contact with men.

Circumstance or choice

Consider the typical lone parent in the media. A teenager, no qualifications, unemployed, living on a run down council estate. How do you explain why she is in this position? Do you see her as a victim, someone overwhelmed by the deprivation she has faced throughout her life? Someone with no access to the resources necessary to 'make a life for herself'? Someone who did not choose sex and pregnancy but to whom sex and pregnancy happened? Or do you see her making choices, calculating that single parenthood is a better option than marriage? Predicting that the Benefits Agency may be a more reliable source of income for herself and her child than one of the unskilled, marginally employed young men she meets in her neighbourhood; noting that, whilst stressed under their workload, Benefits Agency staff may sometimes be rude and inefficient, they do not beat her up or booze away the money for the baby's nappies.

Some lone mothers would vigorously deny that they can be seen as victims. For them lone motherhood is an acceptable or desirable status which they occupy by choice permanently, or at certain stages of their life. It is this prospect of women choosing to be mothers without being wives which so worries some people. Most men traditionally have organised their adult lives around the role of husband. Having to carry out the responsibilities of a husband and father has given stability to a man's life. Without it, suggest some commentators, social problems will develop.

MOTHERS WITHOUT MEN

Increasing numbers of heterosexual women in their thirties are deciding to do without a man and choosing to have children on their own. Women who don't find Mr Right no longer have to settle for Mr You'll Have To Do, nor 'accidentally' get pregnant by a lover reluctant to commit. They no longer have to accept that, if they cannot find a suitable partner, they'll never have children, either.

Donor insemination for single women has made it possible to have a baby without so much as setting eyes on the father. A spokesman for the Donor Conception Network confirms, 'Five years ago, hardly any fertility clinics were providing ID for single women. Today a third do. In the past two years, especially, it has become more common'.

Adapted from an article by Amanda Riley-Jones in *The Guardian Weekend*, 10 June 2000

EXERCISE

Read the article and answer the following questions:

i)   What might a woman consider to be the benefits of 'having a baby without so much as setting eyes on the father'?

ii) List the ways in which a man can contribute towards bringing up a child.

iii) Is it necessary for a man (a) to be married to the mother or (b) to live with the mother in order to make these contributions effectively?

How difficult or easy it is to live as a lone parent will depend on the situation he or she finds him or herself in: how might the experience of lone parenthood be influenced by:

- the attitudes and situation of relatives
- the education of the parents
- government policies
- the attitudes of employers?

How and why might the situation of the lone mother differ from that of the lone father?

Who counts as family?

Sociologists have for a long time been interested in who takes part in the life of a family and in what ways they take part. If you had begun to study sociology in the 1950s this would have been your main focus when considering different family structures in Britain. That today equal, if not more, attention is paid to the differences arising from decisions about marriage and divorce is useful evidence of change in the family. Sociologists have defined two model patterns of participation in family life – nuclear and extended families.

Nuclear family suggests a man and woman living together either as a married or cohabiting couple in a house or flat with their children. This group act as a unit, separate from and independent of other relatives. They might live at a considerable distance from relatives. Sometimes this separation and independence is emphasised by words like 'isolated' or 'privatised'. The words suggest that the nuclear family is largely self-contained and self-supporting. Its members do not have much social contact with, nor do they receive support from, or give support to, a wider set of relatives.

The nuclear family figures prominently in debates about the modern family. Some see it as an ideal unit, bringing up and caring for children at the same time as providing comfort, companionship and affection for adults in a competitive mobile society. The nuclear family is a stable base upon which to face the insecurities and take the risks which economists and politicians keep telling us are inevitable in our lives today. For others though, relationships within the nuclear family are probably based on exploitation, can be unhealthily intense and produce children who are likely to become anxious adults who are easy to manipulate.

Extended family suggests that a wide range of relatives actively involve themselves in each other's lives. The children in the extended family have not only mother and father but also grandparents, uncles, aunts, cousins as part of their life on a daily, or at least, frequent basis. When a couple married they would live close to their parents. Living 'round the corner' makes it possible for members of the wider family to see a lot of and help each other; caring for a sick child, sorting out a nasty neighbour, sending some money until pay day. This strengthens the sense of belonging to the wider family.

Families like this formed the backbone of working class communities in many parts of Britain during the first half of the 20th century. They were established as the children and grandchildren of those who had moved to the towns and cities during the 19th century settled down near to their parents. Son followed father down the pit, into the shipyard or mill, or onto the docks. People living in this way came to share experiences and memories which, whilst sustaining feuds, could be a basis for loyalty to others in the community. Today this kind of family life is recalled by many with warm feelings. It has come to represent a way of life in which problems were shared and neighbours 'looked out' for each other. Some, however, hold a less favourable opinion. A strong attachment to relatives and community could lead to individual ambitions being limited. Someone might be reluctant to accept promotion if relatives with whom a lot of time was spent were likely to see it as a snobby thing to do. The family duty of standing together could also become a source of trade union solidarity when relatives living in the same neighbourhood worked in the same kind of job. This would cause concern to those who believe that an economy is more likely to prosper if there are no, or very weak, trade unions.

Thinking about your own family and those of people you know probably suggests to you that some families are not accurately described as either isolated nuclear or traditional extended families. A married couple may live with their children at a considerable distance from their parents or married siblings and yet maintain regular contact with them – by phone, letter, visits or attendance at family occasions. Although not living in the same neighbourhood the married couple are not isolated from their relatives. Through this contract it is possible for relatives to help each other when necessary. Of course the kind of help may be different from that which could be offered when living in the next street. It is not really practical to dash 150 miles down a motorway to borrow a saucepan. It is practical, however, for the whole family to cooperate in making arrangements for an elderly relative to be looked after. It is practical, for example, for a 17-year-old to be given a bed for the night when attending a university interview far from home. Some sociologists have found the term 'modified extended family' useful when thinking about this kind of family.

WITH SO MANY OF BRITAIN'S OLDER JAMAICANS RETURNING TO THE CARIBBEAN, WHO WILL PASS ON THEIR TRADITIONAL VALUES?

5000 UK based Jamaicans, mainly of retirement age, have been drawn back to their homeland over the last five years. The repercussions are far reaching on those family members left behind.

Grandparents have traditionally played a pivotal role in Caribbean families. In Britain, black families have a one in three chance of being brought up by a single parent, so the support system of the extended family is vital.

Interaction between the generations is an essential socialising process and benefits everyone: youngsters learn deference to age while the elderly acquire patience. More fundamentally, it is in interacting across the generations that culture is passed down. With the older generation gone where will our children learn the traditions essential to shaping a distinctive culture? Older Caribbean children have had the option of seeking refuge with grandparents when tension arises with parents. Caribbean youth used to fear the wrath of grandfathers and uncles if fathers were absent.

Adapted from an article by Eugenie Bryan in *The Guardian* Wednesday, 3 November 1999

EXERCISE

Read the article again and answer the following questions:

i)   List the ways in which grandparents play an important part in the life of Afro-Caribbean families in Britain.

ii)   **a)** Do the items on your list apply less, equally or more to white families and to the families of other ethnic minority groups?

      b) Explain your answers.

It is then possible to see diversity in the pattern of relationships which exist between relatives. Some traditional living-in-the-same-neighbourhood extended families continue to exist amongst the working class and some ethnic minority groups. Such extended families can exist when there is less pressure on members of the family to move from or more pressure to stay in the neighbourhood. For many, however, it has become impossible, even undesirable, to settle down near to their parents. Their family, work, desire to improve their standard of living can all generate pressures to live somewhere else. Despite this, relatives remain important and contact is maintained with at least some of them. Within the modified extended family someone can choose which of his or her relatives to maintain contact with. In the living-in-the-same-neighbourhood extended family, there is less choice.

GREAT BRITAIN			PERCENTAGES		
	Mother	Father	Adult Sibling	Adult Child	Other Relative
Daily	8	6	4	10	3
Less than daily but at least once a week	40	33	25	48	31
At least once a month	21	20	21	16	26
Less often	27	29	45	18	37
Never	3	9	4	1	1
Not answered	1	3	1	7	2
All	100	100	100	100	100

From Social Trends

Figure 5 Frequency of adults seeing a relative 1995

EXERCISE

Look again at the table and answer the following questions:

i)   Do the figures suggest that, when grown up, children are more likely to have relatively frequent contract with their parents or brothers and sisters?

ii) How might this be explained?

iii) What evidence do the figures provide for believing that the extended family is still important to people in British society?

Changes in the pattern of marriage and divorce have resulted in further diversity within extended families today. This diversity is almost never discussed by students. Whenever, for example, the consequences of divorce are considered, the discussion is always narrowly focussed on the consequences for children. No reference is made to the consequences for the divorcing couple's parents and for other relatives. This omission results in the discussion of the consequences for the children being unrealistic since it fails to mention the possibly significant change in the relationship with at least one set of grandparents, uncles, aunties and cousins. It is as if the student sees divorce only in terms of the nuclear family. Recognise that divorce and remarriage can have considerable impact on the relationships which the older relatives are allowed, willing, or expected to have amongst themselves and with the younger generation within the extended family. Tension, division and weakening contacts within this family is a possible result of divorce.

GRAND UNION

Grandparents in the UK who are bringing up their grandchildren are a growing band. We've always had mental illness, and the death of young mothers but today, the breakdown of families contributes more and more to the phenomenon. Also the increase in teenage pregnancy. A major factor is the Children Act of 1989. Before the act, when courts were ruling on who should take care of children whose parents were unable to look after them, the courts were putting children into Local Authority Care, who then often placed them with foster parents and put them up for adoption. Sensibly and happily we've gone from taking the children out of the family to let's keep it in the family.

Adapted from an article by Jeanne Davis in *The Guardian*, Wednesday, 3 November 1999

Female relatives have played a vital role in maintaining social contact within the extended family, their shared interest in children providing a firm basis for the maintenance of relationships. They had frequent opportunities for contact in the 1950s whilst performing their roles as mother and housewife; at the clinic, the shops, the playground gates. Married women in paid employment have perhaps less time for contact – even when living near to each other. Contact has to be organised.

Again, it is necessary to consider the situation of the 'older generation'. The image of the grandmother as someone available for advice, or to look after the children at a moment's notice was dependent on her being a housewife. Many women who are grandmothers today, however, either go out to work or are actively involved outside the house in 'doing their own thing.' The role they are able or willing to play within the family may therefore be different from that traditionally expected. Others, of course, are in a situation which enables them happily to play the traditional role. The situation may be complicated by the survival into old age of the grandmother's mother or father. With the increase in expectation of life, more people live into their eighties and at some point require some sort of care. Traditionally the duty has fallen on a daughter.

DAUGHTER RAILS OVER ABSENT GRANNY

A picture of a woman with her husband and five children appeared in the local newspaper last week under the headline, 'Wouldn't you like to be our grandparents?' Beneath the photograph the woman explained that her own parents simply did not have the right grandparenting qualities. 'My mum is only 46, she works and she would sooner go for a night out with the girls'.

An expert said 'Most women became grandmothers now when they are in their forties or fifties – just when they are beginning to find a new whirl of freedom – a sense of new possibilities. A woman of this age is far younger now both in spirit and in health than her grandmother would have been and is full of energy. Fifty years ago she would have been expected to devote a lot of her time to her grandchildren, now she may resent being asked to do so much babysitting.'

The woman voted Grandparent of the Year 1998 said, 'I think there are plenty of people who would be happy to take on this role, because it's very rewarding both for them and their children'.

Adapted from an article by Amelia Gentleman in *The Guardian* Wednesday, 24 March1999

It is worth noting that someone becomes a grandparent as a result of another person's decision. In a society in which choice is highly valued, people may not be happy about these social roles they did not choose to play.

EXERCISE

Read the article and answer the following questions:

i)   List the ways in which the situation of grandparents today is likely to differ from the situation of those in the 1950s.

ii) What might a grandparent today be expected to contribute to the care and upbringing of a grandchild?

iii) What features of life in modern society might a) help and b) make it difficult for a grandparent to make this contribution?

Another interesting development in the role grandparents play in the family unit is the introduction of 'community grandmothers'. The government-backed scheme is intended to give support to those mothers who do not have the help of close relatives.

EXERCISE

1) Why do you think the scheme supplies 'community grandmothers' rather than 'community grandmothers and grandfathers?'

2) What do you think that those who set the scheme up might see as its benefits?

3) What arguments could be made against the government providing such a scheme?

It is difficult to generalise about extended families today. People are more able than in the past to make decisions about which relatives they see and help out. It might be very useful in your sociology studies, as well as interesting for your relatives, if you were to keep a diary, recording the contacts you have with different members of your extended family. Doing this, even for a month or six weeks, could give you significant findings. If, as you record who the contact was with and where it took place, you also record what it was about, it should be possible to draw some conclusions about the significance of your extended family to its members. Do people help each other out and in what kind of ways? If you decided to conduct this little piece of research you would of course have to decide whether to tell your relatives that you were studying them.

Authority and power

Students often seem reluctant to discuss the politics of the family – perhaps because politics is always seen as Politics – that is, something to do with people such as politicians and institutions like parties and parliament. Within the family, however, decisions are made and carried out, and, unless the family is completely disorganised, a pattern of decision-making will develop. Family members will come to expect a particular member of the family to make certain kinds of decision or that decisions will be made following discussion involving some or all of its members. The family will have an authority structure. If it is accepted and expected that the husband/father makes the important decisions we may refer to a patriarchal structure. If, on the other hand, the general expectation is that all members of the family should play a part in making the decisions we may refer to a democratic structure.

It is commonly suggested that whilst early in the 20th century families tended to be patriarchal, those of the late 20th century were more likely to be democratic. It is important when discussing such change to consider both the relationship between the adults and that between adults and children within the family.

Influences and change

There are many possible influences on the pattern of authority within a family. Consider the situation between husband and wife.

- **Beliefs**
  Both religious and medical beliefs in the early 20th century were formulated to justify the position of the male as the decision maker. Leading doctors, for example, suggested that too much intellectual activity threatened the working of a woman's reproductive system. Men were presented as biologically equipped for thinking; women for bearing children.
  Such religious and medical beliefs have been challenged by more liberal theologies and developments in science. Today fewer people have such rigid ideas about the parts men and women can and should play. Relationships within families which maintain a fundamentalist approach to a religion – Christianity or Islam, say – may still, however, be influenced by the belief that women should obey men.

- **Socialisation**
  Those entering marriage and building a family have been influenced by what they have learned from their own family life, school, and the mass media. They have ideas about what they are, or should be good at, what makes for a good and fruitful relationship and what does not. In the past boys and girls were brought up surrounded by images of men as decision makers, women as those who looked after the decision makers. Such a situation was seen as 'natural'.
  Today things are somewhat different. In recent years, girls have been more likely to be encouraged to see themselves as equal to boys. Boys have been encouraged to respect girls as equals.

- **Practicalities**
  An important source of authority for men during a large part of the 20th century was the division of labour within the family. Men were breadwinners, women were homemakers. It was the man who was handed the money by the employer – it was his money in that it was in his pocket. Both husband and wife knew that whilst he could survive financially without

her, she could not survive financially without him. All those changes which have made it more possible for women to support themselves economically have therefore enabled them to gain more authority within the family.

It is perhaps worth noting that even when men could base their authority on the pay packet it was possible for a wife to have authority in particular aspects of their life together. A husband, for example, may have left the running of the house entirely to his wife – becoming dependent on her. In recent years it seems that some wives have resisted their husband's 'New Man' willingness to share household duties precisely because they feared a loss of authority.

● The Law

Marriage and family life in Britain have always been conducted within a framework of law. For much of the 20th century the law allowed men to maintain their dominance within the family by treating it as an essentially private matter. It was difficult for a wife to use the law and to insist that its official upholders restrain a husband, who therefore had ample opportunity to use violence to enforce his decisions. Since the laws on property and divorce, for example, did not make it easy for a wife to escape, it was difficult to avoid having to do what he told her to do.

The situation has changed and is changing. Property settlements following divorce are now more generous to women and the authorities have developed a more interventionist approach to domestic violence. It may be that the very high levels of domestic violence which occur today are related to the changing authority structure within the family. Losing authority, more men are perhaps trying to manage their relationship with their partner by brute force. The man tries to maintain his authority by using his physical power.

DOMESTIC VIOLENCE SOARS TO EPIDEMIC

'The scale of this problem is mind-blowing, we have to make domestic violence as socially unacceptable as drink driving,' said a spokesman for the Racial and Violent Crimes Task Force.

The figures do not suggest that domestic violence is becoming a thing of the past. Police forces across Britain are being forced to recognise what feminists and women's groups have been telling them for years: domestic violence is the most serious single criminal justice issue facing them today, but one that used to go largely unreported.

The Government believes that changes in society – with people divorcing more frequently – have contributed to the rise. Some feminist writers have observed that a rise in female assertiveness and economic power has coincided with the collapse of traditional male jobs in manufacturing. Some experts believe that increased feelings of worthlessness may have fuelled the increase in male violence.

Adapted from an article by Martin Bright in *The Observer*, 16 July 2000

EXERCISE

Read the article and answer the following questions:

i) Why in the past was domestic violence likely to go unreported?

ii) Why, even today, is the incidence of domestic violence still likely to be under-recorded in official figures?

iii) Look at the comment from the spokesman for the Racist and Violent Crimes Taskforce. What does it suggest about our attitudes to marriage and the family if domestic violence is not already completely 'socially unacceptable'.

For many young Asian women in Britain marriage means abuse or even death to satisfy 'family honour'. This domestic terror inflicted by husbands, parents and other relatives, has long been submerged

In the last five years 21 deaths in Britain can be connected with ideas of 'honour', as well as hundreds of acts of lesser violence. Campaigners claim that the honour code – and its accompanying concept of shame – is a key factor in the repression of the rights of tens of thousands of Asian women in Britain.

Optimists say that, as the Asian community becomes more assimilated and conservative traditionalism dies away, the issue will resolve itself.

Often the victims of violence are women born and educated in the UK whose aspirations are very different from those of older family members.

Adapted from an article by Jason Burke in *The Observer*, 8 October 2000

● Needs

What its members expect to get from their family life can also influence the authority structure. If the family is primarily a source of social and economic security for its members, inequality of authority between them may not matter very much.

In recent years, however, more emphasis has been placed on the family as a source of companionship, fun, affection and emotional support. These expectations may perhaps be more easily fulfilled in a democratic family.

PARENTS ARE NO LONGER A FAMILY'S GREAT DICTATOR

The Victorian approach to child rearing, where children were seen and not heard, has collapsed over the past 30 years with the birth of the new 'democratic family' 78% of British parents consult their offspring on important decisions such as moving house or where to go on holiday.

An expert said, 'It seems parents not only see involving their children in decisions from the outset as a route to family harmony but recognise that their children can actually add value to big family decisions'. Another expert said, 'Many people think that including the kids in decisions makes for happy families but that is not necessarily the result for all members of the household.'

Findings show that some parents find involving their children very difficult as they lose both power and authority within the household. In the same way, children and some adolescents find some decisions too stressful and expect their parents to take responsibility for their welfare.

Adapted from an article in *The Independent* by Cherry Norton, Monday 31 July 2000

Read the article and answer the following questions:

1)   **a**) What advantages of the democratic family are referred to in the article?
    b) What disadvantages or possible problems are referred to?

What explanations might a sociologist give for the changes in the relationships between parents and children during the last 50 years?

You might consider changes in:

➡ the law
➡ public opinion
➡ family structures
➡ what people want from their family life.

Remember, when thinking of explanations, that changes may have taken place both in the situation and attitude of adults and the situation and attitudes of children.

Who does what in the family?

In the 1950s routine childcare and housekeeping were seen as tasks which should be undertaken by women. Of course, in some families life was organised differently. The division of labour – man as breadwinner, women as childcarer and homemaker – was, however, strongly supported by economic circumstances and the culture of the time. The phrase segregated **Conjugal roles** was used by sociologists to indicate the way in which the contributions made by the husband and wife to the running of the family were clearly different.

Since the 1950s many features of the situation within which people conduct their family life have changed. Much attention has been given to discovering the way or ways in which childcare and housekeeping tasks are divided up between the family members today. Is there still a typical way of dividing tasks between members of the family? Have men who entered family life during the 1980s and 1990s played a greater part in routine childcare and housekeeping than their fathers and grandfathers did? It might be interesting to undertake a little investigation of your own.

AIM: To see who does what in a family or families today.

METHOD: Make a list of a range of ordinary tasks which need to be undertaken within a family today – shopping, cleaning, taking the children to school, cooking for example.

Find out which family members do these jobs. Perhaps, if you are investigating the situation in your own family, you could simply observe who does what and record your observations in a notebook. You may be able to do this without anyone noticing – but should you? Might it be a bit sneaky not to tell other members of your family what you are doing, particularly if you are going to compare results with others in your class. If they know you are paying special attention to what they are doing, however, they may act differently. This is the kind of dilemma any researcher may face.

Perhaps you could ask people whether they would help you by ticking some boxes on a simple question sheet. For example:

Would you please indicate by ticking a box which description most accurately fits the situation in your family.

Task	Always done by the woman	Always done by the man	Occasionally done by the woman	Occasionally done by the man	Pretty much shared
Preparing the evening meal					
Doing the washing					
Changing nappies					
Looking after the garden					
and so on ...					

Figure 6 Who does what in the family?

Amongst the tasks – no more than a dozen, since you do not want to put people to too much trouble – select some which might traditionally be seen as 'man's work' and woman's work'. The answers given will enable you to see whether old divisions are becoming blurred.

Look at the information you have obtained to see whether there are any obvious patterns in who does what. Discuss what you have found with other members of your class to see whether their investigations confirm your conclusions.

What influences who does what in the family?

Finding out who does what is a vital first step. Explaining why the tasks are divided in the way you have found is the second. Some reasons are obvious: 'You can't go out/have your pocket money/have your friends around until you have tidied your room.' Authority or power – 'Do that or I'll belt you' can play an important part. Some family members undertake a task because they are forced to. They are punished if they don't. Other influences might include:

- who is considered to be the best at doing the task. Some tasks – baking a cake, for example – require skills which not all family members may have. The way in which adult family members were socialised when young will thus be important, as will be any general expectations of society that men or women are better at doing a particular task.
- who is available when the task needs doing; who has the time. Family members have obligations which take them away from their house – paid employment being the most significant for adults; school for children. In some families a member or members may lack such commitments, being a full time housewife/mother or househusband/father. In other families, however, the demands of paid employment will exert a strong influence on the way in which childcare and housework is organised.

- who are the everyday members of the family. Discussions of 'who does what?' in the family have traditionally focussed on the married couple. It is important not to forget that today the family takes diverse forms – a lone parent has no partner with whom to divide up the tasks.
- the state of health or fitness of family members. Many adults live with some form of disability – limited sight, hearing or movement for example. Such disabilities can influence aspects of the way in which tasks will be divided between partners.

Approaches to the family

An important characteristic of sociology is that within it there are different approaches to society. As a sociologist you will be able to choose between these different approaches. This choice, if it is to be made in the spirit of sociology, should be on the basis of the evidence – the 'facts' – obtained by research. Choose the approach which you believe is most strongly supported by, or fits most closely, the evidence. Of course, someone else, equally within the spirit of sociology, might reasonably make a different choice. He or she may give a lot of weight to evidence which you do not think is particularly important. He or she may interpret evidence in a different way. Recognise that such differences of opinion are a strength rather than a weakness of sociology. They provide a basis for argument and debate which can lead to approaches being improved. They raise issues which provide a reason for doing more research.

Differences in approach can be seen quite clearly in relation to the study of the family, about which some sociologists are very positive and some very critical. Study the photograph below. What do you see? A woman being a good mother, getting real satisfaction and fulfilment from using skills she learned as a child and from the loving smiles of her children? A woman trapped by a daily routine which prevents her from doing other things which would develop her potential as a person? A woman spending her time and the family's income on raising the next generation of office, call centre or supermarket 'wage slaves', out of whose employment the 'fat cats' will continue to make their profits? Three interpretations of the photograph, each suggesting a different approach not just to the family but to what goes on in society as a whole.

Figure 7 The family can be analysed in many different ways.

A positive view

It is sometimes said that the family is at the 'heart' of society. Such an image suggests that just as the heart is vital to the health and survival of a body, so the family is vital to the health and survival of society. The image also suggests that the family has something to do with warmth, affection, deep feelings. Most importantly, however, the image suggests a question. If you were a biologist studying a body you would ask, 'what does the heart do to help keep the body alive?' The equivalent question for the sociologist is, 'What does the family do to help keep a society going?' As is often the case, once you have seen the need to ask the question, answering it looks easy.

If a society could not organise a supply of new members to replace those who had died or migrated it would become smaller and eventually cease to exist. The family is the institution on which is placed the main responsibility for achieving this supply of new members. It is expected that within the family children will be born, protected, cared for and will learn how to live in the society. Sociologists refer to the functions of reproduction, maintenance and socialisation. Within a family the child is someone's son, someone's nephew, someone's grandson. The child has a place, or status, within a family and, through the family, within a community or society. People know what the child is to them – 'He's our Sharon's eldest' – and therefore what they are expected to do for the child. Listen to people discussing other parents and you will very soon get an idea of what are the norms of parenting – that is, what is expected of parents – in that community: 'Tracey's mam never makes her a breakfast, you know. Idle cow. No wonder Tracey is so thin.'

It would perhaps be easy to disregard the part the family plays for adults. Adults can look after themselves, children are vulnerable. Adults also, however, have needs. Life in modern society can be tough, lonely and frustrating. An individual who lacks support can 'break down' under the pressure, presenting society with a variety of problems – illness, suicide, crime, mental instability. For sociologists who view it positively the married couple family can help the adults who are part of it to cope with their lives. Within this family two adults establish a relationship from which, with the approval of society, they are entitled to receive sexual pleasure, love and affection. Through this relationship the couple share interests and build a life together. This life offers fulfilment from, for example, pride in their children, in making their home comfortable. They support each other practically and are 'there for each other'. Being part of a family gives some sort of order, stability and meaning to their life. The family becomes a reason for doing things such as attending an evening course on computers – 'to keep up with my daughter', or doing overtime 'so we can afford a nice holiday this year'. The family can also become a reason for not doing things – 'No more. It isn't worth it. I don't want my kid to have to visit me in jail'.

Looked at in this way the married couple family seems rather attractive. For a child to be brought up by a man and woman living together not only seems natural but also socially efficient. The child satisfies his or her need to be cared for. The satisfactions resulting from parenthood help the adults who provide that care to cope with their life. Society gets a supply of new members. Most of us can easily recall images from our own experience which support this view of the family; the pleasure of people looking at or discussing their family photographs;

the powerful feelings of loss at a family funeral or the joy and pride at a school or college prize ceremony. At the same time most of us recognise that there are other stories to tell about the family – some of them dark and distressing. It used to be proclaimed that 'An Englishman's home is his castle'. Unfortunately few people bothered to ask, 'And who are locked in the dungeons?'

A critical view

If the question was asked some sociologists would answer, 'Women.' Men have exercised authority at work, in churches, in politics, the law and other areas of social life. Men have been able to use the authority they have in the wider society to ensure the subordination of women within the family. The male dominated legal system, until recently, for example, refused to accept that a wife could be raped by her husband – thus effectively denying the wife the right to say no to her husband's sexual demands.

Feminist sociologists and those who sympathise with their approach suggest that crucial to an understanding of the relationship between a wife and her husband is a recognition of the difference in their economic situations. During the 20th century the workplace and the home were typically separate places. Wages and salaries were earned in factories and offices, children were looked after at home. The ideal came to be seen as a breadwinning husband and father in the workplace to support – note the word – his homemaking, mothering wife at home. The wife under this arrangement had no income of her own. She was dependent on what her husband was prepared to give her for housekeeping. Of course there were pressures on him not to be mean. A man risked social disapproval if his wife and children appeared to be worse cared for than others. The wife was, however, in a weak position. What could she do if she wanted money spent in a particular way and her husband said no?

Not suited for the world out there

The separation of women from income earning work outside the home was important not only in a direct 'who controls the money' way. It also influenced attitudes and the identities which men and women developed. Through work men belonged in the wider world. They joined Trade Unions and working mens' clubs, the Rotary Club or the Masons. They discussed politics or economic matters with other men. They read and discussed what was in the newspapers and were expected to be interested in and knowledgeable about a range of issues. The life of a wife was centred on the home. Shopping, baby care, looking nice and satisfying her husband were her areas of expertise. The male's attitude of 'Don't worry your pretty little head about it, I'll take care of it' seems almost a natural response in such an unbalanced relationship. Separated from income earning and the wider world the wife lost status. Her activities were, and often still are, not thought of as work. Even some sociologists do not treat housework and caring for the family as 'proper' work, making no or scant reference to it in the sociology of work chapter. The man with his income earning job was of primary importance. His work routines set a structure for the wife's day, week, year and even life. Father to toddler: 'I've been working all day. Go and bother your mother.'

Motherhood

A second issue of fundamental importance to feminist sociologists has been that of motherhood. For most women a large part of their lives is very much influenced by what society expects of them and what they come to expect of themselves as mothers. Motherhood has demanded and still demands a lot from women. Much, claim some feminist sociologists, that has trapped women and lowered their status in society. From this viewpoint motherhood – as it has been organised in our society – has involved the oppression of women. Picture a mother and baby at home – there is no other adult to have a conversation with: she feels duty bound to put the needs of a selfish, unreasonable creature above her own wants. The baby demands, 'Feed me – put that book down; clean me – I don't care if your breakfast goes cold; carry me around – I don't care that you are having a rest. Do these now or I'll scream and shake so that you get worried.'

To carry out these duties the woman has had to give up her position in the workforce through which she achieved companionship, perhaps the satisfaction of using a skill, and an income. Her role now becomes domestic, menial and unpaid. A role traditionally seen as requiring such limited abilities that any woman could carry it out without formal training. Watching her mum and other women being mothers was all it took. Of course, this is not the whole story. Some feminist sociologists have pointed to the way in which women themselves have drawn attention to the very important contribution to society they make as mothers. The struggle to establish legal rights for and social recognition of mothers was a significant part of the general struggle over the last 200 years for equality with men.

A claim often made, though not by sociologists, is that motherhood is 'natural' for women. It is suggested that there is something in the biological or psychological make up of women that equips them for and pushes them smiling happily towards motherhood. It is woman's nature to be and act as mothers. Sometimes the same claim is made in terms of women's 'maternal instinct' to care for children. This way of thinking can of course be useful to men who do not like the thought of washing nappies and getting up in the middle of the night to give the baby a bottle: 'You do it dear. You will be better at it and happier doing it than me. It comes naturally to you. You've got an instinct for it – I haven't'.

Sociologists, whether feminists or not, take a different approach. For them what women do as mothers in a particular society cannot be explained by reference to female genes, hormones or instincts. Rather, the nature of a woman's relationship with her children should be understood in terms of social rules and expectations, economic and political circumstances. Women were the principal childcarers in Britain during the 20th century because that was what women came to expect of themselves and because, in the circumstances which then existed, that was what it seemed appropriate for them to do. In different circumstances childrearing could be successfully organised with women – and men – playing rather different roles. 'Nature' might – by not giving them wombs – have made it impossible for men to conceive and bear children. Nature neither makes it impossible for men to change nappies, push prams, read bedtime stories nor insists that women do these things. For feminist sociologists, the burden which mothers carried during the 20th century was handed to women not by 'nature' but by men. Dominating parliament, the churches, the mass media, economic institutions, science and medicine, men designed a pattern of motherhood which suited them. As women gain more authority in our society what they feel they should do and what they do may change.

Another critical view

It is hard to think of a satisfactory answer to the child's question: 'Daddy, why wasn't I born into a rich family?' or to argue with the sad, 'It isn't fair', which might follow. Babies are not allocated to families on the basis of any principle of fairness. As long as some families are rich and some poor; some parents are talented and some incompetent; some caring and some abusive, some babies will have a family in which it will be very easy to flourish and some a family in which it will be easy not to flourish. The family helps to pass on the inequalities of one generation to the next, and not just by ensuring that some children are given a 'good start' and some not. Family life generally is linked with inequality. The family home may be a mansion or a council flat, the family savings may be millions or nothing. Much of the wealth of our society is held within families. Some children inherit fortunes, titles, businesses, well-respected names – others do not. It is worth asking yourself – or better a politician bearing promises – how equality of opportunity can be established whilst families are so unequal.

Society is often talked about by sociologists as if it is organised to serve the interests of all its members. But what if it is not like this? What if society has been organised to serve the interests of a small, very wealthy, very powerful group? What if the majority of us are manipulated and exploited? What might be the role of the family in such a society? Any small ruling group is faced with the problem that the majority, who are being exploited, may rebel. Social control becomes crucial. What can the family contribute as an agent of social control? Fathers are expected to love their children, provide support for them and not to take risks with their future. Such expectations traditionally have been deeply embedded in the culture within which young males have been socialised. Spending a life down the pit or in the mill makes some sort of sense. 'We're doing it for our kids,' has been, and perhaps still is, a strong enough reason for putting up with long hours, boredom, lousy conditions and bullying employers. The sense of fatherly responsibility helped, and helps, to maintain a disciplined workforce from which the very wealthy, very powerful can extract their profit.

From this viewpoint, how does the wife help to keep the very wealthy, very powerful in the manner to which they have become accustomed? Firstly, by maintaining her husband in an efficient mental and physical condition for work. This can involve anything from nursing to being a punchbag. Some wives recognise this role when accusing their husbands of, 'Only coming home to recharge your batteries.' Secondly, by making sacrifices to bear and play the major role in bringing up children so that the next generation of very wealthy, very powerful have a workforce to exploit.

The most remarkable feature of the family as an institution sustaining this sort of exploitation is that so few people see it in this way. Adults like to be parents and willingly put themselves under the disciplines of parenthood. To an intelligent outsider such behaviour could seem bizarre. Picture hundreds of thousands of fathers and mothers doing eight hours of tiring, boring work. Why are they working? Picture these mothers and fathers using their leisure shopping, spending their wages for the eight hours work on a pair of designer trainers for

Figure 8 For many women childcare can be very stressful.

their children. The very wealthy, very powerful profit from the parents as workers and from the parents again as shoppers. What do the parents get out of it? The family creates the demand for consumer goods which the parents then have to work to provide.

Politics and the family

Personal privacy is valued in our society. Individuals tend to have a strong sense that, so far as sexual choices, and the making of decisions about their marriages and families are concerned, outsiders should not interfere. At the same time people see, hear about or are victims of behaviour which they do not consider acceptable. They think that 'something must be done' when ten year olds are on the streets at midnight, twelve year olds become pregnant or fourteen year olds snatch handbags from old ladies. Privacy seems less desirable when it appears to shield bad parenting and when bad parenting is thought to result in anti-social behaviour which damages the neighbourhood and society generally.

The family can be seen as individuals who, for their own reasons, have decided to try to build together a life which suits them: it is a private world of intense relationships and deep feelings. The family is also an important part of the wider society to which we all belong – rearing future workmates, neighbours, fellow shoppers and voters. Viewed in this way, what goes on in other people's families can be seen to concern us all.

How we should live in families, the laws which govern marriage and establish a framework for family life, and policies relating to family taxation and family welfare have always been matters of public debate. During the 1990s the debate 'hotted up' as a growing number of politicians, newspaper editors and journalists, religious leaders and even a few sociologists expressed concern about the way family life had developed and was developing in Britain. At the same time members of the public with a particular interest in or strong feelings about marriage and the family set up or joined groups with the aim of influencing the climate of public opinion and the government. The family has become an important political issue.

At the heart of this issue is a division of opinion about the ways in which family life has changed since the 1960s. To some, the greater diversity of family structures suggests progress. It is seen as indicating that people today feel better able to look for and establish a kind of family life which works for them. There is less pressure within society to force people into and keep them in a heterosexual, married couple-for-life structure. Public opinion has become more tolerant of diversity. The law and social policy have become less likely to exclude and penalise those who do not wish to organise their lives according to the morality and conventions of the 1950s.

Greater affluence generally, greater access of women to employment, and a welfare state have all reduced the economic risks of life outside the 'cereal packet family'. Diversity suggests maturity. Adults negotiate their relationships and establish the responsibilities and commitments which they think will suit them rather than trying to force themselves to enjoy being the 'cereal packet husband and wife'.

The worriers point to a range of social problems: rising rates of mental instability, suicide, anti-social behaviour amongst young people and increasing demands on the welfare state have all been linked to what they see as the 'decline of the family'. Various groups of people and developments in society have been accused of helping to bring about the decline. Feminists have been blamed for challenging male advantages and authority and for suggesting that roles within the family should be less gender based. The contraceptive pill and greater access to abortion have been blamed for making casual sex less risky and 'cheapening' relationships. Liberal minded politicians, civil servants, and judges have been blamed for abolishing the privileges which a married couple had so far as the law, taxation and welfare benefits were concerned. Educationalists have been blamed for suggesting that we should be less judgemental in schools so far as family life is concerned. More recently, gays and lesbians have been blamed for suggesting that the caring relationships which they establish are worthy of as much respect as is given to heterosexual caring family relationships. Young parents as a whole have been blamed for becoming more selfish, more concerned with their own satisfactions and pleasures than with their obligations to their children. Some issues raised in this debate have particular interest for sociologists.

What is a family?

A family is . . . Ask yourself how you would complete this sentence to answer the question 'what is a family?' Perhaps you would mention marriage or blood relationships. Perhaps you would write 'A family is made up of mother, father, brother, grandmother and son'. This is the conventional way of thinking about a family. Most of us can remember history books or lessons in which we were shown the family tree of the Queen of England: names of people with titles, connected to other names by little lines with the symbol 'b'– for born to – or 'm' for married. Here is the family seen as structure, as an institution within which people have positions and play roles. Here is the family formed by the officially recorded and significant acts of birth and marriage.

You might give a rather different answer like 'A family is those who are close to you, look out for you and care for you'. Here there is no reference to marriage or blood relationships: here family is not being thought of and defined as a structure. Rather, family is being thought of and defined as something people do – sharing with others, caring for them, feeling obligations towards others. Someone saying of neighbours, 'They were more of a family to me than my mam and dad', is thinking of the family as something people do.

The argument about what family means has been expressed most forcefully in the context of homosexual relationships. For those who see marriage as the only 'proper' basis for family, the word cannot be applied to adult gays and lesbians for whom marriage is forbidden. The Local Government Act 1988 reflected this view when it referred to 'pretended family relationships' between homosexuals. Gays and lesbians are not, however, forbidden to live together as partners in an intimate, caring supportive relationship. Many gays would use the word family to cover their network of close friends and lovers – a family of choice. In 1999 the legal status of homosexual partnerships was tested in the courts. The decision of the Law Lords is very significant for the meaning of 'family' in Britain in the 21st century.

LORDS' GAY RULING RE-DEFINES THE FAMILY

Gay rights campaigners were celebrating a significant victory last night after the House of Lords ruled that a homosexual couple in a stable relationship can be defined as a family. Lord Nicholls said: 'A man and woman living together in a stable and permanent sexual relationship are capable of becoming members of a family. Once this is accepted, there can be no rational or other basis on which the like conclusion can be withheld from a similarly stable and permanent relationship between two men and between two women. The concept underlying membership of a family for present purposes is the sharing of lives together in a single family unit living in one house.'

Lord Clyde added: 'It seems to me that essentially the bond must be one of love and affection, not of a casual or transitory nature, but in a relationship which is permanent or at least intended to be so.

As a result of that permanent attachment, other characteristics will follow, such as a readiness to support each other emotionally and financially, to care for and look after each other in times of need, and to provide a companionship in which mutual interests and activities can be shared.'

Adapted from an article by Matt Wells in *The Guardian*, 29 October 1999

Men as fathers – the future

It is important when discussing the ways in which family life has changed during the last 20 or 30 years not to neglect those changes related to men as husbands, partners and fathers. During the 1990s newspaper headlines sometimes suggested that, whilst the position of women could be seen as having improved in some ways, many men were finding things increasingly difficult. Two changes in particular have been highlighted: changes in employment and changes in the expectations of woman. Look at the following headlines

Fatherhood at Crisis Point

From *The Observer* 21 April 1996

Death of the Dad

From *The Observer* 2 November 1997

Are Men of the Nineties Allowing Women to Trample all Over Them?

From *The Times* 14 October 1996

Floundering Fathers

From *The Independent* 20 April 1996

Ditch your Man and be Happy

Women thrive on their own but single men are sad a new survey claims.

From *The Observer* 17 October 1999

In the 1950s, most adult men under 65 were married breadwinners for a family. This role was a major part of the male identity. Having been brought up to earn a living and be responsible for a family, men knew what was expected of them as adults. Having a job enabled a man to fulfil these expectations – bring in the money – and put him in a position in which he could expect his wife in return to look after him, the home and the children. The difference in the roles of men and women was emphasised by the nature of the work through which many men earned an income – dangerous work, often requiring the kind of skills and/or physical strength which, within society at the time, it was considered impossible or inappropriate for a woman to possess.

The work situation has changed for many men. Jobs requiring physical strength and little skill have become scarce, leaving a section of the male population with limited opportunities for permanent employment and, therefore, of limited value to any woman as a potential breadwinner. Many other jobs carry a higher risk of unemployment than in the past. For other men, and women, the demands put on them by their work create difficulties for them as a member of a family. Employers today insist on 'flexible' workers who are willing, for example, to work 'unsocial' hours. For many the breadwinner role cannot now be performed during the day whilst the children are at school. The time and energy devoted to earning an income may, therefore, make it difficult for a man in this situation to satisfy the other expectations of his partner and children – particularly since neither his partner nor his children are likely to see him just as a breadwinner.

With married women being more involved as income earners the man in a partnership is less likely than in the 1950s to be the sole breadwinner. The roles which a man and woman play in the family are less likely to be rigidly differentiated. Today the division of labour within a family partnership is often on a more flexible basis – both may earn an income at various times and there may be some sharing of household and childcare duties. Some sociologists have found the phrases **symmetrical** family and **joint conjugal roles** useful in this context. Men have had and are having to learn to cope with a situation in which their partners expect to negotiate on a more equal basis how family life will be organised.

A much larger proportion of males than in the 1950s are likely to remain single. Women are no longer in a situation in which they have to enter a marriage on a man's terms. There are many socially acceptable, potentially fulfilling alternatives available today: being single and

	1961	1998/1999
ONE PERSON		
Under pensionable age	4	14
Over pensionable age	7	15
TWO OR MORE UNRELATED ADULTS	5	2
COUPLE WITH		
No children	26	30
Children	48	29
LONE PARENTS	6	10
MULTIFAMILY HOUSEHOLDS	3	1

Adapted from Table in Social Trends 30

Figure 9 Type of household percentages

childless, being single with a child, cohabiting on a permanent or temporary basis with either a male or another woman. There are and will be, therefore, fewer women readily available to become wives.

EXERCISE

Look at the table above and answer the following questions:

ia) For which types of household have the percentages increased between 1961 and 1998/1999?

ib) For which types of household have the percentages decreased between 1961 and 1998/1999?

ii) Which of these upwards or downwards trends might the following help us to explain?

→ the increase in the number of divorces
→ the increase in the average age at which people marry
→ the increase in the number of years people can expect to live
→ the decline in the number of marriages
→ the decline in the average number of children women have.

iiia) What might a woman today see as the advantages and disadvantages of living alone, as being part of a cohabiting couple or as part of a married couple?

iiib) What might a man today see as the advantages and disadvantages of the different ways of living?

iiic) Is the balance between the advantages and disadvantages the same for both men and women?

Children

How children behave will always be a significant part of any discussion of how well or badly the family is doing. Children are a major product of the family – a faulty product may indicate that something is wrong with the way it is being produced. Those who are worried that properly ordered family life is less common in society today often point to what they see as the inevitable result – a rise in anti-social behaviour amongst young people.

Recognise that, whilst it is easy to assert that this or that kind of family is better or worse for children in some way or other, it is difficult to demonstrate on the basis of sound evidence that such assertions are valid. Children are influenced by their family relationships but they are also influenced by the material conditions in which they live, their school, their friends, the mass media and much more. When so many factors are significant it is hard to separate out and weigh the influence of one of them.

Imagine you wished to find out whether having divorced parents was related to children's attitudes and behaviours in some respect or another. You would need to compare two groups of children the only difference between which was that one group had divorced parents and the other group had parents who had not divorced. Any difference in their attitudes and behaviour might then be seen as related to whether or not the child's parents had divorced. Finding children with divorced parents might not be difficult. Finding children with parents whose marriage has 'broken down' but who have got divorced would probably present problems. The comparison must, however, be with children in such families. If it was made with children whose parents had happy marriages any difference between the two groups could be related to how happy the family relationships were rather than to whether the parents had divorced or not.

Recognise that many people with strong convictions of one kind or another want the results from research to support their convictions. Be cautious! Before attaching significance to any conclusions find out how they were arrived at.

Abuse

Of growing concern to members of the public in recent years have been various kinds of child abuse. Shocking cases attracting headlines in the media along with the statistics published by children's charities and helplines have suggested a dark side of relationships between adults and children and children and children. It is no longer possible to think of violent and sexual abuse of children, or bullying as rare and exceptional occurrences. It is, of course, difficult to make comparisons with the past. Reporting abuse has been made easier – through confidential helplines, for example. Adult attitudes have changed, so that a child reporting abuse is more likely to be taken seriously today, whether by a relative or the official agencies. How much greater is the risk of abuse today is difficult to calculate. Parents, however, do see the world in which they are raising their children as more dangerous than the world in which they themselves were brought up. The consequence of this is that many children are very closely supervised by their parents.

Adults can, of course, suffer violent abuse form their children.

WHY SO FEW TEARS FOR CHILDREN KILLED BY THEIR PARENTS?

For more than 30 years, the numbers of child murders by someone unknown to them have remained static, at around five each year. Despite what we imagine they have not been going up. The chances of a child being killed by a parent are considerably higher; between 70 and 80 children are murdered each year by their mum or dad and 10% of all murders are by the victim's parent.

Adapted from an article by Dea Birkett in *The Guardian*, Thursday 20 July 2000.

PARANOIA OVER STRANGER DANGER LEAVES YOUNG PEOPLE UNPREPARED TO COPE WITH REAL LIFE

Twenty years ago 90% of children walked to school on their own; now the figure is 9%. A survey amongst 7–14-year-olds found that fear of abduction was greater than fear of being hit by a car. Latest figures for traffic accidents show that nearly 300 children are killed each year on the roads and 45,000 are injured.

Adapted from an article by Martin Bright in *The Observer*, 1 August 1999

EXERCISE

Read the two articles again and answer the following questions:

i) According to the information in the articles, were children more likely to be killed by
   a) a traffic accident,
   b) a stranger
   c) a parent?
ii) How might a sociologist explain why children are more likely to fear abduction than being hit by a car?
iii) How might a sociologist explain why children being killed by a stranger receives more coverage in the media than children being killed by their parents?
iv) What important beliefs are challenged and perhaps threatened when members of society hear of children being killed by their parents?
va) In what ways might fear of 'stranger danger' influence the ways in which children are brought up?
vb) What might be the consequences for the relationships between parents and their children?
vc) In what ways might fear of 'stranger danger' make public spaces more dangerous for children?

CHARITY PHONELINE FOR BATTERED PARENTS UNCOVERS THE LAST TABOO OF DOMESTIC VIOLENCE.

Horrific levels of violence by teenagers against their parents have been uncovered by a report tackling the taboo topic of adolescent thuggery in the home. Exposing the myth that only a small minority of families have difficulties, the research reveals that it is commonplace for parents to be battered by their offspring. The extent of family rifts was investigated by the charity Parentline plus which has had 10,000 calls within a year of launching its confidential helpline number.

Adapted from an article by Tracy McVeigh in *The Observer*, 9 April 2000

EXERCISE

Consider all the articles on domestic violence in this chapter and answer the following questions:

i) Are there any characteristics of the structures of modern families or the circumstances in which we live in them that might help us to explain the levels of violence discovered.

ii) To what extent does the incidence of violence within the family challenge the idea of the family as a group of people with whom an individual is safe?

Friends

We do not choose our mother, father, brothers or sisters, but the situations within which we live with them and the norms of our society make the relationships we have with them of great practical and emotional significance to us. We are expected to love, respect and care for our close relatives – whether or not they are loveable or worthy of any respect or care.

At the same time we have friends. From an early age we recognise the importance of friendship and attach a positive value to the word friend. An angry seven-year-old can reduce another seven-year-old to tears by snapping, 'I'm not your friend'. The tearful seven-year-old recognises that to lose friendship is to lose something which matters. Adults can use the word friend to distinguish between different kinds of relationship. The divorcing couple who say, 'I hope we can remain friends after the divorce', imply that marriage is not the only possible significant relationship available to them.

A set of friends does not become an institution like a family. You will not find chapters in sociology text books headed 'The Sociology of Friendship.' And yet friends play a vital part in an individual's life in society. Imagine how sad anyone would feel for someone who answered 'No' to the question 'Have you any friends?' As young children it is with friends that we learn how to get on with others of our own age. As teenagers it is because we have friends that we feel able to risk challenging our parents. As adults we can receive advice or companionship from our friends. Do not neglect the status 'friend' when analysing the way in which we live in society.

Contact with relatives and friends, 1986 and 1995

Great Britain		Percentages
	1986	**1995**
Mother	59	49
Father	51	40
Sibling	33	29
Adult Child	66	58
Other relative	42	35
Best Friend	65	59

From Social Trends 30 2000

Figure 10 (Percentage of adult respondents seeing relative or friend at least once a week).

Attitudes towards family and friends 1995

	Males		Females	
	18–44	45 and over	18–44	45 and over
I try to stay in touch with relatives not just close friends	30	48	42	60
I'd rather spend time with my friends than my family	19	10	14	9
On the whole, my friends are more important	9	8	7	6

From Social Trends 28 1998

Figure 11 Percentage of those who stay in touch with family and friends.

EXERCISE

Study the tables and answer the following questions:

- From the first table.
i) Did contact with relatives and friends increase or decrease between 1986 and 1995?
ii) How might a sociologist explain this change?
- From the second table
iiia) In what way do the attitudes of males differ from those of females and do the attitudes of 18–44-year-olds differ from those of over 45-year-olds. Note, the difference is only slight.
iiib) How might the differences be explained?
iv) What would a young woman be trying to communicate if she says 'My mum is my best friend'? What does being a 'best friend' add to being a mum?
v) In what ways might the existence of friendship between people be seen as making a positive contribution to the working of society. In other words, what might a sociologist see as the 'functions' of friendship?
vi) To what extent do you think that it is reasonable to argue that changes in family life over the last 30 years have led to friends playing a more significant part in people's lives.

The limitations of the chapters

Having come to the end of this chapter, the first in the book to deal with a particular sociological topic, you might have begun to realise how difficult it is to organise a sociology textbook or course. Any study of sociology must start somewhere. Yet whichever topic is chosen there will be information which the student will not have until later which would have helped him or her at the start. One aspect of life in society influences, and is influenced by, all other aspects of life in society. Life within a family, for example, is influenced very much by the position of the family within the social structure. Later in the book you will be introduced to various aspects of social inequality. Having read that chapter you may wish to reread this chapter on the family. You will then have greater knowledge of the ways in which some individuals and groups are able, because of their wealth, power and social status, to control their lives – family life included – in ways which are not possible for most of us. The consequences of lone parenthood for someone with his or her own house and an income of £70,000 per year are rather different from those of someone on £15,000 per year living in a rented flat. For most of us satisfying the obligation to care for an ageing parent involves much greater upheaval than for someone in a position to say to their estate manager, 'Redecorate the west wing will you Chivers, memmy's coming to live with us.' In our society we have a 'Royal Family' and a 'Royle Family'.

GLOSSARY

Cohabiting couple family A family formed by a couple who, whilst living together in a stable relationship, are not married.

Conjugal rights The roles which husband and wife, or two partners, play within their marriage or partnership.

Segregated conjugal roles has sometimes been used to suggest a situation in which the man and woman play very different roles: the man goes out to earn the money, the woman looks after the house and children. A man who will never make himself a cup of tea because "that's her job – a kitchen is no place for a man", is thinking in terms of segregated conjugal roles. Segregated also suggests that, to some extent, the man and woman live separate lives – he spends time with his workmates, she with female relatives and neighbours.

Joint conjugal roles has sometimes been used to suggest a situation in which the man and the woman do not think in terms of man's role or woman's role. Joint suggests shared responsibility, whether for earning money, caring for children or housework and doing things together.

Coparenting Many children today have parents who do not have a permanent relationship with each other. Coparenting or shared parenting refers to an arrangement in which a child spends part of the week with one parent and part with the other.

Extended family A family group consisting of three or more generations. "Extended" expresses the continuity of the family by recognising that when someone marries and "has a family of his or her own", he or she remains a son or daughter, brother or sister within the family into which he or she was born. Extended familiy members include grandparents, aunties, cousins, in-laws.

Feminist approach Feminist approaches within sociology focus on showing and explaining why, women have been and still are treated as 'second class citizens' in many areas of social life. These approaches claim that societies have usually been organised so that the interests of men have been looked after and the interests and wishes of women largely disregarded.

Household A household can be a person living alone or a group of people with the same address who share their living arrangements. It is important to distinguish between Household and Family, particularly when looking at tables of statistics.

Monogamy A norm or rule which permits a husband to have only one wife at a time and a wife to have only one husband.

Patriarchal A patriarchal organisation is one in which the men rule over the women. In a patriarchal family, for example, the men have the authority.

Polygamy A norm or rule which permits a husband to have more than one wife at a time or a wife to have more than one husband at a time.

Reconstituted family A reconstituted family is formed when at least one of the two partners in a marriage or permanent relationship has children from a previous relationship (**a step family**).

Serial monogamy This refers to the situation in which someone, whilst married at any time to only one person, has had , during his or her lifetime, two, three or more wives or husbands.

Symmetrical family This phrase was developed to identify families in which the roles of the man and the woman were similar and equal. In a symmetrical family both partners have paid jobs and both partners undertake housework and childcare tasks.

Education

3

Time Scale

1944   The Butler Education Act. Introduces free compulsory secondary education for all based on selection at 11 – the tripartite system.

1965   The Labour government requests that Local Education Authorities submit their plans for comprehensive reorganisation.

1976   Jim Callaghan, Labour Prime Minister, initiates the 'Great Debate' on education about standards and skills – about how well education was preparing young people for work.

1979   Conservative government elected.

1988   The Education Reform Act. Introduced SATs, publication of results, and the National Curriculum amongst other reforms.

1997   New Labour government elected. Abolition of grants and introduction of tuition fees for Higher Education. Selection was not abolished.

What does the education system of Britain look like? Before answering we need to define some terms.

→ State schools: are those which are maintained from public funds – through taxation.
→ Independent schools: are privately financed through charging fees.
→ Selective schools: are those that select their pupils, usually through some form of examination.
→ Comprehensive schools: are those that are non selective, where entry is not dependent upon passing an examination.

It is misleading to talk of the British Education system as there are significant differences between England and Wales, Scotland and Northern Ireland.

● In England and Wales and Northern Ireland pupils take GCSE examinations at 16 (General Certificate of Secondary Education), whereas in Scotland the examination is the SCE, Standard Grade (Scottish Certificate of Education)
● In Scotland all pupils in state schools attend comprehensive schools, as do all pupils at state schools in Wales. In England a minority of pupils of state schools attend selective schools. In Northern Ireland all state school pupils attend selective schools.
● In England a higher percentage of pupils attend independent schools than in Wales or Scotland.

Schooling is compulsory between the ages of five and 16, and it is free at state schools. At the age of 16 pupils may:

- Leave
- Stay on in the sixth form if the school has one
- Transfer to a Sixth Form College or college of further education, or tertiary college.

After two years in England, Wales and Northern Ireland pupils may have obtained A Levels, Advanced GNVQs or Advanced Vocational Certificate of Education, or a BTEC certificate. In Scotland the traditional examination for university is the SCE Higher Grade which is taken in four or five subjects after one year. Vocational courses are also available e.g. GSVQs.

After further or post 16 education some individuals go on to higher education at a university or college. The universities can be divided into two groups. The 'new' universities are those that were previously known as polytechnics but were able to change their names to University in 1993. The 'old' universities are those that were called universities before 1993. Some degree courses are offered, wholly or in part, in further education colleges, and the Open University teaches its undergraduates (those who are studying for a degree) by distance learning, using TV and radio as well as printed material.

As you can see from the above, the idea of an education system in Britain is quite misleading. It is also misleading to think of pupils and students as all being of a similar age. Many adults are now returning to education to obtain qualifications for the first time or to update their existing qualifications. Over 50% of students on degree courses are over 21. Many mature students (over 21) return to F.E. colleges to follow 'Access' courses as an alternative means of gaining entry into university to A Level type courses. The Labour Government elected in 1997 has stressed the idea of Lifelong Learning. This is the idea that we should never consider ourselves too old to study a subject or to obtain new skills.

What is education for?

Many of us will have wondered at some time in our educational careers 'why do we have to go to school, what is it for?' Sociologists have identified three roles that education plays in society:

i)   Education continues our socialisation.
ii)   Education prepares us for work.
iii) Education prepares us to be citizens, it prepares us to take our place as adults in society.

These roles of education overlap quite a lot, as we shall see, but we will deal with them separately in order to explain the role of education in exactly the same way.

There are significant differences between sociologists who believe that society is based upon consensus and those who believe society is based upon conflict between groups. For **consensus theorists** the education system reflects the shared norms and values of society. Going to school continues the socialisation process that has been started at home in the family. We are socialised at school into the norms and values of society as a whole. We learn what is right and wrong and skills that will benefit us as adults. The education system is an important means of passing on the culture of society from one generation to the next. In this way a stable and orderly society continues to exist. We are taught what the rules of society are and we learn to take our place as adults. From this point of view an important task or function of the education system is to select and grade individuals so that the most able and the most talented are able to take up the most important positions in society. From this point of view education is seen to be part of a meritocratic society, that is a society in which people achieve what they can on the basis of their own skills or talents or abilities and not on the basis of how much money they have or who they know, or who their parents are.

Conflict theorists take a different view of the role of education in society. For conflict theorists society is the way it is because some individuals and groups have more power than others and they use this power to look after their own interests. From this point of view education is seen as an important means of passing on the inequalities that exist in society from one generation to the next. Conflict theorists see the education system as being an important way of reproducing inequality. They see the education system as working for the benefit of those who have power in society. In this way those who start their lives at the top of the social scale, growing up in rich and powerful families, are likely themselves to take up powerful positions. Those who start at the bottom of the social scale learn to accept their place, and are likely themselves to take up positions at the bottom of the social scale.

Education, socialisation and social control

Our socialisation starts in the family and continues during our education. At school we are taught how to behave, we learn to mix with other children from a variety of backgrounds, we learn about the history and geography of the country we live in, we learn about some of its cultural heritage in literature, art and science. In the classroom we learn to work as individuals; in organised games we learn to work as part of a team. From the consensus point of view we are being socialised into the norms and values of our culture.

The process of social control is important here too. There are both formal and informal social controls in school or college. There are the formal rules that we have to obey – school uniform, when to walk and when to run, not fighting or bullying, doing our homework – and then there are the informal rules we are bound by in our peer group, for example, how to wear our uniform, how much homework to admit to doing, and the rules about what is appropriate behaviour for a boy and for a girl.

If we break the formal rules we may be punished with a detention, by being put on report, or in extreme cases by being excluded or by being expelled. If we conform to the formal rules of school we may be rewarded with house points, merits, stars or prizes for achievement. If we break the informal rules of our peer group we may be laughed at, teased or ostracised. By conforming to these informal rules we are rewarded with friendship, acceptance or status within the group.

Many sociologists make a distinction between two kinds of education. **Formal education** is that which happens in lessons when we learn subjects like maths, sociology, science and languages. Formal education is what we are supposed to be learning at school. **Informal education** is what we learn in other ways while we are at school or college. As we have already said we learn a lot from our peers, but sociologists have also pointed out how we learn from what is not on the curriculum, from what they call ' the hidden curriculum'.

The **hidden curriculum** refers to what we learn from the way in which school or college is organised and from the way in which education is carried out in school or college. For those sociologists who believe that the education system passes on the inequalities that exist in society from one generation to the next the hidden curriculum is particularly important because it helps the continuation of class inequalities (inequalities of power and wealth), gender inequalities and inequalities between different ethnic groups in society.

The hidden curriculum and class inequalities

According to conflict theorists one of the requirements of a capitalist society (see chapter 6) is that there is a work force that is subservient, that is to say it does what it is told, and that will not challenge the authority of those who run the firms and corporations that it works for. According to this group of sociologists the hidden curriculum helps to produce an obedient and docile work force that is willing to accept the authority of those above them and that will not expect too much satisfaction from the work that it has to do.

At school and college we are encouraged to accept the idea of hierarchy. Some individuals have more power than others. Pupils have to do what teachers tell them. Pupils have very little say over what they are taught or how they are taught it or when they are taught. Learning to accept the authority of teachers over what we do and when we do it is said to prepare us for work. At work we will have to do what our boss tells us, when he or she tells us and we'll have to work how they want us to.

Also, from this point of view, many of the jobs available in a capitalist society are dull, repetitive and boring. Such jobs do not offer much satisfaction and don't require much knowledge of the overall production process. For example if you were employed as a packer in a biscuit factory you would not need to know how to make biscuits or how to advertise and market a new line. Your main source of job satisfaction would probably be in your weekly pay packet.

Schooling is said to prepare us for this kind of dull and fragmented work in two ways. First of all at school we learn to work for external rewards – a gold star, a house point, a GCSE certificate – rather than for the intrinsic satisfaction of studying for its own sake. The real reward of study is not the joy of learning but the certificate which is the route to a job with a decent pay packet. Also at school we study in a 'fragmented' fashion – a maths lesson, a French lesson, PE, science, sociology – with no connection between the subjects. This fragmentation of subjects is said to prepare us for work where most of us will work on a little part or detail of the system in a factory or office with no overview of the whole system. Because the work is dull we'll do it, not for the satisfaction to be gained from the job itself, but for external rewards – for pay.

For conflict theorists the hidden curriculum can be seen as a form of social control. It teaches us to accept the inequalities that exist in the wider society. Because we learn to accept and not challenge these inequalities they continue to exist from one generation to the next. Inequality is therefore reproduced by the education system.

The hidden curriculum and gender roles

Although boys and girls all now have to follow the national curriculum and therefore study the same subjects the hidden curriculum is said to be important in reproducing traditional gender roles. This happens in a variety of ways, but in each case what is being emphasised is that there are acceptable forms of behaviour, abilities and careers for girls and different ones for boys. The role of the hidden curriculum in relation to gender roles is to emphasise the difference between the genders as opposed to emphasising equality.

For example girls may find that they are punished more severely than boys for fighting at school. This difference in punishments emphasises the idea that it is 'unfeminine' to fight, but more acceptable for boys to act in such a way. Girls may also find that teachers are more likely to criticise their work for being untidy than for being wrong. Boys are less likely to find their work criticised for being untidy, but more likely to find it criticised for being inaccurate. Again, this distinction emphasises traditional gender roles. Many school text books also reinforce traditional gender roles. Illustrations in science texts often show men rather than women in the role of scientist. In the 1970s many reading schemes for primary school children were criticised for showing women in a limited number of roles, mainly domestic ones, or in traditional women's jobs such as nurse or primary school teacher. Although publishers of such text books have made efforts to change this many of these books are still used.

Games and PE at school can also emphasise the difference between masculine and feminine gender roles. Some games are seen as more appropriate for boys – football, rugby, cricket; and some more so for girls – hockey, netball, or lacrosse, for example. Although some of these differences are disappearing it is perhaps true that a boy who is not interested in sport is regarded by his peers and by his teachers as more 'deviant' i.e. less masculine than a girl who is not interested in sports. Being interested in sports is not part of the traditional 'feminine' gender role.

Teacher expectations (see later in this chapter) can also affect the subjects that boys and girls choose. Teachers who have themselves grown up at a time when gender stereotyping at school was not questioned are likely to encourage girls and boys to choose subjects that fit with their ideas of appropriate careers for each gender. Girls may find themselves encouraged into subjects that prepare them for careers or jobs in the caring or secretarial fields, boys may be encouraged into construction, engineering, science or computing. Many teachers will still have the expectation that boys will be the main breadwinners in the future and this idea may well be communicated to their pupils in career talks or during the course of lessons.

In these various ways the hidden curriculum is said to contribute to the persistence of gender inequalities in society.

The hidden curriculum and ethnic inequalities

What goes on in schools and colleges also has consequences for equality between different ethnic groups in society. For example some sociologists have pointed out the ethnocentric nature of the curriculum. This means that the curriculum is based on a particular culture – white British culture – and does not take adequate account of the various cultures that exist in

British society. Some sociologists have agreed that this can lead to members of minority ethnic groups feeling that their culture is not valued or is seen as second rate, as somehow inferior, which is said to lead to feelings of low self esteem, and therefore a lack of self confidence. This is said to happen particularly to Afro-Caribbean children. However not all sociologists agree with this point of view. Some say that the expectations of teachers, the lack of role models, racism and stereotyping are more important factors in explaining some of the differences between different ethnic groups in educational achievement. These factors are dealt with later in this chapter.

How does education prepare us for work?

As we have seen in the sections above education is said by some sociologists to be important in preparing us for work by socialising us into having the right kinds of attitudes to take up our place in the work force (this is the conflict view). For others education is important because it grades us according to our abilities so that we can take up a place in the work force on merit (the consensus view). There are other ways in which education prepares us for work.

First of all many schools and colleges now offer vocational courses which prepare us for work by giving us practical experience of a particular job, like nursery nursing or secretarial work, while also teaching us the knowledge and skills required to carry out our chosen occupation. Courses such as GNVQs, AVCEs, BTECs, are designed to give us vocational experience of an area of work. During secondary schooling, too, pupils have to undertake a two-week work placement to find out what is involved in working for a living. This 'vocational education' is dealt with in more detail later in this chapter.

Schools also prepare us for work in other ways. We have to be punctual and we have to meet deadlines (for homework or course work) just as we would have to at work. With the introduction of Key Skills in IT, Communication and Application of Number, schools and colleges are attempting to ensure that their pupils have some grasp of the skills that will be required in most working environments.

While conflict theorists tend to stress the roles of education and especially the hidden curriculum in reproducing the inequalities of the wider society, consensus theorists say that the education system prepares us for work in a different way. One role that the education system plays in society is that of getting us used to being judged on our abilities rather than as who we are. For this group of sociologists the education system helps us to move from being dependent on our family to being independent. Gradually in the move from infant school to secondary school, college, or university we are said to learn that it is what we can do that is important, not who we are. The education system is important because it helps us fit into the wider society on the basis of our abilities.

How does education prepare us for adulthood, for citizenship?

By the time this book is published the present New Labour government (elected in 1997) may well have produced details of its citizenship courses which aim to teach individuals about the rights (what you can do) and responsibilities (what can reasonably be expected of you) of citizens. However schools and colleges prepare us for our adult lives in many ways.

First of all we learn to get along with others while we are at school. We meet people from a range of backgrounds with different beliefs, values and attitudes to our own. An important part of schooling is learning that we are not all the same and learning that it is possible not only to get on with others who are different but also to respect such differences and maybe even learn from them.

Secondly as we go through school we may be given responsibilities, such as being a prefect, which can help us prepare for adult responsibilities. An important responsibility that we all have at school is respecting the rights of others. If we expect to have the right to go through school without being bullied or harassed by others then an important part of schooling is learning to ensure that we extend that right to others. As individuals it is our responsibility to ensure that all our peers enjoy the rights that we want to enjoy. Learning this link between rights and responsibilities is an important part of preparation for adulthood. Some schools build this into their organisation by, for example, having older pupils to whom younger pupils who are being bullied can turn in order to resolve their problem. Other schools have a school council where pupils have the right to discuss some of the rules and regulations that govern everyday life in school. Of course pupils then have the responsibility of ensuring that the rules are obeyed.

Finally there are aspects of the curriculum that are an explicit attempt to prepare us for adulthood. Lessons such as PSE, sex education or parenting skills exist in order to prepare us for our adult lives.

How successful do you think school is in preparing pupils for adulthood?

What aspects of adult life do you think are not dealt with at school? How do you think you could be prepared for adulthood?

Recent reforms to the education system

Over the last 25 years education has become a major political issue in Great Britain. Both the various Conservative governments elected between 1979 and 1992 and the Labour Government elected in 1997 have tried to do two things: raise standards and improve skills.

Conservative governments introduced 'market forces' and greater central government control over education. Their idea was that if 'market forces' or greater competition between schools was introduced then successful schools would flourish (rather like shops in the high street) and the unsuccessful schools would be forced to improve in order to survive (again like unsuccessful shops in the high street). By giving parents freedom of choice over where to send their children, and by making sure that they had the information they needed to make such choices, Conservative governments turned the education system into a market place where schools were in competition for pupils. The more pupils a school attracted the more funding (money) it received.

By taking control of the curriculum, by making pupils take tests at particular stages of their education (7, 11, 14 and16) and by making schools publish their results, Conservative governments were providing the 'rules' for the competition between schools.

According to the Conservative point of view, standards would rise because parents would want to send their children to the 'best' schools. By publishing the results of tests parents would know which the best schools were and they would choose to send their children to those schools. Weaker schools would be forced to improve because if they did not they would be forced to close through lack of money.

The New Labour government has not altered much of what the various Conservative governments introduced although it has placed much less emphasis on competition between schools, and more emphasis on control of education by central government. So they have said that failing schools will be closed, and reopened under a new name with a new head teacher and a reorganised management. 'Failing schools' are those that do not meet the government's targets for achievement. So under a Labour government it is not the 'market place' or competition between schools that decides whether a school survives or not, it is whether or not a school meets the targets set by the government.

Raising the standards – the 1988 Education Reform Act

The 1988 Education Reform Act introduced what were probably the most significant changes to the education system since 1944. The changes included:

- **The National Curriculum**
  All pupils aged five to 16 had to study the 'core' subjects of English, maths and science and 'foundation' subjects which included history, geography, a foreign language and design and technology. For each of the subjects there are set 'programmes of study'. This was an attempt to raise standards by ensuring that all pupils regardless of gender, class or ethnicity studied the same subjects. The introduction of the National Curriculum was also an attempt to raise standards by prescribing what pupils should know at each stage of their school careers. In 1994 the National Curriculum was greatly reduced and simplified because the original was widely seen as too bureaucratic and complicated. Testing was restricted to the three core subjects.

- **Testing and Attainment Targets**
  SAT's (Standard Assessment Tasks) were introduced for children aged 7, 11, 14 and 16. The attainment targets are what children can be expected to know and understand about the National Curriculum subjects. Schools had to publish the results of the SATS and their GCSE, A Level and GNVQ results. These results are now published in the form of 'league tables' which show how well each school is performing. This was an attempt to raise stan-

dards by encouraging competition between schools and also by giving parents information about the quality of their local schools so that they could choose the best for their children.

- **Open Enrolment and Parental Choice**
  This was a further way of encouraging competition between schools. In theory parents can choose the school they want their child to attend and schools have to take pupils providing they have vacancies. In practice many schools are physically only able to take pupils from their 'priority area', which is the area from which they have to take pupils first, and so parental choice is limited. The idea behind this reform was that schools which did not attract the maximum number of pupils that they were able to would lose money.

- **Formula Funding**
  The money that schools receive for books, equipment, teachers' pay, and so on is largely based on the number of pupils they enroll. This was an attempt to raise standards by rewarding successful schools, because they would receive more money, and by providing an incentive for poorer schools to improve. If their results improved they would attract more pupils and so they would receive more money.

- **Local Management of Schools (LMS)**
  Before the 1988 act local education authorities had a great deal of control over school budgets. After 1988 school heads and school governors were given much more control over the way in which the school budget was spent. This particular reform was designed to reduce the power of local education authorities and to make schools much more able to respond to the needs of their local communities and to the wishes of parents (through the parent governors).

- **City Technology Colleges**
  The 1988 act allowed for the creation of City Technology Colleges CTCS which were to specialise in technology. In this way they would not only contribute to raising standards, but also to improving the skills required by industry. The CTCs were sponsored by private industry so that the government did not have to pay the full cost of building them. They are also independent of local education authority control and in competition with local schools.

- **Grant Maintained Schools or 'Opting Out'**
  The 1988 act gave schools the option of 'opting out' of local education authority control. This could only be done if the parents approved of it in a ballot. 'Opting out' meant that a school could, for example, choose to be a selective school even if other schools in its local authority area were comprehensive. Grant maintained schools were funded directly by the government. It was thought that making schools directly responsible for their own affairs, by making them self governing, would help to raise standards. The Labour government abolished grant maintained status in part to prevent such schools 'creaming off' the best students in an area.

Other reforms aimed at raising standards

The system of inspection was altered by the Conservatives. **OFSTED (The Office for Standards in Education)** was introduced. Schools were to be inspected at regular intervals and the results of these inspections were to be published. OFSTED inspections were widely seen by teachers as being more critical and less supportive of their efforts than the previous style of inspections. Publication of inspection reports was thought to be a way of raising standards because it would allow parents and prospective parents to see the strengths and weaknesses of particular schools.

- The Conservative government also introduced the Parent's Charter which was designed to give parents more information about their children's schools. For example under the Parent's Charter schools have to produce a prospectus which shows their exam results in comparison with national averages; they have to produce a governors' report which is sent to all parents giving details of exam and test results and truancy rates and a breakdown of the school budget, and provide a written report on each pupil at least once a year.

- In 1993 all **further education colleges** were taken out of local authority control and received their money instead from the Further Education Funding Council. The money that each college received was directly related to the number of students it enrolled. In this further education colleges were encouraged to compete for students. This competition, it was thought, would help to raise standards. Inspection of further education colleges was carried out by the Further Education Funding Council and the results, like those of schools, were published. Again this was seen as a way of raising standards. In 2001 the Further Education Funding Council was replaced by Learning and Skills Councils introduced by the Labour government. One aim of this particular change was to reduce the competition for students between colleges. Another aim was to encourage the development of Centres of Excellence in post-16 education.

- The Labour government has introduced further reforms. Although the Labour Party is opposed to selection it has not abolished grammar schools. The main change has been a move away from the idea that competition between schools will raise standards to an idea that standards will raise if the government takes direct action to make improvements. This is known as 'state intervention'. So the Labour government has announced targets for improvement together with penalties for failure. Schools that fail to make improvements face closure, and local education authorities that are failing may lose their powers and be taken over by outside agencies.

Particular reforms aimed at raising standards introduced since 1997 are:

- **Education Action Zones**
  These were introduced in 1998 in areas which had high levels of deprivation and low levels of educational achievement. The aim was to raise standards by providing extra help for pupils, by the introduction of homework clubs, and by paying teachers more to work in such areas. Schools in such Action Zones can deviate from the National Curriculum if they wish in order to raise the ability levels of their pupils.

- **Home-School Contracts**

  To try and involve parents more in their children's education all schools have to issue a contract in which parents agree to try to make sure their children do their best at school and the school agrees to meet its responsibilities to the pupils.

- **The Literacy and Numeracy Hour**

  Primary schools have to set aside one hour per week to concentrate on the basic skills of literacy and numeracy.

- **Curriculum 2000**

  From September 2000 there has been a change at advanced level. Pupils now study four or five AS levels for one year and then specialise in two or three which are the equivalent of the old style A levels. It was thought that this would raise standards by giving pupils a broader range of subjects to study in year 12 and perhaps encourage them to mix arts and science subjects, before deciding to specialise. Key Skills were also introduced so that all students in post-16 education would have at least basic skills in Communication, Application of Number and Information Technology. The aim of this change was not only to raise standards but also to improve the skills that school leavers need for employment.

The 2002 National Targets for 16-year-olds are:

50% of 16-year-olds to achieve five or more grades A*–C at GCSE or equivalent. In 1999/2000 49.2% have achieved this target compared with 47.9% in 1998/99.

95% of 16-year-olds to achieve one or more GCSE or equivalent. In 1999/2000 94.4% achieved this target compared with 94.0% in 1998/99.

(Source DFEE SRF/2000 15.11.2000 – First release www.dfee.gov/statistics/DB/SPR)

Higher education

One way of raising the educational standard of the population as a whole is to increase the numbers of individuals in higher education, studying for degrees or diplomas. The number of students in higher education expanded rapidly during the late 1980s and the 1990s. However, higher education is expensive. The Conservatives cut back the value of the student grant and introduced loans for undergraduates. The Labour government, controversially, abolished student grants altogether in 1998 and introduced the idea of students making a contribution of up to £1000 towards the cost of their tuition. The requirement to pay tuition fees is means tested and many students have to make no payment at all.

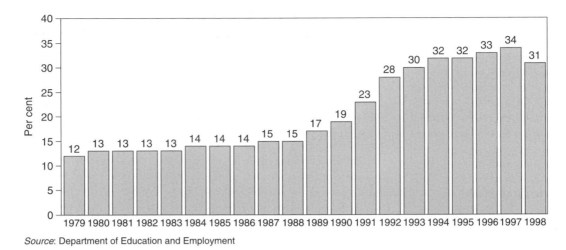

Source: Department of Education and Employment

Figure 12 Proportion of young people entering higher education, 1979–1998.

EXERCISE

Look again at the table and answer the following question

Why do you think the proportion of young people entering Higher Education dropped slightly in 1998?

Criticisms of recent reforms

One main criticism that has been made of recent reforms in education, particularly by teachers in primary and secondary schools, and further education, has been of the speed with which changes have been made and of the number of changes themselves. Many teachers feel that too many changes have been introduced, and not only that, the amount of paperwork associated with the changes has left many teachers feeling that they have become bureaucrats rather than teachers. This was particularly so with the introduction of the National Curriculum – so much so that it was reviewed following action by teachers' unions and slimmed down in 1994.

SATs have also been criticised. Many teachers and parents have said that testing children at the age of seven could lead to some pupils being 'labelled' (see later in the chapter) as 'failures' at an early stage in their school careers. It has also been suggested that testing children at regular intervals puts too much stress on the content of the tests and that children are simply taught how to succeed in the tests and that therefore they do not receive a broad enough education. Activities such as art, drama and music suffer because of the demands of the tests and those of the National Curriculum.

The 'league tables' have also provoked criticism. First of all they have been criticised for not showing the 'value added' by a school. This means that the tables do not show how much progress is made by the pupils in a particular school. For example a pupil with eight grade As at GCSE might be expected to get good grades at A Level, while a pupil with four Cs might be expected to achieve lower grades at A level. If the pupil with four Cs achieves three B grades at

A level her school or college has added considerable value to her education. The Labour government is committed to producing some measure of 'value added' performance in the league tables but has not done so yet.

The existence of the league tables may not affect teachers and pupils who work in or attend schools that do well. But they have been blamed for having a demoralising effect on both staff and pupils in those schools low down in the league tables. Staff are made to feel that they are failing and pupils may also feel that they are failures. They both may be seen as such by outsiders.

The league tables may also have been responsible for encouraging 'fiddling' of the results. For example selective schools can ensure good results by only admitting pupils who are likely to succeed. But comprehensive schools might also ensure that their results look as good in a number of ways, as this extract from an article by Nick Davies shows:

FIDDLING THE FIGURES TO GET THE RIGHT RESULTS

A teacher says that routinely she writes her students' coursework and that a lot of her colleagues do the same. 'I do it for two reasons. First you give the kid a chance and second, you don't get beaten over the head. Otherwise, you would get the blame for the fact that the kids don't do any work, or don't even turn up, and for the fact that the National Curriculum is crap and doesn't do anything for a load of kids. You are bullied. The bullying of staff by senior management in schools is appalling.'

Welcome to the other side of David Blunkett's drive for higher standards, to the world of tests and targets, where the career prospects of a teacher or the future of a school can be broken by one bad set of statistics, a world where teachers have been taught to fear failure with such an intensity that they have learned to cut corners to survive. Welcome to the Big Cheat . . .

The dealing goes far beyond GCSE coursework – to multiple fiddles on SATs and GCSEs, to the wholesale fabrication of figures on truancy and attendance, to the falsification of records on excluded children. It is certain that not all teachers have been driven to cheat; equally our evidence suggests the fiddling is widespread. . . .

Take for, example, the Truancy Game. The object is to make your attendance figures look good. This has been important since the mid 1990s when Ofsted started to log attendance as an indicator of a school's progress and the Department for Education and Employment (DFEE) started to publish annual figures. Now it has become an even higher priority: David Blunkett has announced that by the year 2002 schools must reduce the number of days lost to truancy by 30%. Schools who fail to hit their targets are liable to lose funds.

In the Truancy Game, points are scored by obliterating the evidence of unauthorised absences, and players can score these points in two simple ways: by pretending that an absent child was really in the school, or by admitting that the child was absent but by pretending that there was a legitimate reason.

In the Exclusion Game the trick is to exclude children without admitting it. 'It's jump before you're pushed. You get hold of the parents and say: "'If you leave him here, we're going to have to kick him out. It'll be on his record for ever and he'll never get a job, so why don't you take him out yourself before it happens? It usually works." Some headteachers call this 'cleansing'. Just about nobody admits they are doing it, but just about everybody knows somebody else who has.

Jenny Price, of the Association of Education Welfare Managers, told us: 'Children whose faces don't fit, children who will never get the required number of A to C grades or whose behaviour is disruptive: these children are removed from rolls. You cannot believe how easy it is. Nobody follows it up, nobody chases it.'

There is no doubt that the most demanding play is seen in the Exam Games. SATs have become a central part of school life, the raw material for the league tables which, despite widespread acknowledgement of their failure to tell the truth about schools, have been firmly lodged as the key indicator of a school's success with critical implications for future enrolment and funding. The pressure from the DFEE has been intense since the Secretary of State announced that he would resign if, by 2002, he could not get 80% of 11-year-olds to reach level four in English and 75% of them in maths. There is almost no pattern to the play in SATS, more like an orgy of improvisation as different teachers slip through different loopholes in search of ways to meet the pressure. . .

Some of the loopholes are more or less legitimate, encouraged even: extra classes to prepare children for the tests; practice work on last year's papers, which are being sold in increasing quantities; the teaching of specific test-related skills, such as the layout and style for writing a letter, which is a regular question in English tests. The DFEE says much of this is simply part of improving literacy and numeracy, and they supply £42m for 'booster classes' for children approaching SATs. However in a narrow distinction, they also say that they do not recommend 'cramming or teaching to the test' and there are many teachers who say this whole focus on SATs is a perversion of education.

Some of the loopholes are more controversial, although they are not actually cheating: teachers who tell children that SATs are 'the most important exams you'll ever take' and that their future sets will depend on them; the headteacher who wanders around the exam room, suggesting 'you might want to have another look at that answer'; the English teacher who supplies a list of 'wizard words' – sophisticated unusual words – for the children to memorise so they can scatter them throughout their English answers; invigilators who ignore the clock and let children have as much time as they want to complete the test.

Then there are loopholes which everyone knows amount to cheating. We spoke to some of those who mark SATs and who see the clues in the answers: the school where every single child used almost exactly the same form of words to describe how shadows are made; the incorrect answers which have been crossed out and replaced with correct ones; the school whose children reproduced the wording from an official answer sheet; the papers where tick boxes are filled out in a hand that is stronger and neater than that on the written parts of the paper.

Taken (and slightly adapted) from an article in *The Guardian* by Nick Davies, 11 July 2000

EXERCISE

Read the article again, and answer the following questions:

i) On the basis of what you have read so far in this chapter, why might teachers be under pressure to 'fiddle the figures'?

ii) Do you recognise any of the practices described in the extract from your time in education?

iii) This article produced an angry response from David Blunkett, saying that it cast a slur on teachers. Why might that be so?

iv) According to what is in the extract, why might the official league tables be misleading?

Parental choice and open enrolment

In January 2001 Martin McGuiness, the Northern Ireland Education minister, announced the abolition of league tables. They were abolished because they were felt to be divisive and "did not offer schools the opportunity to give parents a rounded picture of the school", he said.

The idea that parents have a choice as to where to send their children to school has attracted criticism. Firstly because in many parts of the country, and particularly in rural areas, there is no choice – there is only one school within easy reach. Secondly many people argue that it is only the better off, the middle classes, who are able to exercise a choice. Quite simply, they are able to afford to move house into the priority catchment area of a 'good' school so that their children are able to attend it. Many less well off – usually working class – parents are unable to afford this kind of move. Similarly the better off are able to afford the costs of travelling if a child is to attend a school of their choice which is some distance from home. Local schools may well be the only option for the less well off. From this point of view, open enrolment and parental choice do not help in making education more equal, they actually increase the level of inequality.

The changes in higher education have also been criticised. The introduction of tuition fees together with the abolition of maintenance grants for university students (in England and Wales) is said to be putting off students from less well off backgrounds from applying to study for a degree. This reform has certainly caused a reduction in the number of applications from mature students – the prospect of building up a large debt when you already have a house and family to look after is not going to be very motivating. Many full time university students now also work part time while they are studying – during term time that is – to avoid building up large debts. This has led to fears that their education will be affected as they will not have enough time to devote to study, and that their work will suffer because they are too tired to concentrate.

Improving skills – the 'new vocationalism'

Vocational education is education that prepares us for work. The 'new vocationalism' is a term that has been used to describe the developments in vocational education during the 1980s and 1990s. As you will see in Chapters 6 and 7 various economic and technological changes altered the make up of the workforce in Britain. Manual work in heavy manufacturing and in industries such as coal mining became much less significant in the British economy throughout the 1970s and 1980s, and there was an increasing demand for new skills, particularly those related to new forms of technology like computers. At the same time it was felt by many politicians and particularly by employers that the education system was not producing enough individuals with the skills that were appropriate for employment in a technologically advanced economy.

The various initiatives that are known as the 'new vocationalism' are attempts that governments have made to achieve two aims:

→ to raise the level of skills of school and college leavers
→ to bridge the gap between school and work.

73

In order to achieve these aims, governments have tried to:

→ make the curriculum more related to work, especially in post-16 education
→ persuade more 16-year-olds to take part in some sort of education or training
→ to raise the status of vocational as opposed to academic qualifications.

We have already seen how some reforms aimed at raising standards, such as the introduction of City Technology Colleges and Key Skills, were also aimed at equipping school leavers with the skills required in the workplace, but governments have tried to make education much more clearly linked to work in other ways. The idea behind these changes is that economic growth is more likely to happen if the education system produces individuals with the right kind of skills.

- **TVEI**

  In 1983 the Technical and Vocational Education Initiative was started as a pilot scheme. The aims of TVEI were to prepare secondary school pupils for work and to improve their technical skills. TVEI introduced work experience into the school curriculum.

- **NCVQ**

  In 1986 the National Council for Vocational Qualifications was set up. Its main aims were to simplify and standardise the mass of vocational qualifications that existed at that time so that both students and employers would be able to see what was equivalent to what.

- **NVQs**

  National Vocational Qualifications were introduced partly as a way of doing this and partly to bring in a change in the assessment of students.

- **GNVQs**

  General National Vocational Qualifications were introduced in 1993. NVQs are qualifications in a particular skill, such as plumbing or bricklaying, while GNVQs are qualifications in a general vocational area such as Health and Social Care or Construction. GNVQs allow individuals to progress on to a career in a particular area of work, such as in the caring professions, or to progress to university as the Advanced GNVQ is the equivalent of two A levels.

NVQs	GNVQs	Academic
5. Professional and managerial	—	Higher education
4. Higher technician and junior management	—	—
3. Technician and supervisor	Advanced	2 A levels
2. Craft	—	5 GCSEs at grades A–C
1. Foundation	Foundation	GCSEs at lower grades

Source: Smithers (1994)

Figure 13 The equivalence of academic and vocational qualifications.

The introduction of NVQs brought about a change in the way students were assessed. Because they are skill based the assessment is based on what students can do – on their competencies. The introduction of Advanced GNVQs was an attempt to raise the status of vocational qualifications. One of the problems that students on vocational courses had always faced was that vocational qualifications were seen by many as having a lower status than academic qualifications like A levels. By making Advanced GNVQs the equivalent of two A levels and also an acceptable qualification for entry into higher education, it was hoped that this would raise the status of vocational education and encourage more individuals to take these courses.

Post-16 Training

Since the late 1970s various training schemes have been introduced with the aim of improving the skills of school leavers. To encourage (some would have said force) young people to take part in education or training after leaving school at 16, the Conservative government withdrew the right to claim state benefits from 16-year-old school leavers. They were normally only able to receive benefits if they were on a recognised training scheme. Training schemes such as Youth Training combined work experience with education and could lead to an NVQ qualification.

More recently other initiatives have been taken to encourage young people to undertake education and training. For example Modern Apprenticeships are aimed at improving the skills of young people who are in employment by offering training to NVQ level 2 or 3. In 1999 the government announced plans to provide allowances of up to £40 per week to encourage 16-year-olds from low income families to stay on at school or college. This scheme was tested from September 1999 in 12 areas with low staying-on rates.

The New Deal for young unemployed people (18–24) was introduced in1998. Under New Deal young people had to undertake full time education, training or work (through a subsidised job, or in the voluntary sector, or an environmental task force). Individuals refusing any of these options would lose their right to benefits. According to government figures, out of the 284,000 individuals who had entered the New Deal scheme by the end of April 1999, 77,000 had gone into employment lasting more than three months, and 28,000 had other employment. The vast majority of jobs were unsubsidised – that is the employer received no money from the government to take on workers.

The effect of these initiatives can be seen below:

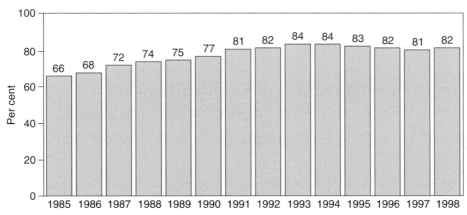

Note: Includes full and part time education, government-supported and employer-funded training.

Source: Department of Education and Employment.

Figure 14 Participation of 16- and 17-year-olds in education and training in England.

Criticisms of the new vocationalism

Many of the training schemes have been seen as measures of social control rather than training. During the 1980s and early1990s when youth unemployment was particularly high schemes such as YTS were seen by many as a way of keeping disaffected young people off the streets. Such schemes were also seen as a way of persuading people that the reason for youth unemployment was not the lack of jobs but the young people's lack of skills. In this way attention was taken away from the failure of the government and industry to provide employment for school leavers.

More recently similar criticisms have been made about the New Deal scheme. Many people see it as a way of disguising the continuing high levels of unemployment among young people. Young people themselves often feel that they are forced into taking up places on New Deal because otherwise they will lose their entitlement to benefits.

Work experience has also been criticised. Some of the work experience done by pupils in year 10 has been described as being dull, repetitive and irrelevant to their future careers. Some pupils simply find themselves acting as unofficial tea makers or 'skivvies' in shops or offices. Work placements on schemes like Youth Training were criticised in two ways. Many young people saw their placements as 'slave labour', doing jobs for benefits that would otherwise have been done by workers on a wage. There were also instances of abuse by employers – taking on trainees with no intention of keeping any of them on in a permanent job after their training period was over, and simply replacing them with more trainees in order to obtain the subsidy from the government. It was cheaper for employers to use trainees than it was to pay wages to workers.

The quality of some vocational courses is also questionable. Because NVQs stress competence rather than understanding, it is felt by some critics that individuals will be able to obtain qualifications without a thorough grasp of the theoretical knowledge behind what they do. In other words they will know what to do but they won't know why they are doing it.

The amount of changes that have been made in courses like GNVQs has also led to criticism, especially from teachers who have had to keep up with them. Teachers and lecturers have also complained about the amount of paperwork involved in GNVQs and NVQs. Such courses are said by many to be over bureaucratic.

Selective or comprehensive schooling?

Before the 1988 Education Reform Act there were two particularly significant changes to the British education system:

- The 1944 Education Act which introduced the principle of free and compulsory secondary education for all for the first time. This act also introduced the tripartite system. Under the tripartite system all children sat an examination at the age of 11 – known as the 11 plus. This examination was to determine whether they would go to a grammar school (for those who were thought to be able to benefit from an academic education); a secondary modern school (for those who were considered to need a general education), or a secondary technical school (for those who were thought to be technically minded). As very few technical schools were built for most pupils the 11 plus examination was a way of deciding whether you went to a grammar school or a secondary modern. This was a selective system. It is a system that still exists in some parts of the country.

● In 1965 the Labour government of the time asked all local education authorities for their plans for reorganising schools along comprehensive lines. This would mean no selection at the age of 11. Pupils would leave their primary schools (which, of course, were comprehensive schools) and progress to their local comprehensive secondary school where they would mix with pupils of all abilities.

In some parts of the country, most notably Northern Ireland, comprehensive reform did not happen. When the Conservative government allowed schools to 'opt out' of local authority control and become grant maintained schools it was felt by many people to be a way of reintroducing selective education into areas that had gone comprehensive. The Labour government that was elected in 1997 said it was against selection in principle, but it has not abolished it where it exists. Many independent schools select their pupils in entrance examinations. The debate about which is the best form of education has gone on for some years. We will look at the main points in the debate.

Selective schools, like grammar schools, for example, are said to offer certain advantages. It is said that the most able will not be held back at a selective school like they would be in mixed ability classes in a comprehensive school. Many long established grammar schools have traditions of learning and excellence that go back over a number of years. It is also said that selective schools provide a route out of the working class (a route to upward social mobility – see chapter 6) for the bright working class pupil. Many of those in favour of selective education argue that as all of us are not the same our education should reflect that. Selection, they argue, allows us to shine at what we are good at.

Critics of selective schooling argue that it tends to favour middle class children. Grammar schools tend to be based on middle class norms and values, the entry examinations are set by middle class individuals and these factors tend to put the working class child at a disadvantage. Critics also argue that selective schools are socially divisive. There tend to be a limited number of opportunities to take the entrance examination (typically at the ages of 11 and 13). Children who do not succeed in this examination may well find themselves labelled as failures – see later in this chapter – and written off. Teachers may well come to expect less of pupils who have failed a selective examination. Therefore their pupils may not be taught as well as those who attend selective schools where the expectations of teachers are higher. The selective system is also divisive because the pupils who fail in entrance examinations are denied the social contacts that are available to those who attend grammar or selective independent schools.

Comprehensive schools are said to offer particular advantages by not being based on selection. Firstly those in favour of comprehensives point out that no child is labelled as a result of failing an examination at 11 or 13 years of age. Comprehensives are also said to offer opportunities to 'late developers'. Those individuals who blossom relatively late in their school careers would find themselves disadvantaged in a selective system with few opportunities to take the all important examination – their talents might well go unnoticed (many of these people enrol on access courses later in their lives). Comprehensive schools are said to allow individuals to develop at their own pace. Because comprehensive schools tend to be large they are relatively cheap to run – the economies of scale meaning that a large organisation can be run cheaper than two or three smaller ones; with only one set of managers to pay, only one gym to maintain and so on. Large schools can also offer a much wider range of subjects and facilities than small schools and so comprehensives are said to be able to cater for a wider range of pupils. They are also said to offer social advantages in that their pupils mix with individuals from a wide range of class and ethnic backgrounds. This is said to make comprehensives less socially divisive than selective schools where, chances are, the pupils will be drawn from a narrow section of society.

Critics of comprehensive schools tend to fall into two groups:

The first group are those in favour of selective schooling who argue that comprehensives hold back those with the most ability. They say that such pupils cannot be 'stretched' in mixed ability classes where the teacher has to divide his or her attention between the able and the less able. Bright working class children are also said to be 'held back' in comprehensives because of the influence of their peers.

The size of comprehensives makes them anonymous institutions. In an institution of 1,000 to 2,000 pupils it is perfectly possible for individual talents and abilities to be overlooked. Individual pupils may well find it very difficult to settle down in such a large establishment.

The second group of critics are those who see themselves as being in favour of 'true comprehensives'. They point out that many so-called comprehensives actually operate some form of selection. This is particularly so when pupils are placed into 'bands' according to their abilities – see later in this chapter. This has the same effect as selection. Those in the lower bands may well face lower expectations from teachers and/or be labelled as low achievers. Teachers may well have higher expectations of those in the higher bands.

These critics also point out that today many comprehensives are in competition with selective schools in their area – either independent or state schools – who have 'creamed off' the most able pupils. So they cannot be said to be truly comprehensive because all abilities are not represented. The comprehensive school tends to have pupils of average to lower abilities. In this way not only is the influence of the most able pupils lost, but so is the influence of their parents.

What is the evidence?

One way to find out about the effects of comprehensives and selective schooling is to compare the results of the two systems. This can easily be done in the British Isles.

INEQUALITY IN ATTAINMENT AT AGE 16: A "HOME INTERNATIONAL" COMPARISON

The UK has four separate education systems, each with different traditions. In Scotland and Wales all state funded secondary schooling is comprehensive, whereas in Northern Ireland it is selective, and in England there are regional differences in the extent of selection. In areas of Britain where many pupils attended selective or independent schools, comprehensive schools could not be considered fully comprehensive because some of their potential pupils were 'creamed' to the selective or private sectors.

Social segregation between schools

If pupils from high social backgrounds attend different schools than pupils from low social class backgrounds there is social segregation between schools. Our study showed that there was more social segregation between schools in England and Northern Ireland than in Scotland and Wales. To some extent this was because more pupils in England and Northern Ireland attended grammar or independent schools, and pupils attending these types of schools tended to have higher socio-economic status than pupils in comprehensive and secondary modern schools.

Sources of inequality in attainment: similarities and differences between England, Wales, Scotland and Northern Ireland systems.

Sex

Girls had higher attainment than boys. This was the same in all four systems.

Socio-economic status

Pupils had higher attainment than average if parents were in professional or non-manual occupations, and if father was in work. The effect of socio-economic status was strongest in England.

School type

Attainment was higher in independent and grammar schools than comprehensive schools and lower in secondary modern schools. More pupils attended independent schools in England.

School composition

Attainment was higher if the average socio-economic status of the pupils in the school was high. This effect was greatest in England.

School effect

Average attainment was higher in some schools than others. Differences between schools were greater in England and Northern Ireland than in Scotland and Wales.

It has been suggested by critics of comprehensive schooling that the overall levels of attainment are depressed by the comprehensive system. Our study found no evidence of this. In Wales, which had a fully comprehensive system, and very few independent schools, average attainment was no different from that of England and Northern Ireland. The different examination system in Scotland makes it less easy to include Scotland in this comparison....

Schools in Scotland and Wales were more comprehensive in every sense than schools elsewhere in the UK. There was less difference in the socio-economic status of the pupil intake between schools in Wales and Scotland. There was less difference between schools in average attainment in Wales and Scotland. Added to this the effect of the social composition of the school was weaker in Scotland and Wales than in England. Altogether we can conclude that in Wales and Scotland it was far less important for pupils to attend the 'right' school than was the case in England.

Adapted from CES Briefing No 19 May 2000, by Linda Croxford, Centre for Educational Sociology, University of Edinburgh.

EXERCISE

Read the extract again and answer the following questions:

i) What does the extract tell you about the effect of comprehensive and selective schooling?

ii) What other factors appear to be significant influences on educational attainment?

Differences and inequalities in education

Independent or state school?

For many people the most significant division in the British education system is that between state schools and independent schools. As we said at the start of this chapter independent schools are those which charge fees for educating their pupils. Some independent schools are day schools, some are known, confusingly, as public schools. Public schools are independent schools that belong to the Headmasters' Conference. These schools include: Eton, Harrow, Winchester, Rugby and Marlborough. Among independent schools public schools are seen as the elite. Many ex-public school pupils occupy positions of power in society – in government or opposition, in the army, in the law, and in business.

Entry to independent schools is normally by selection. Pupils usually have to pass some sort of entrance examination. Many children attend preparatory or 'prep' schools which prepare their pupils for entrance to public or other independent schools. Indeed some children will attend pre-preparatory schools. Both 'prep' schools and pre-preparatory schools are independent schools.

> Pre-preparatory ages 4–8
>
> Preparatory school ages 8–11/13
>
> Public or other independent school ages 11/13–18

In theory entry to an independent school is not restricted to pupils from any particular background, but the level of fees can be quite high. According to the Independent Schools Council, in 1999 the average charge was £5,460 for a year. The fees for Winchester are £15,000 for a year. State schools receive on average £2,372 per pupil. The amount that independent schools can spend on the education of their pupils is not limited by what they receive from fees. The more successful schools 'receive a considerable income from investments and property which they can add to their income from fees, so that a school such as Eton can spend some £20,000 per year on each of its pupils' (Nick Davis 8.3.2000).

Independent schools also have 'charitable status' which means that they do not have to pay tax on their earnings from stocks and shares, investments or their profits. According to an article in *The Guardian* by Nick Davies this charitable status is the equivalent of a state subsidy (i.e. it is the same as the government giving them money) of £1,945 per pupil each year. This is over £200 a year more than the amount of money per pupil that the government puts into state primary schools.

Criticisms of independent schools

Independent schools, and particularly public schools, have been criticised by some sociologists, politicians and other individuals for contributing to class inequalities in society. They are seen as being an important way in which inequalities between the rich and powerful and ordinary working people continue to exist from one generation to the next. The vast majority of parents in our society simply cannot afford to pay fees of £5,000–£6,000 a year for their children to go to school. Independent schools, and especially the public schools, are said to provide advantages for their pupils which ensure that society remains unequal.

Academic success

UK independent schools achieve the very highest academic standards. Of the 500 schools listed by *The Times* as achieving the highest GCSE results in 1999, about 380 were independent schools. About 80% of pupils at independent schools (including special schools) gain five or more GCSE passes at grades A*–C (compared with a national average of 43%). 80% of independent school A level candidates gain three or more passes, compared with a national average of 61%. Nine out of ten independent school leavers go on to higher education.

It is sometimes claimed that this academic success is due to selective admissions policies. Some independent schools do admit only children of the very highest academic ability; many, however, admit a much wider range of ability.

Adapted from the Independent Schools Information Service (ISIS) web site.

Although independent schools educate only 7% of all school children in England they make up a much higher percentage of students at the 'top' universities as the following table shows:

	Actual		Benchmark*	
	No. of young entrants	%	No. of young entrants	%
From independent schools (7% of families**)	10,690	39	7,830	28
From less affluent social classes (50% of families)	3,470	13	4,570	17
Total	27,600		27,600	
From low participation areas (33% of families)	1,740	6	2,290	8

* Benchmark is what numbers should be based on entry qualifications and subjects taught at the institution

** Percentage of families in each category are the best estimates available

Figure 15 Access to top 13 universities.

The academic success of pupils at independent schools is the result of many factors. First of all, as the extract from ISIS shows, many independent schools select their pupils by examination and so only those who are likely to be successful at GCSE and A Level are admitted. Secondly, the classes in independent schools tend to be much smaller than those in state schools, so that pupils can receive much more individual attention from their teachers. Thirdly independent schools have more money to spend on facilities – books, computers, equipment for science labs, for example – and so pupils are more likely to have access to the most recent and up-to-date materials and they are much less likely to have to share textbooks. Also, of course, if pupils are attending a boarding school they are more likely to be supervised throughout the day and the evening. In these circumstances homework is more likely to get done.

Staying at the top

Independent schools do not simply offer academic advantages to their pupils. Young people are also socialised differently in some respects at independent schools. The emphasis in such schools is often on qualities such as leadership. Many of the extra-curricular activities such as the Combined Cadet Force, or the variety of team games available have the effect of developing self confidence and a desire for leadership in pupils. It is probably not an exaggeration to say that independent school pupils are socialised into an expectation that they will be the future leaders of society.

The independent schools, and particularly the public schools, also provide ex-pupils with a valuable network of contacts. This is sometimes referred to as the 'old boy network' (see the section on social mobility in Chapter 6). Sharing the same background and experiences as those who occupy positions of power is said to help individuals gain entry into powerful positions in society. This process is known as **elite self recruitment** by sociologists. Those at the top are said to recruit people who share the same background as themselves. So, in Britain only the very wealthy can afford to send their children to the most expensive public schools. This gives their children an advantage academically and makes it more likely that they will obtain a place at Oxford or Cambridge, for example. This in turn makes it more likely that the children of the wealthy will themselves obtain high status and well paid positions.

> 'Stephen Pollard and Andrew Adonis. . . recorded in their book *A Class Act* that on the latest available figures the 7% of pupils attending independent schools accounted for:
>
> - seven out of nine senior generals
> - 33 out of the 39 most senior judges
> - more than 120 of the 180 officers graduating from Sandhurst
> - half of the 18 permanent secretaries running Whitehall
> - 75% of pupils from independent schools went on to take up professional or managerial jobs, according to research from the Economic and Social Research Council while only 40% of state school pupils reached that level.
>
> (Adapted from Nick Davies in *The Guardian* 8.3.200).

Pupils from independent schools are therefore 'over represented' at the highest levels of society.

Creaming off the best

Another objection that some people have against independent schools is that they tend to 'cream off' the best pupils by examination, and so take only the most able. This is said to reduce the number of talented pupils attending state schools. As a result their results tend to suffer and they are less likely to attract the most able pupils. Another consequence of this process is that parents of independent school pupils will not push for improvements in the state system. The parents of independent school pupils tend to be wealthy and influential people. They tend to be the kinds of people who would be able to exert pressure on the government, local councils and school governing bodies to make improvements. If their children are not attending state schools this is less likely to happen and so, according to this point of view, improvements in state schools will take time to happen because the rich and the powerful have no interest in them.

Many individuals have called for the abolition of independent schools. What do you think? Do they offer unfair advantages or do they represent the freedom of individuals to choose what is best for their children?

Differences in educational achievement

If we look at the figures for success at GCSE, A level, Advanced GNVQ, or the figures for university entrance we can notice certain patterns. For example, the daughters and sons of the better off do better in the education system than those of the worst off. More recently girls have started to do better than boys at A level, though they have out performed boys at GCSE for many years. There are still some subjects, though, that girls are more likely to study than boys.

There are differences in the educational achievements of different ethnic groups too. Students of Indian origin do very well, better than white students. Those of Bangladeshi origin do less well than their white counterparts. As with many other areas of social life there are significant differences in educational achievement according to: Class, Gender, Ethnicity and Age.

In this chapter **class** means your position in society according to your occupation. In Chapter 6 we will look more closely at the idea of social class, but for the time being '**middle class**' means those who work in the professions, in management or in offices. To be '**working class**' means being someone like an electrician or plumber, someone who works in a factory or drives a truck or who is a labourer. In general, to be middle class means to have more money and perhaps a different set of attitudes and values than you would have if you were working class.

When explaining differences in educational achievement sociologists are interested in the social factors determining success or failure. Does the amount of money you have make any difference? Do the norms and values of a particular group make them more or less likely to succeed in education? Do some groups get treated differently to others in schools? This is a different approach to trying to explain educational success or failure in terms of individual characteristics such as intelligence or motivation. A psychologist might say that an individual achieved more because he or she was intelligent or more motivated. A sociologist would try to explain their success in terms of the social groups to which they belonged and how that had affected their chances.

Social class and differences in educational achievement

Look at the table and the graph below. What do you notice about the relationship between social class and educational achievement?

The different rates of educational achievement between children and young people from middle class backgrounds (normally parents in non-manual occupations) and children and young people from working class backgrounds (normally parents in manual occupations) has been a constant feature of the British Education System. This inequality in educational achievement

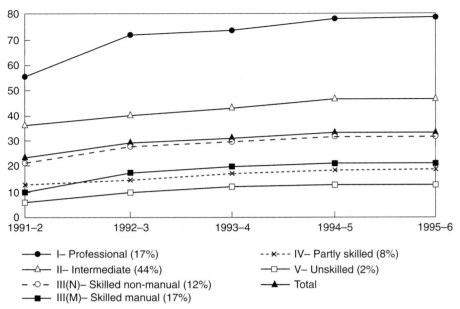

I– Professional (17%)
II– Intermediate (44%)
III(N)– Skilled non-manual (12%)
III(M)– Skilled manual (17%)
IV– Partly skilled (8%)
V– Unskilled (2%)
Total

Numbers in brackets indicate the proportion of participants falling into that particular social class.

Note: This figure uses the Registrar General's class categories. Students were assigned to classes according to admissions data. The distribution of the population by classes was taken from the 1991 Census.

Source: National Committee of Inquiry into Higher Education (1997: 23).

Figure 16 Percentage of young people participating in higher education.

Table 4.2 Attainment of 5 or more GCSE grades A*-C in year 11, by parents' socio-economic group, England and Wales, 1992-98

				percentages
Parents' socio-economic group	1992	1994	1996	1998
Managerial/professional	60	66	68	69
Other non-manual	51	58	58	60
Skilled manual	29	36	36	40
Semi-skilled manual	23	26	29	32
Unskilled manual	16	16	24	20
Other/not classified	18	20	22	24

Source: Department for Education and Employment, Youth Cohort Study: The activities and experiences of 16 year olds; England and Wales 1998 Issue no. 4/99, table b*

Figure 17

is repeated all over the industrial world. The 'underachievement' of many working class children is a problem that governments have tried to solve, but does not seem to disappear despite the implementation of a variety of reforms. By 'underachievement' sociologists mean that, for example, working class children are not represented in universities in the same proportion as they are in the population. If university places were spread out equally among the social classes then the number of places obtained by children from semi-skilled and unskilled backgrounds would be much higher than it is.

There are a variety of sociological explanations for the different rates of achievement of middle class and working class children. They can be divided into:

- those to do with home background.
- those to do with what goes on in schools.

Home background and educational achievement

Material factors, largely to do with money and what it can buy, have an important part to play in the educational achievement of children. (In connection with this part of the chapter you should also read the section on the cycle of deprivation in Chapter 6).

Education today is an expensive business for governments and families alike. Children who have access at home to a range of books and a computer, as well as a quiet place to do their homework are more likely to succeed than those who do not have such facilities. Parents in semi-skilled and unskilled occupations are more likely to be among the low paid and therefore less likely to be able to afford to have such educational equipment in the home.

Growing up in poverty can affect a child's education in many ways. Lack of money can mean fewer educational toys for the pre-school child. A poor diet can mean frequent absences from school because of ill health, which obviously affects a child's progress. A child growing up in poverty is less likely to have a quiet place in which they can concentrate on their homework. People in poverty are less likely to have large, centrally heated homes, and children may have to share rooms with brothers and sisters. As well as this, parents may not be able to replace items of school uniform or provide new shoes or coats when they are needed. Children from poor households may well find that they are teased because of the old clothes they wear or because their garments don't carry the latest brand names. Sometimes children may simply be kept at home because they don't have the correct PE kit or because their only set of school clothes are 'in the wash'.

Poor neighbourhoods may also lack facilities such as playgroups or nurseries which can help a child's educational development. There may not be a library nearby for children to use out of school hours and the cost of travelling to the nearest one may be too much for parents to afford.

Growing up in poverty also means that a child is much more likely to leave school at the earliest opportunity. This is partly because continuing at school beyond the age of 16 involves yet more expense for parents – clothes and equipment for new courses still have to be bought even if a uniform is no longer required. It is also because a child leaving school and getting even a low paid part time job is able to contribute something to the household finances, and is no longer a financial burden.

Lack of money and the material disadvantage it entails can obviously affect a child's chances in education. But some sociologists have said that the working class child is also placed at a disadvantage for cultural reasons.

In other words the norms and values of working class culture that they learn through the process of socialisation are said to put working class children at a disadvantage in education.

Cultural factors that are said to put working class children at a disadvantage include:

- their use of language
- their parents attitudes and values
- the culture of their neighbourhood.

As far as language is concerned the middle class child is said to be at an advantage because the language used by teachers at school is similar to that used by their parents at home. The middle class parent is said to be more likely to use the elaborated linguistic code; the working class parent is said to be more likely to use the restricted linguistic code.

Imagine a young child out walking with her mother, the child lets go of her mother's hand and runs towards the doorway of a large crowded department store. The mother may shout 'Come here, now!' and when the child returns she may say 'Don't do that again!' or she may shout after her child 'You will get lost if you don't keep hold of mummy's hand!' and when the child returns she may say 'You mustn't run into crowded shops on your own because I won't be able to see you and you might get lost.' The first is an example of the restricted code, the second an example of the elaborated code.

The use of the elaborated code is said to be important in a child's educational development because through it the child begins to develop abstract thought. For example, they can link actions (running into a shop) with consequences (getting lost) and reasons (because I can't see you). This kind of thinking and speaking is the same as that used in education. The child who has only been exposed to the restricted code before going to school is at a disadvantage because he or she has a 'new language' to learn. The child who is simply told 'don't do that again' has not been introduced to consequences or reasons, to abstract thought.

The attitudes and values of parents are also said by some to put working class children at a disadvantage. It is said that children will succeed in education if they receive support and encouragement from their parents. Middle class parents are said to be more likely to support their children by attending parent's evenings, for example, and discussing their child's progress with their teachers. Middle class parents are also said to be more likely to encourage their children to stay on at school than working class parents. The values and attitudes of the middle class parent are said to be responsible for the greater success of the middle class child.

But we have to be **careful** with this kind of explanation. The reasons why working class parents are less likely to attend parent's evenings may be nothing to do with a lack of interest in their child's future. Non attendance may be to do with working shifts, for example, or because working class occupations involve hard physical work. It is hard to get cleaned up and ready for a parents' evening starting at 6.00pm if you've spent all day on a building site and you get home at 5.45pm, tired and ready for a bath. It may also be that working class parents find talking to teachers intimidating. Many middle class occupations involve talking for a living. Middle class parents, who are more likely to have achieved some level of success in education, may simply find it easier to talk to teachers than working class parents.

When children have to make decisions about options, about staying on or leaving school, about what subjects to study, about whether or not to think about university, the middle class child may have certain advantages over the working class child. It is easier for parents who have themselves been though the education system, who know a little about courses and qualifications and the demands of A levels and degrees to advise their children and discuss what they might do, than it is for parents who left school at 16 and have no direct knowledge of the system. This does not mean that they lack interest, it is only to say that they are less likely to know how the system works.

Position in society can also influence how we think about qualifications as we grow up. For someone growing up in a family where both parents are solicitors it is probably taken for granted that they will go to university and themselves enter a professional occupation. Their parents, and probably their parents' friends have all done this. They know what is involved, and they are familiar with a certain way of life. For someone growing up in a household where dad is an electrician and mum is a shop assistant, wanting to be a solicitor means thinking about moving upwards in society and therefore leaving behind the kind of people that they grew up with. It means entering a new kind of world that your family and friends are not familiar with.

For this reason the middle class person may well find it easier to make the decision to continue in education than the working class person. For them, doing A levels, or doing a degree, is a way of maintaining their position in society, of not slipping down the social ladder. They may well be pressured by their parents to follow such a course.

Someone from a working class background may experience different pressures. They may feel that by going to university they are somehow deserting their family and friends. The benefits of such a decision have to be very clear for someone to take that step. This can help explain the different routes that people take in education. With the same qualifications (say five Cs at GCSE) the middle class child may well choose an academic course – A levels – while the working class child a vocational course. A working class child with eight As at GCSE may be much more likely to choose the academic route, as the chances of success seem higher and therefore the likely benefits – good job, good pay, good career – are much clearer.

Home and neighbourhood

People don't live in households insulated from their neighbourhoods. For some sociologists many pupils from working class families experience a **culture clash** between the norms and values of the neighbourhood they grow up in and those of their school. This is particularly so when a working class child attends a selective secondary school.

As we have seen earlier in this chapter children in some parts of the country (all children in Northern Ireland) have to take an examination at the age of 11 to decide what kind of school they attend. A child from a working class area who attends a selective school, or grammar school, is likely to find that they are one of a very few from their own area to attend such a school. They are likely to find that in the evenings they are faced with competing demands – going out with their mates or staying in and doing their homework. There is a clash between the culture of the school, which is a middle class institution, and the culture of the working class neighbourhood. The working class pupil has to decide where he or she belongs. Staying loyal to your friends can mean not doing well at school, staying loyal to the school can mean losing touch with friends.

The clash of cultures can affect children in another way. If you have grown up in an area where most of jobs that people do are unskilled or semi-skilled – jobs that don't require any or very few qualifications – then you may well see what you learn in school as irrelevant to getting a job. This is much more likely to be the case in working class areas than in middle class areas where educational qualifications are seen as a necessary first step to a good career.

How do schools influence different rates of educational achievement? To explain how schools themselves might affect the different rates of achievement between middle class and working class pupils we need to look at three different aspects of being at school:

i) The influence of teachers.

ii) The influence of peer groups.

iii) The organisation and location of the school itself.

How might teachers influence different rates of achievement?

'Everyone remembers a good teacher' said the recent government adverts, trying to persuade people to take up a career in education. It is also true that everyone remembers a bad teacher: the one who seemed to write us off, who offered no encouragement; who thought we had no talent, who thought we were just trouble makers and who couldn't or wouldn't explain. The role of the teacher is obviously a key part of any explanation of why some individuals do better than others in the education system. Teachers arouse our interest in a subject or kill it off. They can make us want to work hard or make us want to play them up. They know their subject or they don't.

Teachers can obviously affect our education in many ways but what we are concerned with here is how what teachers do might make it more likely that middle class pupils perform better in schools and colleges than those from working class families. According to sociologists this can happen in three ways, which are all connected:

- Labelling
- Teacher expectations
- The self-fulfilling prophecy.

Labelling

Labelling theory is outlined in more detail in Chapter 4. You may wish to read that section together with this part.

Faced with a class of 20 to 30 individuals teachers have to make judgements about the abilities of their pupils. Teachers tend to have a set of ideas about what the characteristics of a good student are. According to sociological research the stereotype of the good student held by many teachers is not just based on the ability or the intelligence of the individual. Teachers appear to make judgements based on factors such as how well they behave; how they dress and their general appearance; their speech and manners, where they live and what their parents do. In this way children from middle class homes are often seen as more able and more motivated than those from working class homes. The child in the smart uniform who acts as the teacher's pet and who has parents who appear to be supportive is likely to be seen as 'bright'. The child who is scruffy, who speaks with a heavy accent, who has parents in unskilled occupations may well be seen as 'lacking in promise'.

Labels such as 'bright', 'well-motivated', 'disruptive', 'lazy', 'thick', 'slow', or 'uncooperative' are important in two ways. First of all once a child is labelled as 'bright' or 'thick' most of what they do in school will be seen in terms of their label. For example, in a discussion on the sociology of crime a pupil might question the way in which police officers treat young people. If that pupil has been labelled as 'uncooperative' or 'disruptive' that question might be seen as a way of disrupting the lesson, a way of changing the subject and 'having a go' at the police. If the pupil has been labelled as 'bright' the same question could be seen as a reasonable and relevant question about how relations with the police can affect the reporting of crimes. Teachers are much more likely to take seriously and respond to questions and comments from pupils who they believe to be 'bright'. They are less likely to respond to questions and comments from those they believe to be 'disruptive'. The question may just be dismissed as 'irrelevant' or 'off the point.'

This leads on to the second way in which labels are important. If we are treated as though we are intelligent or bright we may come to see ourselves as intelligent or bright. If we are treated as though we are disruptive or uncooperative we may come to see ourselves as disruptive or uncooperative. Labels don't just affect the way other people see us, they can also affect the way we see ourselves. If we are constantly treated as though we haven't much ability we might eventually come to believe it and see ourselves as just average or below average. This will then affect our chances of success.

But we don't have to. It is perfectly possible to react to a label by trying to prove the teacher wrong. This might mean working hard to get good grades or changing our behaviour. Many students of sociology write about labelling as though once labelled as 'thick' an individual has no choice but to become so. This is not so. But labels, especially negative ones like 'thick' or 'disruptive', are hard for individuals to get rid of because of the way that other people judge what we do by how we have been labelled.

How can teachers' expectations affect pupils' achievements?

There is evidence to suggest that if teachers expect pupils to do well at school they tend to do well. Similarly if teachers have fairly low expectations of pupils they will tend not to do so well. The idea behind this is that somehow the teachers' expectations are communicated to the pupil and they behave accordingly. For example, a teacher working with a group of students she believes are capable of obtaining good results may well offer them more encouragement. She may give them more detailed feedback on their work, explain difficult aspects of the subject in more detail, and set more challenging tasks for them to complete. All of this is based on her expectation that the students are capable of high achievement. If, however, the teacher expects little by way of achievement she may not be particularly encouraging or may not offer detailed explanations in the belief that the students are not capable of understanding. The students are not pushed to achieve.

If the teachers have low expectations of children from working class families this will affect how they deal with them in the classroom and may well lead to lower achievement. Unfortunately many teachers learn on sociology courses that working class children are less likely to achieve good results than middle class children. Sociology courses, especially those that present stereotypical views of the working class child, could be seen as being responsible for lower teacher expectations.

The Self Fulfilling Prophecy

Both labelling and teacher expectations can lead to a 'self fulfilling prophecy'. This is when you think something is true and then act in such a way as to make it come true. As we saw above, teacher expectations can lead to a self fulfilling prophecy because the high or low expectations held by the teacher lead them to treat pupils differently. Those whose teachers have high expectations tend to do well because of the high expectations. Those pupils that teachers don't expect to do well are treated differently and so tend to perform less well.

The same applies to labelling – those pupils labelled as 'bright' will be treated by teachers differently because of their label and may well come to see themselves as 'bright', and so work harder and achieve more. In each of these cases the expectation or the label becomes true because of the actions of the teacher – a self fulfilling prophecy.

EXERCISE

Think about your own experience in education. Can you recall instances of 'labelling' or examples of the ways in which the expectations of teachers affected the progress of pupils? Try to think of both positive and negative examples.

Does the organisation of the school itself affect educational achievement rates?

Teachers and pupils work in schools that are organised in certain ways. Some schools teach all their pupils in mixed ability groups, some schools are 'banded' or 'streamed'. Some schools use 'sets' for individual subjects. There is some evidence to show that banding or streaming can act as a form of self fulfilling prophecy.

Some definitions:

- Mixed ability groups are when pupils with a range of different abilities are taught together. This is often the case in primary schools and in comprehensive schools.
- Banding (sometimes called streaming) is when pupils in a school are divided into broad bands or streams of ability. They are taught all subjects within their bands or streams. Many selective schools and a number of comprehensive schools use this system of teaching.
- Setting is where pupils are divided into groups for each subject according to their ability in that subject. So if you are good at maths you will be in the top set for maths. If your French is truly awful you will be in the bottom set.

Banding and the Self Fulfilling Prophecy

If a school is organised into broad bands of ability, placing a child into a band can have two important effects:

i)   The band provides a label for those pupils placed into it. Those pupils placed into the 'top' band are likely to be seen by teachers in terms of their stereotypical view of top band pupils – bright, motivated, hard working and so on. Those in lower bands are likely to be seen in terms of more negative stereotypes – lazy, troublesome, unacademic, for example.

ii) The band also provides a set of expectations for the likely performance of pupils. For example, top band pupils are high achievers and lower band pupils will not achieve much.

Because the band into which pupils are placed effectively labels them and provides teachers with a set of expectations about their future performance, being placed into a band acts as a self fulfilling prophecy. Teachers may prefer teaching those in high ability bands. The high ability bands may have the best teachers, they may be given more encouragement to do well, to be expected to apply for university as a matter of course. In this way the 'prophecy' made by putting an individual into a high ability band becomes true .

In lower ability bands pupils may be given less encouragement because the teachers already know, from the fact that the pupil is in a low ability band, that they aren't going to do very well. They may be taught by the less well qualified teachers, or by a series of supply teachers. The emphasis in the classroom may be more on 'crowd control' than on teaching and learning. Again, in this way the 'prophecy' is likely to become true.

Class and Banding

Because of the factors discussed earlier in this chapter working class children are more likely to be placed in low ability bands than middle class children. In general terms they are likely to be seen as less academic.

Band identities

These are the stereotypical notions that the teachers hold about the bands. As such they are also situational – expecations, that is, expectations about 'what this form is going to be like.'. .

- The Band 1 child 'has academic potential. . . will do O levels (now GCSEs Higher tier). . . and a good number will stay on to the sixth form . . . likes doing projects . . . knows what the teacher wants . . . is bright, alert and enthusiastic. . . can concentrate . . . produces neat work. . . is interested . . . wants to get on . . . is grammar school material . . . you can have discussions with . . . friendly . . .rewarding . . .has common sense.

- The Band 2 child 'Is not interested in school work . . . difficult to control . . . rowdy and lazy . . . has little self control . . . is immature . . . loses and forgets books with monotonous regularity . . .cannot take part in discussions . . . is moody . . . of low standard . . . technical inability . . . lacks concentration . . . is poorly behaved . . . not up to much academically.

- The Band 3 child 'Is unfortunate . . . is low ability . . . maladjusted . . . anti social . . . lacks a mature sense of education . . .mentally retarded . . .emotionally unstable and . . .a waste of time.
  It is apparent that by the beginning of the second year (of secondary school) the majority of the teachers 'see', that is make sense of, the classroom in terms of these preconcieved notions.

(From: Beachside Comprehensive, Stephen Ball Cambridge University Press pp38–39 – words in brackets added)

EXERCISE

i) Explain how teachers' perceptions of the qualities of Band 1 pupils and Band 2 pupils might lead them to treat children differently according to their band.

ii) Explain why pupils in Band 2 might feel demotivated and therefore likely to conform to the band stereotype.

How can the location of the school affect educational achievements?

Read the following extracts.

GAP BETWEEN RICH AND POOR SCHOOLS WIDENS

Schools in affluent areas are enjoying a growing advantage over others by raising the lion's share of £230 million a year in private funding, according to a report by the Directory of Social Change, a London research charity.

A survey of 1,000 schools shows that 20% of primary schools and 5% of secondary schools raise less than £1,000 a year from parents and other private sources. At the other end of the scale 3% of secondary schools supplement their budgets by more than £250,000 a year. . .

A divide has opened up between different types of school, according to the report. 'This is a hidden fault line that is widening, unobserved,' it says.

State schools' fundraising became controversial in 1999 when *The Times* disclosed that the London Oratory had asked parents, including Tony and Cherie Blair, for £30 a month to help meet a projected deficit of £250,000. Most parents already pay £12 a term.

The report underlines the differences in fundraising potential. Location, the involvement of companies and trusts and the ability to make effective applications for grants can all influence how much money is available to a school.

More than half of the primary schools with 50% of children entitled to free school meals raised less than £1,000, compared to only 10% of schools with less than 10% of children entitled to free school meals that raised the same. This division was repeated in the secondary sector.

The contrast with independent schools was even more striking. Almost 40% of independent schools raised more than £250,000 a year, and 21% of them had long term development appeals.

The report says that the pressure to manage fundraising activities has become an additional burden on head teachers, who see the task as time consuming and seldom cost effective. However, children and teachers were also raising more than £30 million a year for charities and community causes.

Adapted from an article by John O'Leary in *The Times, 12* May 2000 .

The social composition of the school had an effect on the attainment of pupils attending the school. Schools in which the average socio economic status was relatively high because the school was attended by a high proportion of pupils with professional and well-educated parents, had higher average attainment than schools with relatively lower than average socio-economic status.

From CES Briefing No 19 May 2000 by LInda Croxford, Centre for Edcucational Sociology, University of Edinburgh.

Read the articles again and answer the following questions:

i) How might the ability of a school to raise money affect the educational achievements of its pupils?

ii) What does the author of the first extract mean when he says 'a divide has opened up between different types of school'?

iii) How might neighbourhood cultures be responsible for the different attainment rates referred to in the second extract?

iv) State education is supposed to be free. Does the information in the first extract support that idea?

v) Why might parents and children prefer to raise money for charity, than raise money for the school?

School 'ethos' and achievement

From what we have seen so far it might seem that schools simply process individuals into success and failure according to their social backgrounds. A reasonable question at this stage is: can schools make any difference? Can they work against the inequalities that exist in the wider society and help pupils to achieve their potential regardless of their social backgrounds.

According to some sociologists schools can make a difference. A study conducted in London suggested that schools can make a difference.

They found that schools with a positive 'ethos' were able to influence the achievements of their pupils in a positive way. The ethos of the school means the values of the school, the way it is organised, and whether or not there is an emphasis on achievement. Good schools, according to the study, were those in which there was a general atmosphere of achievement with all teachers sharing the aims of the school. Teachers were well prepared and organised and were positive roles models for their pupils. There was more emphasis on praise and encouragement of pupils than on blaming and criticising them.

From this perspective the school itself plays an important part in the success or failure of its pupils. The Labour government elected in 1997 tended to support this view with its emphasis on school performance and its targetting of 'failing' schools.

Read the following extract and answer the questions which follow it.

A VISION of RICHES

Mr Harris tells the 400 pupils of Warren Park primary what to do; he even tells them what to think. He tells them they will succeed. Growing up amid the flat roofed maisonettes and broken fences of a huge council estate to the north of Portsmouth it will not be easy to cheat fate. Half of the estate's residents are on income support. More than half of the pupils have special needs and 40% claim free school meals. Most would be among the 4 million children growing up poor in this country, according to a United Nations report.

Colin Harris believes that children can break out of the vicious circle of a life dogged by poverty if they believe in themselves. He tells his pupils constantly, and they tell him, that they 'go to the best school in the world'. When he took over the school was far from the best, but in 1999 three-quarters of 11-year-olds achieved level 4 in English, 72% in maths and 89% in science – all above the national average. These results have been achieved by children who start school with skills far below average.

Warren Park faces the problem that children 'learn to be poor', according to 1998 research by the Joseph Rowntree Foundation. They realise early that their parents cannot afford as much as others which leads them 'to scale down their hopes and aspirations'. They aim for jobs that require no qualifications, or little training – if they aim for jobs at all. Colin Harris' 'best school in the world' challenges this state of mind.

For schools in deprived areas, parents are often the key. They have to back up their children's efforts. Maureen Reynolds, head of Five Elms primary school in Barking and Dagenham, a London Borough that has been working on raising parental expectations, says 'You must remember that parents have a hard time and not judge them. I sometimes tell them their child could go to university and they look at me in amazement. "But no one from my family has gone to university" they say'.

Colin Harris condemns the culture that blames families for being poor. Naomi Eisenstadt who runs the government's Sure Start programme does too: 'It makes me angry,' she says. 'Being a good parent is much harder when you are poor.'

Adapted from an article by Stephanie Norton in the *TES* Friday section 30 June 2000.

EXERCISE

Read the extract again and answer the following questions:

i)   How does the extract illustrate the effects of material deprivation?

ii) How does the extract illustrate the effects of cultural deprivation?

iii) How has Mr Harris tried to tackle these effects through the 'ethos' of his school?

Peer groups, subcultures, and educational achievement

Pupils at school are not just influenced by the way that school is organised and run, or by individual teachers. They are also influenced by their peer groups. How many of us have been told that we are not doing as well as we could at school because we are mixing with 'the wrong crowd'? Broadly speaking sociologists have identified two types of subcultures that tend to develop inside schools:

→ Pro-school subcultures
→ Anti-school subcultures.

Each of these subcultures has a set of names for the other, usually derogatory or insulting. Members of the pro-school subculture may be referred to as 'swots', 'creeps', 'teachers' pets'. Members of anti-school subcultures may be referred to as 'dossers', 'wasters', 'thickies'.

Pro-school subcultures tend to be made up of individuals who accept the norms and values of the school. They want academic success and are prepared to abide by the rules of the school in order to achieve it. Such individuals may well be from middle class backgrounds because of the 'fit' between the attitudes and values of their home background and neighbourhoods and those of the school. Members of pro-school subcultures tend to see the connection between working hard at school and getting a career, maybe by going to university.

Anti-school subcultures can develop in a variety of ways. Those who find themselves labelled as 'no-hopers' and placed in lower bands or streams may well react to the negative identity and low status imposed upon them by creating a subculture in which the norms of the school are challenged. By messing about in class, by 'winding up' the teachers, by teasing the 'swots', members of anti-school subcultures are able to create new identities for themselves as 'hard' or 'smart'. They are able to create a new status in which not doing work, playing truant or ridiculing teachers gives the individual a high status within the group.

Sometimes the values of a subculture that exists outside a school can lead to the formation of an anti-school subculture. For example one sociogical study by Paul Willis showed how particular aspects of working class culture led a group calling themselves 'the lads' to rebel against school. The lads believed that manual work, 'grafting', was superior to mental work – it showed that you were a 'real man'. This belief led to the rejection of the middle class values of education and qualifications and so to the rejection of school. For the 'lads' school was an opportunity for 'having a laff' at the expense of the teachers and the conformist pupils (who they termed the 'ear'oles' because they listened to the teachers). School was something that they had to endure until they could enter the real world of work.

By conforming to the norms of a particular kind of 'macho' working class culture 'the lads' were able to reject the values of the school and to maintain an identity for themselves in an institution which they thought had very little to offer them. This division of sub-cultures into pro-school and anti-school is greatly oversimplified for the purposes of this text book. Many kinds of subcultures exist, in secondary schools in particular. They may be based on music, ethnicity, or extra curricular activities, legal or otherwise. School subcultures may be in favour of or opposed to the values of the school. Some middle class pupils may reject what they see as the unnecessary rules of a school while still believing in qualifications. Members of minority ethnic groups (see below) may reject what they see as a racist education system, but still believe in the importance of obtaining qualifications. Working class pupils may comply with the values of the school in order to escape their backgrounds. The ways in which individuals adapt to their lives at school are varied. **As with every area of sociology it is important not to fall into the trap of seeing social life at school in terms of a series of stereotypes.**

EXERCISE

i)   What subcultures exist at your school or college?

ii) What are their particular norms and values?

iii) Which are anti-school, which are pro-school and which have aspects of both?

Gender and educational achievement

Look at the figures and charts below. What do you notice about the different achievement levels of boys and girls?

What change has taken place in higher education?

The trends which interest sociologists about the relationship between gender and education are:

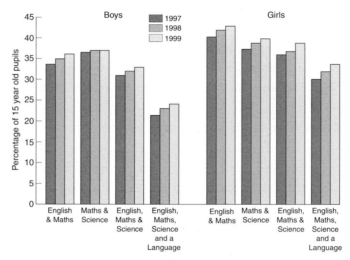

Figure 18 Gender differences in achievement at GCSE level.

	Males				Females			
	All age groups		Aged 16-18[3]		All age groups		Aged 16-18[3]	
	Candidates	Success rate	Candidates	Success rate	Candidates	Success rate	Candidates	Success rate
Any subject								
A Level	118,302	91.3	107,757	93.3	141,117	92.2	123,594	94.6
AS Examination	32,590	68.0	29,943	68.5	35,086	72.9	31,828	73.6
English								
A Level	23,662	91.5	22,115	92.7	56,826	92.9	52,625	94.0
AS Examination	789	86.1	614	85.5	1,514	86.1	1,327	85.9
Mathematics								
A Level	34,667	87.5	33,401	88.2	20,920	90.6	20,165	91.3
AS Examination	8,002	60.3	7,294	61.5	4,953	67.4	4,540	68.6
Physics								
A Level	22,334	88.7	21,724	89.1	6,586	92.2	6,381	92.5
AS Examination	1,488	51.7	1,401	52.7	466	61.6	437	61.1
Chemistry								
A Level	18,957	89.2	18,242	89.7	17,739	92.0	17,034	92.5
AS Examination	787	47.1	709	46.8	769	54.0	712	55.2
Biology								
A Level	18,740	86.6	17,742	87.5	30,240	88.7	28,427	90.1
AS Examination	1,473	50.8	1,319	50.0	2,363	54.9	2,002	55.0
Technology								
A Level	9,737	90.5	9,676	90.6	3,866	93.8	3,851	93.8
AS Examination	151	78.8	141	78.0	71	83.1	63	82.5
Geography								
A Level	18,156	91.4	17,927	91.7	15,249	93.4	15,085	93.6
AS Examination	653	64.5	631	64.7	523	69.0	504	69.0
History								
A Level	15,707	88.0	15.044	89.3	18,781	88.1	18,096	89.2
AS Examination	184	51.6	158	51.9	265	62.3	232	60.3
Music								
A Level	2,620	91.6	2,518	92.1	3,492	94.4	3,391	94.5
AS Examination	550	81.3	509	81.3	528	87.7	491	87.8
Fench								
A Level	4,745	92.2	4,443	92.7	11,278	91.8	10,771	92.0
AS Examination	652	78.5	518	79.9	1,100	73.8	890	73.8
Business Studies								
A Level	17,913	87.5	16,889	89.4	15,264	87.6	14,177	89.7
AS Examination	1,337	73.2	1,265	73.3	1,075	72.3	986	72.9
General Studies								
AS Level	42,224	84.7	41,685	84.8	46,666	84.1	46,080	84.3
AS Examination	6,104	71.0	6,021	71.1	6,819	73.4	6,739	73.3

[1] The total number of grade A-E passes as a percentage of the total number of attempts.
[2] GCE A/AS attempts and passes in the 1999/00 academic year only.
[3] Age at the start of the 1999/00 academic year, i.e. 31 August 1999.

Figure 19 Comparison of male and female success rate at A/AS level.

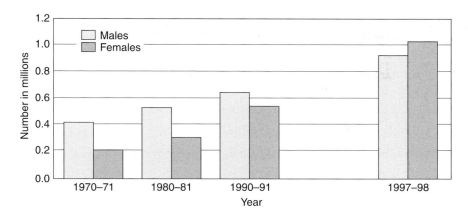

Figure 20 Students in higher education, UK, 1970–71 to 1997–98

- Girls out perform boys at every stage – throughout the SATs in English, maths, and science, at GCSE and most recently at A Level. There are now more females than males in higher education.
- There is still a noticeable trend for subjects to be divided by gender when students have a free choice. For example in the second chart, 22,334 males took Physics A Level compared to 6,586 females whereas 56,826 females took English A Level compared to 23,662 males in 1999/2000.

Why do girls get better results than boys?

There are two kinds of explanation for the different success rates of males and females in education: those to do with changes in the status of women in education and society, and those to do with changes in the status of young men in society.

Explanations for the improved performance of females in education

- **The National Curriculum.**
  The National Curriculum now makes it compulsory for girls and boys to study English, maths and science up to the age of 16. Together with the emphasis on testing, meeting government targets and gaining a good position in the league tables, this means that girls as well as boys are encouraged to do well. This change has not had much of an impact after GCSEs – boys are still likely to choose traditional 'male subjects' at A level, and girls tend to choose traditional 'girls' subjects.

- **The changing job market.**
  There are more opportunities for female employment today than in the past. Economic changes (see Chapter 7) have meant an increase in the number of jobs for women. This is partly because of the decline in the number of traditionally male jobs such as mining or heavy manufacture and because of the increase in the number of service sector jobs. Some service sector jobs and careers such as secretarial work and clerical work are still seen by many people as 'female occupations', but there are also many jobs and careers, for example in entertainment, leisure and tourism, which are not seen as typically male or female.

● **Legal Changes**

Legal changes and equal opportunities policies have not only affected education but also employment. In the 1970s and 80s sociologists pointed out how gender stereotyping could affect the educational performance of girls at school. As a result of this kind of research there were changes made in education to ensure greater equality between males and females. For example reading schemes for younger children were altered to avoid gender stereotyping. There were also initiatives such as GIST (Girls Into Science and Technology) to increase the numbers of girls taking part and succeeding in science and technological subjects. At the same time legislation such as the Sex Discrimination Act of 1975 not only made discrimination in education illegal but also in employment. Because, in theory at least, employers cannot discriminate between male and female applicants for jobs, more women were able to take up employment.

● **Role models**

Partly as a result of economic changes, partly as a result of legal changes, and partly as a result of other social changes (see below) many girls studying for GCSEs and A Levels will have grown up in homes where both parents worked. Many of today's school leavers come from households where both incomes are important. It is not just boys who can relate to dad going out to work. Increasing numbers of girls may also have seen mum return to college to gain qualifications (see the section below on ACCESS courses). Not only have girls grown up with new role models at home but they have also been presented with a range of positive role models in the mass media. From assertive, confident females in music like Madonna to TV shows showing women in a range of roles – from Jennifer Saunders and Dawn French to Kirsty Young and Kate Adie.

● **Feminism**

Underlying many of the changes outlined above is the feminist movement which has challenged the stereotypical views held mainly by men, but also by some women, about what are appropriate roles for women and men. Without pressure from feminists the change described above would not have been possible. Feminists have not only changed the views of women about their expectations but they have at least made some men aware of the lack of equality between the sexes. Many women today do not see their lives purely in terms of family and motherhood, but also in terms of educational achievement and careers.

What is the evidence that such changes have occurred?

Two pieces of research conducted by Sue Sharpe in 1976 and 1994 are important here. In her book *Just Like a Girl* published in 1976 Sue Sharpe said that what was important for girls of school leaving age were 'love, marriage, husbands, children, jobs, and careers, more or less in that order.' But by 1994 when she repeated her study things had changed. By then girls were more interested in gaining qualifications and getting a job or career. However she also found that girls are still socialised to be wives and mothers.

A cautionary note about explanations – an examiner's point of view.

Sometimes in examination papers students refer to two particular explanations to explain girls' improved perfomance. The first one is that girls mature earlier than boys. This may well be the case but unfortunately it is not a sociological explanation, it is a biological one. Also, as it is not a new phenomenon it cannot be used to explain the improvement in girls' performance. Some students also refer to the fact that girls work harder than boys. This is obviously a reason for girls doing better than boys but the question we should be asking ourselves as sociologists is 'why are girls working harder?' The fact that girls work harder is what we are trying to explain, not an explanation in itself.

Gender and subject choice – the other side of girls' improvement

Although girls are now outperforming boys in education up to A level, as we have already seen there is still a pattern of subject choice according to gender in A levels and other post-16 courses. This division also exists in higher education. At university females tend to choose arts and social science subjects. Males tend to choose science based courses.

What are the reasons for different subject choice?

Gender socialisation is an important factor. If boys and girls are socialised into traditional gender roles they are more likely to choose subjects that fit in with their ideas of a suitable adult role. So girls are likely to choose caring or secretarial courses, boys are more likely to choose scientific, computer or technical courses. It is not just gender stereotyping in the home that is important. If teachers themselves have stereotypical views of what is appropriate for each gender they are likely to direct girls and boys into stereotypical options, or give stereotypical careers advice.

Subjects themselves are seen as either masculine or feminine. Partly because of gender stereo-typing in text books, and partly because it is mostly males who take science subjects in post-16 education, it is seen as a masculine subject. The opposite is true for courses such as Health and Social Care or Early Years Education – these are typically feminine subjects.

In the classroom males tend to dominate in mixed sex schools. According to some research boys grab the apparatus, answer the questions directed at girls and generally act in a way which says that they are more important than girls. Alongside this kind of behaviour from pupils, teachers often use examples in their explanations that are likely to appeal to boys rather than girls – such as, using the example of billiard balls to explain forces in a physics lesson. In both of these ways a science classroom can appear to be a male environment.

Some sociologists and teachers have said that single sex classes, even in mixed schools, would help to remove the idea that some subjects were masculine and some feminine. There is some evidence that single sex classes help to raise girls, confidence in subjects that are seen as masculine, such as computing. Single sex classes have also been proposed more recently by some politicians as a way of raising boys' educational achievements.

EXERCISE

i) What do you think would be the advantages and disadvantages of single sex classes in mixed schools?

ii) What do you think are the advantages and disadvantages of single sex schools?

What are the factors influencing the educational achievements of boys?

Over the last two years or so much attention has been directed at the apparent underachievement of boys, and in particular working class boys. Two linked explanations have been put forward to explain this under achievement.

- The change in the economic structure of society which has led to the disappearance of many traditional male jobs, especially manual, working class jobs.
- The development of a so called 'laddish' subculture in which school work is seen to be 'uncool', not 'macho' or masculine.

The laddish subculture adopted by many young males at school is seen by them to be a way of expressing their masculine identity. It is a way that teenage boys have of showing that they are 'real men'. They can express their masculinity through sports such as football, by messing about in class (and so getting behind in lessons) and also by appearing to be 'hard'. This can lead to the development of an anti-school subculture in which not paying attention to teachers and school work is seen as 'cool' and macho.

Many working class boys are said to be lacking in self confidence and self esteem. They are said to be uncertain of what it is to be male and to be a man at the start of the 21st century. By getting involved in the 'laddish subculture' working class boys are said to be able to gain status and 'street cred' from their peer group. Within the group they have an identity as 'one of the lads'.

Part of the reason for this 'crisis of identity' that young working class males are said to be undergoing is the disappearance of many traditional working class occupations. Young working class males today are said to be unable to see a way of expressing their masculine identity in work after leaving school. This lack of traditional male occupations can also be demotivating. If there are no jobs to go on to after school many such students see no point in bothering with school work.

However, we need to be careful about exaggerating the problem of underachievement among working class males. There are still many girls who underachieve at school. After school men still dominate at work, they are still more likely to earn more money and to be promoted than women. The gender differences in qualifications obtained by young men and women mean that they are still likely to be employed in different occupations. Also, it may be that the increasing success levels of many girls has drawn our attention to class inequalities that have existed for many years. By concentrating only on the underachievement of boys we may draw attention away from other inequalities.

Ethnicity and educational success

With this topic, as with many others, it is important to avoid stereotyping, but as the evidence is quite complex no simple stereotypes emerge.

- Although ethnic minorities make up 6.6% of the working age population of Great Britain, 11% of the pupils of primary and secondary schools in England are from minority ethnic groups.
- Bangladeshi, black and Pakistani children perform less well than other pupils in the early Key

Stages. Pupils from these groups tend to achieve less by the end of compulsory education.

● Members of minority ethnic groups are more likely to stay on in full time education than young white people – 85% as compared to 67%.

● At the age of 18, 83% of Indians have a level 2 qualification or higher, compared to 68% of whites, 56% of Pakistani/Bangladeshis, and 48% of black students.

● Ethnic minorities as a whole are over represented in higher education – 13% of under-graduates.

(Source – DfEE Research Topic Paper RTP01 March 2000, Shalini Pathak)

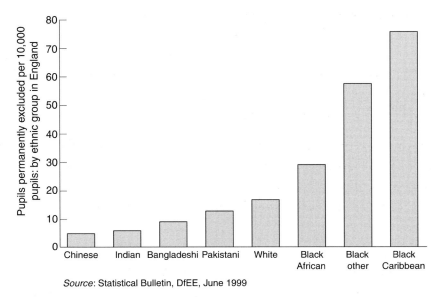

Source: Statistical Bulletin, DfEE, June 1999

Figure 21 Exclusion rates by Ethnic groups.

Figure 21 provides some more evidence.

How are we to explain these differences in educational achievement according to ethnicity?

Class

First of all we need to be aware of class differences between different groups in society. It would be a mistake to assume that just because there are significant differences in the achievement rates of different ethnic groups that the explanation for those differences is to do with ethnicity, or the cultures of different groups of people.

It is also true that we cannot talk about the 'underachievement' of all minority ethnic groups, for two reasons – firstly Indian pupils do better than all other groups, and secondly, all groups are improving.

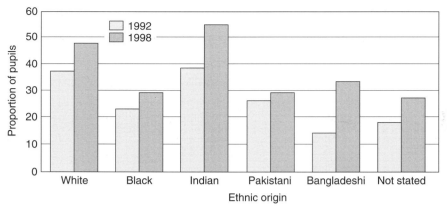

Source: Department of Education and Employment, Youth Cohort Study: The activities and experiences of 16 year olds; England and Wales 1998 issue no. 4/99, Table b.

Figure 22 Attainment of five GCSE passes A*–C in year 11 (age 16) by ethnic origin, England and Wales, 1992 and 1998

Because a larger proportion of Afro-Caribbean and Pakistani/Bangladeshi pupils are from working class backgrounds than white or Indian students it may well be that the lower educational achievement rates of these two groups are best explained in terms of social class rather than ethnic differences. Pakistanis and Bangladeshis are amongst the poorest groups in society with 60% living in low income households whereas Chinese, Indian and white men have the highest full time earnings nationally. As we have seen earlier theses kinds of differences can affect a child's educational chances.

Home background, language, ethnicity and achievement

In the past two explanations relating specifically to the home background of minority ethnic groups were put forward to explain their underachievement.

The first was to do with language difficulties, the second with parents' attitudes to education. It was thought that the underachievement of some Asian pupils was to do with their lack of fluency in English because other languages would have been used in the home (Urdu or Hindi for example), and the underachievement of Afro-Caribbean pupils was to do with the low value placed on education in Afro-Caribbean culture. Recent research shows us that the explanation is more complicated.

Lack of fluency in English partly explains early underachievement of Bangladeshi and Pakistani pupils but, in itself, doesn't adequately explain their poor performance at 16 (research suggests that other pupils with fluency difficulties do make substantial progress). Similarly attitudes towards education among pupils and parents from underachieving ethnic groups don't seem to contribute to lower academic performance; recent research suggests a positive attitude towards education among both black Caribbean and Bangladeshi young men and their parents, although the reality of their school experience may cloud this view.

The particularly negative experience of some black Caribbean boys appears to be an important element in their academic underachievement and contrasts sharply with the experience of Indian pupils. Influences from their peers and from teachers may increase black Caribbean boys' resistance to school, leading to more serious disciplinary responses such as exclusion. Once excluded the majority are unlikely to return to mainstream education, thus disadvantaging them further.

(Source adapted from Shalini Pathak 2000)

Schools and teachers

Why might schooling be a negative experience for black Caribbean boys? Why are black Caribbean boys particularly likely to be excluded?

Various explanations have been put forward for this:

First it is said that teachers have low expectations of black pupils and that these low expectations become a self fulfilling prophecy. Some teachers also experience difficulties in dealing with black Caribbean boys and may well interpret some of their behaviour in the classroom as disruptive and react to it in a fashion that is too punitive and confrontational. The extract below illustrates these points:

> *Attendance and Behaviour in Schools* examines different reasons for excluding pupils and says that black pupils are most commonly barred for 'challenging behaviour'.
>
> The author of the report, Mr Moore, who is responsible for behaviour, exclusion and ethnicity at OFSTED, said that many teachers were failing to get the best out of their black pupils because they were intimidated by them and did not understand them.
>
> Speaking at a conference to discuss ethnicity, identity and achievement in Catholic secondary schools, the inspector said: 'Some teachers clearly find the self confidence of their African-Caribbean boys intimidating and therefore respond to them in a more confrontational and challenging way.
>
> But black youngsters would rather die than back down in front of their friends. So why do teachers continue to treat them in this way? A quiet word after class is far more likely to be effective.'
>
> Father Philip Sumner, chair of governors at Manchester's Thomas Aquinas secondary school, blamed the poor academic performance of black youngsters on a failure to incorporate black achievement into the National Curriculum.
>
> He said; 'How do you think black children feel when the only time they are taught about black culture at school is in terms of slavery and economic dependence, and the only symbol of black achievement is a token poster of Martin Luther King?'
>
> Granville During,17, a pupil at Bonaventures sixth form, Forest Hill, said schools needed to raise their expectations of black pupils.
>
> He said: 'A lot of people still have the idea that black boys are just interested in walking down the streets with their trousers around their bums and that they have no aspirations or desire to succeed at school. This is not the case and it just needs teachers to believe in us a bit more.'
>
> However recent research conducted among 262 African-Caribbean boys in four London schools questioned whether their failings were the fault of teachers. Many of the boys had strong anti-school attitudes and Mike O' Donnell, the author of the research, said peer group pressures had an important influence on success or failure.
>
> Source: Taken from an article by Amanda Kelly in the TES .

The extract above mentions both the curriculum and peer group pressure as well as the actions and expectations of teachers. The National Curriculum has often been criticised for being ethnocentric as we have already discussed in the section on the 'Hidden curriculum'. It is said to be particularly important for young black people to have a macho identity, and this may help to explain their unwillingness to back down in front of teachers and also the ways that peer pressures might influence their apparent attitudes to education. Young black men are subject to the same pressures as their white peers to appear masculine, to be 'a real man' – and backing down in class would make you appear weak and unmanly and would lead to negative comments from your friends – you would appear to be a 'wimp'.

There are very few role models in schools for minority ethnic group pupils because of the lack of teachers and head teachers from minority backgrounds. In 1997/98 only 5% of final year primary trainees and 7% of secondary were from a minority background. This compares with 11% of pupils.

Afro-Caribbean girls have higher achievement rates than Afro-Caribbean boys. For some sociologists this is a result of the position of women in Afro-Caribbean culture. Women are said to be socialised to take up positions which will allow them to provide for their families and so they are said to have the motivation to succeed in education. Afro-Caribbean women are said to be less subordinate than white women. This may help to explain why, even when Afro-Caribbean girls reject the low expectations of their teachers, they still do well in examinations. Their response to low expectations is to show that they can do as well as anyone else.

According to the Swann Report of 1985 very few teachers are consciously racist, but the report did acknowledge that there was a good deal of 'unintentional racism' in schools. This can take the form of stereotypical expectations, as we have seen above, or it can be seen in the use of teaching materials – text books for example – which contain negative and stereotypical images of non-white people. Schools are also not immune to the racism that exists in wider society. Pupils from minority groups may well experience racist bullying, and racist violence at school, which are hardly conducive to successful study. Those pupils who challenge racism in school may sometimes find themselves labelled as trouble makers. Some pupils may also find that they are subject to racist abuse or violence, not just at school, but also on the way there. Again, this does not help their educational prospects.

As the educational achievements of different groups continue to improve it may well be that explanations based on ethnicity will disappear.

Age and education – is it never too late?

LATE LEARNERS

Mature students with few or no formal qualifications are in demand as universities compete to keep their undergraduate lecture halls full.

Among the most proficient at recruiting these types of adult learner are the newer universities, particularly the former polytechnics, some of which have student bodies that boast a clear majority of over 21s. Derby University is a prime example, with almost a quarter of its undergraduates over 30.

Derby runs a modular access programme designed to prepare adults returning to education for admission to a degree course.

Rob Wood, advisor for mature students, explains: 'The university shares the scheme with three local FE colleges and about 500 students pass out of it every year. Perhaps about 300 eventually find their way on to a degree, the majority enrolling at Derby.'

To gain a place on Derby's access course applicants usually have to be over 21. Apart from that there are no formal entry requirements. Like most access programmes up and down the country, there are core compulsory modules covering subjects such as study skills, communication and information technology and further options.

'Roughly two-thirds of access students are women, many of them in their 30s with children in their teens. The men tend to be younger, somewhere in their 20s, Woods adds.

Taken from an article by Graham Wade in *The Guardian,* 15 August 2000.

In 1999, 10,721 of the applicants from the UK who were accepted on to degree courses had access qualifications. Since the late 1970s the access route into higher education has grown and become one of the recognised routes onto a degree course. Access courses are designed specifically for mature students (those 21 or over) and are usually based much more on the skills of studying – writing essays, taking notes, using IT, researching in the library, for example – than they are on the content of a particular subject. They attract adults who want to progress on to a degree to improve their chances of employment, or simply to gain an education they feel they missed out on in their youth. Access courses tend to be provided by further education colleges, often in association with a local university. This kind of collaboration is important as the majority of access students have commitments such as family or partners in employment which mean they are unable to move to another part of the country to study like many 18-year-olds are.

Access courses fit well with two government objectives – to widen participation in education, and the idea of lifelong learning.

According to figures from UCAS the number of home applicants accepted on to degree courses with access qualifications was as follows:

1994 – 14,751
1995 – 16,246
1996 – 16,896
1997 – 13,640
1998 – 11,677
1999 – 10,721

Figure 23 The number of people with access qualifications entering onto a degree course.

EXERCISE

i) Why should about two-thirds of Access students be women?
ii) Why might the average age of male access students be younger than that for female access students?
iii) Why do you think the number of access students accepted on to degree courses fell after 1996? Do your views fit with the extract below?

RISING DEBT HITS ACCESS EFFORTS

Government plans to widen participation in higher education suffered a blow this week as figures showed that spiralling student debt is deterring the poor disadvantaged.

For the second year running English and Welsh institutions are falling short of recruitment targets for students starting full time courses. In Scotland, where students do not pay tuition fees upfront and poor students get maintenance grants, institutions have met their targets.

Some 7,000 full time places were not filled in 1999–2000 and this is likely to be the case this year according to figures from the Higher Education Funding Council for England. Despite the government's efforts to widen participation, a report published this week by the National Union of Students shows that the number of males from skilled, semi-skilled and unskilled backgrounds applying to full time undergraduate courses fell by nearly 7% between 1997 and 1999. The figures in the report were based on figures from the Universities and Colleges Admissions Service.

A spokesman for the Liberal Democrats said: 'If there is a widening discrepancy between recruitment in England and Wales compared with Scotland then that is very strong evidence that the government policy of making poor students poorer by removing means tested maintenance grants is actually destroying the government's aim of expanding access.'

A spokesman from the Department for Education and Employment dismissed the NUS data as misleading, and Higher Education Minister Baroness Blackstone said: 'Younger people from poorer backgrounds do not pay tuition fees. The social class and the ethnic mix of both applicants and entrants to full time higher education has been stable since 1977. From 2001 half of all students will not pay tuition fees.'

Adapted from an article by Alison Goddard in the THES, 17 November 2000.

EXERCISE

What do you think?

Should loans now be abolished and replaced by means tested grants? Should students on degree courses pay something towards the cost of tuition if they can afford to?

How are we as a society to pay for higher education?

You can make your own mind up about the effects of loans and fees by looking at the UCAS website for up-to-date information – www.ucas.ac.uk/higher/stats.

Alternatives to state education

Many people do not send their children to state schools but to independent schools. There are, however, other alternatives to state education.

Steiner Schools

In the UK there are 26 Steiner schools and eight kindergartens. The main reason why many parents choose to send their children to a Steiner school rather than to a state school is that the teachers place more importance on the moral and personal development of the child than on academic performance. One major difference between Steiner schools and state schools is that pupils have one teacher from the age of 7 to 14 so that continuity in the relationship between student and teacher is maintained. Another major difference is that each day there is one 'main lesson' which is two hours long. During the main lesson pupils will study one topic but from many different angles – using stories, pictures, song and dance for example. Reading as such is not taught until the second or third year although pupils will be introduced to letters. The emphasis is on creativity and the development of the whole person. Parents who find the state system rather oppressive and regimented are likely to send their children to a Steiner school, although because they are independent they have to pay a fee. One criticism that is made of such schools is that sometimes pupils find it hard to adjust back to a state system. This is particularly so if the child is of primary age, as their reading ability is likely to be behind children in state schools, because they start to learn at a later age.

Education at home

Increasing numbers of children are being educated at home by their parents. This is allowed by the Education Act of 1994 which makes education, not school attendance, compulsory. A pressure group, Education Otherwise, exists to support and advise those parents who wish to educate their children at home. This may be because they object to aspects of the National Curriculum – for example, parents might feel it does not allow enough time for studying music or art. Individual pupils may be educated at home because their parents feel that conventional schools do not allow children to develop their imaginations or creativity because of the emphasis on testing and examinations. Pupils may be educated at home because they have been bullied at school or because conventional schooling has been negative in some other way – children feeling bored and not stimulated by the lessons, for example.

One major criticism made of home education is that children do not mix with the variety of children that they would meet in an ordinary school. Critics of home schooling feel that children educated in this way will lose opportunites to develop their social skills. However many home educators meet regularly in groups in order that their children do not miss this important aspect of schooling.

CHILDREN TAUGHT AT HOME LEARN MORE

Children taught at home significantly outperform their contemporaries who go to school, the first comparative study has found.

It discovered that home educated children of working class parents achieved considerably higher marks in tests than the children of professional middle class parents, and that gender differences in exam results disappear among home taught children.

There were virtually no home educated children 20 years ago. Now there are about 150,000, about 1% of the school population.

Paula Rothermel from the University of Durham conducted the survey. She questioned 100 home educating families from across the UK. She conducted face to face interviews and made detailed appraisals of their children's academic progress in line with government tests. She found that 65% of home educated children scored more than 75% in a general mathematics and literacy test, compared to a national figure of only 51%. The average score on the test for school educated pupils was 45%; for home educated pupils it was 81%.

Rothermel said: 'The improved exam results could be down to the sheer quantity of parental attention and the sense of long term security that gives them. . . It could also be down to the fact that families who home educate from birth had worked with their children from the word go and without the disruptive transition at an early age to the very different environment of school.'

Alison Preuss, a mother of three, has been home teaching for six years and is director of Schoolhouse, a Scottish support group for parents who have opted out of conventional schooling. She said: 'In school children have knowledge poured into them, while they're at home they can decide what they want to learn. It's a better preparation for university because they are used to motivating themselves.

'Their social skills and general knowledge are more advanced because they are not restricted by the National Curriculum. They can explore a huge variety of subjects, concentrating in depth on whichever captures their imagination.'

Adapted from an article by Amelia Hill in *The Observer*, 13 August 2000.

EXERCISE

Read the article again and answer the following questions:

i)   How does the article explain the better performance of home educated children?

ii) What do you think would be the advantages and disadvantages of being educated at home?

iii) Why do you think the number of children educated at home has increased so much over the last 20 years?

In the recent past education has become a major political issue in Britain. There have been many changes to the education system in this country, some popular, some less so. What would your ideal education system look like? Would it, for example, concentrate on preparing individuals for the world of work? Would it concentrate on developing well rounded individuals with an understanding of the arts, science and the importance of their own physical well being? Would it concentrate on producing citizens with an understanding of their society and respect and tolerance for the ways of others? Would it try to combine all of these?

Teachers and the Education System – What about the Workers?

Getting people who want to teach has become quite a problem for schools in many parts of the country. Some schools have gone onto a four day week. In many schools lessons are only possible because of supply teachers. The government has introduced various financial incentives to persuade individuals into teaching. At the same time increasing numbers of teachers are leaving the profession, and many more would like to. Why has teaching become such an unattractive occupation?

The article on pages 109 and 110 suggests some of the answers. What do you think they are?

'I was scared that I'd be stuck for life'

A former teacher explains why he quit – but might yet go back

Interview by Simon O'Hagan

7 January 2001

Joe Hallgarten, aged 30, went into teaching when he was 23, working in primary schools in Manchester and London before leaving the profession in 1998. He is now a researcher at the Institute for Public Policy Research in London, and is carrying out a project on the future of the teaching profession.

I left teaching before disillusion really kicked in – before the point came when I felt I would be unemployable anywhere else. I was scared I'd be stuck for life, because there's the feeling with teaching that other professions don't see it as relevant experience. I would disagree, but I got the distinct impression that if I'd tried to get a job in, say, advertising, then they would rather I'd spent five years in Thailand than five years as a teacher.

I'm not sure why that should be. Maybe people have strange memories of their own schooldays. Plus, teachers are quite closed about their experiences. The profession probably needs to go further in promoting itself, and being more transparent.

For me, the desire to teach started with youth work, taking kids camping. I think you either have a passion for a subject or you really enjoy working with kids. I believed it was going to be a very creative profession, and I don't think the National Curriculum need prevent that. There were other obstacles to creativity though.

I read politics at Manchester University and then did my PGCE. To begin with, I could compare myself with my friends quite favourably. The pay wasn't great, but they weren't earning much more than me, and in terms of the independence and responsibility I had I was far better off. But over three or four years, all that changed.

One reason why the creative side was hampered was the pressure of league tables. Inner-city schools feel the heat in particular, although it's not just a question of leafy schools on the one hand and deprived schools on the other. It's about schools being confident, and teachers having space to prioritise their own values and passions, which are the reasons why people go into teaching in the first place.

The money is obviously crucial. I was on £19,000 when I left, and that included London weighting. I guess I could have gone down the road to a well-paid headship. But that's not really the point.

There was also the question of status. It was Lord Puttnam who said that too many teachers have to work in slums, and certainly conditions weren't good. I don't like to talk in terms of stress. There is stress in many walks of life. But there was a kind of fatigue attached to teaching that is very draining. Physically and mentally it's very demanding. Call it adrenaline, but it makes you knackered. Then there's the Ofsted regime. The build-up to an inspection was just awful, and afterwards I had this strange sense of apathy. That had a lot to do with my departure.

I considered journalism, but I went and did some work for the National Union of Teachers and then this job at the Institute for Public Policy Research came up. There are 40 or so of us, including three ex-teachers, and there's no doubt in my mind that we bring unique perspectives and skills to the organisation. I feel valued, and my pay is about half as much again as it was when I left teaching.

Having said that, I'm not saying I've left teaching for good. There's a possibility I'd go back. Once you've worked in a vibrant school community anything else can feel soulless.

Taken from the Guardian, 8th March 2001

Sociologists have contributed a great deal to our understanding of what goes on in the education system but it is not their role to decide on the nature of the education system. That is the role of the citizen.

Glossary

Culture clash: refers to the idea that working class pupils in particular experience a degree of conflict between the norms and values of their homes and neighbourhoods and those of their schools. Schools are often dominated by middle class norms and values which may be at odds with working class values. This "clash" may be experienced in terms of accents, career expectations, the kind of language used at school and home or in terms of the value placed upon education.

Cultural deprivation refers to the idea that some pupils do not do as well as they might in education because they do not possess particular cultural attributes. For example, middle class children are thought to be at an advantage because they have access to a range of books and educationally valuable materials at home, such as computers. Middle class parents are also said to use the same kind of language as teachers at school.

Material deprivation this term is used to explain the relative failure of working class pupils. It refers mainly to economic factors. That is to say, because some working class people are less well off than others, and less well off than middle class people in general, the physical environment of some working class houses may not be conducive to successful study. It is harder to work in cramped or overcrowded rooms with little or no privacy. Parents may not be able to afford important 'extras' like educational visits. Some working class neighbourhoods may also be materially deprived with few facilities for young people such as libraries, sports centres or youth clubs.

Ethnocentricity

refers to the way in which we might make decisions or judgements from the point of view of a particular culture, that is from the point of view of a particular ethnic group. The national curriculum has been described as ethnocentric because it concentrates on the history and literature of the white majority without recognising, and therefore appearing to devalue, the history and literature of other ethnic groups.

The Hidden Curriculum

refers to what we learn from the way in which schooling is organised and carried out. The hidden curriculum is contrasted with the overt curriculum which consists of the subjects we learn like Maths, English and Science. The idea of the hidden curriculum has been used to explain how stereotypical gender roles are reinforced through the process of schooling and also how the class inequalities of society are reproduced by the education system.

The self-fulfilling prophecy

this refers to a prediction (or prophecy) that turns out to be true because we think it will be true. For example "banding" in schools is said to be an example of a self-fulfilling prophecy. Pupils who are thought to be low achievers are placed in lower bands. Because they are in lower bands not so much is expected of them and they may not receive the same quality of education as those in higher bands. In this way the original prophecy becomes true. Labelling and teacher expectations may also result in self-fulfilling prophecies.

Tripartite system

this was introduced by the 1944 Education Act. At the age of 11 school pupils sat the 11 plus examination which was supposed to indicate the type of education - grammar (academic), technical (technological) or secondary modern (general) - from which they would benefit most. The tripartite system was therefore based on selection by examination. This system was criticised by many as it was seen to favour the middle class child and the 11 plus exam was abolished in many parts of the country after 1965. However, the idea of selection is still favoured by some. Entry to private schools is often subject to passing an entrance exam and the 11 plus still exists in many parts of the country most notably Northern Ireland.

Conformity, Deviance, Crime, and Social Control

4

Our lives are governed by rules; social rules make social order possible. Some are written down, some are not. Some of them we obey, some of them we don't. Some of us conform, some of us don't. Some people get a reputation because they break rules, some don't. This chapter is about rules, what kinds of rules we encounter in our lives, what happens when rules are broken, and the possible explanations for some people breaking rules.

In Chapter 1 we introduced the idea of social control, and how it could be formal or informal. We also saw how rules could be formal or informal. Imagine that you and a group of friends are going out together. Someone is going to drive and you are all going across town to another friend's house to listen to music. What formal rules will you be subject to? What informal rules might exist in this situation?

If you are driving from one place to another you will be subject to the formal rules – the laws – regarding road traffic. You'll have to drive according to the speed limits, on the correct side of the road, taking account of one way streets, traffic lights and so on, and also in a fashion that shows due care and attention to other road users. If you break any of these formal rules – laws – in this case you can expect to be punished with a caution, a fine or maybe a ban. But in this situation the rules of your peer group will also apply. You will be expected to obey the norms of your group. Maybe this means wearing the 'right' kind of clothes, maybe it means paying your share of the petrol. It might also mean liking the 'right' kind of music, having the 'right' opinions, and having the 'right' accent. If you break any of these informal rules you will find out. If all your friends have taken 12″ singles of obscure DJs and you turn up with an easy listening album you can probably expect some gentle teasing at least. If you don't pay your share of the petrol you may find yourself uninvited next time.

Social rules are important in society as a source of social order. If everyone obeys the rules society is orderly. If no one obeyed the rules there would be chaos. For some sociologists the rules that make social order possible arise out of **consensus**. This means that these rules are based on general agreement about what is right and wrong, good and bad. They believe that most of us agree on the norms and values that govern our actions. As we have seen in Chapter 1 we are socialised into the norms and values of society – we learn the rules that make order possible. Other sociologists believe that rules are imposed upon those who don't have power by those that do. This view of social order stresses **conflict** in society, like that Karl Marx said existed between the bourgeoisie and the proletariat (see chapter 6). From this point of view social order is the result of the operation of power. The powerful make the rules and impose them on the rest of society.

- **Formal social control** is the process of making sure that individuals conform to formal social rules. The most obvious formal rules in any society are laws. The police are formal agents of social control because a large part of their role in society is to ensure that we obey the laws. There are penalties for disobeying laws. These penalties, or sanctions, are at least partly there to encourage us to conform to the laws. I know that if I am caught speeding I will be fined and get some points on my licence and so, to avoid this happening, I obey the speed limit. Sanctions like fines also exist to punish us if we do not conform, and seeing others punished also acts as a form of deterrent. As we saw in Chapter 1 other important formal agents of social control are magistrates, judges, probation officers and the armed forces. We may also be subject to formal social control at school, college or work because in all of these contexts there are written rules which we are expected to obey, and formal sanctions for disobeying or not conforming to the rules.

- **Informal social control** is also a process of making sure that individuals conform to social rules. But informal social control is 'unofficial'. Informal social control is carried out by 'unofficial agents of social control like members of our family, our peer group, our work mates. It is called informal because the rules are not written down, and because the rewards and punishments are also not specified exactly, as they are if we break road traffic laws for example. Approval or disapproval from our friends, family or colleagues is an important aspect of informal social control. The reward (the positive sanction – see Chapter 1) for conforming to the rules of our peer group is that we get their approval – they accept us, they like us – and we also know that if we break the rules they will show their disapproval and this makes us more likely to conform. For example parents can show their approval of our actions by rewarding us with praise or presents, they can show their disapproval by grounding us or by stopping our pocket money. Our peers can exercise peer pressure by teasing us (disapproval) or showing us friendship (approval).

The process of informal social control is an important part of our social rules by a system of rewards and punishments. We see what happens to people who break the rules and to people who conform. We may also experience punishments and rewards ourselves. In this way we are encouraged to conform.

Not conforming – criminals and deviants

Sociologists distinguish between two groups of people who break social rules:

- Someone who commits a crime, that is someone who breaks the law, is a **criminal**.
- Someone who does not conform to the norms of society, or of a particular group, is a **deviant**.

Separating these two ideas is not always easy. After all law breaking is not only criminal, it is also deviating from the norms of society. Most law breaking acts are not only criminal they are also deviant. But many deviant acts are not criminal, they do not break the law. For example we would all probably regard a perpetual thief as not only criminal but also as a deviant, but someone who dresses in a bizarre fashion, turning up for lessons wearing a gold lamé suit and blue suede shoes is not breaking a law, but they would probably be seen as deviating from the norms of student dress.

Deviant? Who says?

While it might be possible to provide a list of actions that would almost certainly be regarded as criminal, it is not possible to do this for deviant acts. This is because what is regarded as a deviant act can change according to three important factors:

- **Context**
  Where an act takes place can affect whether or not it is seen as deviant. The context could be a place – it is normal to be naked in the bath, it could be seen as deviant to be naked in the supermarket. The context could be a social group: someone wearing the gold lamé suit and blue suede shoes we mentioned above would probably not be regarded as deviant at an Elvis impersonators convention, they might be regarded as deviant if they turned up for an interview for a head teacher's post in such an outfit.
  The context could also be a culture. Some acts which are regarded as deviant in one culture are not so regarded in another. For example, drinking alcohol is not regarded as deviant in Britain, but is not only deviant but also illegal in some Moslem countries.

- **Time**
  When an act takes place can also affect whether it is seen as deviant or not. What is regarded as deviant behaviour changes over time. For example smoking was once seen as normal for adults but now is regarded as deviant by many in Britain (but perhaps less so in France). Women wearing trousers was also regarded as deviant 100 years go but not today.

- **Who**
  Who commits an act also affects whether or not it is seen as deviant. For example we might not think twice about seeing a group of young people rollerblading through town but if it was a group of nuns we might regard this as deviant.

However it is not simply who commits acts that affects whether or not they are seen as deviant. A lot depends on how other people react, and on how much power they have.

Some people in society have more power than others to define certain acts, and the people who commit them, as deviant. Newspaper editors have more power than most of us to define individuals or groups as deviant. Over recent years New Age Travellers, single parents, lager louts and eco-warriors have been described in some sections of the press as though they were deviants. If we do not come across any of these people in our daily lives the way they are written about in the papers, or described on TV, can affect how we think about them.

Deviance is quite a complicated idea then. What is seen as deviant can change from place to place, from group to group, from culture to culture, from time to time. What is seen as deviant also depends not just on what is being done but also who is doing it. Maybe the most important factor in determining whether or not a group or individual comes to be seen as a deviant is power. Some people in society have more power than others to label individuals or groups as deviant.

The relationship between crime and deviance is also complicated. Not all deviant acts are criminal, some deviant acts only break norms not laws. But not all criminal acts might be seen as deviant. For example using cannabis is seen as perfectly normal among many groups in our society like rastafarians, people with multiple sclerosis who use it for pain relief, and many others who use it as a recreational drug in preference to alcohol, but the use of cannabis is illegal and so all of these people are breaking the law. They may not see themselves as deviants, and indeed many others may not, but they are committing a criminal act.

Not only does deviance vary across time and cultures so does what is criminal. At present in our society the use of cannabis is illegal. As we are writing this book many people are calling for its legalisation: MPs, Cabinet ministers and members of the Shadow Cabinet are admitting to having used it, and some senior police officers are admitting they turn a blind eye to its use. It may be that in sociological terms we are seeing behaviour that was regarded as deviant 20 years ago being no longer regarded as deviant. It may also be that the use of cannabis changes from being wholly illegal to legal, or legal for some groups on prescription, or just decriminalised (staying illegal but its use would be tolerated in certain places like coffee shops in Amsterdam).

EXERCISE

i)   What do you think?

ii) Is the use of cannabis 'normal' in your area or is it deviant?

iii) Should the use of cannabis be made legal, for all or for some, or should it just be decriminalised?

Here are some figures on cannabis use for you to consider.

According to the 1998 British Crime Survey 42% of 16–29-year-olds have tried cannabis; less than 0.5% of 16–29-year-olds have taken heroin, crack or methodone in the year before the survey, but 3% had taken cocaine. According to a MORI poll in 1999 61% of the public feel that cannabis was 'not very or not at all harmful'.

Deviance: when, where, and whom?

Using figure 24 for each of the following activities try to identify a situation in which it would be seen as 'normal' or 'deviant', legal or illegal, or any combination of these. For example, as we have said above, drug taking can be seen as normal but illegal by some social groups.

EXERCISE

	NORMAL	DEVIANT	LEGAL	ILLEGAL
Killing someone				
Breaking the speed limit				
Having sex				
Hitting a teacher				
Drinking alcohol				

Figure 24 Classifying types of behaviour.

Labelling theory

So far we've looked at social control and the concepts of 'deviance' and 'crime'. Labelling theory is the way of linking all of these together. Labelling theory has been very influential in sociology because:

→ It shows how social control can actually create deviant or criminal behaviour.
→ It shows that the reactions of people who have power to make labels stick is important when thinking about how individuals become 'criminals' or 'deviants'.
→ It shows how people may come to see themselves as 'criminals' or 'deviants'

In labelling theory a '**master status**' is a particular characteristic of a person that is seen by others as more important than any other characteristics that a person has. So if we are seen as a thief this status or characteristic is likely to be seen as more important than the fact that we

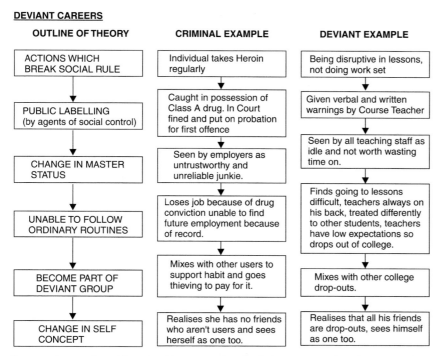

DEVIANT CAREERS

OUTLINE OF THEORY	CRIMINAL EXAMPLE	DEVIANT EXAMPLE
ACTIONS WHICH BREAK SOCIAL RULE	Individual takes Heroin regularly	Being disruptive in lessons, not doing work set
PUBLIC LABELLING (by agents of social control)	Caught in possession of Class A drug. In Court fined and put on probation for first offence	Given verbal and written warnings by Course Teacher
CHANGE IN MASTER STATUS	Seen by employers as untrustworthy and unreliable junkie.	Seen by all teaching staff as idle and not worth wasting time on.
UNABLE TO FOLLOW ORDINARY ROUTINES	Loses job because of drug conviction unable to find future employment because of record.	Finds going to lessons difficult, teachers always on his back, treated differently to other students, teachers have low expectations so drops out of college.
BECOME PART OF DEVIANT GROUP	Mixes with other users to support habit and goes thieving to pay for it.	Mixes with other college drop-outs.
CHANGE IN SELF CONCEPT	Realises she has no friends who aren't users and sees herself as one too.	Realises that all his friends are drop-outs, sees himself as one too.

(1st two columns adapted from Outsiders: Howard Becker (63) Free Press and Stephen Moore, (96)*Sociology Alive*, Second edition (Stanley Thomas).

Figure 25 Classifying deviant careers.

are also a student, a part time shop assistant or a baby sitter. People will also see us in terms of other characteristics of being a thief – not to be trusted, not to be left alone with money, unreliable and so on.

Our '**self concept**' is literally how we see ourselves, what kind of person we think we are.

Labelling theory shows us how individuals might follow a '**deviant career**' or '**criminal career**'. That is to say, just as with a career in an occupation, there are certain stages that individuals have to go through before they come to see themselves as deviants or criminals. One stage does not automatically lead to the next though. In the example below it is possible that our heroin user can show her employers that she is not a 'typical junkie', perhaps by going for drug counselling or rehabilitation. In this way her master status might not change, she might keep her job, and a possible deviant career would be ended.

Look at the examples of deviant careers above. Think about the college 'drop out'. For each stage of his 'deviant career' try to identify actions that might be taken by our 'drop out' or other people that would stop his 'deviant career'.

Labelling theory is important in sociology because it shows us how the interaction between agents of social control and particular groups or individuals can create deviance. It shows us that sometimes it is people's reactions to rule breaking that are as important as rule breaking itself. What labelling theory doesn't tell us though is WHY people break rules in the first place. We'll return to that later on in the chapter when we look at possible explanations for criminal behaviour.

Religion and social control

Religious beliefs can have a powerful influence over what people do. Catholics, for example, are against birth control and abortion. Religious teachings enable us to tell right from wrong, good from bad. They give us a moral code to live by, such as that enshrined in the Ten Commandments or the Koran. In this way religious organisations of one kind or another can be seen as agents of social control. We conform because we have a set of beliefs. If we know, because of our beliefs, that we will be punished in some sort of way by our God or Gods, we are likely to conform to the teachings of our religion in order to avoid such punishment.

Karl Marx, writing in the 19th century, said 'religion is the opium of people'. What he meant by this was that religious beliefs offer people who hold them a dream which stops them acting in the real world to make their situation better. If you believed, for example, that 'the meek shall inherit the earth', then it would be no good to go around shouting about injustices and trying to put things right. Your beliefs told you that being 'meek' was the answer and making a fuss was not being meek!

Marx thought that religious beliefs were an important factor in keeping the proletariat poor and oppressed. Again if you really believe that God made the world and God decreed that there would be rich people and poor people then there wouldn't be much point in arguing – because you couldn't argue with God and anyway your main opportunity would come after your death.

The poor and oppressed did not rebel against the way society was because according to Marx, they thought that the inequalities in society were the result of God's actions, not the result of conflict between the powerful and powerless. They also believed, according to this point of view, that they would be rewarded in the after life, that they would get their reward in heaven. So, as well as knowing that the meek would inherit the earth, the poor knew that it would be 'easier for a camel to pass through the eye of a needle than for a rich man to get to heaven,' which offered some real comfort in an oppressive world.

Religion, or at least the particular beliefs of 19th century Christianity, was a source of social control for Marx because the beliefs that people held stopped them from acting to change the unequal world around them.

How does this verse from 'All Things Bright and Beautiful' illustrate what Marx was saying?

> The rich man in his castle
>
> The poor man at his gate
>
> God made them high and lowly
>
> And ordered their estate.

(Bob Marley's song 'Stand Up For Your Rights' puts forward a similar view to that of Marx.)

Feminist sociologists have also shown how religious beliefs and teachings can be seen as forms of social control, as the following extract shows:

> Religious institutes advocate traditional family structures. This helps to place women in a more subservient role at the expense of their own careers and opportunities. In this respect religion

acts as an agency of social control of women and children. The Koran says 'Men are in charge of women...hence good women are obedient.' In the Bible, Ephesians 5, 22-24 says: 'Wives, be subject to your husbands ... for the husband is the head of the wife...'. In Judaism there is a prayer in which males say 'Blessed art thou, o Lord ... that I was not born a woman'.

(from Religion (Access to Sociology Series), Seife and Starbuck (1998), Hodder and Stoughton).

Religion and change

There is a lot of evidence to show that religious organisations need not be a source of social control. In the USA. the Reverend Martin Luther King was a prominent leader in the Civil Rights movement. In Poland the Catholic church was an important part of the resistance to the Russian regime, and in South America, the 'Liberation Theology' put forward by some priests has been an important source of opposition to some of the inequalities existing in some countries. Nearer to home we have also seen attempts to bring about change based at least in part on religion in Northern Ireland. Some of the opposition to the apartheid regime in South Africa came from the Church of England. The Church of England was critical of some of the politics of the Thatcher government between 1979 and 1990. Quakers have been active in the peace movement in Britain and some refuse to pay that part of their taxes which is spent on armaments. It is difficult to generalise on the basis of the available evidence that all religious organisations are necessarily sources of social control all of the time.

Are religious organisations and religious beliefs still important? Many sociologists believe that the mass media are more significant as agents of social control in the 21st century than religious organisations. They say this for the following reasons:

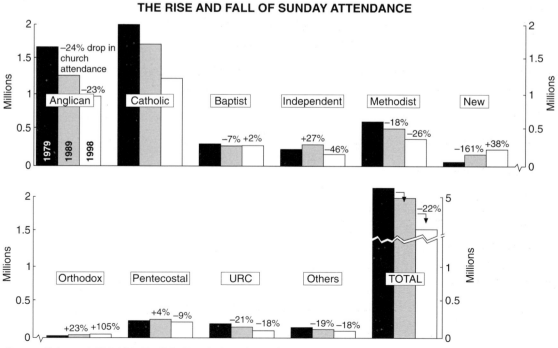

Figure 26 Church attendance statistics.

- There has been a steady decline in the number of people going to church on a Sunday.
- Fewer people believe in a personal God, 43% 1950s, 31% 1990s. More people do not believe in God at all, 2% 1950s, 27% 1990s.
- Major religious organisations such as the Church of England have less power in society than they used to. Margaret Thatcher, for example, was famously 'too busy' to meet the Archbishop of Canterbury, when she was Prime Minister, a situation which would have been unheard of 100 years before.

On the other hand the mass media are everywhere and they have audiences of millions. For example, on Monday 20 November 2000 14.9 million people watched Judith Keppel become a millionaire on ITV while over 13 million watched the last episode of *One Foot in the Grave* at the same time on the BBC.

The mass media and social control

What are the mass media?

The mass media consist of newspapers, television, radio, magazines, CDs, cassettes, the Internet, computer games, films, videos, DVDs, books and advertising posters. A mass medium is any medium of communication which can reach a mass audience.

Most of us probably spend a great deal of our time exposed to various mass media. We get up in the morning thanks to our radio alarm, go downstairs and switch on TV, read the paper on the way to work, see advertising hoardings. In the evening we might listen to a little music, read a magazine, play on the computer, watch more TV, and perhaps read a book before we go to sleep. It is this all pervasive, all surrounding nature of the mass media that gives it such influence. In countries where there is a revolution or a couple what is one of the first institutions that the rebels try to capture? The radio, or a TV station. Why? Because capturing the means of communicating allows them to put their message or their propaganda across to the population. The mass media is seen by many sociologists as an important agent of social control.

There are two particularly important ways in which the mass media might be said to act as an agent of social control.

i)   How it affects **public opinion**. The mass media might have an influence on how we think about issues that affect us as citizens. What gets into the papers and onto television news and current affairs programmes may well affect what we think about and how we think about it. For example if there was no reporting of lone parents we might not think of lone parents as an issue. If there is reporting of the increase in the number of lone parents and this is reported in connection with fraudulent claims for welfare benefits we are encouraged to think of all lone parents as 'social security scroungers,' and not to think, for example, of the problems that face many women in providing for their children and themselves after divorce.

ii)   How it encourages **conforming** to particular social norms. The mass media has been said to encourage individuals to conform to traditional gender roles by, for example, tending to show women as either sex objects or as mothers and housewives. Many of us get our role models from the mass media. If all we see are people playing traditional roles we are more likely to behave in a similar fashion. The mass media are often said to present us with gender stereotypes.

Stereotyping does not only happen in the mass media in relation to gender roles. Many young people complain that you can read or see nothing good about young people in the papers or on TV. They complain that the press and the television companies present stereotypical images of young people as hooligans, or as mixed up with drugs, for example. Many black and Asian members of society feel that they too are portrayed in a negative and stereotypical way in the media. If the majority of images we see of black and Asian people are to do with crime, public disorder and inner city decay, or as helpless victims of famines or natural disasters then this can affect how we think of all black and Asian people.

Sometimes this kind of stereotyping is linked to the consequences of breaking social norms. If we read stories about convoys of New Age Travellers being broken up by the police this can be seen as showing us what happens when we deviate from the social norm of living in a fixed place and having a steady job. The reporting of AIDs as a 'gay plague' or as resulting from sharing dirty needles can be seen as showing us the consequences of deviating from the norm of heterosexuality, or of not taking illegal drugs. This process is known as **norm setting**. Those who break social norms are treated in a negative way and presented as outsiders.

EXERCISE

Look at a selection of daily newspapers. What social norms are being emphasised in them? (You may want to look at the stories that emphasise the consequences of wrong doing.)

Are the social norms emphasised ones that we would all agree with? (the consensus view)

or do they represent the norms of powerful groups in society? (the conflict view).

For example we would probably all agree with the idea that murder is wrong. We might not all agree with a norm that said homosexuality was wrong.

The mass media and public opinion – does the mass media influence our political opinions?

In Chapter 8 we talk about the ways in which the mass media might have become more influential over recent years. One way in which the media is said to influence our political opinions is through the process of agenda setting. This means that the mass media act like the person who sets the agenda for a meeting. In a meeting you can only discuss what is on the agenda – the person who sets the agenda, therefore, has a lot of power over what is discussed and how it is discussed. For example look at the different views of the underclass in Chapter 6. If the mass media report poverty in terms of what they see as the characteristics of the poor themselves (criminal, promiscuity, unwillingness to work, welfare dependency) we will see poverty as resulting from these characteristics. We might then think that the way to remove poverty is to change poor people themselves by, for example, strong policing in poor areas and by making welfare benefits harder to get, or conditional on work, and stressing the importance of the traditional family. If the media report poverty as resulting from discrimination, low wages, inadequate benefits, substandard housing and lack of jobs such as investment in particular areas then we may think that the way to remove it is through policies that tackle these issues such as investment in jobs and housing. Controlling the agenda for political debate is an important element of political power.

EXERCISE

Think about the following issues. How have they been reported in the mass media? How might they have been presented differently?

- Asylum seekers
- Failing schools
- The price of fuel

Those sociologists who consider that the mass media can set the agenda for political debate tend to stress how the newspapers and television companies (and record companies, computer companies and magazine companies) are owned and controlled by a small number of individuals or organisations. They also stress that the people who decide what gets into the papers or onto television are drawn from a relatively small section of society. Newspaper and television news editors tend to be middle class, middle aged, male and white. The point is that what gets into the papers is reflecting what middle class, middle aged, white men feel is important or significant. The views of other groups tend to be ignored. Those who make the decisions about what gets into the news are known as 'gatekeepers' – they decide whether or not to print or broadcast a story.

These gatekeepers are said to act broadly in line with the interests of powerful groups in society and especially the owners of the paper or TV company and so are unlikely to print stories that are critical of those in power or that threaten their position. So, for example, stories about money lost through tax evasion and tax avoidance are much less likely to be reported than stories about single mothers fiddling social security benefits. Stories about accidents, deaths, injuries and ill health resulting from failure of big companies to observe health and safety regulations are less likely to be reported than stories about workers going on strike.

There is a different view of the role of the mass media in society, however. If the view we have just described represents the **conflict** view, where the powerful use their power to their own advantage, this view is based more on society as consisting of lots of groups, each with their own interests but none of whom manage to dominate the others.

This point of view is known as the **pluralist idea of the media**. Those who put forward this point of view say that the newspapers, for example, give us what we want. If the papers didn't print the kind of stories that we want to read we would not buy them. Accordingly what we want is what we get. The influence of owners is limited by the fact that the newspapers are in competition with each other. If one paper does not give us what we want, we'll buy another. So if we are supporters of the Conservative Party we will tend to buy a newspaper that presents them favourably, not one that criticises them. If we support the Labour Party we'll buy a different paper.

Those who put forward the pluralist point of view tend to stress the range of newspapers and magazines available. We can go into our local newspaper shop and buy anything from *Playboy* to *Gay Times*; from *The Spectator* to *The New Statesman*; from *Mojo* to *Q Magazine*; from *Cosmopolitan* to *Woman's Own*; from *Homes and Gardens* to *Climber*. What is successful is what sells, what sells is what people want. The range of media products available ensures that every point of view is represented. Many people suggest that the Internet is the ultimate forum for free speech. Anyone can set up a website and put forward their views on any subject.

The mass media and gender stereotyping

As we saw in Chapter 1, the mass media is an important agent of socialisation. As we watch TV, read papers and magazines, listen to CDs, play computer games, or listen to the radio we see or hear our role models and we are presented with images of what it is to be a woman or a man in Britain today. This is why the mass media is said to be important in the process of socialisation. Through the mass media we can:

- See what people do and how people act. In other words we can see women and men performing various social roles.
- See what people look like. In other words we can get an idea of what counts as 'attractive' in our society. We can also get an idea of whether or not it is important for us to look right, to have the right 'body image' from what we see and how individuals are described in newspapers.

The mass media is often accused of gender stereotyping. It is said to present us with fixed ideas about what is appropriate for men and women. According to this idea women are said to be presented as 'sex objects' or as housewives/mothers or in a limited number of occupational roles – cooking, cleaning and caring – these roles being clearly associated with domesticity. Women are often described in terms of their appearance – 'attractive blonde' for example. Men on the other hand, are presented to us in a wide range of occupational roles: they are the powerful, the decision makers, the leaders. They are also fearless and aggressive where women are often presented as rather passive and dependent. Men are rarely portrayed as emotional; women often are.

EXERCISE

Try writing a tabloid headline and brief paragraph about a bank clerk, who is married with two children, aged 28, slim, good looking, with a lively, outgoing personality, who foils a robbery at the bank.

Write one headline and brief paragraph for a male, and one for a female, fitting the characteristics above, using as many gender stereotypes as you can. Then compare your paragraph with stories from actual newspapers. To what extent do newspapers use the language of stereotypes?

Researching stereotypes in the mass media

Content analysis

Content analysis is perhaps the best way to research the extent to which the mass media present us with stereotypical images of women and men. Content analysis is what it says, a good away of analysing the content of newspaper articles, TV programmes and so on.

There are a number of ways of doing content analysis:

- **Measuring**

  A page of a newspaper is divided into two columns. By simply measuring how many 'column centimetres' or 'column inches' are devoted to a type of story we can see how important it is meant to be. We could also measure the amount of time taken up by men and women talking on news programmes by timing them.

- **Counting**

  If we wanted to find out if a school reading scheme showed women and men in traditional gender roles we might use this method. First we would have to draw up a list of traditional roles for males and females, and then make a chart as shown in figure 27.

ROLE	WOMEN	MEN
DOMESTIC		
Cooking	☐	☐
Cleaning	☐	☐
Child care	☐	☐
DIY	☐	☐
Car maintenance	☐	☐
Nurse	☐	☐
Teacher	☐	☐
Cleaner	☐	☐
OCCUPATIONAL		
Postal worker	☐	☐
Doctor	☐	☐
Driver	☐	☐
Head teacher	☐	☐

Figure 27 Traditional and occupational roles.

The next step is to go through the reading scheme and simply tick the appropriate box for each character. A separate chart could be drawn for pictures.

This is like the measuring method – you are effectively measuring how much of something there is. This kind of content analysis could be used to examine the roles played by characters in soaps, and it could be used to assess the extent of gender stereotyping in science textbooks.

- **Interpreting**

  This is a slightly more complicated variety of counting. Imagine that for your course work you have decided to investigate whether or not TV soaps such as East-Enders or Brookside portray female characters as passive, dependent individuals and male characters as active, independent individuals.

  Firstly you would have to define what you mean by each of the characteristics. For example a passive character is one who has things done to them, an active character does things. A dependent character has to rely on others, an independent character does not. Secondly you would have to interpret the actions of the characters in the soaps you have chosen. Finally you would have to allocate each character to a box, as below, but you would also have to have some evidence to support your decision.

	M	F	Active	Passive	Dep.	Indep.
1st Character	✓		Reason			Reason
2nd Character		✓		Reason	Reason	

Figure 28 Interpreting characteristics.

EXERCISE

i) Measuring – what proportion of the sports section of daily papers is devoted to women's sports?

ii) Counting – in TV documentaries or newspaper articles on family issues how often are men's opinions quoted as (a) 'experts' (b) fathers, and how often are women's opinions quoted as (a) 'experts', (b) mothers?

iii) Interpreting – a tricky one to try – how far do men's magazines portray the 'new man' who is in touch with his feelings?

Stereotypes or variety? Does the mass media stereotype us now?

While there is much evidence to show the extent of gender stereotyping done by the mass media, the situation now is less clear. Take computer games. One of the most popular games is *Tomb Raider*, whose main character is Lara Croft. Lara is an action heroine – so cast in a non-stereotypical role, but what about her appearance? Likewise we have female newsreaders, female leads in cop shows such as *Prime Suspect*, and many TV advertisements play with our expectations about gender roles (we have seen Robbie Coltrane doing the washing up in a Persil advert and Melanie Sykes advertising beer for Boddington's). Gay characters are also shown on our screens, and not just as victims or as exaggerated stereotypes which might have been the case in the past. (Think about the difference between Mr Humphries in *Are You Being Served* and Dr Fonseca in *EastEnders*.) Members of the government such as Chris Smith are open about their sexuality without harm to their careers, and Eddie Izzard can appear on prime time TV wearing nail varnish and a dress.

As a result many sociologists feel that we are now presented with a variety of ways of being a woman, of being feminine, or of being a man, of being masculine.

Finally, it is possible that while women are shown in a greater variety of roles there is still a great deal of pressure on younger women in particular to conform to a particular body image, and that this is becoming true for young men too.

What do you think? What evidence do you have?

It is also possible that while women are portrayed in a wide variety of new roles, they are still portrayed as having the main responsibility for child care and housework and that very few men are shown within this dual role.

What do you think? What evidence do you have?

All of the ideas we have outlined above can be applied to the process of **ethnic stereotyping**. Try some of the exercises to find out the extent to which the mass media stereotype members of ethnic minority groups.

Look at the photographs below – which individual is closest to your idea of a real woman or a real man? You might like to discuss your ideas with someone else.

Figure 29 Are these examples of 'real' men and women?

Can the mass media increase the amount of deviant behaviour?

Look at the chart below. It shows the process of **deviancy amplification**. Some sociologists believe that the mass media can actually increase the amount of crime or deviance that occurs.

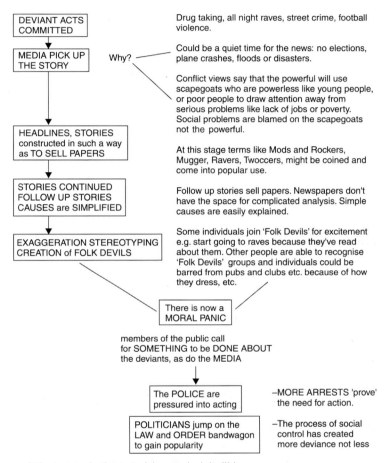

Adapted from Ken Browne (98), *An Introduction to Sociology*, 2nd ed, (Polily).

Figure 30 The process of deviancy amplification, the creation of folk devils, and moral panics.

Folk Devils are groups of people who are 'visible reminders of what we should not be' according to Stan Cohen in *Folk Devils and Moral Panics*. They are groups of individuals who are portrayed as being responsible for problems in society; they are portrayed as posing a threat to society because of their deviant ways.

Moral panics arise when the press, the public and politicians call for 'something to be done about' a group portrayed as Folk Devils because they are seen as representing a threat. Since the 1960s there have been moral panics about Mods and Rockers, lager louts, teenage drinkers and Alcopops; raves, muggers, joy riders and 'twoccers', and falling standards in schools.

Crime

Sociologists are interested in three aspects of crime:

- How much crime there is
- Who commits crime and why they do so
- What the consequences of crime are for individuals and groups in society.

How much crime is there?

One way of finding out how much crime there is is to look at the official figures of crimes recorded by the police, as shown in the table below (figure 31) for England and Wales.

	England and Wales		
	1981	1991	1998–99
Theft and handling stolen goods,	1,603	2,761	2,127
of which: theft of vehicles	333	582	391
theft from vehicles	380	913	681
Burglary	718	1,220	952
Criminal damage	387	821	834
Violence against the person	100	190	231
Fraud and forgery	107	175	174
Robbery	20	45	66
Sexual offences,	19	29	35
of which: rape	1	4	8
Drug offences	–	11	21
Other notifiable offences	9	23	42
	2,964	5,276	4,482

Figure 31 Notifiable offences recorded by the police: by type of offence.

EXERCISE

According to the information in the table:

a) What is the most common crime?

b) Did the overall number of offences recorded by the police fall or rise between 1991 and 1998–99?

c) Which offences increased in number in 1991 and 1998–1999?

The official statistics can also tell us about the proportion of the population who are found guilty of offences.

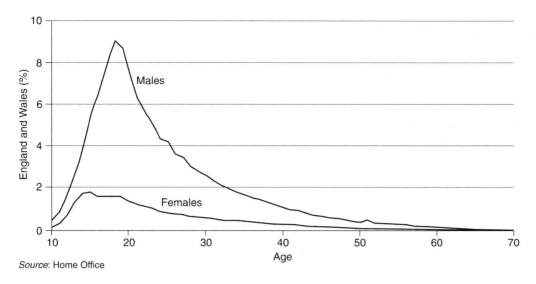

Source: Home Office

Figure 32 Offenders as a percentage of the population: by gender and age, 1997–98.

EXERCISE

According to the information in the graph above.

a) What is the peak offending age for males?

b) What is the peak offending age for females?

Official statistics can also be used to see the trends in crime over time, that is they can tell us if the crime rate is going up, down or staying the same. The crime rate tells us how many offences were committed in a particular year for every 1000 people in the population.

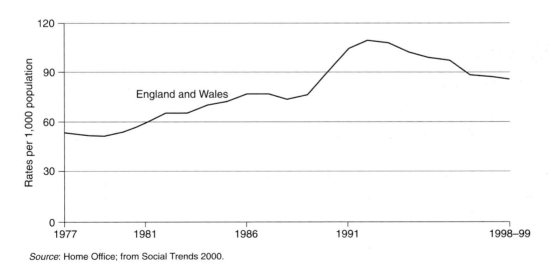

Source: Home Office; from Social Trends 2000.

Figure 33 Notifiable offences recorded by the police.

EXERCISE

According to the information in the graph above:

a) In which year was the crime rate for England and Wales highest?
b) In which year was the crime rate for England and Wales lowest?

The official statistics for crime can apparently tell us a good deal about crime – how much of it there is, what kinds of offence are committed, who commits crime. **But what these official statistics tell us may only be useful if the figures are accurate.**

Where do the official statistics come from? There are three stages in the 'production' of a crime statistic.

i) An offence is committed
ii) The offence is reported to the police
iii) The police record the reported offence as a crime.

Think about the following questions:

i) Have you ever been the victim of a crime and not reported it to the police?
ii) Is it possible to be the victim of an offence and not realise it?
iii) Is it possible that the police could decide that there is not enough evidence that a crime has actually been committed?

If you have answered yes to any, or all, or these questions then we can see that the official figures might not be completely accurate. Sociologists have been critical of the official crime figures for three reasons.

i) We know that not all crimes are reported to the police
ii) We know that not all crimes that are reported to the police are recorded by them as crimes
iii) We know that policing policies can affect crime rates.

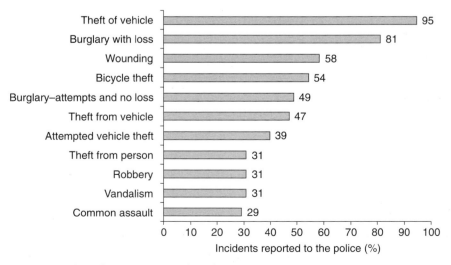

Source: British Crime Survey 2000, Home Office Statistical Bulletin 18/00.

Figure 34 Proportion of offences reported to police in 1999.

As a result we know that there is an amount of crime that does not appear in the official statistics of recorded crime. Sociologists refer to the amount of crime that goes on unrecorded as 'the dark figure'. The British Crime Survey 2000 estimates the dark figure as 77%. The table on page 131 shows the percentages of particular offences that were reported to the police in 1999 (Burglary with loss means a burglary in which something was actually stolen).

EXERCISE

i) Why do you think that 'theft of a vehicle' was the most likely offence to be reported to the police in 1999?
ii) Why might individuals not report common assault?

You have probably identified the need to report theft of a vehicle for insurance reasons in your answer to question (i) – insurance companies require evidence that the theft of a car has been reported to the police before they will deal with a claim. What about the 5% of vehicle thefts that were not reported? Perhaps the owners were not insured and had no wish to let the police know they were driving without insurance.

Why aren't all offences reported to the police?

The British Crime Survey 2000 asked victims of crime why they did not report incidents to the police. The reasons why victims of crime said they did not report crime to the police are shown below.

Reason for not reporting offence	Percentage of incidents in which this reason was given
Too trivial/No loss	46
Felt police couldn't do anything	30
Private/dealt with ourselves	22
Felt police would not be interested	17
Inconvenient to report	5
Reported to other authorities	4
Fear of reprisal	3
Dislike/Fear of Police	1

(N.B. – these figures don't add up to 100 as respondents could give more than one reason for not reporting.

Source: BCS 2000 – Home Office Statistical Bulletin 18/00 Crown Copyright

Figure 35 Why don't people report crimes?

As we can see from the above the most common reason for not reporting an offence was that people thought it was too trivial, or not serious enough, to bother reporting it to the police, or they hadn't actually lost anything. For example if someone had a couple of cassettes or some loose change for parking meters stolen from their car they may well feel that it devas not serious enough to report to the police. Minor acts of vandalism may also go unreported in this way.

Sometimes the victims of theft may feel that the police are unlikely to find the stolen property and catch the criminal and so they feel it is a waste of time reporting such offences. This is particularly likely to be true when the victim and the offender are both teenagers and it is something like a mobile phone that is stolen.

Domestic violence is an offence that many victims see as private, they want to deal with it themselves in their own way without involving the police. Other victims of violence might prefer to take revenge themselves. Sometimes people feel that the police just won't be interested. This is particularly true of bike theft. It may be that the people who have had their bike stolen feel that the police wouldn't be interested in solving such a small crime.

Sometimes people won't report a minor offence if it is going to cause them some inconvenience. In rural areas, for example, people may not want to take up a lot of their own time travelling to a distant police station or waiting in for an officer to call at their home, so they don't report it. Some crimes are reported to people other than police – if something is stolen from us at school or at work we may inform our teacher or our boss, rather than the police. Sometimes people do not report crime for fear of reprisals. This is especially true when the victim knows the offender – women who are beaten by their husbands or partners may not report these offences through fear of being attacked again as a result.

Very few people fail to report crimes because they don't like the police or are frightened of them. In some instances victims of racist attacks have found the police to be unsympathetic and have felt themselves treated as a criminal and not a victim. Such treatment has led to some members of ethnic minority groups actively disliking the police.

Another important reason for not reporting offences concerns rape and sexual assaults. Many women do not wish to relive the experience, or feel too embarrassed to report such incidents to the police. They may also be fearful of what might happen should they have to go to court and be crossexamined about their sex lives. Many victims of sexual assault or rape also feel that the police will not deal with the matter in a sensitive fashion. All of these factors of course apply equally to male victims.

Sometimes offences are not reported because the victim is unaware that a crime has been committed. We may have been the victim of a pickpocket, for example, and think that we have simply lost our wallet or our purse.

White collar crime and official statistics

It might appear that all crime is committed by those in the lower social classes. This is not so. Crimes are committed by people across the whole social scale. Sociologists use the term '**white collar crime**' to refer to those crimes committed by individuals, usually in high status positions, in the course of their occupations. It can also include offences such as tax evasion. A typical white collar offence is fraud: for example, insider trading which happens when someone has inside information about takeovers or mergers and uses their inside knowledge to make money on the stock market by buying or selling shares. This is, of course, illegal. Other offences include embezzlement, 'fiddling expenses', and professional misconduct.

White collar crime is thought to be under reported for various reasons. Quite often there are no obvious victims – it is often seen as a 'victimless crime'. For example, insider trading may well benefit the perpetrator, but there are no obvious victims in the same way that there might be with a burglary or robbery. Trust has been broken, but no one individual has lost out.

Very often when individuals are found to be committing offences at work their cases do not get to court as this would cause bad publicity for their company. Guilty parties may be dealt with by the firm's own internal procedures to prevent such bad publicity.

In cases of bribery or corruption it may well be that none of the parties involved will report the offence. This is because they all see themselves as benefiting and so are unlikely to report it to the police. Bribes may be offered to individuals to secure financially lucrative contracts or information about the activities of commercial rivals. Sometimes white collar crimes are not reported because no one is aware that they have been committed. This may be the case when the public is misled by misrepresentation in advertising.

Corporate crime is also under reported. Corporate crime is crime that benefits corporations rather than individuals. For example, firms that do not follow anti-pollution legislation in order to maximise their profits are guilty of corporate crimes. Other examples include industrial espionage and failure to follow health and safety laws. Although there are victims, such breaches of the law may only result in a reprimand or an official warning from government bodies.

Infamous examples of white collar crime include the case of Nick Leeson whose activities led to the bankruptcy of Barings Bank; Robert Maxwell who used money from the Mirror Group pension fund for business purposes; and Jonathan Aitken, the ex-Conservative MP, who was imprisoned for conspiracy to pervert the course of justice after trying to cover up accepting hospitality at The Ritz from Mohammed al Fayed, the owner of Harrods, in return for asking questions in the House of Commons.

Sometimes the police may regard an offence as too trivial to be worth pursuing formally. For example if someone reports some minor vandalism the police may decide to deal with it informally by 'having a word' with the perpetrators. Occasionally offences are reported to the police but then the victim decides not to take the matter any further. If, for example, someone has a bike stolen and it is then returned to them, they may decide not to prosecute. The police may also feel on occasions that no crime has actually taken place. They may decide that someone is making a malicious complaint, or there might not be enough evidence to show that a crime has actually taken place.

How can policing policies affect the crime figures?

If the police decide to crack down on a particular offence the figures for that offence will rise. In Cleveland, for example, at the time of writing this book, the police have targeted speeding motorists and are using speed cameras on many roads. This will probably have the effect of inflating the number of speeding offences. It may appear that motorists in Cleveland are particularly likely to drive too fast, but the figures will simply reflect the policy of Cleveland police force to target speeding motorists.

What other ways are there of measuring the amount of crime that happens?

If we think about it there are often three groups of people involved in crime.

→ The victim
→ The offender
→ The police and courts.

If the official statistics on crime come from what the police record or from who gets found guilty, then there are two other groups we could ask – the victims and the offenders. As there is no obvious way of knowing who these individuals are sociologists have devised two types of survey which basically ask people either:

i)   What crimes they have been victims of – **a victim survey.**
ii) What crimes they have committed – **a self report survey.**

By using either of these types of research sociologists can estimate the amount of crime that actually happens.

The British crime survey – a victim study

Every two years since 1982 (from 2000 it will be carried out annually), the British Crime Survey has measured crimes against people living in private households in England and Wales. The 2000 British Crime Survey used a nationally representative sample of 19,411 people aged 16 and above, and had a response rate of 74%. Face to face interviews were carried out to obtain responses. The idea behind the British Crime Survey is that individuals are asked whether or not they have been victims of crime since the previous survey was carried out. In this way it can measure reported crime and unreported and unrecorded crime. A victim survey is said to provide a more reliable measure of trends in crime. The table on page 135 shows a comparison of the advantages and disadvantages of the British Crime Survey and police recorded crime.

The 1998/99 Youth Lifestyles Survey – A Self Report Survey

Because the official statistics only tell us about who gets caught they cannot tell us about what kinds of people offend and how often they offend. If the police only give informal cautions to offenders they won't appear in official figures either.

Self report studies can show us how much crime is committed, what kinds of offences people commit, how often people offend and what groups are most likely to offend.

The 1998/99 Youth Lifestyles Survey used a representative sample of 12–30-year-olds living in private households in England and Wales. The survey was conducted in two parts – a face to face interview and a self completion questionnaire were used in the part of the survey about offending because of the sensitive nature of the subject matter. A sample from the questionnaire can be seen on page 136.

One of the problems that sociologists face when doing this kind of research is being sure that

THE BRITISH CRIME SURVEY	POLICE RECORDED CRIME
• Starting in 1982, it measures both reported and unreported crime. As such it provides a measure of trends in crime not affected by changes in reporting, or changes in police recording rules or practices	• Collected since 1857. Provides measure of offences both reported to and recorded by the police. As such they are influenced by changes in reporting behaviour and recording rules and practices
• In recent years has measured crime every two years. From 2001 the BCS will move to an annual cycle	• The police provide quarterly crime returns, and figures are published every six months
• Measures based on estimates from a sample of the population. The estimates are therefore subject to sampling error and other methodological limitations	• Only includes 'notifiable' offences which the police have to notify to the Home Office for statistical purpose
	• Provides an indicator of the workload of the police
• Does not measure crime at the small area level well, but from 2001 the sample size will be increased to 40,000 respondents per annum	• Provides data at the level of 43 police force areas
• Does not include crimes against: – Those under 16 – Commercial and public sector establishments – Those in institutions, and the homeless	• Includes crime against: – Those under 16 – Commercial and public sector establishments – Those in institutions, and the homeless
• Does not measure: – Victimless crimes (e.g., drug, alcohol misuse) – Crimes where a victim is no longer available for interview – Fraud – Sexual offences (due to the small number of incidents reported to the survey, estimates are not considered reliable)	• Measures: – Victimless crime – Murder and manslaughter – Fraud – Sexual offences
• Collects information on what happens in crime (e.g., when crimes occur, and effects in terms of injury and property loss)	• Collects information about the number of arrests, who is arrested, the number of crimes detected, and by what method
• Provides information about how the risks of crime vary for different groups	• Does not show which groups of the population are most at risk of victimisation

Figure 36 Comparing the British Crime Survey, and police recorded crime.

their respondents are giving accurate replies. If you were doing coursework on offending among 12–16-year-olds do you think they would be more likely to answer such questions honestly if you asked them in person or if they could fill in a questionnaire alone?

Young people in particular may well be reluctant to answer questions face to face. They may be embarrassed about their behaviour or they may feel that the interviewer will tell someone in authority about what they have done. They may be more likely to tell the truth in an anonymous questionnaire that they fill in themselves. Researchers are increasingly likely to use lap top computers in this kind of research. The respondents key in their answers alone. Because the researcher is not able to see their responses it appears that individuals are more likely to admit offences.

Problems of self reporting

- Sampling: the sample used may miss out potential high rate offenders. For example the Youth Lifestyles Survey did not include children in care, homeless people, or those in custodial institutions. These groups are only a small percentage of the relevant population but the sample could have been biased by missing them out.
- The non-response rate. If many individuals refuse to take part in the survey the results could be biased.
- Are the responses true? People may exaggerate their offending or they may not admit to particular offences.
- Counting offenders – sometimes self report studies can give us a false picture of the amount of offending that takes place because they don't always distinguish between petty offences and serious offences.

Offences included in the 1998/9 Youth Lifestyles Survey

* Have you ever.

* In the last 12 months, have you.

Criminal Damage

1. ... damaged or destroyed, purposely or recklessly, something belonging to someone else (e.g. a telephone box, bus shelter, car, window of a house, etc)?

2. ... set fire, purposely or recklessly, to something not belonging to you? It might be to paper or furniture, a barn, a car, a forest, basement, a building or something else.

Property Offences

3. ... stolen money from a gas or electricity meter, public telephone vending machine, video game or fruit machine?

4. ... stolen anything from a shop, supermarket or department store?

5. ... stolen anything in school worth more than £5?

6. ... stolen anything from the place that you work worth more than £5?

7. ... taken away a bicycle without the owner's permission, not intending to give it back?

*8. ... taken away a motorbike or moped without the owner's permission, not intending to give it back?

*9. ... taken away a car without the owner's permission, not intending to give it back?

Figure 37 A sample from the Youth Lifestyles Survey.

EXERCISE

i) Why might some individuals refuse to take part in a self report study?

ii) Why might some individuals exaggerate what they do?

iii) Why might some individuals not admit to particular offences?

The main findings of self report studies

The various self report studies that have been carried out in Britain since the 1950s tell us:

→ Delinquency is more common than official figures show.

→ Class differences in offending are much less than official figures show.

→ Gender differences in offending are much less than official figures show.

Crime

What and who do we think of when we think of crime? Maybe our first thought is of gangs of threatening looking young men looking for trouble in the town centre. Maybe it is of drug users breaking into houses to steal videos or CD players to raise cash to support their drug habit. Maybe we think of the vandalism and damage that blight some parts of our town. Maybe we think of the consequences of crime. Perhaps crime means increased premiums for

England & Wales					Rates per 10,000 population
	10–15	16–24	25–34	35 and over	All aged 10 and over (thousands)
Males					
Theft and handling stolen goods	133	221	88	18	152.6
Drug offences	15	177	70	9	96.0
Violence against the person	31	74	33	8	51.7
Burglary	40	66	18	2	37.2
Criminal damage	11	18	8	1	12.4
Robbery	6	11	2	–	5.6
Sexual offences	3	4	3	2	5.5
Other indictable offences	11	104	61	12	74.3
All indictable offences	250	674	282	53	435.9
Females					
Theft and handling stolen goods	73	75	30	7	56.8
Drug offences	2	18	10	1	11.5
Violence against the person	11	12	5	1	8.9
Burglary	4	3	1	–	2.0
Criminal damage	1	2	1	–	1.3
Robbery	1	1	–	–	0.6
Sexual offences	–	–	–	–	0.1
Other indictable offences	3	21	13	2	15.0
All indictable offences	95	131	61	12	96.1

Crime rates in England and Wales

Figure 38 Crime Rates in England and Wales.

our car insurance policy, or even not being able to afford to insure the contents of our home because we live in a high crime area. Perhaps crime means the possibility of racist abuse, graffiti or violence. Perhaps it means that because of where we live, or the colour of our skin, we are likely to be stopped by the police more frequently than we think is right. Perhaps crime simply means that everyday life is more stressful for us.

In this section we will look at sociological explanations of crime and differences in crime according to gender, ethnicity, class, age and where we live. We will look at the consequences of crime in terms of who suffers from crime and how. Before doing that, though, look at the table above.

i)   What is the most common crime committed by males and females?
ii) What age group of men are most likely to have committed an offence?

Social class and offending

A variety of data shows a link between social class and offending. For example, 41% of prisoners are from social classes 4 and 5 against only 18% of prisoners from social classes 1, 2, or 3. But self report studies show less difference in offending between social classes. In the 1998/99 Youth Lifestyles Survey men in social classes 4 and 5 were more likely to be serious or persistent offenders than others. The same pattern applies for women. Men from different social classes commit different offences. Those in social classes 4 and 5 were more likely to be involved in fighting, to both buy and sell stolen goods and to commit workplace theft. Men in social classes 1 and 2 were more likely to commit fraud.

The official crime figures, self report studies, and victim studies all show us that there is less

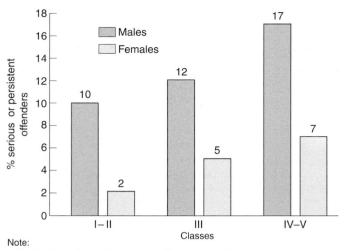

Note:
1. The Registrar General's social classification is used to measure social class. The individual's social class is derived from their father's occupation (or their mother's, if father's is unknown or not applicable). I – professional, II – managerial or technical, III – skilled manual and non-manual work, IV – partly skilled, V – unskilled

Figure 39 Serious or persistant offending, by social class.

crime in rural areas than urban areas, and that crime rates are highest in inner city areas and on poor council estates. From the official crime figures, from the figures about the prison population, we could perhaps say that the typical criminal is a young working class male living in an urban environment, most likely the inner city or a council estate. This image is probably what fits with our view of the typical criminal. As we will see later in this section there may be good reasons to cast doubt on this stereotype, but many sociologists' theories have tried to explain crime in terms of the characteristics of the young, urban, working class male. Here are some of the influential ideas.

How might position in the social structure affect our chances of committing crime?

According to Robert Merton, who was writing about American society in the 1950s, the socially accepted goal in society is to achieve success. Having wealth and what goes with it – a big house, car and these days a computer, a good sound system, DVD player and so on – all of these are symbols of success. Not only are there socially approved goals, but there are also legitimate means of achieving the goal of wealth. According to the norms of society we should achieve our wealth by hard work. Hard work at school, at college and when we get a job is the route to success. For many people in society this does not pose a problem, they go to school and college, get jobs, work hard, get promoted and are rewarded with varying degrees of success. For Merton these are the **conformists**, they conform to the socially accepted goals and they use the legitimate, socially approved means to achieve them.

However there are groups in society who find themselves disadvantaged because of their position in the social structure. These people want success but they find they cannot achieve it legitimately. The strain that arises because they find they cannot achieve success legitimately causes them to find alternative ways of be coming wealthy – drug pushing, organising prostitution, robbery or burglary, for example. This group Merton calls **innovators**. The innovators turn to crime because the legitimate means do not work for them. Perhaps it is because of poor quality education – a lack of qualifications means low paid work or maybe no work at all. Perhaps it is because of discrimination; perhaps it is because of high levels of unemployment in certain areas. The pressure on individuals to succeed means that some will turn to illegitimate means to obtain the symbol of success – money and all that it brings.

EXERCISE

i) What kinds of crime in Britain today could be explained using Merton's ideas?

ii) What kinds of crime cannot be explained using Merton's ideas?

How might the norms and values of our subculture affect our chances of committing crime?

Although Merton's explanation for crime was influential it was unable to explain crimes which brought no obvious reward for the criminal, such as vandalism, fighting or criminal damage. Some sociologists put forward ideas that linked the norms and values of working class culture or of youth subcultures to criminal behaviour. For example some sociologists felt that the norms of working class culture which stressed toughness, the need for excitement and the ability to be 'smart' – to always have an answer – would lead to working class youths eventually coming into conflict with the law. To be tough you would have to act tough, maybe through fighting. To get excitement you would do things for kicks – joyriding or maybe getting your 'tag' on the subway or underground train. To show you were smart you might have an 'attitude' when stopped by the police. Any of these norms could get you into trouble.

A similar explanation of crime and the young working class involved the idea of '**status frustration**'. According to this idea working class youths are likely to end up in low paid jobs because they are less likely to succeed at school than middle class children. This lack of status leads them to create their own subcultures in which they have a chance of achieving the status they cannot achieve in a mainstream society dominated by middle class rules. In the subculture the norms and values of society may well be turned upside down. The lad who can break into and 'hotwire' a car the quickest has a high status within the subculture.

EXERCISE

Is it only working class youths who are vandals and who fight?

Find out from self report studies or official statistics.

What is the link between deprivation and crime?

Throughout this book there are examples of the way in which society has changed. During the 1980s and 1990s many people (at least 3.5 million) found themselves out of work. Many jobs disappeared for good – in the mines, the car factories and the steelworks for example – while at the same time some individuals became extremely wealthy. Young people in particular created a whole range of subcultures and lifestyles, which often involved spending reasonably large sums of money on clothes, CDs and other consumer goods. As unemployment rose, so did crime, and for some people the link between unemployment, poverty and crime was quite simple. Unemployment caused deprivation and deprivation caused crime.

However for some sociologists, the link between deprivation and crime is not such a simple one. For some it is not deprivation itself that causes crime, but relative deprivation.

Relative deprivation is not the same as absolute deprivation. **Absolute deprivation** refers to joblessness, poor education, poor housing but relative deprivation refers to a situation where we feel deprived when we compare ourselves to others around us. For example if we live on a large, run down housing estate outside town; if we don't have a job, but nor do many people on the estate, and we rarely go to town we may not feel ourselves to be relatively deprived. But if we live on a small estate alongside newly done up houses occupied by fairly well off people who have well paid jobs while we only have one casual and low paid work in a burger bar, we may well feel relatively deprived. Sociologists like Jock Young feel that it is not deprivation but relative deprivation that leads some individuals to commit crime. It is the feeling of discontent that arises from not having a job or having very little money, while at the same time seeing the symbols of wealth and success all around you. The mass media is important here – it constantly shows us what we could have or how we could live. It is, as Young puts it, like being barred from the racetrack which will allow you to win the prizes (see below). If you feel unfairly treated you may find your own way of getting what you want.

Relative deprivation need not always lead to criminal behaviour. People develop a variety of subcultures to cope with their situation in society. Sometimes these subcultures might be based upon religious values, for example the Pentecostal Church could be seen as providing a set of norms and values for many Afro-Caribbean individuals facing racism in their everyday lives. The church provided a focus for people who found themselves excluded from mainstream society because of racism. Rastafarianism too could be seen as doing something similar, but with a set of values which were more clearly opposed to mainstream society. Subcultures could, however, lead to crime.

Some young men, especially those living on the large, bleak, and desolate estates in large towns and cities, may well form subcultures based on 'macho' values. These subcultures may well lead to violent crime. Changes in the economy lead to many people being unemployed (see Chapters 6 and 7), but especially the unskilled and unqualified. Jock Young shows us the link between relative deprivation and the development of subcultures like this.

> The shrinking of manufacturing industry produces relative deprivation particularly among unskilled workers clustered round the empty factories on the desolate estates. Although the young women in these areas can find a role for themselves in child rearing and, very often, work

in the service sector, young men have no social position and no future. They are locked into unemployment and not even available to offer the stability of 'marriageable partners'. They are barred from the racetrack of the meritocratic society and yet remain glued to the television sets and media which alluringly portray the glittering prizes of a wealthy society. Young men facing such a denial of recognition turn, everywhere in the world, in what must be almost a universal criminological law, to the creation of cultures of machismo. They mobilise one of their only resources, physical strength. They form gangs. They defend their own 'turf'. Being denied the respect of others they create a subculture that revolves around masculine powers and 'respect'.

Adapted from Jock Young (99)

EXERCISE

Read the extract again and answer the following questions.

According to the extract above:

i) Why are unemployed young men not 'available to offer the stability of marriageable partners' ?

ii) What has caused the young men in the extract to be 'barred from the racetrack of meritocratic society'?

iii) What examples of subcultures can you think of that fit Young's description.

iv) How do such subcultures lead to violent crime?

v) What other criminal subcultures might develop in the areas Young describes? (see below and Chapter 7)

Drugs and crime

Using illegal drugs is of course criminal, and widespread use of drugs has devastating effects on communities (see Chapter 7). However the link between drugs and crime is not always straight-forward as this extract from *The Guardian* shows.

> The Cleveland police said there was a strong link between crime and drugs but added that there was a product of prices remaining high because drugs are illegal. A serious heroin user needed to find £50 in cash each day and so turned to crime, mainly shoplifting, selling drugs and burglary. The report noted that nationally about a third of all crime was geared to the purchase of heroin, cocaine or crack.
>
> The officers insisted that most drug users did not commit significant amounts of crime and their only offence was to choose a drug which was illegal.

EXERCISE

i) how might drug use be a response to relative deprivation?

ii) What are the consequences for communities of a high concentration of drug use?

The consequences of crime

The kind of explanation of crime put forward by Jock Young shows us how groups who are relatively deprived, or who are socially excluded, may turn to crime. This kind of explanation is important because it also shows us one of the consequences of crime. One of the effects of criminal subcultures is that they also affect other people's lives. For example, people, in areas where violent crime is common, can feel afraid to go out at night. They feel themselves socially excluded, they are unable to live normal lives because of what they see as the risk of crime.

The British Crime Survey examined the impact that concern about crime had on people's lives. Here are some of their findings.

> Overall 24% said that they never walked alone in their local area after dark and a further 16% said they went out less than once a month. Women were more likely to say they never walked alone in their local area after dark (36% of all women), particularly those aged 60 or over (59% of this group).
>
> There are many reasons why people may not walk alone in their area after dark. The most common reasons given were that people had no reason to – that is they were broke or content staying at home or did not want to go out. Fear of crime (mugging, physical attack, burglary or vandalism) was given by 19% of those who never went out or went out less than once a month (this group made up 8% of the whole sample).
>
> Adapted from BCS 2000.

According to the British Crime Survey the groups who were most likely to say that crime greatly affected their quality of life were:

➜ Women aged 60 or older
➜ Asians
➜ Those in poor health or with a limiting illness or disability
➜ People in low income households
➜ People living in council or housing association accommodation
➜ People living in run down areas.
    Source BCS 2000.

EXERCISE

For each of the groups listed above identity one reason why they would be particularly likely to say that fear of crime affected their quality of life.

In this section we have seen how social exclusion and relative deprivation might be linked to crime in two ways:

● First feelings of relative deprivation might lead individuals to engage in criminal activity.
● Secondly those very criminal activities can affect the lives of others in their neighborhoods or communities, leading them to experience forms of social exclusion.

Crime and ethnicity

We are all familiar with the image of the uncontrollable pre-teens stealing car after car on deprived estates; we are all familiar with the portrayal of 'muggers' as being, on the whole, young black men; we are all familiar with the derogatory terminology of 'rat boys', the barely concealed message of 'bogus asylum seekers'. These messages help us look for solutions.

Lord Davnit Dholakia OBE Chair, National Association for the Care and Resettlement of Offenders, July 1999.

The term institutional racism should be understood to refer to the way the institution or the organisation may systematically or repeatedly treat, or tend to treat, people differently because of their race. So, in effect, we are not talking about the individuals within the service who may be unconscious as to the nature of what they are doing, but it is the net effect of what they do.

From evidence given by Inspector Paul Wilson of the Metropolitan Police Association Black Police Association to the Stephen Lawrence Enquiry.

- British Afro-Caribbean people are seven times more likely to be in jail than whites, despite being no more likely to commit crimes.

- Ethnic minorities are more likely to be the victims of crime. Data from the British Crime Survey shows that Pakistanis and Bangladeshis are worst affected.

- Afro-Caribbean people are six times more likely to be stopped and searched by the police and arrested.

- After arrest the same amount of ethnic minority people are charged as whites – 59%.

- Afro-Caribbeans are far more likely than any other group to be imprisoned. In June 1998 the rate of imprisonment per 100,000 of the general population was 1,245 for black people, 185 for whites and 168 for Asians.

- Francis Cook, Director of the Howard League said: 'The number of black people in our prisons is out of all proportion to the size of the black community, yet there is no evidence to suggest that black people commit more crime.

  'The reasons for this are complex. It is partly a matter of social deprivation. But it is also clear that discrimination operates at every stage in the criminal justice system, from the chances of being arrested to the decision of the court and the length of the sentence.'

  Adapted from an article in *The Guardian*.

The above extracts tell us a number of things about ethnicity and crime.

- Stereotyping is an important factor in looking for criminals
- Racism exists throughout the criminal justice system.
- Minority ethnic groups appear to commit no more crime than any other group.
- Minority ethnic groups are more likely to be the victims of crime.

In the last section of this chapter we looked at explanations of crime and also possible responses to relative deprivation. In this section we will look at two aspects of the relationship between ethnicity and crime which are both linked by racism.

→ Differential treatment by the criminal justice system
→ The consequences of crime for ethnic minority groups in particular

Discrimination, racism and institutional racism

Since the Stephen Lawrence Inquiry, and with the publicity attached to other cases such as those of Ricky Reel and Michael Menson, much attention has been given to the way in which individuals and organisations can treat individuals and groups in unjust ways. Before looking at racism we need to define some terms.

- **Prejudice**

  When we 'pre-judge' an individual or a group on the basis of one particular characteristic like the colour of their skin or their nationality.

- **Discrimination**

  This exists if we treat someone less favourably because of their ethnic background, their gender or their religion than we would treat other people.

- **Racism**

  This exists when we believe that members of a particular 'race' are superior or inferior just because they belong to a particular 'race'. Racism can sometimes be unintentional when individuals act in such a way as to suggest that they hold negative beliefs or stereotypical views about particular individuals or groups.

Why is the term 'race' in inverted commas? This is because the term itself was used in relation to people at a time when it was thought that individuals and populations could be categorised usually on the basis of skin colour and facial characteristics. These differences were thought to be based on biological differences and were also thought to be linked to factors like intelligence. There is no scientific basis to this idea. The concept of 'race' is not a valid one in this sense, but it is an idea that people refer to in everyday life and so sociologists are interested in how the idea is used, for example, by racist groups. To show that it is an idea without foundation scientifically it is often placed in inverted commas.

The Stephen Lawrence Inquiry found that there was evidence of institutional racism in the following:

i) The investigation of the case included the failure of many officers to recognise Stephen Lawrence's murder as a purely 'racially motivated' crime.

ii) The disparity in stop and search figures (see above): Although factors such as unemployment and school exclusions were relevant there was 'a clear core conclusion of racist stereotyping'.

iii) The inadequate response of the police service to reports of 'racial incidents' which led victims to lack confidence in the police and their willingness to take such reports seriously.

iv) Police training – there was evidence of a lack of significant training in racism awareness and race relations.

(Adapted from Macpherson report)

The Macpherson report did stress that not all police officers were racist, and since the report was published many practices have been altered including that regarding the reporting of 'racial incidents.'

What is institutional racism?

The Stephen Lawrence Inquiry report defined it as:

> The collective failure of an organisation to provide an appropriate and professional service to people because of their colour, culture or ethnic origin. It can be seen or detected in processes, attitudes and behaviour which amount to discrimination through unwitting prejudice, ignorance, thoughtlessness and racist stereotyping which disadvantage minority ethnic people.
>
> (Report p 28)

How does institutional racism persist?

In the last section of this chapter we looked at the way in which subcultures can develop in response to relative deprevation so that people have a way of dealing with their problems. Subcultures arise in all walks of life. Police officers are faced with all kinds of problems as a routine part of their job. Many sociologists have seen the 'canteen culture' of the police as being a way of coping with the problems that face them as they do their job. The following extract shows how negative stereotypes of black people can arise while officers do their job.

> Much has been said about our culture, the canteen culture, the occupational culture. How and why does that impact on individuals, black individuals on the street? We would say the occupational structure within the police service, given the fact that the majority of police officers are white, tends to be the white experience, the white beliefs, the white values.
>
> Given the fact that these predominantly white officers only meet members of the black community in confrontational situations, they tend to stereotype black people in general. This can lead to all sorts of negative views and assumptions about black people, so we should not underestimate the occupational culture within the police service as being a primary source of institutional racism in the way that we differentially treat black people.
>
> (Macpherson report p 25 evidence of Insp. Paul Wilson.)

EXERCISE

Read the extract again and answer the following questions:

i) Why would officers only meet black people in confrontational situations?
ii) Why is 'the canteen' so important in developing stereotypes?
iii) There have been some well-publicised reports of sex discrimination in the police force. How might 'canteen culture' produce a kind of institutional sexism?

The consequences of crime for minority ethnic groups

The Stephen Lawrence case was just one example of a racist murder. Members of ethnic minority groups are subject to verbal abuse, criminal damage and arson, as well as physical violence. Asian respondents to the British Crime Survey were the most concerned about physical attacks. Fear of attack as well as actual physical violence can affect the lives of individuals as is illustrated by figure 40.

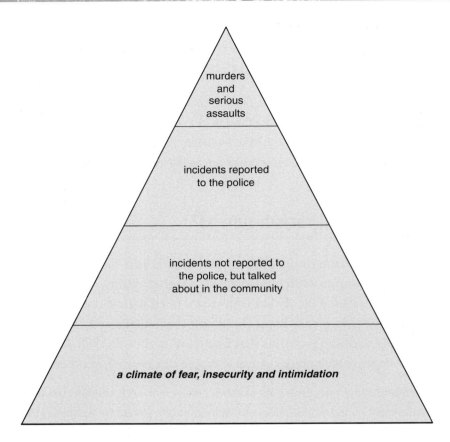

Figure 40 A cime pyramid.

Questions

i)   What ordinary daily activities would be affected by living in a climate of fear?

ii) How might a family protect itself against fear?

Gender and crime

Both official statistics and self report studies show us that males commit more crime than females.

Why do females commit fewer offences than males?

- Socialisation

  Girls and boys are socialised differently by their parents. Girls are not usually expected to act in a tough or aggressive fashion while this is thought appropriate for boys. Being tough and acting aggressively are forms of behaviour associated with crime. Look at the table on page 147 and compare the percentages of males and females admitting to fighting and other violence.

	12–13	14–15	16–17	18–21	22–25	26–30	All 12–30
MALES				Percent			
Fighting	26	13	36	18	11	3	15
Other violence	16	8	9	3	1	3	5
Buying stolen goods	1	10	16	20	25	20	18
Selling stolen goods	3	4	5	16	4	11	9
Shoplifting	4	15	5	5	5	1	6
Other theft	7	17	17	8	7	3	9
Theft from the workplace	n/a	n/a	1	9	22	15	10
Fraud	n/a	n/a	2	15	21	44	17
Criminal damage	42	34	9	5	3	1	11
All offences	100	100	100	100	100	100	100
FEMALES							
Fighting	3	17	9	19	4	0	9
Other violence	0	0	2	0	0	1	1
Buying stolen goods	12	10	48	23	30	25	26
Selling stolen goods	0	1	14	7	4	5	6
Shoplifting	27	41	5	9	5	22	18
Other theft	23	10	7	0	10	1	8
Theft from the workplace	n/a	n/a	4	20	14	6	7
Fraud	n/a	n/a	7	22	25	40	14
Criminal damage	34	21	2	0	8	0	10
All offences	100	100	100	100	100	100	100

Note:

1. Questions on fraud were not asked of respondents aged under 16. Workplace theft figures are not reported for under 16 year-olds due to small numbers.

2. Not all columns add to exactly 100% because of rounding.

Figure 41 Profile of crime admitted by offenders of different ages.

EXERCISE

Look at the table again and answer the following question:

i)   What offences are females over 16 particularly likely to admit to?

ii) What offence do increasing numbers of females admit to with age?

iii) Why do you think this is ? (compare your ideas with what follows).

● **Social control**

For some sociologists this is perhaps the most important reason that females offend less than males. These sociologists say that females are subject to a greater degree of social control in their lives. For example while growing up at home girls are probably subject to stricter rules than boys. Parents are more likely to have strict rules about what their daughters can or cannot do than about what their sons can get up to (check this out among your friends).

A similar sort of control exists when a woman sets up home and has children. Women are generally still expected to take on the role of housewife and mother. A woman who is seen to be failing in this role might well be subject to various informal social controls – gossip in the neighbourhood, signs of disapproval ('call yourself a mother. . .') from her family or her partner's family, and maybe threats from her partner, or even physical violence because of her 'failure' to be a 'proper' wife or mother. Being expected to be at home means that women have fewer opportunities to commit crimes.

The kinds of crime that women are likely to commit – shoplifting, benefit fraud – are linked to the fact that women are more likely than men to experience poverty. This is dealt with in more detail in Chapter 6, but the feminisation of poverty can help to explain why women are likely to commit crimes for financial reward. If the money coming in is not enough to feed the children or pay the bills some women will resort to shoplifting or 'working on the side', or cashing Giros and then reporting them lost to make ends meet.

The 'chivalry factor'

Some sociologists have said that magistrates and judges treat women more leniently than men when they appear before them in court. This is said to be because they see women in a stereotypical way, as housewives and mothers and so issue lighter sentences 'for the sake of the children'. Men are not thought to have the main responsibility for house and children and so are dealt with more harshly. However it also seems that women who commit serious offences receive harsher sentences than men because they are thought to be 'doubly deviant' – first because they have committed a serious offence like assault or murder, and second because this does not fit with the stereotypical view of appropriate feminine behaviour.

The police are also said to be more lenient in their dealings with women who commit offences because of the same kind of stereotyping. It is thought that police officers are more likely to caution female offenders than males because they are less likely to see females as criminal, or because they feel that female offenders have been 'led astray' by males.

Public space, private space

In general we can say that women are subject to two sets of controls.

In the private world of the home and family girls and women find their opportunities limited by the controls placed upon them. The rules they have to live by are often made by men – fathers, husbands or partners. These rules are themselves often based on a stereotypical view of each gender – the male as rapacious predator, the female as passive victim.

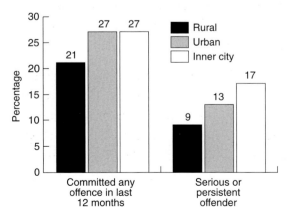

Figure 42 Area differences in offending (males only).

England & Wales			Percentages
	Inner city	Urban	Rural
Vehicle crime (owners)			
All thefts	23.7	16.2	12.0
Vandalism	9.2	7.2	4.9
Bicycle thefts (owners)	8.9	5.2	2.4
Burglary	8.5	5.9	3.4
Home vandalism	4.3	3.7	2.6
Other household	8.4	6.8	5.4
Any household offence	32.2	28.6	22.8

1 Percentage victimised once or more.
2 Area type classification based on CACI ACORN codes, copyright CACI Ltd 1994.
Source: British Crime Survey, Home Office

Figure 43 Proportion of households which were victims of crime[1]: by type of crime and type of area[2], 1997.

In public spaces – pubs, clubs, shopping centres, and so on – girls and women are also in a social situation dominated by male rules. A woman may still find going into a pub alone at night an uncomfortable experience. Walking home alone at night is often a threatening experience for a lone female, especially when the only other people around are gangs of, usually male, youths. A woman or girl who is out is subject to stereotyping in two ways. First of all if she's been up to fairly small misdemeanours she must have been led astray because the stereotype tells some men that women are weak and easily led. Secondly if she's done something serious she's not a 'proper' woman (according to the stereotype) and therefore must be severeley punished.

Why is crime lower in rural areas?

Look at the charts and tables above. They both show what the official figures also show – that crime rates are higher in inner city areas than in other urban areas and rural areas. What the tables do not show is that poor council estates also have high rates of crime. Why should this be so?

The most obvious point is that there are more **opportunities** for crime in the inner city and on poor council estates. The concentration of shops and people in the inner city offer many opportunities for crime – shoplifting, fighting with other youths, large and anonymous car parks, and individuals with purses, handbags and wallets full of money and credit cards. Run down council estates with empty buildings and sometimes isolated properties also offer many opportunities for vandalism and theft.

Secondly the inner city in particular offers more opportunities for escape. Very few people are likely to know offenders personally, and the crowds and the network of streets offer good escape routes. In rural areas, however, as in many suburban areas, strangers are more likely to be noticed, and the chances of escaping are limited.

In rural areas where people are more likely to know one another social control may well be much more informal. If everyone knows you it is harder to step out of line because there is a good chance it will get back to your parents. The village police officer – where he or she still exists – is able to get in touch with the parents of petty offenders easily and is more likely to issue an informal warning to such offenders. People who live in such areas often comment that 'everyone knows your business'. Tonnies, a sociologist who looked at the difference between urban and rural communities called this 'the tyranny of observation'.

In the city it is said that formal social control is more likely to operate. Because the city offers anonymity – probably no one knows who you are – the police are much more likely to arrest and charge young people committing offences because they won't know them or their parents. Similarly it is easier to rob a shopkeeper if you don't know them or their family. Such a shopkeeper is more likely to press charges if she doesn't know the offender or their family. The police presence is more likely to be high in the city – the chances of being caught are greater because there are simply more police officers about.

However this kind of distinction between informal social control in rural areas and formal control in the city doesn't apply totally. In rural areas people are still subject to formal controls – speeding, drinking and driving, for example – and formal social control is still likely to be used in serious offences. Young people in rural areas are still subject to formal social controls at school, and TV licence dodgers and benefit fraudsters are just as likely to be prosecuted.

Informal social controls are important in cities too. Peer groups will exert pressures on their members to conform; the informal controls operated by the mass media will still apply as will the informal controls in the family.

People in both rural areas and cities are subject to both types of control. It is therefore difficult to generalise. The informal controls that might keep a young person from a rural village in line will have no effect on the burglars who drive into that village from the nearest town. These informal controls won't work either on the village lad who goes into town to steal a car for joyriding.

Glossary

Self concept	this is our idea of what kind of person we are. For sociologists, our self concept, or our image of ourselves, is formed in interaction with other people, but particularly in interaction with people who are important to us like family or friends. This is a significant idea because it helps us to understand how labelling theory works.
Labelling theory	this is a theory which says, in a very simplified form, that we may come to see ourselves as others see us. Some people in society, like newspaper editors or teachers, for example, have the power to apply labels to others. People who are labelled as deviants, trouble makers or good students may come to see themselves in terms of their label. They may change their self concept. It is important to remember that labelling theory does not say that those who are labelled will change. It is now an automatic process. Individuals can, however, reject their labels. The pupil labelled a "no-hoper" can change in such a way as to change their identity.
Peer group	a peer group is a group of people who have something in common, usually their age or their gender. If you are reading this in a classroom at school, your classmates are your peers.
Subculture	a subculture is a smaller culture within a larger culture. Some of the shared norms and values of a subculture are different to those of the larger culture. For example, in Britain there have been a variety of youth subcultures with their own distinctive norms of dress and behaviour. Activities such as drug-taking, which are viewed as deviant in the majority culture may well be considered normal within a subculture.
The crime rate	is the number of crimes per head of population. It is usually shown as the number of *recorded* crimes per head of population. Expressing the crime

rate in this way, rather than the actual number of crimes recorded, allows us to see whether crime is becoming more or less prevalent without having to take into account population increases or decreases.

The dark figure   refers to the number of crimes that are not reported to the police. Official statistics can only tell us about reported or recorded crime. Sociologists use self report or victim surveys as alternative means of measuring crime.

Self report surveys   are surveys in which respondents are asked what offences they have committed.

Victim surveys   are surveys in which respondents are asked whether or not they have been the victim of particular offences.

Folk devils   are groups portrayed as a problem or a threat to society in an exaggerated or distorted fashion. Folk devils are often seen as symptomatic of all that is wrong with society. The mass media have a particularly important role in the creation of both folk devils and moral panics.

Moral panics   are said to occur when people say that "something must be done" about a particular social problem. The reaction to an apparent problem may well exaggerate the extent and effects of the problem involved. Moral panics often result in calls for tougher policing and harsher sentence –i.e. for "something to be done".

Coursework and Examinations

Introduction

Sociology – if not a science in the way that chemistry and physics are sciences – is a subject which attaches great importance to research. Sociological statements about what happens in society, and why, need to be supported by evidence collected by appropriate methods if they are to be taken seriously. Sociological theories are judged ultimately on the basis of the extent to which they 'fit the facts'. Because of this, sociology syllabuses give students an opportunity to undertake some research. This enables the student to become familiar with research methods in practice and also to see how the findings gained by using such methods help sociologists to draw conclusions about our society.

Many students – if the work they produce is anything to go by – seize the opportunity gladly and become genuinely excited as they investigate an aspect of social life which interests them. Others appear never to get really involved and merely go through the motions. Often the work of the latter group seems to be saying to whoever reads it, 'What can I do? I'm only a GCSE student. I've virtually no sociological experience, hardly any resources, and little time. I'll copy the stuff from the books. It will be better than anything I could do'. Such a view is mistaken.

All tutors and examiners have read coursework which was as interesting and informative as anything a professional sociologist might achieve. Being an amateur or a beginner is no disadvantage provided you recognise the limitations it imposes on you. In fact, being an amateur or a beginner you may be more likely to ask some questions which professionals have forgotten are important. As an amateur, sociology is not your job. You may be at school, a nurse, a retired policeman, for example. Your situation gives you access to experiences and research possibilities denied to professionals. A 16- or 17-year-old has much better access to some of the attitudes and behaviour patterns of fellow 16- or 17-year-olds than any 35-year-old researcher. Use this access and with persistence and a basic understanding of sociology you may produce a piece of work that you and those who read it will remember. One example, from many which the authors could have mentioned, was an investigation into racism in soccer. The student who conducted the research was still at school, was an English Asian and a good soccer player who had represented his town. At the heart of the research was a participant observation study on the basis of which the student offered the reader significant sociological insights into racism on the field of play, in the dressing room, on the coach. I doubt whether anyone else was in a position to do such a study and thereby give us these insights.

Aims

The importance of selecting an appropriate aim for your coursework research cannot be overemphasised. Most students who underachieve on their coursework do so because they do not give sufficient thought to their aim. Not consulting their tutor on this matter makes it worse. The aim – or aims – you select should influence every aspect of your research. Your choice of method – or methods – will be influenced by your aim(s). Whichever sources of information are likely to be useful will depend on your aim(s). The way you sort out and analyse the information you gather will depend on your aim(s). A relevant conclusion will relate to your aim(s).

Some students seem to select aims without considering what kinds of research and analysis they will have to do in order to achieve them. It is almost as if these students see their aims as separate from the rest of their coursework and believe that tutors and examiners will be impressed if they see lots of aims, some of which are complicated. The opposite is generally true. Seeing a long list of aims a tutor immediately wonders how the student is going to find enough time to do all the necessary research. Remember that for those who will mark your work your aim is a measure by which the whole project will be judged. 'Has the student dealt with all the aims satisfactorily?' becomes a key question. The longer the list of aims the more difficult it is for the student to ensure that the answer will be 'Yes'. **Do not set yourself an unrealistic – overambitious – aim or set of aims.**

Be aware of your limitations

The amount of time you can expect to spend on your research is limited. You may be studying other subjects which put demands on you. Select aims which you will be able to achieve. Try to avoid becoming one of those students who find themselves having to write in a conclusion – 'I think I could have improved it if I had had more time'. Recognise that you may be uneasy using particular methods of gathering information. Asking people, particularly strangers, to fill in a questionnaire or give an interview can be a worry to most of us. Try to avoid becoming one of those students who begins with the intention of questioning a wide range of members of the public and ends up having questioned only friends and relatives. Be modest.

> I might face the problem that I am not very experienced in research methods. Although I know them in theory, I have not put them into practice yet.

Be aware that some information or types of information may be difficult or impossible to obtain

Material you need may not be available in libraries – or you may have to wait for it. Organisations to which you write may not reply. Permission to observe or interview people may be refused.

A student researching students who were also parents:

> I tried the college library for newspaper clippings but couldn't find anything related
> to my topic. I had a go on the library computer but still found nothing.

A student researching unemployment:

> I drew up a questionnaire to use at the local job centre. This did not work out as planned. The first person I approached told me that he didn't come to the job centre to be harassed by students. He then complained to the centre manager who escorted me from the building.

A student researching teenage crime:

> I intended to include an interview with a police officer to get their views. I wrote a letter and called the station. They didn't get back to me. So I couldn't get the interview with an officer which would have been good for my research.

Be aware that the longer your list of aims the greater the chance that you will neglect – or even forget – one of them when collecting, analysing or drawing conclusions from your information.

Be aware how easy it is to set yourself aims which push you in different directions

Consider the following aim:

'To find out if men are helping out with the household duties and, if they are helping, are they taking sole responsibility for jobs or are they sharing responsibility with their partner? To try to find out if the main responsibility for the upbringing of the child is more of a shared job or is it still mainly a job for the mother?'

It is appropriately modest and well focussed. The student has given him or herself a clear idea of what he or she needs to do. Anyone reading this aim has a good idea of what to expect – that is, a piece of research into which household and childcare duties men and women actually carry out when partners. The second paragraph suggests, through phrases like, 'more of' and 'still mainly', that the student is also going to make some comparison of what happens now with what happened in the past.

The student, however, decided to express this aim in the following **hypothesis**:

'I think that when it comes to gender roles concerning housework and the main upbringing of the child women no longer see household chores as their responsibility and that the main upbringing of children is now seen as more of a shared job.'

Here a rather different piece of research is proposed. The focus is now on what men and women 'see' or expect. The student is, without being aware of it, suggesting two different pieces of coursework. The aims coursework would look into changes in how household and childcare duties are actually divided up. The hypothesis coursework would look into changes in attitude. Whilst the two are related, they are not the same. The **conclusion** suggests that the research undertaken was focussed on the aims.

CONCLUSION

'My findings suggest that women still take greater responsibility for both childrearing and household duties. However, men share some responsibility for most household jobs and the upbringing of the children.'

Perhaps the lesson to be learned from this example is that you should make sure that your hypothesis fits in fully with your aim(s). If in doubt, do not bother with an hypothesis. An aim – or aims – can be stated quite satisfactorily in the form of clear questions.

Be aware of any ethical implications in your aims

'Candidates at GCSE, when undertaking research, enter into personal and moral relationships with those they study, as individuals and groups. The pursuit of knowledge, or need to complete a project, as an aim must not provide an entitlement to override the rights of others. Candidates must remember their responsibilities as researchers when undertaking research. This should be kept in mind at all times.'

From S.E.G. GCSE syllabus support material 1998

As members of society most of us try to live according to certain principles and rules. It is considered wrong, for example, to hurt other people or to risk hurting them. Occasionally, however, students seem to forget this and other principles and rules of decent behaviour when doing their sociology coursework. It is as if they think that when doing research such principles and rules do not apply. Would a relative or friend go up to an overweight 13-year-old girl and ask, 'Excuse me, but do you feel ugly because you are fat?' Or ask an 11-year-old boy whose parents divorced a year ago, 'Would you tell me how you feel about not seeing your father any more?' Of course not – it would be cruel. Yet ordinary, decent students include such questions in their questionnaires. They appear to believe that they are acceptable because the answers may help them to draw conclusions about the causes of anorexia and the effects of divorce on children.

It is not difficult to anticipate ethical or other problems if, when thinking about your aim(s), you ask yourself some simple questions:

If I choose this aim:

- What information will I need?
- From whom or what will I get this information?
- How will I get this information and what will the getting of it involve?
- Will getting this information hurt or offend anybody?
- Would I mind giving the information if somebody asked me?

Consider the following typical example:

Aim: To find out why teenagers take drugs.

- **Information needed:** The attitudes of drug-taking teenagers; their relationships with other drug-taking teenagers and non-drug-taking teenagers; their family relationships and their relationships with the 'authorities' about the ways they spend their time.
- **From whom or what?** From other sociological studies, publications by government agencies or voluntary bodies. It may be possible to get information from, for example, the police, social workers, teachers, members of the teenagers' family. The drug-taking teenagers and their friends are clearly going to be an important source of information.

So far as the police, social workers and teachers are concerned the students' ethical problems are limited. Members of these groups are bound by professional and ethical codes of conduct.

This may make them a poor source of information since it would not be proper for them to tell you much of what they know. The prospect of your research requiring contact with drug-taking teenagers and their families should, however, set ethical alarm bells ringing.

- **How will the information be obtained?** Methods involving contact with the drug-taking teenagers themselves present problems. Interviewing them or getting them to complete a questionnaire may make them feel good or important. Their drug taking has made them interesting to you. This interest may, in a small way, confirm them in their anti-social activities. Getting to know teenage drug takers by 'hanging around with them' – that is, using some sort of observation or participant observation method – presents a more obvious problem. By reporting their activities to the authorities the researcher may provoke hostility and make it impossible to continue the research. By not reporting the activities the researcher may seem to be accepting them. What is more, there is always the risk of being drawn into the activities.

This is only one of many examples which might have been given. Investigating any section of society engaged in illegal or anti-social activities can present ethical problems. Football hooliganism, underage sex, underage drinking are topics frequently investigated by students. Very seldom is there any suggestion in the resulting coursework that thought has been given to the ethics of the research. The same indifference is often evident in research which involves getting information from vulnerable or potentially vulnerable people. Recognise that questions may remind people of their problems. Divorce, poverty, being discriminated against, medical conditions, for example, bring hurt to those affected. Put yourself in the place of the person being questioned. How would you feel answering your questions?

Tutors and examiners are reluctant to forbid students to study certain topics. A topic which, researched in one way may produce all sorts of ethical problems, may be problem-free when researched in another way. Recognise that some sorts of contact with some kinds of people is probably best left to professionals. Formulate your aims with this in mind.

Make sure that your aim is sociological

There should be two starting points for designing any piece of sociology coursework. Firstly, there are your own interests and the opportunities for sociological research arising from your situation and the things you do. Secondly, there is the syllabus. A satisfactory aim has two basic characteristics: that it can be achieved and that what is achieved is thoroughly sociological and on the syllabus. To make the latter more likely it is worth identifying which section(s) of the syllabus the aim(s) fall within. Ask yourself what are the social structures and processes with which the topic you have chosen is linked. It might be worthwhile, as you put your coursework together, to look through it occasionally, checking that the contents of each page are sociological. Remove anything which is not. Doing this will help you to maintain the sociological focus of the work. It will also spare tutors and examiners the necessity of reading, for example, detailed descriptions of the biochemistry of nicotine and looking at pictures of diseased lungs in projects on smoking, or of reading detailed medical descriptions, with illustrations, of the way in which condoms and inter-uterine devices help to prevent pregnancy in projects on contraception.

An illusion which seems widespread amongst students is that an essentially non-sociological piece of work can be transformed magically into sociology by the mere inclusion of a questionnaire investigating people's attitudes. A traditional example would be a project on alcohol. The main part would consist of information about how much alcohol it is safe to consume; about the alcohol content of different drinks – sometimes with pictures of the bottles; about the short and long term effects of alcohol on the body; about how to spot if a friend or relative is an alcoholic. The student would then try to magic this into sociology by getting half a dozen friends to fill in a questionnaire which asked whether public houses should be open all night, whether 13-year-olds should be able to buy alcohol and so on.

It is possible, of course, to undertake genuinely sociological research into alcohol use. Gender or class differences in drinking habits would lead the student to examine drinking in the context of important sociological processes such as socialisation, peer group pressure or of inequalities of income or time within the social structure.

Problems also arise when students confuse moral issues and sociological issues. Two common examples of this involve capital punishment and abortion. Many students over the years have stated as their aims – 'to find out whether capital punishment should be reintroduced' or 'to find out whether abortion should be allowed'. Questions like this cannot be answered by sociological research. They are questions for moral philosophers, theologians or, so far as practical policy making is concerned, politicians. Research can, of course, find out whether, for example, there are more murders in countries which do not inflict the death penalty on murderers. 'Should capital punishment be reintroduced?' cannot, however, be answered on the basis of that kind of information alone. Keep your coursework within sociological territory. Avoid the word 'should' in your aims.

Questions which cannot be answered by sociological research	Questions which can be answered by sociological research
Should men help more in the house?	Are men helping more in the house today than in the 1970's?
Should criminals be punished more harshly?	In what ways are those who commit or might commit criminal acts influenced by punishment?
Should the monarchy be abolished?	Is the monarchy less popular amongst younger than older generations?

Figure 44 Keeping your coursework in sociological territory.

Do not misunderstand your aims

It is perhaps surprising, but a significant number of students do not seem to understand the aims they set themselves. The rather serious consequence of this is that the research undertaken does not then match the stated aims. Sometimes linked with 'should' aims this misunderstanding occurs most commonly when the student thinks that he or she is setting out to investigate either the causes or the effects of a particular social phenomenon.

Consider the aims below. You could perhaps assess them by raising some of the issues highlighted in this section:

i) To investigate what makes people bully others.

ii) To find out whether bullying has an effect on a child's education.

iii) To find out whether bullying will ever be stopped.

➡ Are the aims overambitious?

➡ Might any of the information needed be difficult or impossible to obtain?

➡ Do the aims fit together nicely?

➡ Are there worrying ethical implications?

➡ Are the aims sociological?

Your attention should have been drawn immediately to the third aim. A student, or anybody, can make an informed guess about what might happen in the future. Sociologically based predictions are acceptable and are important to those planning services for the public. There is, however, a great difference between predicting and 'finding out'. The latter probably requires the use of a time machine which, because of underfunding, schools and colleges would not be able to afford – even if it had been invented. If the student really meant 'to predict' rather than 'to find out', the aim is no longer impossible to achieve but it would be difficult. Such a wide range of factors is involved that the making of a convincing prediction would be a very complicated process – far beyond what it would be reasonable to expect in a piece of coursework.

Whilst the unrealistic nature of the third aim attracts attention immediately, a second reading reveals the general lack of clarity in the others. What kind of bullying – physical, verbal, or sexual harassment? Bullying in what context – at work, school, in the home or in a racial context? The second aim, by referring to 'effect on a child's education' might suggest that the student is thinking about bullying at school – but at what age? Bullying which could 'affect a child's education' could be taking place in the home or the neighbourhood. The first aim gives no clue as to which of the many contexts in which bullying can occur the student has in mind. The second aim gives no clue as to what kind of 'effects' the student has in mind: on examination results? On the pattern of social behaviour at school? On attitudes to fellow pupils or teachers? Lacking clear aims, the research is likely to lack a clear direction. The student has not provided him or herself with a clear measure of what should be included and what left out.

Consider now the method the student used to achieve these aims:

'I will achieve my aims by using a questionnaire which will ask members of the public questions on what they think makes people bully others (this question will answer aim number 1). Do they think that bullying has an effect on a child's education (this question will answer aim number 2), and do they think that bullying will ever be stopped (this will answer aim number 3).'

As it turns out, the lack of clarity in the aims, which might have presented a problem, did not matter. There was a more serious problem. The student misunderstood the aims. He or she confused finding out what makes people bully others with finding out what people think makes people bully others.

Sometimes it seems that this particular confusion is more likely when a student sets him or herself an ambitious aim which would be very challenging if researched appropriately. Consider again the aim 'to investigate what makes people bully others'. This could be approached wholly through secondary sources. If, however, a student felt that he or she should undertake some primary research what would it involve? Clearly the most useful source of information would be those whose relationship is under investigation – the bully and the victim. What they can give a researcher is not the speculation of an outsider. A bully can say, 'I bullied this or that person because . . .'. A victim can describe the circumstances in which he or she came to be bullied. Obtaining and using this information may, however, present difficulties. How does a student find sufficient bullies and victims who are willing to give interviews or complete questionnaires? Can the student handle the contact with these people and the information they reveal in an ethical way? The student may be in a position to observe bullying. Again, ethical issues may be raised. By treating 'what makes people bully others?' as 'what do members of the public think makes people bully others?' potential difficulties are side-stepped. Finding information is reduced to the relatively simple task of handing out a few questionnaires, in most cases to people known to the student. Unfortunately, the coursework which results is of limited value.

It is vitally important that a student understands what kind of research particular aims will require of him or her. Finding 'causes' can be difficult and complicated. For the last 50 years, for example, researchers have studied whether violence on television can lead those who view it to acts of violence. The conclusions which have been reached are rather modest, limited and uncertain. This has not prevented many students over the years from reaching very definite conclusions. On what evidence have these conclusions been based? The results of questionnaires which asked the public, 'Do you think that violence on TV leads people to be violent?'

Recognise that answering sociological questions usually involves much more than simply asking a few people what they think the answer is. They might not know.

Method

The impression given by many pieces of coursework is that the high spot of the whole process for the student was the printing, distributing, collecting in of the questionnaires, and the conducting of observation or interviews. Students seem willing to devote considerable time to collecting their data. Tutors and examiners have often felt that were such enthusiasm matched by an equivalent level of thoughtfulness most projects would be very good indeed. Unfortunately, students often seem to choose a method without any serious consideration of its appropriateness for their particular aims. It is as if some would use a questionnaire and interviews whatever their aims.

Recognise that it is you undertaking the research

'A postal questionnaire has the advantage of being a cheap way of getting the opinions of many people. Conducting interviews on the other hand is expensive.'

Students continue to offer this reason for preferring the postal questionnaire – clearly not, however, having weighed up the costs but because they have read it in a book. It is as if the student is playing at being a professional interviewer with a decent salary and expenses. Far better to stay in the real world – that of the GCSE student – when discussing the choice of method. In this world stamps and stationery are expensive and you do not have to pay yourself to conduct interviews.

When choosing a method start with your aim

Consider the following explanation of why a particular method was chosen by a student:

> I must select a research method to use to gather information to test my hypothesis. Sociologists use questionnaires, interviews or observation methods.
>
> Questionnaires are a set of questions on a sheet. The advantage of using a questionnaire is that they are cheap, fast and accurate. The disadvantage is that people often cannot be bothered to fill them in.
>
> Interviews can be structured or unstructured. Structured interviews are when someone is asked questions from a list of pre-set questions. Unstructured interviews are like a normal conversation. A structured interview is good for getting facts. The advantage of an unstructured interview is that the interviewee can elaborate on his answers and provide more indepth information. The disadvantage is that the answers may be long and complicated. This makes it difficult to compare what different interviewees say. Observation is what it says. The advantage is that you know this is how people really act. The disadvantage is that people may act differently if they know they are being looked at.
>
> After considering these methods I have chosen questionnaires. Using questionnaires I can collect information from a lot of people quickly and accurately.

It is worth reminding yourself, having read the passage above, what the student thinks he/she is doing – that is, explaining why a particular method was chosen. What is so striking here is that the discussion makes no reference to the aims of the research. The student seems to be judging the advantages and disadvantages of methods independently of what they will be used for. It is difficult to believe that anyone would think about choosing any other tool in this way. Can you imagine a passage in a piece of horticulture coursework in which having listed the 'advantages and disadvantages' of hoes, rakes and spades the student concluded – 'after considering these three tools I have chosen the hoe. Using the hoe I can cover a lot of ground quickly and accurately' – without making any reference to the job that needed doing? If you were asked, 'Has the spade an advantage over the rake?' or, 'Has the spanner an advantage over the screwdriver?', you would, probably impatiently, reply, 'for doing what? How on earth do you expect me to answer if you don't tell me what purpose you have in mind?' Yet every year many students write page after page trying to explain and justify their choice of method without reference to their aims.

> I have chosen postal questionnaires because unlike interviews they do not involve face to face contact between the researcher and the subject. Postal questionnaires being impersonal are a good way to get answers to questions which might be embarrassing for a person to answer face to face.

In itself this is rather pleasing. It suggests that the student has some sensitivity to the situation of those answering his questions. Since the research did not involve any remotely embarrassing questions, however, it was clear that this sensitivity was not that of the student but of the textbook writer or tutor. The following passage is very different:

> I realised that there might be difficulties interviewing elderly people about their attitudes. These days elderly people are scared of young people and might worry if I asked them to talk to me. Because of this I used a snowball sample. I have got to know two elderlies who came into the

shop where I do my Saturday job. I asked them if they would let me interview them. They agreed. I also asked them if they would introduce me to some elderly friends who might let me interview them. This worked quite well. I arranged to go with them to see three of their friends. By doing it this way the people I interviewed were relaxed and happy to talk . . . I tried to keep the questions simple. Elderly minds are not as sharp as when they were young. If the questions were not simple they might not understand them and get upset . . . Elderlies do not have much energy because they have worn themselves out. I decided to keep the interviews short. I did not want any of them to fall asleep while I was interviewing them . . .

This is not a routine recitation of the general advantages and disadvantages of the methods available. Here the student has thought about how to obtain the particular information she needs from the particular people who can give it. The student has focussed on her particular use of a method. Elderly people and what the student sees as their characteristics are at the centre of the discussion. Interviews are not treated here as an abstract possibility. The student is thinking things out and giving explanations in the real world of her own research. The following passage has a similar feel:

I felt that most people would be willing to complete a questionnaire about housework while they may not wish to be interviewed on the subject. Being able to complete the questions in privacy and in their own time would allow each respondent time to think. This was important because most of the questions required some maths to be done. Additionally, the embarrassment factor of having to admit during a face to face interview to doing no ironing, hoovering or washing up may have led to considerably more exaggeration than in an anonymous questionnaire.

A method then is not 'good' or 'bad' in some sort of absolute way. A method is 'better than' or 'not as good as' another method for getting the particular kind of information you need from the kind of people who can give it. Would it, in the particular circumstances of your research, be more ethical to use one method rather than another? In the particular circumstances of your research, is it likely that the data collected by using one method would be more accurate or relevant than that collected by using another? In the particular circumstances of your research, might one method be more practical for you than another? By outlining the considerations given to these and other such issues and the reasons for the decisions, you have made you can demonstrate both commitment to a 'real' piece of research and, almost certainly, much sociological understanding.

If you have taken the trouble to use a pilot study, also take the trouble to describe what you did, to explain why you did it and to assess how useful it was

The reference to 'doing a pilot study' is often one of the least convincing paragraphs in a piece of coursework. Some students appear to believe that simply reporting that they have done one will itself gain them some credit. The following is typical:

To do my research I made a list of questions for my questionnaire. The questionnaire then underwent a pilot study to find out what information I could gain. I changed a few questions and changed the layout. My questionnaire was then ready to be handed out and filled in.

The questionnaire as it was before the changes was not in the coursework submitted. The impression given was that the student had read that pilot studies are a good thing and thought that she had better claim – truthfully or not – to have done one. Treated in this way the pilot study becomes a kind of ornament stuck on the research to make it look more attractive.

It might be sensible not to think of a pilot study at all. No student has the time – or the need – to carry out a complete small scale study before undertaking their real, larger scale study. What students generally mean when they refer to a pilot study is that they have tested the method or methods they will use to collect information. This may or may not be a sensible way to use scarce time. It may, for example, be useful to conduct a test interview or two – if the student has never conducted one before. If it is difficult to decide whether to phrase a question in one way or another, it might be useful to try it out on people. If it is not obvious whether a question will offend, be answered willingly or seriously, it is useful to try it out. There are many excellent reasons for a student researcher to test methods and to find out certain things before starting the study proper. Each student must work out whether these reasons apply in his or her particular situation. If some sort of pilot work is undertaken it should be fully described and justified.

Take the trouble to understand the importance of sampling – why and how sociologists do it

Very few topics within sociology seem to trouble students more than sampling. A large number avoid it completely, making no reference to it in their coursework and substituting another question for any question involving sampling in an examination. When an examiner asks, for example, 'How would you choose people to take part in your research?' many students read it as, 'How would you get information from the people who are taking part in your research?' These students then write about questionnaires. Students seem to like writing about questionnaires. They refuse to write about sampling. This is a shame because sampling is a very significant procedure for much sociological investigation. Why?

Imagine you want to find out something about the attitudes of students in a school or college. There are 1,000 enrolled. Does contacting and interviewing or giving a questionnaire to each one of them sound like a seriously practical proposition? Not really. Not only would it take a long time to get the information but when it had been collected there would be so much that an analysis could take months. Even if you had as much time as it took, would it be necessary?

Not if you selected 100, say, of the 1,000 students in such a way that the smaller group represented the larger group. If you did this the statistics which you got from your research into the attitudes of members of the smaller group should be the same as the statistics you would have got if you had studied all the students in the school.

Your sample will be representative if the proportion of people in the sample with a particular characteristic is the same as the proportion of those with that characteristic in the survey population. If, for example, there were 500 boys and 500 girls in the school, a representative sample of 100 should include 50 boys and 50 girls. If there were 300 boys and 700 girls in the school, a representative sample of 100 should include 30 boys and 70 girls. In this case the number of boys and the number of girls in the sample should not be equal because the number of boys and the number of girls are not equal in the survey population. This might seem – and is – a simple point. It is emphasised for the sake of that very large number of students who, year after year, tell examiners that a sample will be representative as long as it contains an equal number of boys and girls – whatever proportions they are of the survey population.

EXERCISE

To assure youself that you understand what a representative sample is, answer the following questions:

If a population to be surveyed consisted of:

- 50 Muslims
- 50 Jews
- 200 Catholics
- 500 Anglicans and other Protestants
- 200 Non-believers

how many from each group would you need to form a representative sample of 100 people?

Is the sample below representative of the population being surveyed?

	Survey Population	**Sample**
Professional	100	5
Managerial, Technical	100	5
Skilled non-manual	600	35
Skilled manual	500	15
Semi-skilled manual	600	35
Other	100	5
TOTAL	2,000	100

Figure 45 A sample population survey.

How then might the sample of 100 be selected for the survey into student attitudes mentioned above?

An inappropriate method, but one often chosen, would involve the student researcher asking his or her friends at the school to fill in the questionnaire or be interviewed. This – **convenience sampling** – has the advantage of being convenient. In some studies students make up their sample from relatives, neighbours, friends of the family. If the student researcher does not personally know sufficient people to make a large enough sample he or she might ask some of those in the sample to ask their friends and so on to take part – **snowball sampling**.

Unfortunately, samples selected in these ways will not be representative of any survey population likely to be studied. Friends are usually people with whom we have things in common – age, interests, social background, for example. Neighbours may well have similar incomes, relatives may well belong to the same social class. Convenience samples or snowball samples are biased. Imagine the attitudes to alcohol consumption which the student researcher would discover in his school if he was a keen rugby player and the most convenient people to ask were therefore rugby players and their friends!

The most obvious way to prevent a researcher's biases from influencing the selection of people for the sample is for the researcher him or herself not to select them. Leave the selection to chance. Put all the names of the people in the survey population in a hat and draw out the number required. A professional researcher might give each person in the survey population a number and ask a computer to select randomly as many as are wanted. Since each name, or number, has an equal chance of being selected it is likely that, so long as the sample is large enough, it will include people from each of the different groups in the survey population in the correct proportions. This is **simple random sampling**.

Before a researcher can put the names into a hat, he or she needs some names. A **sampling** frame is a list of names of those in the population to be surveyed. Student researchers often use college or school class registers, for example, from which – using **systematic random sampling** – they select every seventh or tenth or whatever name.

In particular circumstances, systematic or simple random sampling may be unlikely to produce a representative sample. Consider a year group of 135 white and 15 black students from which a sample of ten is to be selected. It is possible, perhaps probable, that the first ten names drawn from the hat will be of white students. Since black students make up a tenth of the survey population they must make up a tenth of the sample if it is to be representative. To ensure the inclusion of the black student it might be sensible to use two hats – one for the black and one for the white students. The researcher can then take one name from the first hat and nine from the second – thus obtaining a representative sample. This is **stratified random sampling**.

A method of sampling sometimes chosen by students is **quota sampling**. Used with care, this method can produce a representative sample without the need for a sampling frame. As with stratified random sampling, however, the researcher must know something about the structure of the population being surveyed so that the sample can be selected in such a way that it has the same structure. The researcher might need to know what proportion of the population being surveyed is male, what proportion female; what proportions belong to different age groups; what proportion is middle class; what proportion working class, for example. Sex, age and class are usually thought to be significant influences on the behaviour or attitudes being studied. The researcher would not need to know what proportions of the population had brown or blue eyes.

If the researcher has found out that a third of the survey population are boys and has decided use a sample of 30 people, ten boys and 20 girls must be questioned. Simple enough, but it comes more complicated when other factors are taken into account. If half of the survey pulation is aged 12–15 and half aged 15–18, five of the boys selected must be aged 12–15 d five aged 15–18. If two-fifths of the survey population is middle class and three-fifths rking class then four of the boys selected – two in each group – must be middle class and of the boys – three in each age group – working class. Having calculated this, the researcher es out looking for appropriate numbers of people in each category to question.

EXERCISE

Look at the paragraph above and calculate how many girls are required for each category.

Quota sampling is often used by professional polling organisations. Most of us have seen Clipboard Women lurking in a shopping precinct looking for a class A, 50–65-year-old female, or whoever is necessary to complete her quota for the day.

EXERCISE

Consider the advantages and disadvantages of using the different methods of sampling when undertaking research into:

● the attitudes of college or school students to their academic work
● the kinds of conjugal roles which exist in marriages today
● the voting behaviour of over 80-year-olds
● leisure activities of people with disabilities
● the attitudes of members of the public to street beggars.

Do not discriminate against secondary sources

Students often discriminate against secondary information by not treating its collection as the use of a method. Tutors and examiners regularly read 'method' or 'methodology' sections which discuss at great length, for example, the advantages or disadvantages of interviews or questionnaires but which make no reference at all to the use of secondary sources. In some cases the 'method' section comes after the section in which the secondary information has been presented. By doing this the student seems to be saying that distributing questionnaires, conducting interviews or observation is 'proper' research whilst looking at the results of other people's research is not.

Recognise that your use of secondary sources should be as significant to you as your use of questionnaires or interviews. Treat them with equal respect. Explain why the secondary sources you have selected are appropriate for this particular piece of research – just as you would with your method for collecting primary information.

Analysis

To many students analysis presents a special problem. They do not know what it is. Not that most of these students lack commitment to this aspect of their coursework. They produce what they think – incorrectly – is an analysis with tragic enthusiasm. The result – page after page, of colourful, statistical charts and diagrams. 'I plan to do a short write up of my findings for each question. I will then show this information in pie and bar charts and do some graphs.'

Presenting your data – stating what you have found out by using your method – is not the same as analysing your data. You may have found by interviewing adult males in relationships, for example, that only 10% of them enjoy doing the ironing. Or by getting a sample of teenagers to fill in a questionnaire, that only 3% of them can name the Chancellor of the Exchequer. Such statistics are results, findings, pieces of information, data, and however many different ways you present them they remain just that. They are not analysis.

The potential of the information gained from secondary sources is often starkly unrealised. Dumped in a kind of ghetto, this information, apparently forgotten, is unused. Locked away behind the heading 'Background Information', material from textbooks, government statistical records, and the mass media play no part in the coursework. Why do students take so much trouble collecting information which they are not going to use? In extreme, cases a plastic wallet full of pamphlets, photocopied or downloaded sheets is offered – appropriately, since they are not used – as an appendix.

Recognise that analysis involves sorting out the information you have collected and using it to answer the questions asked in the aims.

Sort out the information so that it relates to your aims

Tutors and examiners often come across projects which do not fulfil their early promise. Appropriate aims are stated, an appropriate method chosen and used effectively. At the analysis stage, however, it becomes clear that things are not proceeding as they should. The student seems unable to sort out the material so that it gives him or her the information needed to achieve the aims. Often such projects involve the use of questionnaires:

'AIM: I will find out if people's attitudes to women at work have changed, or if they are still the same.

Question on questionnaire. What age group do you belong to?

Under 20   21–30   31–40   41–50   Over 50

Reason for asking the question: I chose this question because people would have different views depending on their age. Some old people might think that a woman working is a bad thing and today's younger generation would probably think that it's better if women work.'

So far so good. The student appears to understand that to investigate changes in attitude, it is useful to compare the attitudes of different age groups. The questionnaire – by asking individuals to indicate which age group they are in – enables this comparison to be made. Unfortunately, in this case, the questionnaires remained in one pile. The student was unable, therefore, to compare the attitudes of the different age groups. All calculations related to the sample as a whole. The findings presented were all in the form: x per cent of my sample thought this; y per cent of my sample thought that. The reader began to wonder why the student had bothered to get information about people's age in the first place. By the conclusion he or she seemed to have forgotten the aims of the research.

Yet the questionnaires can be sorted so easily into piles – one pile for each age group – enabling the researcher to work out what percentage of people in each pile, therefore in each age group, had this or that attitude. The sorting can be taken further. Each age group pile can be sorted into two subpiles – one for males, one for females. The student researcher can then calculate what percentage of, say, 21–30-year-old females thought this or that. Alternatively, each age group pile could be sorted into subpiles for different social classes or ethnic groups, for example. There are many bases on which the pile of questionnaires can be sorted. Each different sorting enables a different comparison to be made. No shortage of material to relate to the aims here.

Use your secondary information in your analysis

Do not insult any of your secondary information by thinking of it and labelling it 'background information'. Ask yourself what part or parts you want it to play in your study. How do you want to use it? You will probably want to use different elements of it in different ways. Lumping these elements together under a single heading can make this more difficult. 'Secondary information' regularly contains three elements, each of which can play a vital part in your analysis.

Firstly, there may be information about the meanings of the sociological terms which will be used in the research. A student investigating an aspect of poverty may, for example, identify the different ways in which poverty can be defined and explain why he or she has chosen one rather than another. A student researching the division of labour within the household may explain the difference between segregated and joint conjugal roles, or what is meant by the symmetrical family. This sort of information is important and remains important throughout the research.

Secondly, there may be information about social structures and patterns of behaviour or attitudes, either in the present or recent past, which have a bearing on the issue being investigated. A student looking into the academic achievement of girls during the last 20 years might appropriately include statistics relating to women's employment or make reference to the introduction of the National Curriculum. A student studying lone parenthood might make reference to changes in the divorce law or include statistics relating to the attitude of the public to sex outside marriage. This information describes the social context. It will help you to make sense of – to explain – what you have found out by using your questionnaires or whatever. It will help you to do some analysis.

Imagine, for example, that by observing young children in a playground or by questioning their parents a student had found that boys tended to be more boisterous than girls. An interesting fact, supported by evidence, has been established. It would, however, be rather frustrating for a tutor or examiner if it was left there. 'I have found that little boys are more boisterous and aggressive than little girls.' Yes, and so? Go on. It would be particularly frustrating if, buried within the 'background information' were references to and facts about socialisation, gender stereotyping with regard to toys, role models and so on. Kept active these references, these facts could have transformed the findings from the observation or interviews into an analysis. If the findings had been considered in the social context an explanation is likely to have been developed.

'Little boys are more boisterous and aggressive than little girls **because** they are treated differently by parents, relatives, the media and so on. Little boys are treated like this . . . which would perhaps lead them to adopt such and such a pattern of behaviour. Little girls are treated like this . . . which would perhaps lead them to adopt such and such a pattern of behaviour.'

At this point, the student can allow him or herself to feel a little satisfaction.

Thirdly, there may in the 'background information' be references to the work of other sociologists. For example, tutors and examiners routinely find in coursework on conjugal roles brief outlines of the approaches and conclusions of Young and Wilmott and Ann Oakley. These references established the sociological context within which the research was being undertaken. In this case the context is a long running debate about men's participation in household and childcare duties. References to how other sociologists have approached the issue, to the research methods they used and to the conclusions they reached are, when used properly, a wonderful stimulus to analysis. The student can compare his or her work with theirs. 'Sociologist 1 did it like that in 1980 and found such and such. Sociologist 2 did it like that in 1990 and found such and such. I have done it like this in 2001 and found this.'

Set out in this way it is difficult to avoid 'doing some analysis'. Questions jump from the page. What have the findings got in common? In what ways do the findings differ? Are any differences in the findings likely to have resulted from the methods used? Have conjugal roles changed between 1980 and 2001? Why have they changed? Discuss the answers to these questions and, there you have it – an analysis.

How strongly do your findings support your hypothesis? How strongly do your findings support a particular answer to the question(s) you set out in your aims?

Imagine two students who, independently, undertook research to test the hypothesis – 'most males today share household chores equally with their partner.' One student found that 100% of males in her sample shared the chores equally. The other student found that 51% of males in his sample shared the chores equally. Both students reported – 'My findings support my hypothesis.' Although correct, such simple general statements can mislead. The impression given here is that both students came up with very similar findings. This is clearly not so.

Even the addition of one or two words would have helped to match the conclusion and the findings more closely. The first student might have concluded. 'My findings wholly – completely – support my hypothesis.' The second student might have concluded: 'My findings barely – only just – support my hypothesis.'

The additional word also, perhaps, suggests that there is more to say. 'My findings support my hypothesis,' has a 'that's your lot, I've finished' feel about it. 'Completely supported', or '. . . barely supported' raise questions. 'Completely supported – you mean there were no exceptions? I don't believe it. How do you explain that then?' There is more to discuss. Perhaps those who answered the questionnaire lied. Why? Might the sex of the interviewers have had something to do with it in the example above? Perhaps the first student had received information only from 'new men'. How might that have come about?

To some of the questions raised by the findings the student researcher may not be in a position to offer more than a sociologically educated guess. His or her research may not have produced the information necessary for more firmly based answers. It does not matter. This after all is how sociology progresses. A piece of research will help the sociologist to answer some of the questions he or she asked at the start. It will also raise questions and so create a need for further research. 'Loose ends' like these should not be seen as a problem, either in an analysis or a conclusion. A student demonstrates understanding just as much by identifying the questions still to answer as by answering the questions which can be answered.

The conclusion

In some ways an easy part; in some ways a difficult part of a piece of coursework. Easy because planning the study, doing the fieldwork, analysing the results is behind you. The work is nearly finished. Difficult because having done so much it is not easy to see what is still to be done. This perhaps helps to explain why so many conclusions merely repeat and summarise what has already been said.

Remember when planning your conclusion why you were asked to do a piece of coursework. By doing coursework you had an opportunity to find out for yourself something about the way we live in modern British society. What you have found out should be discussed in the conclusion. By doing coursework you had an opportunity to use – and gain skills by using – sociological research methods. Whether your chosen method or methods worked well, or not, and why should be discussed. Put simply, you should see the writing of a conclusion as an opportunity to show what you have learned from your research.

Some students, although producing a project, seem to have gained little from the experience. It is as if they have sleepwalked through the entire research process. With no memories of anything he or she has done the student can only dream of starting again. Few statements embody this more clearly than, If I did this project again I would have

- conducted more interviews and got more information.
- the main change I would make to my project is to have done a bigger survey.
- I could expand my findings and cover a wider area. I could do a more in depth analysis of the issues.
- I would have got a wider range of answers and could have made a more definite conclusion.

Such statements are empty. They reveal no insight into the practice of sociology gained by the student as a result of the coursework. They could have been written before the coursework was even started. Rather than offering such 'wish lists' a student should reflect on his or her real experiences of thinking up some aims, selecting and using a method, trying to make sense of the information collected. It would be very surprising if there had not been occasions when the student researcher was prompted to ask him or herself whether the aims fitted together, whether people were telling the truth, whether the right questions or the right people were being asked, whether this bit or that bit of information was useful. By reflecting on the answers to such simple questions the student can demonstrate real understanding. The conclusion may come at the end of the coursework but it relates to all that has been thought and done from the moment the student began to work out his or her aims.

Make the most of things which did not go according to plan

Even if you have considered your aims very carefully, chosen an appropriate method and taken a sensible and conscientious approach to your coursework, things will not always work out as planned. You may, for example, find that questionnaires which you have distributed are not returned. This is perhaps more likely to occur when someone else has distributed them for you. Use of a third party is often the only way to reach a group you want. A year 11 student would probably find it impossible to distribute in person questionnaires at an office or in a factory. Asking an adult relative or friend to do so for you at their place of work is a sensible way to tackle the problem. Equally, the help of a son or daughter could prove invaluable to a mature student who wished to research some aspect of teenage life. If such help was not available the range of topics it would be possible for a particular student to research would be narrower.

Not being there to remind those who are completing the questionnaires that you have deadlines can, however, be a disadvantage. You might have to try something else if your planned source of information looks likely to produce nothing. This can obviously cause worry and annoyance. It can, on the other hand, have a positive outcome.

Outlining how you coped with the problem and discussing its consequences for your research can provide an excellent opportunity to demonstrate an understanding of sociology.

> I had decided to distribute my questionnaires through a doctor's surgery. I left the questionnaires at the surgery and put up a big sign on the wall asking people to take one and fill it in. Unfortunately by the end of the week only a handful of people had done so. As I had not got the time to wait, I gave some questionnaires to people I knew. This limited the kinds of people who gave me information and may have affected my results. It also meant that since the people who filled in the questionnaires knew me they may not always have written what they really thought.

Handled in this way, the problem with the distribution of the questionnaires did not put the student at a disadvantage.

Check that your conclusion relates to your aims

Imagine a project which has been well planned and in which the research has been undertaken successfully and according to that plan. It should be possible for anyone reading the conclusion to work out simply and accurately what were the aims. If this is not possible there is a problem. It may be that the conclusion has been badly written. In this case the conclusion could be rewritten to make clear what has been found and how it relates to the aims.

There may, however, be a more serious problem, one resulting from a problem with the aims. (See the section on aims.) The aims may have been so ambitious or complicated that parts have been neglected during the research. There may therefore be no findings and no conclusion relating to these parts. It may be that the student did not fully understand the aims and collected data which only now he or she realises is not relevant. Drawing a conclusion relating to the actual aims of the research may be impossible.

It is important for a student who discovers a lack of fit when checking a draft conclusion against the aims to respond to the discovery in an honest and positive way. It is not a good idea to say nothing and hope that the problem will not be noticed. It will. The appropriate response is to identify where things 'went wrong' and to analyse why they 'went wrong'. This should then be discussed. Recognise the conclusion as an opportunity for final comments, the chance to consider and discuss the research process as a whole.

Consider whether what you have found can be explained in any other way

In your analysis you should have considered your findings in detail. You should have related the various pieces of information gained from your questionnaires, interviews, observations and secondary sources to your aims. You should have considered what credibility you wish to give to the different sources of information. You are now in a position to stand back from the detail and to look at what you have found as a whole.

'Hypothesis – children in lone parent families do not get as good academic qualifications as children in married couple families.

Findings – the average GCSE scores for children in lone parent families were lower than those for children in married couple families.

Conclusion – the hypothesis is supported by the findings.'

In the example above the student found evidence to support the hypothesis. The explanation he offered for their relative underachievement was that children in lone parent families had less stable and satisfactory relationships. A good workmanlike project had been produced. It would, however, have been even more impressive had the possibility of an alternative explanation been suggested – 'Lone parents tend to be poorer than married couple families. Income inequality might therefore be at least part of an explanation of academic underachievement.'

'Hypothesis – Elderly people are more likely than those in younger age groups to attend church.

Findings – The proportion of elderly people in church congregations was greater than their proportion in the population at large. The proportion of younger people in church congregations was smaller than in the population at large.

Conclusion – the hypothesis is supported by the findings.'

In this example the student explained why elderly people were more likely to attend church by suggesting that as people get closer to death they get worried and want to 'make peace with God'. Having, however, explained how this might work and what were the grounds for thinking it might be so, the student offered an alternative explanation – 'Elderly people might be more likely than younger people to go to church because when they were younger it was more of a rule go to. They might have got used to it and kept going. Younger people are less likely to have got into the habit.' As if this was not sufficiently impressive she finished – 'In order to discover which explanation is better I would have to question the younger people in 30 years time to see whether they had started going to church.' It is difficult to think what more could reasonably be expected of a student who was taking an introductory course in sociology.

Examinations

Sociology examination papers have changed a great deal since they were first introduced. In the early days all of the questions demanded essay style answers. Today, most examination papers contain different types of question requiring different kinds of response. A candidate now has to understand not only a lot of sociology but something about how the examiners would like different types of question to be answered. Examination boards help students and those who teach them to gain this understanding by publishing the question papers and marking schemes. Finding out, by looking at these, what the examiners intend to award marks for is one of the most useful ways in which a student can prepare for an examination.

Examination questions today are often based around a piece of 'stimulus material'. This might consist of a newspaper article, a graph or a chart, a picture or diagram relating to the topic being examined by the question. The question is then made up of a set of subquestions on this topic. The question which follows examines a student's understanding of the 'family' section of a syllabus.

	Millions					
	1971	**1976**	**1981**	**1986**	**1991**	**1996**
Number of one parent families	0.57	0.75	0.90	1.01	1.30	1.60
Number of dependent children in one parent families	1.0	1.3	1.5	1.6	2.2	2.8

Table from Population Trends 100, Summer 2000

Figure 46 Best estimates of the numbers of one parent families and their dependent children 1971–1996, Great Britain

Subquestion

(a) How many one parent families were there in Great Britain in 1981? (1 mark)

(b) What was the trend in the number of dependent children in one parent families between 1971 and 1996? (1 mark)

The answers to these subquestions can be found in the stimulus material – that is, in the table of figures.

Answer:

(a) 900,000 (1 mark awarded)

(b) upwards (1 mark awarded)

Although the marks here seem easily obtained, had these subquestions appeared on an examination paper many students would not have obtained them. Some would have written: (a)

0.90 – disregarding the millions. Other students would not have known what a trend was and offered no answer to (b). A trend may be observed when over a period of time the figures change in a particular direction. That is, the figures consistently increase or decrease, enabling us to say that the trend is upwards or downwards. In the table above the number of dependent children in one parent families increase as we moved from 1971 to 1996. There was an upward trend.

Subquestion

(c) Identify one reason why there were more one parent families in 1996 than in 1971. (1 mark).

This subquestion is related to the stimulus material but the answer cannot be found just by looking at the figures. Here, students are being questioned on their knowledge of those social, economic, legal and other changes which are associated with some types of family becoming more common and some less. By using the word 'identify' the examiner is indicating that he or she expects a clear straightforward statement, rather than a detailed description, of a reason. The question indicates that only one reason is required.

Answer:

(c) The number of divorces increased between 1971 and 1996. (1 mark awarded)

Or

Answer:

(c) During the last 30 years women have become less likely to think that they needed a husband to help them to raise a child. (1 mark awarded)

These answers are adequate and would be awarded the mark. No more detail is necessary. Students should not, however, risk losing the mark by offering anything less:

Answer:

(c) Divorce. (0 marks awarded)

Or

Answer:

(c) Attitudes have changed (0 marks awarded)

Answers like these suggest that the student might know what he or she is talking about but they are too vague.

Answer:

(c) Teenage girls get pregnant and do not marry their boyfriends.
   (0 marks awarded)

This would be an answer to the question 'State one reason for there being one parent families' which is not what was asked. It does not identify a reason for the change, for the way in which things were different in 1971 and 1996. Answers stating that 'teenage girls were more likely to get pregnant in 1996 than in 1971,' or that – 'when teenage girls got pregnant in 1971 they were more likely than in 1996 to marry their boyfriend,' would be acceptable. Note the significance of the word 'more'.

Subquestion

(d) What do sociologists mean by serial monogamy? (2 marks)

This kind of question examines a student's knowledge of the terms commonly used by sociologists. The mark scheme would probably make a distinction between a simple, unclear or incomplete statement which would be awarded one mark, and a clear, reasonably complete statement of what the term means:

Answer:

(d) Serial monogamy is when a husband can have only one wife at a time. (1 mark awarded)

Or

Answer:

(d) Serial monogamy is when a man or woman gets married to one person, gets divorced from that person, gets married to another person, gets divorced from that person, gets married again and so on. (2 marks awarded)

The first answer is alright as far as it goes. There is no hint, however, that the candidate knows what 'serial' contributes to the meaning of the phrase. The second answer offers a clear and complete statement of the meaning.

Sometimes, knowledge of sociological terms is examined by asking the student to explain the difference between two terms.

Subquestion

(e) Explain the difference between laws and norms. (3 marks)

Answer:

(e) Laws are passed by parliament and norms are not. (1 mark awarded)

Or

Answer:

(e) Laws are made by parliament. When a person breaks a law he can get put in prison. When a person breaks a norm he will not. (2 marks awarded)

Or

Answer:

(e) Norms are informal rules. If someone breaks a norm people might gossip. Laws are official rules made by parliament. Someone who breaks a law is punished officially with a fine or prison. (3 marks awarded)

The first two answers show an incomplete understanding of the difference. Typically, both students know more about laws than about norms. The third answer shows a fuller understanding by referring to the nature of the rules and to what happens if they are broken.

One of the phrases most frequently employed by examiners is 'Identify and explain'. Questions starting this way often carry three marks: one mark for an appropriate identification; two marks for an appropriate identification, plus the beginnings of an explanation; three marks for an appropriate identification with a clear and reasonably complete explanation.

Subquestion:

(f) Identify and explain one way in which a pressure group might try to influence the government. (3 marks)

Answer:

(f) A simple reference to either demonstrations or to lobbying MPs or to petitions would achieve the mark for the identification. It is worth noting that if the student mentioned four or five ways he or she would still receive one mark. If, having identified 'demonstrations', say, the student continued by saying that such action will attract publicity to the group's cause two marks would be awarded. An explanation has been started. Something is being said about why the group thinks that demonstrations are worthwhile. Left there, however, the explanation would be incomplete. The question contained the phrase 'influence the government'. To be complete, the answer must link the actions of the pressure group with the hoped–for response of the government. 'The pressure group hopes that its cause will gain public support through the publicity and that the government will therefore be worried that it will lose popularity by opposing it. In that case the government might listen to what the group has to say.' Such a statement completes the explanation.

The mini-essay

The final subquestion will generally attract the most marks. It will offer an opportunity to show a deeper or wider understanding by asking the student to write an essay, or mini-essay. This subquestion will often begin 'To what extent is . . . ?', or 'To what extent do sociologists . . . ?', 'How far is . . . ?' or 'How far do sociologists . . . ?'

Make sure that you refer to both sides

Consider the question 'To what extent/how far do the poor bring poverty on themselves in Britain today?' If you disregard the 'To what extent/how far' the question reads, 'Do the poor bring poverty on themselves?' From your study of poverty you are aware that some sociologists answer 'Yes' and some 'No – there are other explanations. There are two sides. The question is inviting you to explain what each side says and to indicate which side you believe is supported more strongly by the evidence. You may, of course, sympathise with or know more about the argument put by one side. You may wish, therefore, to explain that argument more fully than the other. Fine, the balance of your discussion is up to you. Recognise, however, that if you explain only what one side says you will not have answered the question.

EXERCISE

Look at the following and consider what are the two sides of the issue:

- To what extent/how far do all pupils have an equal opportunity in Britain to achieve educational qualifications?

- To what extent/how far is an ageing population becoming a problem for British society?

- To what extent/how far is it appropriate to see routine clerical workers as members of the middle class?

You do not need to remember dates but you must have a sense of time and period

Examiners often emphasise that students should focus on the present or very recent past. Sometimes questions specify, 'in the 21st century'; 'since the 1970s; 'During the 1990s'. Sometimes the wording is less precise – 'recent or recently'. Often students disregard this emphasis. Some, for example, seem more prepared to discuss the Butler Education Act and the Tripartite system than the 1988 Education Reform Act. The issues surrounding the first two are interesting and an important part of the history of our education system. A discussion of such issues is not an appropriate focus, however, in a mini-essay written in response to a question starting 'To what extent have recent reforms to the education system . . .?'

Note whether the question is asking you to compare two time periods or to consider a trend

Some questions ask students to consider the way things have changed in recent years. Sometimes the word 'changed' will itself be used – 'To what extent/how far has the class structure of British society changed in the last 40 years?' Sometimes it is made clear in other words that change must be at the centre of the discussion – 'To what extent/how far does the increase in the number of lone parents suggest that marriage is less important today?' Occassionally, the indication that the essay should be about change is more subtle – and more likely to be missed by students: 'To what extent/how far is class still an important influence on voting behaviour in Britain?' Here, 'still', is the key word.

Whatever the wording, this kind of question is inviting the student to discuss both what things were like before and what things are like now. Having done this the student is in a position to indicate what has stayed the same and what has changed and, hopefully, to explain why. A student who referred only to what things were like before or, more commonly, only to what things are like now would not have answered the question.

How long should an essay or mini-essay be? The answers 'As long as you have the time to write it', and 'As long as it takes to deal with the issues raised by the question,' never satisfy students. They are the best tutors can give. The important point is that a student who allocates time appropriately to the different subquestions improves his or her chances. Every examiner has marked with sad disbelief scripts in which more words have been devoted to answering questions which carry one, two or three marks than to essay or mini-essay questions carrying nine or ten marks.

GLOSSARY

Ethical considerations the ordinary rules and principles which guide our conduct in everyday life should be applied by anyone undertaking a piece of research. Ethical considerations involve the researcher being concerned about being honest and sensitive to the feelings of others, when carrying out his or her research.

Hypothesis a piece of research is usually undertaken to answer a question which the researcher sets him or herself. Sometimes the researcher predicts what the answer will be thus stating an hypothesis. For example, a question might be "Are men more likely to help around the house in 2001 than they were in 1970?" The prediction, or hypothesis, associated with this question might be "Men are more likely to help around the house in 2001 than they were in 1970".

Interview an interview traditionally involves the researcher asking questions by word of mouth, face-to-face or by telephone. Today, since people are said to 'hold conversations' over the Internet, the meaning of interview has perhaps to be expanded.

Method to sociologists a method is a means of obtaining information.

Observation a means of obtaining information by observing the ways in which people act. Participant observation involves the researcher becoming part of the group being observed. In **open** participant observation the researcher tells the group that he or she is observing them. In **covert** participant observation the researcher does not tell the group that he or she is observing them.

Pilot study this refers to any work done before the 'research proper' gets under way – pilot in this context means 'trying out'. It can be sensible, for example, for the researcher to try out on one or two people the questions he or she is thinking of using before asking a full sample of 20 or 30 people.

Primary data this is data which the researcher has gathered him or herself by asking questions or observing.

Questionnaire a list of printed questions which a researcher can give to someone to write in the answers. The questionnaire can be filled in whilst the researcher waits. Alternatively, it can be taken away and returned later.

Respondent the person who answers the questions put to them by a researcher in an interview or on a questionnaire.

Sample a small part of a population being studied selected in such a way that it is representative of that population as a whole.

Secondary data this is information, discovered by someone other than the researcher, which is used by the researcher. The Tables in 'Social Trends', for example, are popular secondary data for students.

6 Inequality

Inequality is one of the facts of social life. It is difficult for any of us to ignore it. If we look around us on our way to school or college inequalities of all kinds present themselves to us. We may pass homeless people selling the 'Big Issue'; we may catch the bus while others walk or drive; we may notice that it is mainly women who work in the shops we pass, or that, on our journey, we pass through richer and poorer areas, and that some parts of our town are mainly populated by white people while other areas are more mixed or are mainly black or Asian. We may also notice newspaper headlines announcing huge profits for a company, job losses in a particular industry, or an outbreak of racist violence in another part of the country. Some people may be queuing up outside the benefits office while others are on their way to work, or even on their way home after the night shift.

Once we get to school or college it is hard not to notice more inequalities – some students simply have more money than others, some courses have more males than females, and some members of staff have more power than others. This may seem like an unlikely series of events to some, but it does show that you can think and do sociology even when staring idly out of the window of a bus.

Inequality is one of the main themes of sociology. In the paragraph above are the four types that we are going to cover in this chapter: Class, Gender, Ethnicity, Age.

Sociologists are interested in inequality for many reasons: they may want to make society more equal, they may wish to bring to our attention just how unequal society is, or they may wish to argue with someone else's ideas about the causes of inequality. Whatever their interest, there are usually two aspects of their work:

1) **Description:** trying to show how much inequality there is, or trying to show **how** people are not equal (like the fact that although men and women are legally equals, women still earn less than men, on average).

2) **Explanation:** trying to say why certain types of inequality exist.

In the rest of this chapter we will describe the extent of the types of inequality above and outline some sociological explanations for them. But before that we need to introduce some of the terms you will need to know.

- **Stratification:** refers to the way that society is divided into layers. For example we could put people into groups according to what their weekly income is, with the richest at the top and the poorest at the bottom. Societies are stratified in all sorts of ways: Under apartheid South Africa was stratified by race.

- **Class:** In sociology the term class is used to identify economic differences between individuals and groups. What that means is that there are differences between people according to how much money they have and what they own. An important aspect of this is that if you have a lot of money you can make a lot of choices that people who are less well off can't; and if you own property like a block of flats or you own a company, you may have a lot of power over other people's lives. Unfortunately sociologists do not have an agreed definition of class and so you will be introduced to more than one later in the chapter. But we are all familiar to some extent with the terms upper class, middle class, and working class.

- **Status:** This term refers to the extent to which people look up to us or look down on us. To put it in more academic terms it is about the amount of honour or prestige we have in society. For example, there are those who will look down on a single mother or someone who is unemployed regardless of their circumstances. They see the single mum or the person signing on as having less status than themselves. If you have a high status in society, and many people look up to you, you will have more power and influence than someone who has little or no status.

- **Life chances** are your chances of enjoying all the things that are seen as good in society, and avoiding those things that are seen as bad. Are you likely to enjoy good health? Will you live in a pleasant area, in a large house? Will you take your holidays abroad? Will you be able to go to the cinema, the pub, the theatre when you want to? Or will you spend a lot of your life ill, maybe through living in a polluted area, or having a dangerous job, or living in a cold, damp house that is expensive to heat? Maybe you won't be able to afford holidays very often, or at all, and your leisure activities may be limited to a trip to the pub on a Friday night, or a take away, and a video once a fortnight; or just a couple of hours in front of the television once the kids have gone to bed. Sociologists sometimes divide society into groups who share the same Access to Life Chances, with some having more of the good things in life, and some having less. Obviously this is affected by your income, which is most often determined by your job.

Inequality and Social Exclusion

It is not just sociologists who are interested in inequality. Governments may wish to introduce policies to reduce inequality, like, for example, introducing a minimum wage to help the low paid, or extending child care provision so that more women can obtain full time jobs. People who experience inequalities of one kind or another are said to be excluded from mainstream society. They may not be able to take part in the same way as the majority. For example, individuals on low pay or living on benefits may not be able to buy the things that most of us take for granted: the occasional meal out, a weekend away, or some new clothes. Some might find it hard to go to an evening class or to take a job because of child care difficulties. People living in high crime areas might find their life is blighted by vandalism or burglary. Those living in poor housing could find their health is affected by damp or cold. Often these factors act together: someone in a high crime area with a poorly paid job cannot afford the high rates of household insurance. If they are then the victim of a burglary and lose their video or TV it is doubly difficult to replace – the effect of crime is greater.

The Labour government elected in 1997 set up a Social Exclusion Unit to examine the effects of various aspects of inequality on individuals. The Social Exclusion unit defines the term as 'a short hand label for what can happen when individuals or areas suffer from a concentration of linked problems such as unemployment, poor skills, low income, poor housing, high crime, bad health, and family breakdown.' Thus social exclusion is more than poverty.

(Source: ONS Social Inequalities 2000 edition)

EXERCISE

i) What happens to an area suffering from the linked problems described above?

ii) Why might some individuals find it harder to move away from such areas than others?

iii) Why is Social Exclusion more than poverty?

The ideas of Karl Marx and Max Weber on inequality

Before going any further we need to look at the ideas of Karl Marx (1818–1883) and Max Weber (1864–1920) whose work continues to influence sociologists today despite the fact that they were both born in the 19th century. There are many reasons for their continuing influence, but the two most important are:

i) They both stress the role of conflict between groups in making societies the way that they are.

ii) Both tell us that the really important difference between individuals and groups in society is in terms of how much power they have.

One of the questions that all of us ask about our society at some time or other is 'how did it get to be like this?' Another question we often ask is 'what makes society change?' According to Marx and Weber, the answer to both of these questions is to do with power and conflict. Changes in society come about when a group gains or loses power. This is not just to do with elections or revolutions, but could be because of a variety of factors. In the 1970s many people said that the trade unions had too much power. During the 1980s and 1990s there were certainly laws passed to limit the power of the unions, but there was also a high level of unemployment which meant that fewer individuals were members of unions and so their power declined. However, as we are writing this book, unemployment is falling and the newspapers are starting to talk about an increase in the power of the unions so there may be more changes.

This is a very simplified example but it shows what Marx and Weber believed in. They both thought that society is based on a constant struggle for power, for some sort of control over our lives and those of other people. Some individuals or groups have this power and some do not, but they would like to have it. This means there is a conflict of interests between those who have power and those who don't. Changes in society come about as the balance of power between groups alters. At any particular moment in history, society is the way it is because of the views and opinions of those who hold power at that time.

Karl Marx

Karl Marx saw all history as being the history of struggle between those who had power and those who did not. In 19th century capitalist society he thought that the two most important groups or 'classes' were the bourgeoisie and the proletariat, what today we might call the ruling class and the working class.

The bourgeoisie were the property owners. Not any old property but that which could be used to create wealth. They owned the mills and the factories, the land, and had enough capital (in the form of money) to pay others to work for them. The bourgeoisie were capitalists: they used their property to make goods that could be sold at a profit. If they paid their workers as little as they could and made them work long hours then their profits would be high.

The proletariat were those in society who owned nothing that could be used to create wealth. They were the workers. Because they had no capital of their own they had to work for those who owned the mills, the factories, and the land. For Marx all they owned was their ability to work. By working in the factories owned by the capitalists the workers created wealth in the form of the goods that were sold at a profit.

So Marx defined class in terms of what you owned or did not own. This was important because ownership of capital (land, factories, machinery, and money to pay wages) gave the owners power, especially over those who did not own this kind of property and so had to work for those who did.

Marx also thought that the relationship between the two main classes in capitalist society was one based on conflict. The bourgeoisie wanted to make a profit, the proletariat wanted higher wages and a better standard of living. If the workers were paid more, it would reduce the profits of the capitalists. So what was good for the workers was not so good for the capitalists and vice versa. A conflict of interests was built into the very nature of capitalist society. The workers were exploited by the bourgeoisie because they made the goods that were sold, but only received a small part of the price that the goods were sold for. The rest, after the cost of raw materials, went to the bourgeoisie in the form of profits. To put it very simply, for Marx, the rich got richer at the expense of the poor.

Marx's ideas about class were part of a much larger analysis of capitalist society that he undertook in order to bring about change. Marx was not a sociologist working from a university like many today – he was a political activist who thought that the situation of the proletariat could only be improved by the abolition of the kind of property ownership described above. He thought that men and women could never develop to their true potential in a capitalist society, and so it was necessary to change it. However, in order to change society you had to understand how it worked, and you had to demonstrate to those who had the most to gain from change how they were being held back and exploited so that they would act. In this way Marx influenced many sociologists – not just through his ideas, but also through the idea that the point of doing sociology was to change society for the better.

Max Weber

Weber gave a more complex explanation of inequalities than Marx. For him there was more to inequality than just economics. There were three aspects of stratification according to Weber: Class, Status, Party.

- **Class** – According to Weber, individuals who shared the same access to life chances could be put in to the same class position. Your access to life chances is determined by two things:

whatever skills you have to sell on the job market, and whatever assets you have to sell. For most of us our access to life chances is determined by our job, as most of us do not own much that we could sell and make enough to live off. This is different to Marx's definition of class which was based on ownership.

- **Status** is different to class as your status in society, as we have seen above, is based on how much prestige or social honour you have. Much of the time this is linked to your class position. For example if we are successful we may spend our money on status symbols like a big house, a flashy car, or lots of gold jewellery so that we can let others know that we've 'made it'. But our status can be completely separate from our class position. For example many men in our society still think that women have a lower status than themselves just because they are women and regardless of how rich or poor they are. In the same way there are still many white people who regard members of ethnic minority groups as automatically being of lower status. The same can be said of the way in which some able bodied individuals regard people with disabilities.

- **Party** – Weber also thought that there were inequalities in society which were not necessarily based on class or status. For example if a group of football fans decide that their team's manager is not doing as good a job as they think he ought to be doing, and they organise a series of protests to persuade the board to sack him, and they are successful, then they have become quite a powerful group at their club. They may be made up of working class and middle class supporters, both male and female, and come from a range of ethnic groups, but as a group they are still powerful, regardless of their class or status positions. When Weber uses the term party he is talking about any group of people who are organised to achieve a particular goal: this might be running the country, which is the goal of political parties, or it might be changing the rules at the local leisure centre. The important point is that sometimes differences in the amount of power or influence that people have cannot be explained in terms of either class or status.

Why is 'class' an important idea for sociologists?

Most of us, most of the time, probably don't think about social class very much. We may never have thought about whether we are working class or middle class or upper class until we started doing sociology. Other aspects of our lives may seem to be much more important to us – whether we are male or female, young or old, white, Asian, or Afro-Caribbean, for example. So it is not an unreasonable question to ask why does sociology appear to be all about class?

Class and money

First of all class tells us something about the economic differences between people and groups in society. We probably know that if we are middle class we are likely to have more money in the bank than if we are working class. Having more money means that we have a bigger choice about where we live, what we eat, where our children go to school and so on. This aspect of social class is probably how most of us think about it.

Class, power and control

We are also probably aware that some people in society have more power than others. As we have already seen for Marx and Weber this was an important aspect of class. When we use the word power in connection with social class it can mean power over other people – getting them to do what you want them to do – or it can mean how much control we have over our own lives. In some occupations people have much more freedom to choose what they do, how they do it and when they do it than others. In other occupations the workers might be much more closely supervised and told what to do. People who do not have an occupation – those who are not in paid employment – may have a lot of control over their own lives (if they do not work because they have an unearned income) or they may find they have a lot of free time but not much control over what they can do (perhaps they are unemployed and living on benefits). Sociologists are interested in this aspect of class – power and control – because it affects many aspects of our lives but especially our working lives, as we discuss below and in Chapter 7.

Class and culture

As we have seen in Chapter 3 there are other aspects of class that are not directly to do with economics or with power and control. We saw how children growing up in different classes are said to learn different norms and values, different uses of language and different attitudes to education from their parents. Some sociologists talk of the 'culture clash' between the middle class school and the working class family as a means of explaining the underachievement of working class children in education. Similarly the values of working class or middle class cultures can lead to members of those cultures voting for a particular political party.

Class and identity

We mentioned the issue of identity in Chapter 1. For some individuals the most significant aspect of their identity is their own class background. Some people think of themselves as acting to improve the situation of the worker class; they see themselves in class terms. The idea of class identities crops up from time to time in popular music, for example John Lennon's 'Working Class Hero,' and Pulp's 'Common People'. Class identities are important for sociologists because the way in which we see ourselves can affect how we act. Perhaps the last time large numbers of people in Britain saw themselves in terms of their class was during the miner's strike of 1984–85. The campaign anthem of the miner's wives support groups contained the lines: 'united by the struggle, united by the past/Here we go, here we go, we're the women of the working class'. In this example both gender and class are sources of identity.

For some sociologists class is much less important than it used to be as a source of identity. Gender, ethnicity, sexuality, or simply patterns of consumption (what we spend our money on) are said to be more significant. For Marx in the 19th century class identity, or class consciousness as he called it, was particularly important. This was because Marx thought a change in society would only come about when the workers realised that they were all in the same situation and act together as a group to improve their position. As we discuss in Chapter 8 class consciousness and class identity are issues that particularly interest sociologists investigating the possible links between social class and political action.

Class and handling information

Being able to put individuals or families into social classes is also important for sociologists (and many others including market researchers or government statisticians) for a practical reason. It allows us to handle information about large numbers of people relatively easily. We can see if there are patterns in the population, for example, in health, death rates, housing, leisure activities, according to social class. In order to cope with vast amounts of information sociologists and others often use occupation as a quick and easy way of allocating individuals to social classes.

Class inequalities in britain

Income

In April 2000, according to the new earnings survey, average earnings were as follows:

Full Time	£ per week
For manual workers	321
For non-manual workers	465
For all workers	411

(Source New Earnings survey 2000 ONS)

Figure 47 Average earnings sample.

During the 1980s the top 10% grew by 38%, but the earnings of the bottom 10% grew by only 5%. Although there was a little more stability in the 1990s earnings at the top grew more than those at the bottom. At the start of the 1970s the incomes of the top 10%. By the end of the 1990s they were four times higher.

(Source: ONS quoted in www,guardianunlimited.co.uk.)

Wealth

The distribution of wealth has altered very little over the past 20 years. Wealth is distributed more unevenly than income. In 1996 1% of the population owned 20% of the wealth (about £388 billion). 10% of the population owned over 50% of the wealth. The wealthiest 50% of the population owned 93% of the wealth, almost all of it.

Education

In 1998 only one-fifth of those whose parents were in unskilled manual jobs achieved five GCSEs at grades A–C. But more than two-thirds of children of the professional and managerial classes obtained five A–C grades at GCSE.

Class and occupation

In the last section we looked at some evidence of class inequalities in Britain. In many of the figures we used, occupational groups have been used to illustrate class differences. So we have talked about manual and non-manual workers, professional and unskilled occupations and so on. In this section we will look at the link between class and occupation.

The Registrar General's Classification

I Professionals – e.g. doctors, solicitors

II Intermediate – e.g. teachers, nurses

III (N-M) Skilled non-manual – e.g. clerical workers

III (M) Skilled manual – e.g. electricians, plumbers

IV Semi-skilled manual – e.g. postal delivery workers

V Unskilled manual – e.g. labourers

The Standard Occupational Classification (SOC) 2000

(i) Managers and senior officials

(ii) Professional occupations

(iii) Associate professional and technical occupations

(iv) Administrative and secretarial occupations

(v) Skilled trades occupations

(vi) Personal service occupations

(vii) Sales and customer service occupations

(viii) Process, plant and machine operatives

(ix) Elementary occupations.

Why do sociologists use occupation to allocate people to social classes?

It is quick and easy. Sociologists only have to ask one question, like what is your occupation, and the individuals can be given a class category. Most people are prepared to answer such a question where they might be less happy answering questions about what they earn or what they own or how much money they have saved, for example. This willingness of people to answer makes it easier for sociologists. Individuals can be put into categories according to classifications like the Registrar General's or the Standard Occupational Classification.

Occupations do give us a good indication of some important aspects of class inequality like income, education and health. In Weber's terms knowing what someone does for a living is a pretty good guide to their access to life chances. For example, we know that a doctor is likely to earn more than a labourer and so the doctor will enjoy a greater access to life chances than a labourer.

How has occupation been used to allocate people to social classes?

The Registrar General's scale uses the 'standing in the community' of occupations to put them into a hierarchy. The SOC 2000 uses two factors: the type of work done, and the level of skill required to do it.

However it is done, occupational scales usually produce a hierarchy. Some occupations are at the top, some occupations are at the bottom. It is also usually possible to group occupations together into 'the middle class' and 'the working class'. For example in the Registrar General's Classification:

I	Professional	
II	Intermediate	The Middle Class
III	Skilled non manual	
III	Skilled Manual	
IV	Semi-skilled Manual	The Working Class
V	Unskilled manual	

The boundary between the middle class and the working class has usually been between manual and non manual workers, or as they are sometimes known as the 'blue collar' and 'white collar' workers. The distinction was between those who worked with their hands in, for example, factories, building sites, textile mills, and the mines and those who worked in offices, dealing with insurance claims, issuing Giros to benefit claimants, collecting tax, teaching, designing buildings and managing groups of workers. The terms 'blue collar' and 'white collar' came from the fact that manual workers would wear overalls and office workers would wear white shirts.

EXERCISE

i) Look at the list of occupations in the Standard Occupational Classification 2000 list on page 185. Where would you put the boundary between working class and middle class occupations?

ii) Do you think that this distinction between working class and middle class is still relevant in the 21st century?

Problems of using occupation as a means of allocating individuals to social class

While considering the questions above we need to understand some of the problems with using occupation as a mean of allocating individuals to social classes. We can identify two types of problems: practical problems and theoretical problems.

Practical problems

- Not everyone has an occupation (in the sense of paid employment). So using occupation means that those who do not have paid employment are left out. This would include, for example, the very rich, the unemployed, housewives, students, and lottery winners who give up their jobs.
- The categories used are very broad and may well gloss over differences between individuals doing the same job. For example there are wide variations in the access to life chances of different doctors and farmers. The junior hospital doctor working for the NHS and the private specialist; the tenant farmer on a hill in Wales and the owner of thousands of acres in East Anglia, would not share the same access to life chances.

Theoretical problems

At the start of the chapter we said that sociologists wanted to be able to describe and to explain certain aspects of society. If the practical problems above prevent us from describing social classes then using occupation can also cause us problems in explaining social differences.

- Having people who do not have occupations left out is not just a problem for describing. If we remember Marx and Weber's ideas on class, for both of them power was an important element of class. Using occupation to allocate individuals to classes means that the very powerful in our society are likely to be left out. These very wealthy individuals, who do not need to work, but whose decisions on investment, for example, can affect us all, would not appear in a classification based on occupation. At the other end of the scale the very powerless would also be left out, for example, the widow living off state benefit. Classifications based on occupation tend not to tell us enough about the differences in power in society.

- Classifications based on occupation do not tell us much about what people think. We saw earlier that class identity, class consciousness and class cultures are important for sociologists in many different ways. What class is the girl from a council estate whose dad is a bricklayer, but who goes to university and becomes a solicitor specialising in employment law and working for a trade union? Is she working class because of her background and who she works for, or middle class because of what she does? Occupational classifications can't tell us much about how people see themselves.

- The final difficulty with occupational classifications is connected with a much bigger problem in the sociology of stratification. Male sociologists might refer to it as the problem of women and class; female sociologists might broaden it out and call it the problem of male sociology. The problem arises from the fact that occupational scales often use the job of the 'head of the household' to allocate individuals to a social class. So traditionally a woman was allocated a class position on the basis of what her husband's or partner's occupation was. In this way the class structure became based on men, and women were invisible.

Men and women, families, households and class

Feminist sociologists have pointed out that traditional sociology has ignored women in many ways. The term 'malestream' sociology was coined to show how much, if not all, mainstream sociology was written by men. One important problem is that this 'malestream' sociology ignores significant changes in society such as:

→ The increasing number of families where both the male and female work.
→ The number of households where the woman is the main breadwinner either because her husband/partner is unemployed or in a lower paid job or because she is a lone parent.
→ The differences in income and status between men and women doing the same job. Men may be able to work overtime where women feel they are unable to because of their domestic role. Some occupations, like clerical work, may be seen as just a job for women, but as the possible start to a career for men.

There are two possible ways in which this problem could be solved.

i) Allocate individuals to social classes. In this way women and men would be allocated to a social class on the basis of their own occupations.
ii) Allocate families/households to social classes. In this way the problem caused by the greater access to life chances of double income families would be avoided. The incomes of both males and females would be taken into account when calculating the class position of a family or household unit.

EXERCISE

You are doing your coursework on the relationship between class and educational achievement and you have interviewed some children from a number of families. Into what social class would you put:

i) The daughter of a male plumber and a shop assistant?
ii) The son of a male secondary school teacher and a female solicitor?
iii) The daughter of a female primary school teacher and a male electrician?
iv) The son of a female filing clerk who is only able to work part time?

The occupational structure and the class structure

We have looked at the problems of using occupation to allocate individuals to social classes, but there is a link between the occupational structure and the class structure. If the number of middle class jobs increases then we will find more individuals in middle class occupations. For many people this means that the middle class has got bigger. This is effectively what has happened in Britain.

The primary sector of the economy has decreased in size. This is the extractive industries. There are now fewer people employed in mining and fishing, for example, than in the 1960s. The secondary, or manufacturing, sector of the economy is also smaller than it was. Think of the decline of the British motorcycle industries. The tertiary, or service sector, however, of the economy has grown. There are now many more jobs in finance, banking, teaching, retail and leisure and entertainment than previously. So, if we can define occupations in the traditional way we referred to earlier in the chapter as either middle class (non manual) or working class (manual), then it would appear that the middle class has grown.

What is the class structure of modern Britain? How has it changed?

If we define class in the traditional way then the class structure of Britain has altered as shown in the diagram below.

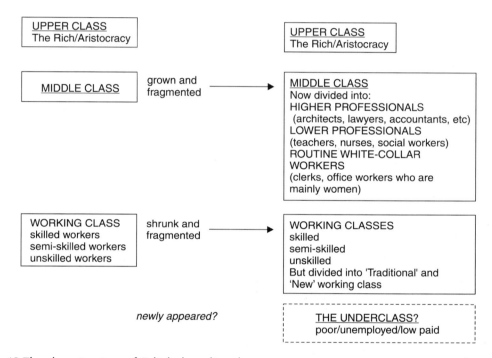

Figure 48 The class structure of Britain has altered.

Looking at figure 48 we can see that the main changes to class structure that sociologists have identified are that the **upper class** remains a small but influential group; the **middle** class has increased in size relative to other classes; the **working** class has decreased in size relative to other classes.

There are now divisions in the middle class between those at the top and those at the bottom. The middle class is said to have fragmented so it is now more true to speak of the middle classes rather than a single middle class.

The working class is also said to have fragmented. It is divided into a traditional working class and a new working class. There is also said to be an underclass, cut off from mainstream society.

Who are the upper class?

The upper class are the very richest people in society and represent a small proportion of the population as a whole. We can divide the very rich into three main groups.

i)   Owners of industry and commerce. According to *The Sunday Times* 1999 rich list the richest man in the country is Hans Rausing whose wealth comes from packaging. He was said to be worth £3,400 million in 1999. Sir Richard Branson and the Sainsbury family would also come into this category.

ii)   The aristocracy and land owners: this group would include the Royal Family and individuals such as the Duke of Westminster.

iii) Those who have made their money through entertainment or sport like David Bowie, David Beckham or Sir Paul McCartney.

The list below gives us an indication of where the very rich get their money from. Many land owners and individuals in industry or commerce have inherited their wealth – that they have not had to earn it. Although *The Sunday Times* list states that 709 of the richest 1000 are self-made millionaires it is worth noting that many individuals who became millionaires themselves inherited large sums of money, though less than one million. The 'Rich List' also gives us an indication of the extent of gender inequalities in our society.

The 1999 Rich List is made up of . . .

1,022 men and 71 women

709 of the richest 1,000 are self-made millionaires
291 inherited their wealth
137 are aristocrats

There are:

155	in land and property
142	in industry
86	in food production and retailing
82	in finance, banking and insurance
74	in computers, technology and software
70	in media and publishing
61	in construction
60	in non-food retailing
52	in music and entertainment
51	in leisure
38	in distribution and car sales
37	in transport
26	in pharmaceuticals and healthcare
24	in textiles and fashion
19	in business services and recruitment
12	in mobile phones
11	in the internet

Inherited wealth is included under its original source

Figure 49 The Rich List 1999.

Being wealthy can obviously make a big difference to our lives. For a start we do not have to work. Wealth itself can provide us with income – we could put our money into a building society savings account and receive interest on our savings. We could also buy shares in a range of companies and receive income in the form of a dividend.

Before we consider the middle class and the working class, we need to think about where the boundary between them should be. Some sociologists say that because of changes in work it is no longer appropriate to simply say that manual workers are working class and non manual workers are middle class

Social change and social class

Where do we draw the boundary between the working class and the middle class?

Think about the following.

> But what if a bus driver was married to a teacher? By that reckoning he'd be working class all day and middle class once he was at home. He'd leave the garage shouting 'Alright guvnor, see you tomorrow you old plonker,' then get indoors and say 'Hello poodlekins, I hope my little teacher-weacher hasn't had any nasty marking to do tonight.'
>
> The working class are the section of society who have no control over how society produces the wealth, and as a result, have no choice but to sell their labour. A call centre packed with clerks, each with microphones strapped on so they can talk and tap in details at the same time, is not fundamentally different from a factory or a mine. They can hardly be described as middle class, just because no one lives in fear of a tragic accident involving the collapse of a photocopier.
>
> Supermarket checkout staff, bank clerk, salesmen, radio and television producers and especially teachers are part of an endless list of jobs once considered as middle class, but now made harder, longer and with less reward in order that the £87 billion owned by the richest can become £88 billion.
>
> Adapted from an article by Mark Steel in *The Guardian*, 20 January 1999

Q u e s t i o n s

---

i)   Is the author putting forward a Marxist or Weberian view of class?

ii) What evidence is there in the article to support your answer?

iii) Why do you think the author thinks that working in a call centre 'is not fundamentally differ-ent from working in a factory or a mine'?

Proletarianisation and routine clerical work.

Proletarianisation refers to the idea that some middle class occupations are becoming working class. The reasons put forward for this are:

- The work carried out by clerks and office workers has become routine in the same way work on an assembly line is routine. Clerical and office workers will often spend their day repeating a limited number of tasks over and over a again. See the piece on call centre workers in the next chapter.
- Linked to the above is the idea that clerical work has become deskilled. The growth of office technology – computers, calculators – means that many complex tasks can now be carried out by machines. Office workers do not need to be as skilled as they were in the past.

- The rates of pay for office work has declined in relation to other types of work. Clerical workers can no longer expect to be better paid than manual workers, and in many cases they will be paid less.
- In the 1960s and 1970s many white collar workers were not only joining trade unions but also taking strike action. This was seen by some as evidence that white collar workers saw themselves as working class.
- Clerical workers have become much more closely supervised at work. Their work is more closely controlled than it was in the past – they have lost much of their autonomy.

If we consider these changes from a Marxist point of view then it is proper to regard clerical workers as working class as they are as much a part of the proletariat as manual workers. They have little control over what they do. They sell their ability to work to an employer, and they act like members of the working class. From a Weberian point of view they share the same, or possibly worse, access to life chances as manual workers.

It is important to remember that the vast majority, approximately 75%, of routine clerical workers are women. Male clerical workers tend to fall into two groups: young clerks who have started out on the first rung of a career, possibly in management, and older men ending their working lives in an office environment rather than on the factory floor. Whether or not routine clerical work can be seen as working class is not a simple issue though. There are certainly some reasons why it should not.

- Over a lifetime male clerical workers, at least, are likely to earn more than manual workers. This is because they are likely to be promoted or at the very least receive a salary with yearly increments.
- Clerical workers tend to work in close physical proximity with management. The offices of management and clerks are often separate from the factory floor. Clerks are often seen by other workers as part of the management.
- There is still a certain status attached to office work. It is often seen as a 'better' job than manual work. This may be because the environment is cleaner, because the hours are shorter, or because of the association of clerical work with academic rather than vocational qualifications.
- While many white collar workers may join trade unions they do not see themselves as working class. They see themselves as middle class.
- Office technology may well have simplified some tasks but its introduction has also meant that workers have had to learn new skills – they have been reskilled (see Chapter 7).

Maybe the best way to resolve the argument is to look at the job separately from the people who do it.

- Clerical work may well be routine and similar to many manual occupations.
- The people – young males – can't really be seen as proletarian as they are starting off in a middle class career.
- Older males can't be seen as becoming working class because they have been in working class occupations before entering clerical work.
- Females can be seen as proletarian when compared to men in the same job because women clerical workers are less likely to obtain promotion, so their job is not a route to a truly middle class occupation.

How has the middle class altered?

We can divide those in middle class occupations other than routine clerical work into two main groups:

i) The higher professionals
ii) The lower professionals.

The main difference between these two groups lies in their access to life chances.

The higher professionals are individuals with occupations in the law, accountancy, and engineering, for example. These individuals are likely to have full time and secure employment, high salaries and may enjoy perks such as expense accounts, private health care, company pensions and company cars. They have a high level of control over their own working lives and also control over their employees.

The lower professionals are individuals mainly employed in the public sector, such as teachers, lecturers, nurses and social workers. Such employees are likely to receive lower salaries than higher professionals. Their employment is likely to be less secure – for example approximately 22,000 lecturers in further education have been made redundant since 1993. Lower professionals are likely to enjoy few of the perks that are enjoyed by higher professionals. They are also more likely to be employed on temporary contracts. Lower professionals enjoy less freedom at work than higher professionals. Think, for example, of the way that the introduction of the National Curriculum has affected the role of the school teacher. Lower professionals are also more likely to be supervised or controlled by others.

Social change and social class: What has happened to the working class?

Apart from the fact that there are fewer individuals in manual occupations sociologists have noted other ways in which the working class has altered: it has divided into a 'traditional' working class and a 'new' working class, with the possible emergence of an underclass.

The Traditional Working Class

Although there has been a reduction in the number of people employed in manufacturing industry there are still many 'traditional' working class individuals and communities. These people are likely to be employed in industries such as mining, steel and shipbuilding. They tend to be concentrated in southern Scotland, south Wales and the north east and north west of England. The traditional working class' belief in trade unions as a means of improving the lot of their class as a whole is still held by many. People in these areas are likely to live in housing rented from the local council. Politically such individuals and communities are likely to be strong Labour Party supporters.

The New Working Class

This class is said to be found mainly in the south of England. Individuals in the new working class are likely to be employed in new light industries. They are likely to take an instrumental attitude to the trade unions: they belong to the union only because of what it can do for them as individuals. Many members of the new working class are not union members at all. New working class individuals are much more likely to own their own homes than members of the traditional working class. They are also more likely to be 'floating voters' who will vote for the party that will benefit them the most.

The Underclass

During the late 1970s and the 1980s some sociologists thought that significant numbers of people were becoming 'detached' from mainstream society. Different sociologists interpreted the change in different ways. However certain factors appeared in many of the descriptions about the rise of the underclass.

→ High levels of unemployment, and particularly long term unemployment, especially among young men.
→ The increase in the number of lone parent families, particularly among teenage girls.
→ The apparent increase in crime in inner city areas, and especially crimes that were drug related or anti-social in nature such as 'joyriding.' There was also an increase in disorder on the so called 'sink estates' such as the Meadowell in Stockton and the Blackbird Leys in Oxford.
→ Rising levels of poverty and deprivation especially among the elderly, solely dependent upon a state pension, and among women bringing up children alone.

These groups of people found themselves 'detached', 'excluded' or 'marginalised' from mainstream society.

The underclass as a threat

Sociologists like Charles Murray portrayed the underclass in a particularly negative way. He referred to the underclass as 'the new rabble' and thought that they represented a threat to mainstream society. Murray thought that the very existence of welfare benefits encouraged some people to live on them and not to look for work. Murray linked this welfare dependency with the numbers of single teenage mothers. The existence of the welfare state meant that young girls could be promiscuous without having to worry about the consequences because they could be looked after by the state.

Murray argues that the underclass have developed their own sets of norms and values – young men do not want to work nor are they willing to settle down and look after the children they have fathered. Large numbers of children were growing up without an adult male role model and also without any respect for the law. Members of the underclass would commit crimes because they had no particular respect for the law – they had not been socialised to. This 'criminal, promiscuous, work shy rabble', in Murray's words, were a threat to society because young people would be attracted to this lifestyle when times were hard, and also because their criminal activities would pose a direct threat to non underclass communities.

Before going any further read the section on the culture of poverty later in this chapter. What similarities do you notice between Murray's ideas and the theory of the culture of poverty?

Criticisms of Murray

Murray's ideas were controversial when they first appeared, and remain so. Much of the controversy concerns the language that he writes in. When he visited Britain in 1989 he referred to himself as 'a visitor from a plague area come to see if the disease is spreading' – hardly the words of an objective sociologist.

Many sociologists criticised Murray for 'blaming the victim'. Murray appears to blame the poor and the disadvantaged for their situation. According to Murray the poor and disadvantaged are in that situation because of the rules of their subculture. Their norms and values are not the same as those of the rest of society.

Look at the table below which shows the worries of young people in four different areas of Edinburgh, ranging from middle class (Corstorphine) to Wester Hailes with high rates of unemployment and single parenthood. It is an estate thought of by some as housing the underclass.

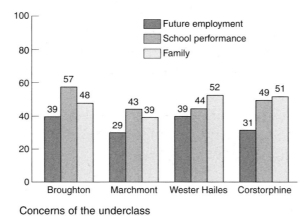

Concerns of the underclass

Source: Anderson *et al* (1994) Cautionary Tales: Young People, Crime and Policing in Edinburgh. (Avebury).

Figure 50

EXERCISE

Look at the table again and answer the following questions:

i) What differences are there in the worries expressed by different groups according to the research done in Edinburgh?

Different views of the underclass

Sociologists who do not agree with Charles Murray's view put forward other ideas for the existence of an underclass.

The first of these is the **failings of the welfare state**. Because of inadequate state benefits and services groups such as the long term unemployed, lone parents and state pensioners are unable to take part in society fully. The **poverty trap** means that they find it particularly difficult to escape from poverty and may adjust their lifestyles to suit their situation. There is no evidence according to many sociologists, that their attitudes are any different to the rest of us – it is the failure of the welfare state that keeps them poor and on the margins of society.

Racism and discrimination are to blame for the disadvantaged position of many members of minority ethnic groups. Because of racism and discrimination in employment and education individuals are more likely to find themselves unemployed or in low paid and insecure employment. If an underclass exists, it is one made up of individuals who are excluded from society by the racist attitudes of others.

Those of us in secure or relatively secure employment tend to conform to the norms and values of mainstream society because we gain the benefits of conforming. Our jobs provide us with wages or salaries that allow us to buy the consumer goods that we want – CD players, computers, brand name clothes, houses, cars and so on. The disadvantaged in society are subject to a different kind of social control. Because the poor are not able to play a full part in the consumer society (because they don't have much money to spend) they are unlikely to conform to the norms and values of a society which gives them few benefits. Therefore their actions have to be scrutinised and controlled, especially by the welfare state. People on benefits are used to form filling and to hanging around in dismal buildings. From this point of view the kind of social control exercised over the poor stigmatises them and works as a reminder to the rest of society of the benefits of conforming. From this point of view the underclass would be those people we see in a negative way – social security scroungers, the work shy, the idle.

The concept of an underclass has been so controversial that many sociologists have said we should not use the term because of the negative messages it conveys about particular groups in society. Whatever we think about that idea there are certainly groups in British society who live on the margins of mainstream society for a variety of reasons. Using the term underclass is one way of conveying that idea, social exclusion is another.

Social mobility

Social mobility refers to the movement of individuals up or down the social scale. It can be intragenerational (within one generation) – for example, a woman working as a care assistant who does an access course, goes to university, gets a law degree and becomes a solicitor, would be upwardly mobile. Mobility can also be intergenerational. For example, the son of an electrician who becomes a doctor would be upwardly mobile in comparison with his father.

Why do sociologists study social mobility?

Studies of mobility can tell us how open or closed a society is. **Open societies** are those with a great deal of movement up or down the social scale. They allow the talented and able to rise to the level of their abilities and the less able may well drop down the social scale. Open societies are more meritocratic – where you end up in society is determined by your ability and not your background or the connections you have. A **closed society** is one in which little or no movement between social categories is possible. Caste societies are the best example of closed societies. You are born into a particular caste and movement either up or down is extremely restricted. A society with high rates of social mobility is said to be an open society; one with very low rates of social mobility is said to be closed.

Politicians often make reforms, such as in the education system. Studies of social mobility allow us to find out whether or not such reforms are successful. One of the reasons for the introduction of comprehensive schooling in the 1960s and 1970s was that the previous selective system was said to be a barrier for working class pupils. If rates of social mobility increased after the introduction of comprehensive schooling then that reform could be judged to be successful. (See below for the outcome of Goldthorpe's mobility study.)

Studies of social mobility can also tell us something about the ways that classes form and change. If a social class is self-recruiting, if the members of that social class are drawn from the sons and daughters of its own members, then it is quite likely that the norms and values of that class will remain the same from one generation to the next. If the members of a class are drawn from a variety of backgrounds then it is much less likely that the same norms and values will exist from one generation to the next. It is probably much less likely that individuals will see themselves in terms of a class identity.

Look at the diagram on page 198 and think about which class (service, intermediate or working), is most likely to have a common set of norms and values, or a common class identity. This diagram uses Goldthorpe's division of the classes into a service, intermediate and working class.

What are the patterns of social mobility in Britain today?

There are two terms you will need to know before we can look at the extent of social mobility in Britain.

- **Absolute mobility** refers to the actual numbers of people who are socially mobile.
- **Relative mobility** refers to your chances of moving up (or down) the social scale in comparison with someone from a different social class. In a perfectly open society all individuals would have the same chances of movement.

The evidence on patterns of social mobility is quite complicated. What we find, as is often the case in sociology, depends on which measure we use. The evidence shows us two main trends.

- The degree of absolute mobility is quite high. Many individuals who are born into working class families obtain service class jobs.
- Patterns of relative mobility show us a different pattern. Your chances of obtaining a service class job are much greater if you are born into a service class family than if you are born into a working class family. When Goldthorpe conducted his first study in 1972 boys born into the service class had four times the chance of obtaining a service class job than boys born into working class families. In his updated study, conducted in 1983, the relative chances of working class individuals had increased, but not by a great deal.

For some sociologists the high rates of absolute mobility are important as they show the way in which class barriers are breaking down. For others the way in which relative mobility rates are fairly constant is important because it shows how Britain remains a society which is dominated by class barriers.

How do we achieve social mobility?

- **Education**

  Getting qualifications and getting a better job than you have now is one of the main ways of becoming upwardly mobile. Likewise if we fail to obtain qualifications we may move down the social scale in relation to our parents.

- **Acquiring new skills**

  This is an important avenue to social mobility. We may acquire skills through work or through education and training that allow us to move up the occupational ladder.

- **Promotion**

  If we are promoted at work we may move out of one social class into another. For example, we may move from routine office work into middle management. A primary school teacher who becomes a head is also upwardly mobile.

- **Marriage**

  A woman who marries someone from a higher social position may be said to be upwardly mobile.

- **Talent**

  Having a particular talent may allow a few people to achieve upward mobility. This applies particularly to people in sport or entertainment.

- **Luck**

  Winning the lottery or the pools can make us very wealthy and increase our 'access to life chances' and can be a way of achieving upward mobility.

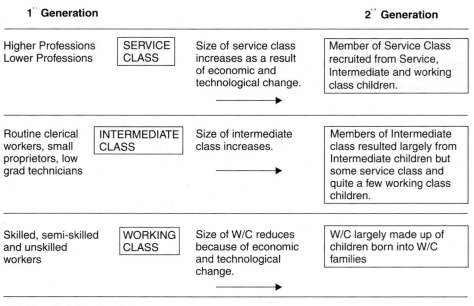

Figure 51 Shift in class make–up.

All of the above are explanations of mobility based upon individuals. They are also mainly ways of achieving upward mobility. We also need to think about some other factors.

One of these is the change **in the occupational structure**. We saw earlier in this chapter how the number of traditional working class jobs has decreased in recent years, and the number of service and intermediate class jobs has increased. This means that there are more jobs available higher up in the class structure and an opportunity for individuals lower down to move upwards to fill vacancies. For some sociologists such changes in the occupational structure are more important in explaining increasing rates of upward mobility than changes in education. But changes in the occupational structure can also mean downward mobility for some people.

What are the obstacles to upward social mobility in Britain? Which groups are likely to face obstacle to upward mobility?

- Discrimination is a major obstacle which is faced particularly by women, members of ethnic minority groups and older people. Women may encounter a 'glass ceiling' (see Chapter 7) at work because of the sexist attitudes of some employers and managers. Black and Asian people may be denied equal opportunities of promotion or employment because of racist attitudes and assumptions (see later in this chapter). Older employees may find it difficult to obtain promotion or a new job because of ageism. (see Chapter 7.)

- Although education is traditionally seen as the means to achieve upward mobility, educational opportunities are not distributed equally amongst the population. Better off members of society may be able to afford a private education for their children but many working class children face the disadvantages outlined in Chapter 3 and fail to obtain as many qualifications as their middle class peers. It is not only working class children who are at a disadvantage in education. Girls and members of some minority ethnic groups also face discrimination.

- Lack of appropriate skills, especially those connected with Information Technology, can be an important obstacle to social mobility. It is not only important to have these skills to get a job, it can be equally important to have them to obtain promotion. Individuals without appropriate training may find they are unable to gain promotion or move to get a better job.

- Some occupations, such as the law, are still dominated by the old boy's network, men, usually, who went to public schools and then to Oxford or Cambridge. People who did not go to these schools and universities may still find it difficult to get in those occupations. This may be because of the culture that is passed down from one generation to the next at these institutions, making it difficult for those who do not understand the norms to get in. It may also be because of the network of social contacts that can be made at the gentlemen's clubs that exist in London whose membership is largely drawn from the public schools.

Why might social class be considered less important today than in the past?

Some sociologists now see social class as a less important source of division in society than it once was. In the past (up to about the end of the 1970s) they say individuals were much more likely to see themselves as belonging to one of the main classes in British society – either working class, middle class or upper class. In other words individuals were likely to have a strong class identity. Sociologists were able to identify distinctive class cultures and indeed much of the comedy on British TV in shows such as *Steptoe and Son*, *Just Good Friends* and the *Likely Lads* was based on class differences.

However, class is said to be in decline both as a source of identity in society and as a source of division in society. It is said by some that we no longer see ourselves as being working class or middle class, and that aspects of social life other than social class are more likely to be potential causes of conflict or division. We can identify a number of reasons for this.

1). Other aspects of inequality in society have become more important, such as gender, ethnicity, age, sexuality, nationality. A woman may feel that it is her gender, not her class, that is the reason why she is paid less than a male colleague. Young unemployed Afro-Caribbean males may well feel that ethnic divisions in society are more responsible for their predicament than class divisions. Pensioners may feel that their interests (in pensions, healthcare etc) arising from their age, unite them more than their class differences divide them. Lesbians and gay men may see the world divided into the homophobic and the non homophobic. Welsh and Scottish nationalists may find that their national identity overrides class differences in a conflict with a government based in England. For many sociologists social class is just one out of a number of possible sources of identity and division.

2). Lifestyle and consumption patterns have become more important to us and can be seen as an important way in which we emphasise the difference between 'us' and the rest. We may share the same access to life chances as our next door neighbours but live in a different way to them. We see ourselves as different because we have a different lifestyle. We're vegetarian; they're meat eaters. We buy furniture from junk shops and do it up; they shop at Ikea. We listen to Radio 4; they listen to a local commercial station. There are a range of possible lifestyles for us to choose from today. Those lifestyles provide us with a sense of our social identity. It is not only sociologists who have identified a variety of lifestyles, advertising agencies do the same thing as a means of selling goods.

Marketing makes tribes of us all

The social classes may be dead but now there is a new range of pigeonholes to put us in, reports Richard Reeves

Observer

Sunday 18 July, 1999

Mods, Hippies, Yuppies, Sloanes, Dinkies, Lombards, New Men, Soft Lads, New Ladettes, Generation X-ers, Generation Y-ers, Wide-boys, Young Fogeys, New Agers, Permakids … the list of labels we hang on ourselves grows almost daily.

It may be that social class is dead (or, as Tony Blair believes, that we are all middle class now), but social classification is alive and kicking. Never before has our society been under such microscopic scrutiny, so prodded, analysed, dissected and polled. Never has our need for a tribal tag been so strong.

Alex McKie, author of a new report, Tribes, says the lack of foundations based on class, occupation, gender or geography fuels our need for new identities.

'There are two factors driving the demand for our own tribes. One is the desire to feel that other people are feeling the same as you. The other is we all want to see the world with ourselves at the centre – to do that we have to know who we are.'

Freer family structures, greater job mobility and greater tolerance have enhanced life choices, says McKie, but at a price. 'There is a sting in the tail. Because there is so much choice and fragmentation, it is easy to feel that you don't belong anywhere at all.'

Hence the hunger for new ways of describing ourselves instead of the old class-based life stories. McKie's report describes the new 'tribes' emerging in Britain, based on survey evidence and focus groups – the factory floor of the booming label industry.

The tribes range from Nomadic Networkers, living and working on the move using high-tech equipment; Barbie Babes, who live by their looks; Elders, who are poor but wise; to Villagers who recreate idealised community life around a welcoming supermarket.

One of the difficulties for the army of social analysts is that one of the strongest social trends of the past 30 years is the desire not to be pigeonholed.

'In the past we could put people in boxes and pretty much rely on them to stay put,' McKie says. 'Now the social classification is more like a solar system, with people rotating around each other at different times. Someone may be part of one tribe during the day, and another altogether at night. It is shifting all the time.'

While advertisers and firms lap up new labels, mainstream social scientists fear that the once noble pursuit of describing the dynamics of society is being degraded by upstart think-tanks and trend-spotters.

McKie admits that the groupings are necessarily subjective. 'Of course there is an arbitrary element to it,' she says. 'But when we are describing culture, lifestyle and attitudes it is hard to be completely academically rigorous.'

But this unscientific categorising for any client who will pay is irritating to academics, who often struggle to interest the media in long-term, meticulous research. Many are critical of this social trendspotting industry.

'It is not social science at all,' says Jonathon Gershuny, head of the Centre for the Study for Micro-Social Change at the University of Essex and a leading quantitative researcher. 'Proper qualitative research is vitally important and goes hand in hand with robust survey evidence. But merely to listen to people you have paid to talk to you in a focus group and base classifications on that is simply bad science.'

Gershuny admits that labels are more accessible than sociological treaties. For example, whoever came up with the label Yuppie to describe young upwardly mobile professionals helped our understanding of a late 20th century phenomenon.

Gershuny worries, however, that the serious side of the profession might be seen as guilty by association, particularly when jokey labels dreamt up by marketing types in wine bars start determining social policy.

'It's great, colourful stuff, and great copy. It's great for everyone except those trying to do serious social science.'

The apparent fragmentation of the middle and working classes is seen by some sociologists as a reason why people no longer see themselves in class terms. The very terms middle class and working class no longer seem to mean what they used to do. Skilled manual workers may well earn more than clerical workers. They may live on the same estates, drive the same cars, take the same holidays as each other. It is harder to distinguish between two great blocks of society than it was in the past, for example in the 1950s and 1960s.

Although class differences may be less visible in some ways, class remains an important division in society for many sociologists because class differences in education and health in particular appear to be remarkably resistant to changes in society. However we define class, the middle class child is still more likely to obtain a university place than the working class child. The middle class child is still more likely to live longer and suffer fewer illnesses than the working class child.

Some of the divisions in society that are said to have replaced class can themselves be said to be the result of class differences. Where we live, what we buy and how we live are all influenced not simply by how much our income is, but also by how much control we have over our lives. Both of these factors are important aspects of class.

Perhaps it is best to see social class as an important factor in the way that society is structured (see Chapter 1). We may not be aware of class differences in our day to day lives but as sociologists we can see how class influences our lives in such a way as to make life easier for some and more of a struggle for others. At times, maybe in extreme circumstances such as the miner's strike, perhaps because of our own particular values or political opinions, some of us may identify ourselves with one class or another, but for most of the time class remains a hidden mechanism producing regular differences in society.

Gender inequality

Inequalities according to gender occur throughout all aspects of social life. Gender inequalities exist within the family, education, work, income, political organisations, our dealings with the law, and in our leisure time. Gender inequalities pervade our society to such an extent that many sociologists feel they are more significant than class inequalities. We can get some idea of their extent by thinking about very small scale social interaction.

In some pubs barstaff will still ask if a half of lager is to be served in a lady's glass (when was the last time you heard anyone ask if a drink was to be served in a gentlemen's glass?) In the same situation a woman may be addressed as 'pet', 'love', or 'darling'; a man as 'mate', 'guv', or 'chief' – words which carry a different message about the status of the person being addressed. Until fairly recently, women have been almost invisible in sociological research. This situation led many feminist researchers referring to mainstream sociology as 'malestream' sociology.

The extent of gender inequalities in Britain

Details of the particular inequalities below can be found in the appropriate chapters, but here is a summary of some important areas of inequality.

- In the family women are still more likely to do most of the housework.
- There may well be different rules for girls and boys about staying out late.
- Women are more likely than men to be the victims of domestic violence.
- After divorce women are more likely to obtain custody of the children than men which can affect their ability to obtain paid work.
- In education although girls are performing better than boys at GCSE and A Level there is still a 'gender bias' in subject choice. This affects future employment chances.
- Although more and more women are entering paid employment women's average pay is still less than men's. Women are more likely than men to be part time workers. Women are most likely to be employed in low paid occupations and they are less likely to obtain promotion.
- Women are more likely than men to experience poverty. Some married women may find their access to welfare benefits is determined by their husband's situation and not their own.
- Women are more likely to feel worried about being the victim of crime than men.
- In politics there are far fewer women MPs than men in parliament.

There are, then, significant inequalities between women and men in modern Britain. As well as describing these inequalities sociologists try to explain them. One possible explanation is that because men and women are different biologically it follows that they will behave differently in society. This explanation says that men and women are naturally different, that women are naturally the ones who stay at home and care for the children because they are genetically programmed to do so.

Many sociologists would reject this idea based on nature and instead put forward an argument based on nurture. Women and men carry out their roles in society because they have learned them through the process of socialisation. So girls learn to be carers and boys learn to be breadwinners. Girls learn that their role in life is primarily a domestic one (their main role is in private life), where boys learn that their role in life is primarily to do with getting somewhere and earning enough to support a family (their main role is in public life, outside the house).

The importance of socialisation for sociologists is that just as we learn our roles, norms and values, people in other societies learn different ones as they are brought up in other cultures. It is also possible for people growing up in a society to learn different roles, norms and values as the society changes.

So we can distinguish between what we are given by nature and what we learn from society some sociologists make a distinction between our sex and gender.

➡ Sex refers to our biology – whether we are biologically male or female.

➡ Gender refers to what we learn through socialisation, about how to be 'feminine' or 'masculine'. This can refer to the roles that we play or the characteristics associated with being feminine or masculine e.g. being emotional or logical, passive or aggressive; intuitive or rational.

Nature or nurture

How do we know if gender roles are biologically determined or learned?

One way of solving this problem is to look at different cultures to see if males and females have the same roles in all cultures.

If we can show that social roles change as society changes then it is likely that our gender roles are learned and not biologically determined.

REAL MEN DON'T EAT QUICHE. THEY BAKE IT.

Will you pamper yourself with L'Oreal this weekend because you're worth it? Will the kitchen floor sparkle after you give it the once-over with the Dyson and a dab of Flash?

You will? Congratulations: you are a typical British man.

As evidence grows that caveman is giving way to man about the house, leading firms are for the first time targeting traditional women's products at the male market.

Forget the "sex, booze and more sex" sales pitch which has been used to sell men anything and everything. Advertisers are adopting the soft sell for the stay at home generation who get their thrills from doing the dusting and cooking.

New research shows more than one third of men are putting on their aprons and elbowing women out of the kitchen. More than half are regular supermarket shoppers.

Melanie Howard, co-founder and director of the Future Foundation, says advertising firms are responding to men's complaints that they are being pigeon holed as lads. "All our research shows that men don't like commercials where they bring home the bacon and the stay-at-home woman cooks the tea."

Adapted from an article in *The Independent*, Nov 2000.

i) This article describes a change in 'the typical British man'. According to the article what actual proportion of men are 'elbowing women out of the kitchen'.

ii) Do you agree that men are changing? What is your evidence?

Socialisation and gender roles

In the not so distant past we would have found it quite easy to write this part of the book. There was a time when it was easy to talk of straightforward gender stereotyping in the home, at school, in the media, and in the workplace. One of the interesting things about doing sociology is that the findings of sociologists can influence who they study. Findings about the way in which school reading schemes, like the old Peter and Jane series, presented stereotypical images of male and female roles led to changes in many reading schemes for young children and a positive attempt to move away from gender stereotypes. While it is true that some parents, schools, teachers, advertising agencies, TV companies and newspapers have made efforts to try and move away from traditional stereotypes, many examples still exist.

The family

Our primary socialisation takes place in the family. If our parents have traditional views on gender roles we are likely to be socialised differently to children in families where parents hold non traditional views on gender. In families with traditional views girls are likely to be dressed in different clothes and colours right from birth. Boys will be given boys' toys (guns, model planes, Meccano, boxing gloves, football games) and girls will be given girls' toys (dolls, tea sets, prams, cookers). There will be one set of rules for boys and a different set for girls.

There are families, perhaps not very numerous, where parents (or the parent) attempt to treat girls and boys in a similar fashion. They may dress babies in neutral colours (not blue or pink); they may seek out unisex toys (such as Lego kits), and encourage daughters and sons to do equal shares of the housework.

We also learn from role models in the family. There are increasing numbers of children growing up in families where both parents work. Not only do increasing numbers of women work full time, but more members of the labour force work flexible hours. In a traditional family setting the father who went out to work was the role model for his son, the mother whose main role was a domestic one was the role model for her daughter. While it is likely that this is still the norm in some families the situation is changing.

There are increasing numbers of lone parent families where there is only one role model for the children – usually a woman – and in those two parent families where both parents work it may be that dad cooks the tea as often as mum, or that dad picks the kids up from school when it is his turn. These tasks are still likely to be seen as the women's in the majority of families, but again things may be changing. What do you think?

Our peer group is also important in our gender role socialisation. The girl who acts like a 'tom boy' may be teased by some of her friends for not being feminine enough. There is likewise a great deal of pressure on boys and young men to act in a 'macho' fashion. They have to look 'cool' and act tough even when they don't feel like it or risk being an outcast in their particular group. Young boys will avoid being called a 'cissy' and older boys may feel they have to conform to the norms of masculinity for fear of being thought effeminate.

Other aspects of gender socialisation are dealt with in the chapters on Education and Crime Deviance and Conformity. You may wish to read these sections now.

Ethnicity and inequality

We live in a multi-ethnic society. Perhaps most of the time we don't think about it, but it would be difficult to talk about everyday life in Britain today without acknowledging the influence of a wide range of ethnic differences – the people, the shops, the mosques, synagogues, churches, the banks, the restaurants and cafe's – our everyday life is affected by many different cultures in many different ways.

Fish and chips is no longer our most popular meal – it is curry. But it isn't just our national taste for curry that shows the multi-ethnic nature of society. Most small towns will have an Indian and a Chinese restaurant; there may also be a Caribbean or a Thai one too. We can stop off at a cafe and drink Italian cappuccino together with a French pain au chocolat or a Jewish bagel. If we fancy a night out listening to music, what will we choose? American rock, pop, blues or rap? A night in an Irish bar listening to airs, jigs and reels? Pehaps some Rai, Soukouss or Township Jive? If we want a quiet night in reading a book what will we choose? The poems of Benjamin Zephaniah or perhaps a novel by Zadie Smith or Kazuo Ishiguro? Maybe we'd rather watch TV – *Goodness Gracious Me* is on, or maybe we'd rather watch someone show us how to do Cajun cooking.

At the end of the day we might fancy a drink at our local – an English pint? A rum? (Jamaican or Cuban?); a lager? (Belgian, French, Australian, Jamaican?), tequila? vodka? It isn't just the mix of people that makes society multi ethnic. As individuals we are all multi ethnic to a degree – in our habits, as we've outlined above, as well as in our communities or neighbours. Read the followng extract:

> This has been the century of strangers, brown, yellow and white. This has been the century of the great immigrant experiment. It is only this late in the day that you can walk into a playground and find Isaac Leung by the fish pond, Danny Rahman in the football cage, Quang O'Rourke bouncing a basketball, and Irie Jones humming a tune. Children with first and last names on a direct collision course. Names that secrete within them mass exodus, cramped boats and planes, cold arrivals, medical checks. It is only this late in the day that you can find best friends Sita and Sharon constantly mistaken for each other because Sita is white (her mother liked the name) and Sharon is Pakistani (her mother thought it best – less trouble). Yet despite all the mixing up, despite the fact that we have slipped into each other's lives with reasonable comfort...despite all this it is still hard to admit that there is no one more English than the Indian, no one more Indian than the English. There are still young white men who are angry about that; who will roll out at closing time into the poorly lit streets with a kitchen knife wrapped in a tight fist.
>
> From *White Teeth*, Zadie Smith, Hamish Hamilton 2000 p.281–282.

Read the extract again and answer the following questions:

i)   Why do you think the author talks about children whose first and last names are on 'a direct collision course'?

ii) What evidence is there for ethnic conflict in the extract?

iii) What evidence is there in your area that 'we have slipped into each other's lives with reasonable comfort'?

We are all members of an ethnic group. This section is about how members of some minority ethnic groups suffer various forms of inequality in our society. In terms of access to life chances the most significant types of inequality are those connected with education, work, and housing. Education is the key to a career: the money we earn from our job can affect both where we live and how we live. Losing out in education can mean losing out in both housing and work. Alongside education housing and work goes access to justice. As we have already seen in Chapter 4 many members of ethnic minority groups are denied equal access to justice – either in terms of not having complaints believed, or being stopped and searched too often. All of these factors can affect our quality of life. But the major factor affecting the quality of life of members of ethnic minority groups is racism. Racism leads to unequal treatment in schools, jobs, housing, and in relation to law. Racism can affect our lives in many ways from the violence of racist attacks with the inevitable consequences of fear and anxiety, to the more casual even unintended 'joke' or offensive or insulting remark. If our access to life chances are defined as our chances of obtaining what society thinks is good and avoiding what is bad, then the very existence of racism means that to be a member of a group that is subject to racism is to be unequal.

Racism adds a layer of extra inequality to inequalities that already exist. However all of the inequalities experienced by members of minority ethnic groups cannot be explained by racism alone. There are inequalities of class, for example, in the education system. There are inequalities of gender within families, and there are inequalities of age in terms of access to work. The experiences of all members of society are best understood in terms of the way that their gender, class, age, and ethnicity interact. For example to be a middle class, middle aged Asian male may mean that we have the money, because of our class position, to insulate us against many forms of inequality. We can drive to work so we don't have to hear remarks on the street. We can choose where we live and perhaps avoid the worst kind of neighbourhoods but we may not be able to avoid the attitudes of our neighbours. Class inequalities will make others more vulnerable to the effects of racism. Without money our lives are more public and less private. We'll have to use public transport, if we can't afford cars or taxis. We're more likely to live in rented houses or flats which have less privacy, and we may have to spend a lot of our time waiting in public spaces for benefit claims to be sorted or even just to make a phone call. For some of us these kinds of class inequalities can make us more exposed to some aspects of gender or ethnic inequalities – the sexist remark, the verbal abuse. Of course racist and sexist attitudes can have the effect of magnifiying class inequalities, if we can't get a job because we are black or because we are female. In these situations our status gets in the way of our access to life chances. Our status can affect our class position.

Where does racism come from?

As we said in Chapter 1, we all belong to social groups. The groups we belong to are mostly made up of 'people like us'. We are the 'insiders' and we can recognise 'outsiders'. Outsiders are often viewed with suspicion, if not always hostility. In small communities, especially in rural areas, people may still be referred to as 'incomers' even though they have lived in that community for ten or 15 years. Strangers and outsiders are 'not like us'. They may have different accents or languages, eat different food, worship different gods or no god at all, or wear different clothes – they have different norms and values. Outsiders and strangers can sometimes be seen as a threat. In small rural communities 'townies' or 'incomers' may be seen as posing a threat to the way 'things have always been done around here'. Problems can be blamed on outsiders – they've changed the way things were. If the strangers or outsiders also have a different coloured skin they are more visible, easy to see, easy to identify as outsiders and easy to blame because they are different.

It is one thing to enter a community or society where you are viewed as a stranger. It is another to enter a society which is likely to see you not only as different but also as something 'less' than the 'native' population.

History, culture and 'rank'

The history of the British Empire can help us to see why some people might regard individuals or groups as being automatically of a lower status. The colonisation of many countries was justified on the grounds that the 'natives' were less civilised than the white man. The white man was thought to be superior and it was 'the white man's burden' to bring civilisation to the supposedly less civilised peoples of the colonies.

The barbarity of slavery could be justified if the slaves were thought of as inferiors. These kinds of thoughts were made easier to hold in a culture where 'white' stood for goodness and purity and 'black' stood for the negative and the bad. For example in British culture the white knight rescues the damsel in distress, the bride gets married in white, the black prince is evil and we talk of 'black days', 'blacklegs' and 'black' meaning dirty – all negative associations. These ideas existed before many British people came into contact with black people and so it made it easy to see them as something alien and threatening.

In the 19th century it was widely believed (at least in Europe) that the 'races' (see Chapter 4) could be categorised and ranked. The white 'race' was seen by many (whites) to be superior to the black 'race'. Today such ideas are known to be without scientific foundation but the three elements of history, culture and ideas of ranking can still influence how people think.

Stereotypes and scapegoats

When things go wrong we like to find someone to blame, and it is usually easy to blame the 'outsider', someone who is different. If we have only come across stereotypical and negative images of the 'outsider' then this process is easy.

If the mass media constantly refer to 'bogus' asylum seekers we are likely to imagine they are all fraudulent. We will stereotype the asylum seeker as someone looking for an easy time at our expense, especially if we never meet any, and we are likely to be mistrustful about stories of oppression, of beatings, torture, rape and murder in the countries from which they have fled. If politicians speak on television about the country being 'swamped' by people of another culture we may see them as a threat.

Figure 52 Asylum seekers can easily become the target of stereotyping.

These kinds of feelings can be exaggerated if somehow we feel that we are in competition with 'outsiders' for houses, jobs or education. The 'outsider', the immigrant, the black Britons, can find themselves blamed for the decline of the neighbourhood, for high rates of unemployment and for declining standards of education. They can become the scapegoats, the people who get the blame for problems in society, especially if those problems are complex and difficult to unravel. It is easier to find a simple solution – to find a scapegoat.

The causes of racism are themselves complex. Racism is connected with British history and culture, with discredited ideas about 'race' from the 19th century, with the process of stereo-typing and scapegoating.

The charts on page 210 show the make up of the population of Britain by ethnic groups. What they do not show is the different age profiles of different groups.

The minority ethnic group population is younger than the white population. In 1997 6.4% of the population as a whole belonged to a minority ethnic group but 9.1% of the total population under 25 did.

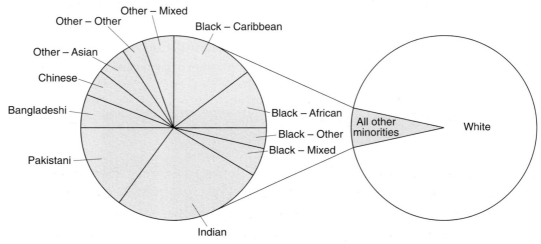

Source: Population Trends, Office for National Statistics. © Crown Copyright 1999.

Figure 53 Composition of the British population by ethnic group, 1997.

Housing

There are two aspects of housing to think about: where your house is; what kind of house you live in.

Figure 54 shows the distribution of ethnic groups in the worst off and better off areas.

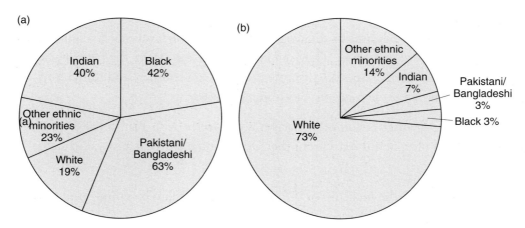

Source: Department of the Environment, English Housing Survey. © Crown Copyright.

Figure 54 Population by type of area – percentage of population living (a) in council estates and low income areas, and (b) in affluent suburban areas 1994–95

There are many reasons for the patterns shown in the charts above, and you should read Chapter 9 on Migration and Movement together with this section.

● **Institutional racism**

The rules that many local councils had regarding who could obtain a council house or flat in the 1950s and 1960s meant that many minority group members were unable to get housing. The rule was that you had to be resident in the area for two years even to get onto the waiting list. This rule meant that if you'd just arrived in the country to take up a job you couldn't get a council house. The result was to put minority ethnic group members at a disadvantage.

- **House prices**
  Unable to rent from the council many individuals bought houses. They tended to buy houses in the inner city areas because they were cheaper. These houses haven't gone up in price which makes it hard for people to move away.

- **Cultural factors**
  Large urban areas are more likely to have the facilities that people want. If these are specialised – like access to a mosque, specialist food shops, clothes shops, specialist day centres or interpreters, for example – people may choose to stay in the areas where they know the facilities exist. So although the area might be seen as deprived many of the minority ethnic members that live there may well not be deprived themselves. Many professionals, for example, will continue to live in the area so that they can use the facilities which might not exist in the suburbs or the countryside.

- **Increased risk of racial harassment**
  An important factor that prevents many minority group members from moving out into the suburbs and rural areas even though they can afford to do so is that they fear the increased likelihood of racial harassment. Without the support of friends and community individuals may well be wary of being exposed to increased levels of racism.

Signs of change?

One way of finding out if racism is declining in society is to look at popular leisure pursuits. If members of all ethnic groups are represented in popular pursuits and are able to enjoy themselves without harassment then we could say that racism has declined significantly. Professional football is one such activity. Thousands go to support their team each week (both males and increasingly females) and there are many black players.

So what is the situation in football?

Racial abuse aimed at black or foreign players at football grounds is still rife, according to university researchers who carried out a survey of 33,000 fans.

Fans from Everton, Rangers and Celtic topped the league table for the largest number of racist comments heard, the survey found.

Arsenal, Charlton Athletic and Wimbledon won praise for reducing racism through campaigns inside their grounds, but according to Sean Perkins of the Sir Norman Chester Centre for football research at Leicester University, racism overall has remained much the same since the last survey, in the 1996–97 season. . .

Dr Perkins said that although abuse overall did not appear to have diminished, it did seem to be changing. More overt abuse such as throwing bananas on to the pitch and groups chanting abuse was rarer, and most examples were confined to individual bigots. . . .

'The fact that racist abuse in all its forms is being reported so readily could be an encouraging sign that the high profile campaigns make people aware it is going on, he said.

Since the 1980s, however, football has tackled racism. Many clubs have signed up to anti-racist initiatives and tried to attract non-white fans to their grounds. Figures continue to show that few black fans attend matches.

The campaign is led by Kick it Out, which has enlisted the help of leading footballers to highlight racism, organises anti-racist days at the clubs, had Kick It Out banners erected at the clubs, and is launching an anti-racist campaign.

The chart below reflects the scale of the problem.

Racism on the terraces

Club	Value
Everton	38
Rangers	36
Celtic	33
West Ham	32
Newcastle	31
Blackburn	29
Sheffield Wednesday	28
Leicester	27
Middlesbrough	27
Liverpool	26
Tottenham	26
Chelsea	24
Leeds	23
Aston Villa	22
Coventry	21
Nottingham Forest	20
Manchester United	20
Arsenal	16
Southampton	16
Derby	14
Charlton	12
Wimbledon	11

From an article in *The Guardian* 7.1.2000 by Paul Brown and Vivek Chandary.

Figure 55 Percentage of fans who heard racist abuse directed at players.

Questions

i) What evidence is there in the extract above that racism is declining or changing?

ii) What evidence is there in the extract that racism is still a serious problem in football?

iii) How successful do you think campaigns like Kick It Out can be?

This section of the chapter has looked at only two aspects of inequality. You can read about differences and inequalities in education, work, crime, politics, migration and family in the relevant chapters.

Age inequality

As you read this you are getting older. Ageing is something we cannot escape. But we need to distinguish between different views of the ageing process. The most straightforward way of thinking about ageing is in chronological terms. Our **chronological age** is simply the number of years we have been alive. There are often legal restrictions on what we can or cannot do which are defined in terms of our chronological age. At 17 we can drive a car, at 18 we can vote, at 60 or 65 we can retire.

We can also think about age in **biological** terms. We go through particular physical changes according to our age. When we are chronologically quite young we go through the process of puberty and as we get older we develop wrinkles and our hair turns grey, we may also lose some of our physical strength.

Sociologists, though, are interested in the way in which different age groups are treated in society. For sociologists 'age' is a 'social construct'. What that means is that the expectations we have of what is appropriate for a person of a particular age may well vary from culture to culture and over a period of time.

Read the extract below. The girl concerned was born in 1848.

Lucy Luck – Straw Plait Worker

Well I was not quite nine years old, when I was sent back to Tring to work in the silk mills . . .

The first day I went to work I was so frightened at the noise of the work and so many wheels flying around, that I dared not pass the rooms where men only were working, but stood still and cried. But, however, I had to go, and I was passed on to what was called the fourth room.

I was too little to reach my work and so had to have what was called a wooden horse to stand on. At that time children under 11 years of age were only supposed to work a half-day, and go to school the other half. But I did not get many half days at school, as Mr D. was a tailor by trade, so I had to stop at home in the afternoon to help with the work. But I have never been sorry for that, for I learned a lot by it. Neither was I 11 when I had to work all day at the mill.

From *A little of my life* London Mercury, edited by J.C, Squire

---

Q u e s t i o n

How would we regard a nine-year-old doing this kind of work today?

This extract shows us how expectations of particular age groups change over time:

No one could fail to notice Joseph's standing in the community. Dealings with him (as with the elderly in many societies) are marked by a jocular respect, a celebration of an old man's importance and authority . . . And from time to time the young men call on his authority: is this the

line along which to cut a horse's hooves? Do you ever find Lynx on such and such a hillside? . . .
He had not only the expertise but also the authority of his 80 some years.

(from Brodice H (86) *Maps and Dreams* p 24 Faber and Faber. Quoted in Bradley H

In a society like ours we can identify two age groups who generally have a lower status than others: the young and the old.

We are probably all familiar with songs such as 'My Generation' by The Who with its reference to 'hope I die before I get old'. We're probably familiar with the way older workers talk about 'being on the scrapheap' and we are probably familiar with stereotypical views of older people as cantankerous old so and so's with nothing better to do than complain, especially about the younger generation. We may also be familiar with the lack of status given to young people in our society. Young people are often seen as feckless and irresponsible, idle and rebellious.

There are two important questions we can ask: why do the young and the old have lower status? Are the stereotypes accurate?

Dependency and age

Look at the table below:

	Wages and salaries, plus self-employment	Social security benefits (excl disability benefits)	Social security disability benefits	State retirement pension plus any income support	Other pensions	Investments and other sources
Age	%	%	%	%	%	%
16-24	68	15	1	-	-	16
25-34	87	9	1	-	-	3
35-44	88	7	1	-	-	3
45-54	86	4	2	-	3	5
55-59	75	5	5	1	10	6
60-64	54	5	7	6	21	8
65-74	18	4	5	35	28	9
75-84	9	8	6	43	25	9
85+	5	11	8	46	21	9
All	73	6	3	6	7	5

Table 3.2 Components of gross weekly household income, by age of head, Great Britain, 1997-98

Source: Department of Social Security Family Resources Survey Great Britain 1997/98, table 3.3

Figure 56 Components of gross weekly household income.

Q u e s t i o n

i)   Which age groups were most reliant on sources of income other than wages, salaries or self employment?

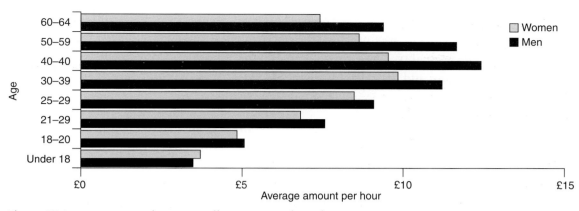

Figure 57 Average pay per hour according to age and gender.

Questions

i) Which age groups had the highest average earnings per hour?

ii) What is the relationship between men's and women's earnings?

The information in the tables can help us to explain the relatively low status of young people and old people. Both belong to dependent age groups.

Children are obviously dependent upon their parents but they are increasingly dependent upon both their parents and the state once they reach school leaving age. Child benefit continues to be paid in respect of young people over the age of 16 continuing in full time education. Young people on training schemes receive money from the state. Students at universities may well have to rely more upon their parents than they did in the past now that maintenance grants have been abolished and (in England and Wales at least) there are possibly contributions to tuition fees to be made. Because young people in work lack experience their wages are often lower than older, more experienced workers, similarly they do not have the experience necessary to obtain promotion.

People over 60 and 65 qualify for state retirement pensions (and may also have occupational pensions) but may well find their opportunities for employment limited because of ageism (see Chapter 7). The elderly may also be more dependent on the state or on the local authority for a range of services. We are more likely to suffer ill health as we get older, we may require specialist services like meals on wheels or sheltered accommodation.

In a society like ours where our identities are connected to what we do, to our occupations, to the fact that we are productive, it is perhaps easy to see how those who are not productive will have a lower status than those who are. Young people and older people form significant parts of the dependent population.

We cannot generalise about the status of all young people and all older people, however. The class position of some young people and some older people will make them less dependent on others. Gender differences will also affect how dependent we are on others – most lone parents are women and women have a longer life expectancy than men. Likewise ethnicity can affect the degree of inequality we experience – see the sections on poverty and fear of crime.

As with all aspects of inequality we cannot, as sociologists, examine age inequality by itself. We have to take into account the way in which other sociological variables interact with age to produce patterns of inequality. The retired company director with a large house that is paid for, with a company pension and considerable savings is likely to enjoy greater access to life chances than the retired labourer living in council accommodation on a state pension.

Throughout this book there are references to stereotyping – gender stereotyping, ethnic stereotyping and teacher expectations based on stereotypes of working class pupils, for example. By looking at the dependent nature of the elderly population we are in danger of adding to those stereotypes.

Poverty

What is poverty?

Everyone reading this book will have some idea of what poverty is. Our experiences put us into contact with poverty either at first or second hand – perhaps both. We may ourselves be living in poverty. We may have neighbours or friends who are in poverty. We may encounter those in poverty at school or church, through paid or voluntary work. We may see obviously poor people when we go to town or for a walk in a park. We read articles, hear or see documentaries about poverty in the media.

All of us have a sense of what poverty looks like: it is an old man wearing three threadbare jackets laying out the cardboard he sleeps on in a shop doorway; four-year-olds playing in a burnt out wreck of a car outside a dilapidated tower block or a teenager shabbily dressed in last year's fashion who is the only one in the class not putting their hand up to go on a school trip. We might even have a sense of what poverty smells like. Standing in a post office queue or sitting on a bus next to someone who cannot afford to have a frequent bath, change into clean clothes regularly or buy deodorants is an unfortunately memorable experience. From these impressions and images those of us who are not in poverty can work out that poverty is about being without.

At this point in a sociology text book the reader would generally be introduced to sociological definitions of poverty. Having clear definitions is vital. 'One in five British children are in poverty' will mean something only if you know what poverty is. Such quantitative information about how much, how many, or what percentage plays a crucial part in helping sociologists to understand and explain what is going on in society.

It is important, however, not to forget that out there are people for whom poverty is not the definition typed on a page but day after day, week after week, possibly year after year of deprivation. Few sociologists have lived in poverty. Along with many in society they stand outside poverty looking in at it. Through observation, questionnaire and interview much information about what it is like to be in poverty can be gathered. You should recognise, however, the limitations of the information. Ask yourself to what extent the question 'what is it really like to be poor?' can be answered by using these methods. Consider what additional information a sociologist might gain from living in poverty for two or three years, practising participant observation. However sensitive a sociologist might be, the disparity between the situation of the person doing the research and those in poverty make understanding difficult. A sociologist might spend an afternoon with someone in poverty, visit their house on a run down estate to conduct an interview. After the interview the sociologist goes back to his or her home in a 'better' part of town. It is worth reminding yourself of this, particularly when any sociologist, politician or newspaper editor claims that there is no real poverty in Britain today, or dismisses those in poverty as idle scroungers.

SUFFER THE CHILDREN

Stuart is 10, he has a hyperactivity disorder and lives in Beeston, Leeds, with his mum and little brother in a house overrun with mice.

Stuart says "My mum cries if she needs food and hasn't got enough money. It makes me sad. I don't like my mum crying. All people need food . . . Bad people came to our house and took my tape, records and TV and my mum's brand new shoes. They set fire to our house . . . Some other kids beat me up and say I've got second hand clothes on It's not just me, my friend's mum doesn't have a lot of money either. But if they say my mum's mean I beat them up."

The following are the words of a mum, 27 years old with three children Jake 11 months, Wesley 6, Thomas 4: "They put me on the ninth floor with three kids. I have to keep all the windows locked and it's so cold. Jake always has numb hands and feet. The schools around here are terrible. Yesterday this little boy goes up and punches Wesley in the face. Another time Jake got it when he was in the playground. I mean he's just a baby, he ain't done nothing wrong . . .

This area is scum. You see old people getting pushed over, people breaking into people's houses, my door's been kicked in three times. A baby fell out of the block the other week . . .

My best mate, she's a big woman, six feet tall, she got mugged outside the post office. They nicked her child benefit book. If my kids ever mugged an old lady i'd break their fucking legs. You've got to give kids values . . .

I'm cracking up. I keep telling them but no one will help me".

Adapted from an article by Nadene Ghouri in the *Big Issue*, 21–27 February 2000

Kinds of poverty

If poverty means going or being without it is obviously possible to use the word in a variety of contexts. Religious leaders may warn us about the '**spiritual poverty**' of the present consumption-focused age or the '**moral poverty**' of global commercial enterprises concerned only with producing large dividends for shareholders. 'Green' groups may argue that the economic growth on which rising consumption is based is leading to '**environmental**' poverty. Some critics of the mass media suggest that the desire to attract large readerships of audiences is leading to 'dumbing down' and '**cultural poverty**'. All of these poverties raise issues of interest for sociologists.

Our principal concern here, however, is with **material poverty** – lacking things or the money to buy things. Until the1950s material poverty was seen essentially as destitution. A person was in poverty if his or her income was not sufficient to buy enough food, warmth or shelter to maintain his or her body in a healthy – physically efficient – state. This is absolute poverty. To work out the income level – poverty line below which a person would be in absolute poverty – a researcher would have taken the following steps:

→ He or she would have consulted a medical expert who could say how many vitamins, carbohydrates, proteins and so on a typically active person needs in a week to stay healthy.

→ He or she would have consulted a dietician who could say what quantity and sort of food would supply these vitamins as cheaply as possible.

→ He or she would have gone round the shops to see how much this food would cost.

→ He or she would have added a small amount for clothes, heating and shelter. In this way a **poverty line** could be calculated.

It is worth noting that sociologists were not amongst those whose expertise were needed to calculate the poverty line. There is no recognition here that people live in a society and therefore have cultural and social needs. So far as the absolute definition of poverty is concerned the human being is just a biological machine. Anyone with sufficient income to fuel that machine and keep it in working order is not in poverty!

Since the 1960s poverty has been defined and measured in ways which recognise that people do live in a society. As a member of society an individual comes to expect to do certain things and be certain things. Other members of society expect the individual to do certain things, have certain things, and be certain things. In this way people share and recognise that they should share a way of life even though there may be different patterns within it. A poor elderly woman in the UK might, for example, expect and want to give her grandson a little present at Christmas. If she goes without her meals for two days in order to save some money to pay for it, what do we think? That she has strange priorities and is wasting money that should be spent on fuel for her biological machine? Not really. She is doing what grandmas do in our society. Her desire to be a good grandma is more powerful than her biological need to eat. If this is so the absolute measure of poverty is inadequate. It makes little sense to focus on biological-physical needs whilst disregarding social needs, which for real people are just as important or more important.

Relative poverty

Sociologists have therefore developed the concept of **relative poverty**: an individual is in poverty when his or her standard of living is significantly below that considered normal in the society in which he or she lives. An individual is poor relative to or compared with others who live in the same society. The higher the general standard of living in society, the more and better possessions an individual will need to avoid being in poverty. In Britain in the 1950s not having a television was not an indication that someone was poor. Today, with television viewing being such an important part of everyday life, not having access to one could perhaps be a sign of poverty. It is not true that everyone without a television set is in poverty. A small number of people choose not to spend their money in that way, believing that there are more important things to do with their money and their lives. Poverty is to do with not being able to afford, not with not wanting something.

Some politicians have at times expressed reservations about the concept of relative poverty. It is easy to understand why: if we measure poverty in relative terms there will be greater numbers of people in poverty than if we use the absolute poverty measure. Poverty embarrasses governments and they want to find as little of it as possible. Despite this the relative measure has become widely accepted by governments and official bodies as well as by sociologists.

BRITAIN SHAMED BY CHILD POVERTY

A report by Unicef, the children's arm of the United nations, says that Britain has one of the worst records on childhood poverty in the industrialised world. Nearly 20% of young people – between 3 and 4 million – live in families which are below the official poverty line – judged on household income below half average earnings.

Adapted from an article by Kamal Ahmed in the *Observer,* 11 June 2000.

Its use, however, is not without problems. Comparisons can on the face of it be confusing and seem to go against common sense. Many people would have been surprised to read that a higher percentage of children are in poverty in the United Kingdom than in Turkey, Poland or Hungary. After all the general standard of living in the last three countries is lower than in Britain. Such a statistic is surprising, however, only if poverty is thought of in absolute terms. Clearly more people who are hungry and destitute can be expected in poorer countries.

Once the idea of relative poverty is understood the surprise disappears. Relative poverty involves a comparison between the lowest incomes with the average income in the society. If there is a higher proportion of British children in relative poverty it means that a higher proportion of British children live in households with incomes which are much less than the average. The average income in Turkey, Poland and Hungary is lower than the average income in Britain, but a higher proportion of households than in Britain receive an income closer to that of the average. Relative poverty is to do with how much inequality there is in a society rather than how well off the society is.

Poverty and its duration

The consequences for an individual or family receiving an income below the poverty line will depend very much on the length of time the income remains at such a low level. It can sometimes be useful when describing the situation of the poor in Britain to recognise this by distinguishing between **long term** and **short term poverty**. Someone whose income falls below the poverty line for a month is unlikely to be faced with the same problems as someone who has endured poverty for a year. At the start of a period of receiving an income below the poverty line an individual or family have savings and the clothes and household goods and so on that were bought before their income dropped. These help to maintain their standard of living during the early months. As time passes, however, clothes wear out, household equipment needs to be mended or replaced, putting pressure on the low income. If money has to be borrowed interest payments add further pressure. This pressure can be intense if the poor are rejected as 'bad risks' by 'respectable' lenders. They may be forced to turn to loan sharks who charge huge rates of interest and who may use violence to enforce repayment. It may no longer be possible to run a car, making bulk buying at distant superstores impossible – even if the money could be found to bulk buy. Having to buy a bit now and a bit later can be expensive.

In this way having an income below the poverty line for week after week makes it much more difficult for an individual or family to keep control over their finances. The kind of planning by which the better off try to make sure they get value for money becomes less possible. Being poor can be expensive not only because good financial management becomes difficult but because it can create expenses. Getting through another day might be possible only with the help of cigarettes, drink or harder drugs, the consumption of which can be costly 'habits' – as can gambling, which might come to be seen as a way out. The poor have not only the problems which led them to being poor in the first place; being poor itself presents them with further problems. 'Poverty trap' seems not too strong a phrase to describe these problems.

Who are the poor?

Perhaps the best starting point for an answer is another question: what are the main sources of personal income in our society? The answer: income may come from paid work, welfare benefits or from savings. Those most likely to be in poverty are those least likely to be in a job for which they receive a decent wage and other rewards – a pension, use of car, for example; those least likely to be receiving adequate welfare benefits; those least likely to have substantial savings.

Approached in this way it is the **children** who are the most vulnerable. Babies are not capable of working and the hours older children can spend doing paid work are legally restricted. Benefits are not paid directly to children. Few children have direct access to substantial savings. The material situation of a child depends very much on the adults with whom the child lives; whether a child suffers poverty depends on the income of those adults and on how they choose to spend that income.

Because children do not have an income of their own it can be difficult to calculate accurately the numbers in poverty. From taxation or welfare benefit records the number of households receiving an income below the poverty line can be estimated. What cannot be known, however, without rather intrusive investigation, is how that income is distributed within the household. In a household of two adults and two children an income below the poverty line could be distributed in such a way that the adults suffered severe material deprivation whilst the children were at least warm, well fed and properly clothed. Even so the adults would not be able to protect the children from the problems arising from living in poor housing in a poor area. None the less the situation would be significantly different from that of children in a poor household in which the adults spent most of the income on themselves. It is of course possible for children to suffer at least some aspects of material poverty in a household that has an income above the poverty line if the adults choose not to spend sufficient money on them.

Because children are such a dependent section of society child poverty seems to be particularly distressing. A child cannot bring his or her poverty on him or herself. Children are poor because of the actions or inactions of others, whether parents or people in the wider society. Child poverty is also worrying since it can so easily, and in so many ways, make it difficult for the child to develop to his or her potential. Child poverty can in this way damage the future of society.

PERSISTANT PEST

The children who are currently poor may include someone whose dad is newly unemployed who has fallen on hard times for a few months but who will shortly bounce back with a well paid job, and a child in a lone parent family who has been poor since birth. The longer a child is poor, the greater the deprivation entailed. Moreover, poverty during childhood has long term effects, reducing the chances of being successful in adult life.

During 1991–1996 more than one in five pre school children lived in households where the income was below the poverty line for at least half of this period, compared to just one in 10 people in the population as a whole.

Adapted from an article in *The Guardian* Society.

Another section of society vulnerable to poverty because of its lack of access to an earned income is the **retired elderly**. Some may be in a similar or near total dependency – very like children. Severe physical disability or mental incapacity can make it impossible for some elderly individuals to run their own lives. They are vulnerable to unscrupulous relatives or others who may be handling their affairs. Most of the retired elderly are in a position to manage their own lives. Income may come from welfare benefits, savings or other sources such as company pension schemes.

It is important to recognise that whilst many of the retired elderly may be poor, many are not. Some will be amongst the richest individuals in society. The elderly retired whose only income is the retirement pension, or other state welfare benefits, are likely to have an uncomfortably poor old age. Those who, in addition to what the state pension provides, have income from other pension schemes, and savings and investments may have a very high standard of living until they die. If you find it impossible to avoid using stereotypes when discussing the situation of the elderly, recognise at least two: an elderly 85-year-old woman in a council flat counting her pennies, unable to afford to keep warm in winter let alone afford a holiday, who has to make little sacrifices in order to keep intact the savings which will just cover the cost of a respectable burial. The other a 70-year-old couple who holiday abroad for six weeks a year, spend money regularly on their home and garden, help their grandchildren financially when at university. Whichever stereotype fits best the reality of an elderly individual's life will be linked to the following factors:

- The **age** of an elderly retired person will be important. The older he or she is the more years will have passed since the last wage packet was received. During this time savings may well have been used up or their value reduced by inflation. Health may have declined, putting the elderly person in the position of having to buy care as relatives and neighbours, themselves becoming more frail, are no longer able to provide it. A person's age indicates which times he or she has lived through. The working lives of most ordinary people aged 80 or more in 2000 are unlikely to have left them at retirement with great savings or a company or private pension. People of this age lived through the economic depression of the 1930s which produced mass unemployment, and the Second World War. For a large proportion of their working life wages were low and very few employers provided pension schemes.

- **Gender** is also important. Whilst women under 35 may expect to approach their retirement on a footing almost equal to men, this was an unrealisic expectation for their mothers and inconceivable for their grandmothers. For much of the 20th century women tended to rely on their husbands from altar to coffin. With access to well paid, long term employment restricted by social expectations and discrimination women over 60 are unlikely to have accumulated large savings or pension rights to see them through their years as elderly people. It is also significant that women tend to live longer than men – they have longer to become or stay poor.

- Finally, and obviously, the kind of job which an individual has had during his or her working life is important. Some people are paid as much each week as others earn in a year. This kind of money is able to support not only a high standard of living in the present but also allows large sums to be invested to provide for a high standard of living in retirement. What is more, those who receive high pay also tend to receive lots of 'perks' or extras, one of the commonest of which is a large retirement pension. For such people the National Insurance retirement pension, on which millions of pensioners have to survive is an irrelevance, simply 'beer money'. Inequalities established in working lives thus continue in retirement.

The economic situation of many elderly retired is made worse by their not claiming benefits to which they are entitled. There may be several reasons for this. Some pensioners may remember their parents talking about the shame of receiving handouts under the old 'poor law'. Even though people today have a 'right' to benefits – which they have paid for through their National Insurance contributions – old ideas remain powerful. Many elderly people would hate to be thought of and to think of themselves as 'charity cases'. Others may not be aware of benefits which may be available to them. Some elderly people – particularly the older ones – may not have contact with people who know about such things. With failing eyes, legs and ears it may be difficult for them to read information circulars, contact 'Age Concern' ask at the Post Office or Citizens Advice Bureau. They may not, therefore, find out about new benefits for which they are eligible.

Bringing home a decent wage on a regular basis is the best way to avoid being in poverty. With a wage an individual can avoid being in poverty in the present and perhaps put something aside to help avoid it later in life. To answer the question 'which sections of the working age population are most likely to suffer poverty?' ask yourself what makes it more likely and less likely that someone will be able to earn a decent wage regularly. The following factors suggest themselves:

- **Possessing qualifications, skills, experience** make it easier to earn a decent wage. Jobs that require skill tend to be better paid and, so far as having a job at all is concerned, a skilled person can always apply for an unskilled job whilst the reverse is not true. Of course having skills does not guarantee a decent job. What economists – who seldom seem to be unemployed – celebrate as 'restructuring' industry or the economy can leave thousands of well trained men and women without a job as the global market determines that coal will be mined in Poland, ships built in Korea, or cloth woven in the Far East. Over the past 30 years boilermakers, coalface workers, pattern makers and weavers have become part of our past. Their importance is still proclaimed in the names of some public houses but the only context in which a few have opportunities to use their skills is for the education and entertainment of tourists in industrial museums. Nonetheless, it is possible to make the generalisation that the more skilled the less likely someone is to become unemployed and face poverty.

- **Being responsible** for the care of young children – or a sick or elderly relative – can make it more difficult to earn a decent wage. Such responsibilities which are still more likely to fall on women than men can severely restrict the time that is possible to be away from the home earning money. Full time work might be impossible as might taking on well paid jobs unless it is close to home. Significant care commitments may make it difficult to establish the continuity of employment or undertake the out of hours training necessary for promotion to a better paid position. It might, of course, be possible to leave a child with a relative or pay for childcare. The latter may be expensive. Alternatively childcare can be combined with paid work through 'home working'. Most of those who employ homeworkers, however, recognise the very weak position of their workers and pay them very little.

- Being chronically sick can make it more difficult to earn a decent wage as can being a member of a group against which employers – and perhaps society in general – may discriminate. People with disabilities might be quite capable of doing a job but might find it impossible because of transport problems or working conditions. Members of some ethnic minority groups may find it difficult to obtain a job or achieve promotion because of racial discrimination – despite laws prohibiting it.

Poverty and place

The question 'who is in poverty?' cannot be answered solely by reference to individual characteristics and personal circumstances. The opportunities to avoid poverty are not distributed evenly throughout the country. People living in some areas have a better chance of avoiding poverty than those living in others. This point has often been made in the contrast between a prosperous south and a depressed and poor north. Alternatively affluent towns have been contrasted with deprived inner cities. Whilst at a general level these contrasts might be appropriate, the situation is clearly more complicated. There are poor areas in the south and wealthy areas in the north. Towns have their run down estates and sections of inner cities become trendy and 'up market' as yuppies move in.

If having a decent wage is the key to avoiding poverty, the distribution of jobs which pay good wages is going to be very important. Whether an individual of working age avoids poverty or not depends very much on whether there are enough jobs paying decent wages in the area in which he or she lives. In cities and towns which are 'doing well' and developing economically there may well be plenty of jobs for semi- and unskilled workers, building offices, homes and shops, for example. In other places, perhaps where mining or the manufacturing industry has finished, young unskilled and semi-skilled school and college leavers compete with those made redundant for the few jobs which are available. Long term unemployment becomes a real possibility in such circumstances.

Area and place are significant not only in relation to the availability of decent wages – they are significant in relation to the cost of living. An interesting example which has been well publicised during the last few years is that of those on low incomes in rural areas. During the last 40 years the situation in many rural areas has changed. The fashion for high technology farming has led to loss of jobs on the land. A significant number of the affluent middle class have decided that they would like to own a cottage for the weekend. As the belief that services should be provided only if they make a profit increasingly came to dominate government and business thinking rural areas have lost their trains, buses, shops, banks, post offices, and pubs. A car has become essential for families – including the poor – in rural areas to run the children to school, go to the shops and get to work. Running a car, however, is expensive. A family on a low income in an urban area where there remains at least some sort of public transport system is spared this expense. In many other respects, however, the low income family in a city faces a higher cost of living.

Living in a poor urban district can be expensive. Poor areas are, for example, often high crime areas. Even if a company is prepared to insure a family's belongings, the premiums may be very high. If the poor family pay the premiums it reduces their income. If they do not pay the premiums and their belongings are stolen the family has to buy replacements – if and when they can afford to do so. Again this reduces the money available for other things. If replacements for stolen goods are bought on credit, the interest paid makes this even more expensive.

Area and district are thus linked to the chances of individuals avoiding poverty – through job availability and the cost of living. Not only that, having to live in certain neighbourhoods can itself be counted as an aspect of poverty. Simply walking round some neighbourhoods might suggest that those living there are deprived of an environment which people in our society might normally expect. Being able to walk down a street without seeing hypodermic needles or used condoms amidst the rubbish, or obscene graffiti on what remains of a vandalised bus shelter; without being snarled at by some dogs or jeered at by teenagers can hardly be seen as a special privilege in our society. Being able to let a child toddle in a local playground free from the fear of serious cuts from broken bottles seems a rather ordinary expectation. For many, however, the only way in which they could secure these rights for themselves and their families would be to move to a better 'area'. The poor condition of their neighbourhood becomes part of their poverty.

Why poverty?

At one level this question is answered when those sections of society most likely to suffer poverty are identified. Some are poor because they haven't got a job, others because their job is badly paid; others because they don't claim the benefits to which they are entitled. Particular sections of society suffer poverty for particular reasons. Sometimes, however, sociologists want to explain not why this or that section of society is in poverty but why anybody in society is in poverty. What is it about our kind of society and/or the people in it which leads to there being people in poverty?

Social and economic factors

For many sociologists poverty exists because within our society are powerful forces generating and maintaining inequality. Wealth is distributed unequally and so the income which comes from wealth is distributed unevenly. Some members of our society own houses, land and/or shares, for example. By letting a house or some land the owner is entitled to collect rent from the tenant. By holding shares, the owner is entitled to yearly dividend payments from the company which issued the shares. At the end of every year, therefore, the owner is richer than he or she was at the beginning of the year. Those who do not own houses or shares have not received any rent or dividend payments. They are not richer at the end of the year. The inequality between the owners and the non owners is greater at the end of the year than at the beginning of the year. And so it will be for the next year, and the year after next, so long as some people collect rent and some cannot, some people receive dividend payments and some do not. What is more, the value of the houses, land and shares is likely, in the long term, to increase. At the end of the year, therefore, what the owner owns is worth more than at the beginning of the year. The value of the nothing which is owned by many people does not increase.

There are equally powerful forces leading to inequality in the amount of money different sections of the working population receive as wages, salaries or fees. Contrast 'we need to pay the top salaries to make sure that we attract the best people' with 'workers must moderate their wage demands or else they will price themselves out of a job'. Statements like these have been made regularly during the past 20 years by politicians, economists, business executives, business pressure groups and newspaper editorials. How much an individual or section of the workforce is paid is influenced very much by competition – market forces – not just within the society but on a world wide basis. We hear much of globalisation, the global economic market. As suggested above, the consequences of market forces for different sections of the workforce can be rather different. Some skills might be in great demand and those who possess them can claim great rewards. Other skills might not be wanted. If some jobs can be moved around the world to the cheapest workforce there will be constant pressure to lower the wages of British workers doing these jobs. These workers will be under constant threat of unemployment and in a weak bargaining position so far as their pay is concerned.

Whilst how much is earned depends on power within the free market those sections in the working population with great power will receive great rewards and those sections with little power will receive relatively little. Consider the situation if those who have great power in the 'free market' are the same people who own the houses, and shares, and those with little power in the market are the people who own nothing from which an income is received. It is not difficult to understand how the level of inequality generated might result in sections of the population facing relative poverty.

Recognise that this kind of approach focusses on the structure of society and social forces. The character, attitudes, values which individuals have are not mentioned. They are not relevant to the explanation. There are poor people in society not because there are certain kinds of people in society, but because there are certain kinds of position in society. In our competitive, market-based society poverty positions – or statuses – have been created. The people selected to occupy them will become poor people.

The characteristics of the poor

There is a very different approach which continues to be popularised by politicians and newspaper editors. This approach does focus on personal characteristics, attitudes and values. It suggests that a majority of the poor bring poverty upon themselves by being the kind of people they are. They are lazy and if they can scrounge or fiddle enough to get by they will not bother to go to work. They are incompetent and waste what money thay have. They have bad habits – gambling, drinking, sexual promiscuity, drug taking – which keep them from living the ordered, respectable life which is expected to keep them out of poverty.

It is not difficult to see how this view of the poor could be attractive to the non-poor. If the poor have brought it on themselves; if their poverty is the result of anti-social or immoral behaviour, they do not deserve to be helped. Someone seeing a scruffy young adult sitting on a pavement with 'hungry and homeless – please help me' written on a piece of cardboard can walk past thinking, 'Idle beggar! I'm not giving you anything to waste on more drink.' At a society-wide level such a view could justify thinking that it would be wrong to tax the respectable, hard working, better off in order to support such an undeserving section of society. What is more the taxpayers might well suspect that any benefit payments would be wasted. After all it is because the poor can't run their own lives properly that they need help.

In recent years the sociologists who emphasise the importance of people's character, attitudes and values in their explanation of why, in our rich society, we have poor people, have used some distinctive words and phrases to express their ideas – '**culture of poverty**', '**culture of dependency**', '**underclass**'. Use of the word 'culture' is very significant. To a sociologist culture means 'way of life'. To refer to a culture or subculture of poverty is to suggest that a large section of the poor accept that they are and are likely to remain in poverty and have built a way of life on that basis. If people see their poverty as acceptable it becomes unlikely that they will do what is necessary to get out of it. If this outlook is communicated to their children they are unlikely to 'better themselves'. Poverty as a way of life is passed down from generation to generation.

The lifestyle of this section of the poor has become highlighted in recent years. Concern in certain political quarters and sections of the media has, at times, almost reached the level of a moral panic:

- this way of life is seen as tolerating or encouraging criminal or grossly antisocial behaviour. Television documentaries and newspaper articles have introduced us to children, teenagers and young adults who seem to have no sense of responsibility to those around them, no ability to put themselves in someone else's shoes, to feel a sense of shame or guilt. These are individuals who will steal the pension from an elderly person, throw a brick through a baby's bedroom window, and steal or set fire to someone's car for fun.

- this way of life is seen to tolerate or encourage casual sex from an early age and promote fragmented family structures. Babies are conceived and born without those responsible having any clear idea of how they will raise the children. Many are lone parents who have erratic relationships with the father(s) of the baby(s). Conventional father figures, traditionally seen as performing some sort of controlling and stabilising role in the child's upbringing, are absent. Living in such disorganised families it is hardly surprising, suggest those who see a culture of poverty, that the children fall into anti-social behaviour.

- this way of life is seen to tolerate or encourage idleness and dependency – the 'dependency culture'. 'Why work when you can get money from the social?' The picture presented in some newspapers of benefit claimants happy to live on money collected through the taxation of working people who may not be very well off themselves causes understandable anger. 'Paying your way', 'working for a living' remain important values in society. If people of working age claim benefits week after week without any apparent gratitude, sense of shame or indication that they are doing their best to get a job these values are challenged. Some sociologists and politicians believe that the poor who live within this culture have become a sufficiently large, permanent and distinguishable element within our society for them to be seen as part of the social structure. They are an underclass.

The cycle of deprivation

Sociologists, occasionally politicians, refer to a 'cycle of deprivation' to which those in poverty may be subject. At the heart of any cycle of deprivation is the idea that poverty in one generation leads to poverty in succeeding generations. Poor parents have poor children who, when they grow up, will have poor children themselves – and so the cycle continues. It is important to recognise this core element of the 'cycle of deprivation' and to avoid confusing it with 'life cycle poverty' or the 'poverty trap' as students sometimes do. The cycle of deprivation is often represented by a diagram. Look at figure 58. Such diagrams are useful for showing the continuity of the process.

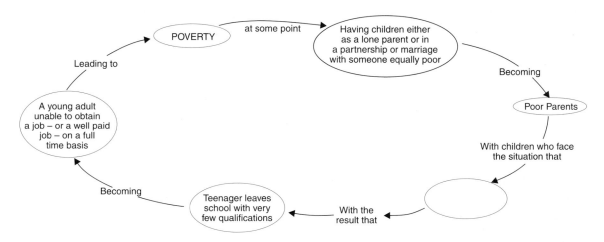

Figure 58 The cycle of deprivation.

Note the empty box – perhaps the most important part of the diagram. In it should be described what leads children of poor parents to achieve low qualifications. The box has been left empty because there are several ways in which it can be filled in, each suggesting a rather different interpretation of the problem.

- For those who have sympathy for the 'culture of poverty', 'culture of dependency' approach the contents of the box might make reference to an inadequate, incompetent parent or couple not bothering or not able to carry out their responsibilities. The child sees a parent or parents who don't care about upholding the 'normal' social standards, who don't try to get on and are happy to muddle through on benefits. This then becomes 'how things are', 'how people should be' for the child, who consequently takes to school neither the desire to do well nor the skills which are necessary to fit in and benefit from what school has to offer.

- The box could be filled in rather differently with emphasis not on the deficient, inadequate culture of the parents but on the poor material circumstances in which the child is forced to live. Inadequate money in the household for food leads to the child being more sickly than others and thus missing more schooling. Money to buy books, computers and all those educational toys by which better off children are surrounded is not available, nor is money for bus fares and entrance fees for museums and art galleries. The child is being limited here not by parental attitudes and behaviour but by material deprivation and the way in which material deprivation can influence the child's morale. Material deprivation can lead to exclusion – not having the money to join in with what better off children are doing – and self exclusion – not trying to join in out of fear of being laughed at, rejected.

- Alternatively, the box can be filled in with an emphasis on the way in which poor children might be failed by the education system. Poor children living in a deprived area were in the past and may continue to be offered depressingly inadequate facilities. The staff working in such conditions might lose hope or might label the pupils 'no hopers'. Such low expectations would perhaps initiate a self- fulfilling prophecy. It only takes one or two extremely disaffected or disturbed children to burn down part of a school, beat up a teacher or terrorise children in a playground to turn a difficult situation into an impossible one, where pupils are very unlikely to leave with reasonable qualifications.

The cycle of deprivation can thus be very helpful when you want to outline some of the ways in which poverty may be passed from one generation to another. It can also help you to identify the sorts of things which would have to be done to break the cycle – change parental attitudes, guarantee all children a reasonable level of resources in the home to enable them to benefit from their education, help schools to offer poor children better chances. The cycle of deprivation – or cycle of poverty – is not, however, an adequate explanation of why poverty exists. The cycle starts with the poor parents. Why were they poor? Because their parents were poor. And why were they poor? Because their parents were poor. At this point the limitations of the cycle of deprivation as an explanation become very clear.

The functions of poverty

Most people will see poverty as something negative. It is occasionally useful then to take an alternative view and consider the ways in which groups within society might benefit from there being people in poverty. Is poverty at all functional? Worryingly, once the question has been asked it is not difficult to think of the ways in which poverty can be seen positively:

- Since it is socially dangerous and unacceptable in terms of social values for a government to do nothing about poverty, the existence of poor people creates jobs. Welfare benefits need to be distributed. Poverty causes individuals and neighbourhoods to have problems which must be tackled. Social control needs to be maintained in what can be particularly difficult circumstances. Here are jobs for civil servants, welfare and social workers, police officers and the probation service.

- The poor provide a demand for low quality goods, food past its sell by date, clothes passed over by the better off which are later sold cheaply at a market.

- The poor are available as an easy scapegoat for newspaper editors and politicians with particular agendas. The image of the 'benefit scrounger' or lone mother can play a powerful part in a variety of campaigns for lower taxes, for example, or a return to the 'traditional' married couple family.

- In a less public context the poor can be used as an effective teaching aid or method of social control: 'You don't want to end up like that do you? – so listen to your teacher and do your homework,'or 'Don't insult the poor boys and girls by leaving that cabbage. They would be glad of it. Eat it up'.

Looking at poverty in this way does not provide an explanation of why poverty exists. The idea that some person or group invented poverty to achieve these benefits is rather far fetched. What this view can reveal is a side to poverty apart from its undoubted cost to the individuals who suffer it and to society generally. It might also suggest that given poverty does exist, for whatever reason, there might be sections of society who will be hoping it doesn't go away.

Glossary

Class structure	this refers to how we can think of society as consisting of a number of social classes – for example, an upper class, a middle class and a working class. The class structure of a society also tells us something about the relative size and importance of the different classes. In the 1950s and 1960s the working class was the largest class in Britain. Because of various economic and technological changes the class structure is now said to be different with a larger middle class and a smaller working class. The class structure is also said to have fragmented (or broken up) – it is probably accurate now more to speak of the middle class in terms of higher professionals, lower professionals and routine office workers. Likewise, the working class can be seen as divided up in various ways – a 'new' working class and a traditional working class, for example.

Social Exclusion	some people find themselves unable to fully take part in society. They are excluded from activities that most of us take for granted. This is usually a result of material deprivation though it need not always be so. The young single mother on benefits may find herself excluded from the labour market because she cannot afford decent childcare, or because no adequate childcare facilities exist in her area. The Bangladeshi mother may be afraid to go out alone because of the activities of racists in her area. An elderly couple may be confined to their home because of their fear of crime. All are forms of social exclusion.

Bourgeoisie	in Karl Marx's theory the bourgeoisie were those who owned the means of production. They owned land, they could pay for labour, or they owned capital in the form of factories or machinery – they owned the things needed to make saleable goods. In Marx's view this gave them power in society: they had power over the workers (the proletariat) and their economic power gave them political power.

The middle class are not the same as the bourgeoisie. The middle class are usually distinguished from the working class by the fact that they are non-manual or white collar workers. The middle classes today might include accountants, architects, doctors, teachers, nurses and clerical workers. When sociologists refer to the middle class(es) today they are usually referring to a group or groups that can be identified by some aspect or aspects of their occupation e.g. qualifications, status, skills, amount of control over others, or earning power.

The proletariat for Marx this group were the workers, without property, who had no means of making a living other than by selling their "labour power" to a capitalist. For some sociologists today this definition of "the workers" means that, for example, clerical workers could legitimately be seen as part of the working class.

Open societies are societies where social mobility, upward or downward, is possible. Social mobility studies are often undertaken in order to see exactly how open a society is.

Closed societies are societies where social mobility is not possible. Such societies would include caste societies based on religion or, for example, South African society under apartheid which was based on "race". In both of these examples your status would be *ascribed* at birth (by the caste that you were born into or by your colour) rather than *achieved* during your lifetime, as it might be in a meritocracy.

Meritocracy a type of society where your social position is based on merit rather than any other factor such as wealth, gender or ethnicity.

Absolute Povery an individual is in absolute poverty when he or she lacks the resources necessary to maintain him or herself in an active, healthy stae.

Relative poverty a situation in which an individual cannot afford to do and have those things which are considered by its members to be a normal part of life in their society.

People and Work

7

What are the first couple of questions you ask someone you have just met?

Probably you will say, 'What's your name?', and 'What do you do?' The fact that this is a very common way of starting a conversation with a stranger tells us something about how important work is in our society. We spend a good proportion of our lives working: our jobs generally determine how much we have to spend (in other words our access to life chances) and we see ourselves and are seen by others in terms of our jobs – our work is an important part of our identity. What we do also gives us a position in society, it affects our status. Work can also affect the rest of our lives in other ways: it can make us tired or stressed; it can inspire and excite us; it can make us bored and fed up; it can limit our social lives (especially if we work shifts), and it can expose us to danger or even injure or kill us. Our job can affect where we live and how often we move house. Not having a job or not being able to work can make us feel useless or inadequate, and losing a job can affect us in the same way. It is no wonder then that sociologists are interested in work.

However, having got this far into this book, you will be used to the idea that there is often a difference between the way that we use a word in everyday life and the way that sociologists use the same word. What, then, do sociologists mean by work? It is in fact quite difficult to give a straightforward answer to this question.

Draw a chart with a space for each day, divided into 24 hours, then fill it in according to what you are doing in each hour for example.

SATURDAY

07.00 Sleeping.

08.00 Getting washed and dressed, eating, then travelling to job in shoe shop in town.

09.00 At work, dealing with customers.

    and so on until

17.00 Travelling home.

18.00 Making tea, washing up, cleaning the living room.

19.00 Watching TV, doing homework.

20.00 At the cinema with friends.

Now look at what you have written and make three lists from the activities on your chart, one headed Work, one headed Leisure, and one headed Other for actvities which are neither work nor leisure. So using the extract above, we might have dealing with customers down as work, going to the cinema as leisure, and getting washed and dressed as other. But what about making the tea? Washing up? Cleaning up? Travelling to work? Doing homework? We don't get paid for doing any of these things, but apart from travelling to work when we might read the paper or a magazine or doze off on the bus, they all feel a lot like work when we do them. To make all this a bit clearer we can use some of the terms that sociologists use.

First of all we can distinguish between three ways in which we can spend our time: these are work, leisure, and committed time. Some things are quite easy to categorise using these terms. For example taking part in paid employment is obviously work, going to the cinema is leisure, and travelling to work is neither, it is something we have to do in order to do our job, so we can regard it as committed time.

Work itself is usually defined as 'the production of goods and services by physical, mental, or emotional effort'. So if we work in a factory and make bookshelves, or we add up figures as a book keeper, or we act as a counsellor for troubled individuals, then we are working. These kinds of work would most likely be paid work – we would be employed by someone else to give up our time to perform that particular task – and usually in a particular place – a factory or an office, for example, but we can't just define work as paid employment. We could make a bookshelf for our home; we could do the books for a local voluntary organisation for nothing; we could do the books for a shopkeeper friend for some cash in hand; we could give up some of our time to work for the Samaritans. All the same activities as above except that we're not getting paid or we're being paid unofficially to avoid paying tax.

The production of goods and services in a society is what we call the economy of a society and sociologists and economists divide the economy up like this:

- **The Formal Economy**
  This is the official economy, where you pay tax and National Insurance as either an employee working for an employer, or as a self-employed individual. In the formal economy formal records are kept. Firms know how many people are working for them and how many vacancies there are.

- **The Informal Economy**
  In this part of the economy either no records are kept or no money is paid. The informal economy is divided into three parts:

→ The Hidden Economy is unofficial paid work – 'working on the side', working 'cash in hand'. We possibly all know of people who are signing on at the benefit office but who are also doing a bit of work that they are not declaring to boost their weekly income, or perhaps we know of people who have paid a plumber or a builder in cash so that they don't have to pay VAT. This is the hidden economy: it is unofficial and unrecorded, usually so that benefits won't be affected, or to avoid tax.

→ The Domestic Economy refers to all the work done in the home: childcare, DIY, cooking, cleaning and gardening, for example. This is not usually paid employment.

→ The Communal Economy includes voluntary work and helping others in the community. It includes working unpaid for charities or voluntary organisations. For example, doing two afternoons a week in the local Oxfam or PDSA shop or going shopping for elderly neighbours.

So for sociologists it is not always easy to separate work and leisure. What I do for work you may do for leisure, like gardening or decorating the house. I may go running for relaxation or for fun but a professional athlete may do it as part of their regular training (think of tennis players or footballers). As a teacher I may read sociology text books as part of my job, but I may also read them just because I'm interested in the subject. But I may also have to spend some of my time at home marking students' work or preparing lessons. Likewise I may spend some of my time at work talking about last night's TV, something for which I am not getting paid.

Most of the rest of this chapter will be about paid full time or part time employment, in other words it will be about the formal economy. Before that we will look at the significance of the informal economy and introduce some terms you will need to know.

- **The Division of Labour** is the way that tasks or jobs are divided up in a society or an organisation. Our society is a complex one and not everybody can do everything, so some are doctors, some are teachers, some are electricians and so on. This kind of sharing out of tasks or jobs also happens within companies, schools and other organisations. Sociologists are interested in the division of labour because it shows us who does what in a society.
- **The Domestic Division of Labour** is more specific. It refers to the way that tasks are divided up in the household, between males and females, and between parents and children. Sociologists are interested in this because it shows us how far there is equality between men and women, and between parents and children at home.
- **Patriarchy** – when men have power and dominate women.
- **The 24-Hour Society** is a term used to describe a society which is open 24/7, as they say. In other words where not only are some people working through the night, but increasing numbers of shops, supermarkets and clubs are too, so there are also buses, trains and taxis operating 24 hours a day.
- **The Primary Sector** of the economy is the extractive industries such as mining, fishing, north sea oil and gas.
- **The Secondary Sector** is manufacturing industry, everything from the heavy industries such as steel, to cars and textiles, and light industries such as printing.
- **The Tertiary or Service Sector** includes banking, insurance, transport, communications, all the leisure industries, and of course the retail and catering industries.

The household economy – housework and domestic labour.

From the definitions given earlier in the chapter it is hard to argue with the idea that housework is work, even if you don't get paid for it. Sociologists tended to ignore housework for many years, spending more time investigating the formal economy which was mainly occupied by men. More recently feminist researchers in particular have highlighted the significance of housework in a variety of ways. Some of the questions they have been interested in are:

i)   Do women and men do equal amounts of housework and childcare?

ii) Does the fact that women tend to be seen by other people as being the person responsible for housework and childcare affect their employment prospects?

iii) Does the fact that women tend to do most of the housework and childcare affect their chances of getting full time employment, of earning more when they are employed, or of being promoted?

iv) How much is the amount of work done in the house worth? Or to put it another way, what would a man (or a woman) have to pay to get someone to do all the jobs that a housewife does?

v)   Are the recent changes in the economy having any effect on the domestic division of labour? These changes include the increase in the service sector, and the decline in the number of traditionally male jobs such as mining and shipbuilding, and the growth of the '24-hour society'.

In this section we will only be concerned with the last two questions. The first question is dealt with in the chapter on the family, and the second and third are dealt with later on in this chapter.

What is housework and childcare worth?

There are two ways of answering this question. We can look at all the jobs that are done in the home and then work out what it would cost to have someone to do them for us or we can look at what people actually spend on household chores and childcare.

> **EXERCISE**
>
> Make a list of all the jobs done around the house. Find out the hourly rates for these jobs. Then calculate the cost of housework and childcare.

Changes in paid employment

So far we have looked at the nature of work and non-work. In this part of the chapter we will look at the various ways in which paid employment has altered in Britain. This will involve us looking at the changes in the sort of work that people do; the ways in which contracts of employment, hours of work and time of work have altered; and the way changes in paid employment affect people's lives outside their work. In the chapter on inequality we saw that there has been a change in the occupational structure of Great Britain. To remind you the main changes can be seen in the charts on page 235.

These show us that there has been a shift from the primary sector (mining, fishing etc) and the secondary sector (manufacturing) towards the tertiary or service sector. Indeed many people now talk of Britain as having not so much a manufacturing economy as a service economy. In other words there are now fewer people employed in making things and more people employed in providing various services. These services consist of banking, selling goods, advertising, education, health services, providing IT services, and the communications industry.

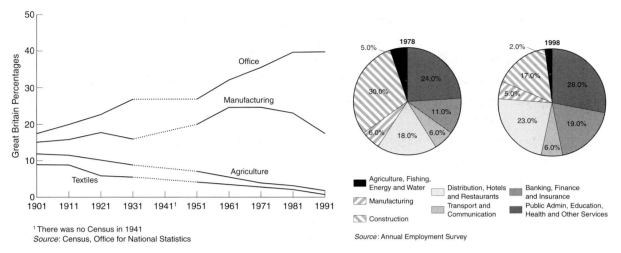

Figure 59 Percentages working in four key areas of employment.

Figure 60 Employee Jobs by Broad Industrial Sector.

The charts and diagrams above can tell us about the distribution of paid employment but they can't tell us why the kinds of jobs that people do have changed or who does what jobs (men or women, young or old, black or white) or why.

What are the reasons for the changes in paid employment?

There are many reasons why the kinds of work available in a society change over time:

● Industries or companies face **competition** from firms abroad. If it is cheaper to build ships in the Far East then people will buy those ships instead of those made in Britain, and so the shipyards in towns like Sunderland, Birkenhead, Newcastle, Belfast and Glasgow decline or close altogether. Apart from shipbuilding other industries that have lost out in competition from abroad include the British motorcycle and textile industries.

● **Government policies** can also affect what kinds of jobs are available. For example the Conservative government of the mid 1980s wanted much less reliance on coal to run power stations. This was one of the factors that led to the decline of the coal industry. Government can also increase the number of jobs available by offering subsidies or reducing the amount of tax that firms have to pay if they move to particular parts of the county. Local government can also try to attract industry in this way. Ships may no longer be built in Sunderland, but Nissan now make cars there.

● **New forms of technology** can also influence how many jobs are available in a particular industry. Look at the photographs on page 236. What do you notice?

The first picture shows a production line with many workers, the second shows the effect that automation and the introduction of robots and computers can have on employment levels. Over recent years workers in many industries have been affected by the introduction of new technologies, but not always in the same way. We will discuss this more later in the chapter.

● **Consumer demand** – what people want and can afford to pay for can affect the demand for

Figure 61 Technology can have a drastic effect on employment levels.

goods and services. As people have become better off, their tastes have changed and having bought the 'essentials', they spend their money on luxuries. If most of us have a washing machine, a TV, and a car of some kind then we might want to eat out more, or go to the cinema more, buy a DVD player, or take an extra short break holiday. In this way we are creating a demand for more goods and services.

Before going any further here are some terms you will need to know.

- **Mechanisation** is the use of machines to do a job previously done by hand. For example an electric or petrol driven lawnmower will take the physical effort out of cutting the grass. Power tools of all kinds are now used in industry to perform tasks that once involved physical effort. We talk of mechanisation when the machines are controlled by people.

- **Automation** refers to the situation in which the machines are controlled by other machines. These days that is most likely to be a computer or a micro-chip. In the car industry robots are used to perform various tasks like welding and painting. In these circumstances people are only needed to supervise the running of the machinery. Automation and computerisation have removed the need for human labour in a variety of industries; not just in car manufacturing but also in banking, travel, and communications:

  Think of the times during the day when you deal with a machine which does a task automatically. You may have taken some money out of a cash machine, where once you would have dealt with a bank clerk; you may have bought a train or tube ticket from a ticket machine instead of from a kiosk; you may have made a phone call and listened to pre-recorded instructions telling you what numbers to press on your phone before you get to speak to a real person.

The examples of automation or computerisation above refer to situations where automatic processes mean that people are no longer needed to carry out certain tasks. Of course if tasks are being carried out by computers we do need other people to build, programme and operate them and so on, so the effects of new technology are not always the same. In some instances people will lose their jobs, as in the car industry; in other instances new jobs will be created, for example in computer programming or other areas of new technology like web design or in mobile phone technology.

The effects of technology on jobs

Over the last century one of the biggest changes in industry, as you have seen above, has been the change from the production line or assembly line to automation. Sociologists are interested in two particular effects of technology:

→ How does technology affect the jobs that people do?
→ How does technology affect the people who do the jobs?

In this section we will look firstly at the way in which technology affects the jobs that people do.

In the early part of the twentieth century Henry Ford developed the assembly line or production line technique. In this method of production the task of building a car was broken down into specific tasks each of which could be carried out by a worker who did not need to have all of the skills or knowledge necessary to make a car. The workers simply needed to know how to carry out their own particular task. Indeed the workers on the assembly line might not even see the finished product if it was finished off in another factory.

Throughout the twentieth century this kind of production technique was used in many industries from car manufacturing to televisions, from clothing to food. In the latter part of the twentieth century this kind of approach was also applied to many kinds of office work. For example, in the 1970s if you applied for unemployment benefit your claim might be handled by a number of people dealing with different aspects of your claim: filing your application, conducting the interview, calculating your benefit, writing your Giro and so on.

In both factories and offices production of goods or the provision of services was based on the division of labour – the breaking down of the work that had to be done into a series of relatively simple tasks that could be learned fairly quickly and repeated often during the working day. With various technological advances many of these jobs disappeared as assembly lines became automated. Machines, often controlled by computers, can now carry out many tasks like spray painting a new car, welding and dispensing cash through a hole in the wall. In some instances new technology makes it possible for a series of tasks to be carried out automatically. For example in some shops and supermarkets when the person at the checkout scans the barcode on your tin of soup or CD it not only registers the price of the item but also orders more stock at the same time. The system also provides bosses information on how quickly the checkout operator is working and how many mistakes they have made. (How does this link technology to social control?)

Deskilling or reskilling?

The ways in which technology has changed what people do in some kinds of work has led some sociologists to say that certain jobs have become deskilled. **Deskilling** means that the level of skill that is required to do a particular job is reduced. The job itself requires a lower level of skill, perhaps even to the extent that it can be performed by an unskilled worker. For example in the early history of the car industry cars were produced by individuals with a range of engineering and design skills. With the arrival of the assembly line cars could be built by

237

workers who had very few, or none, of those skills. They simply had to know how to perform their part of the process, like fitting the gearbox or the seats. In offices and banks deskilling is said to have happened because clerks may not need to be able to perform complex calculations because computers can do them.

Deskilling is said to have two important consequences:

1) Many jobs have become simple, boring and repetitive and so the people doing them can be paid less and are likely to get little job satisfaction.

2) The amount of control that workers have over what they do has been reduced. This is because the important knowledge connected with how to do a particular job (like building a car or performing complex calculations) isn't in the workers' heads anymore. The people who have that knowledge are likely to be the managers or employers. This makes it difficult for the workforce to bargain over pay or conditions at work, because they can be easily replaced because they are relatively unskilled. This process of deskilling is linked to the process of proletarianisation dealt with in the chapter on inequality.

However not all sociologists agree that deskilling has been taking place on a large scale. Some say that the introduction of new technology has the opposite effect, that of reskilling. **Reskilling** refers to the way in which workers have to learn new skills to do a particular job because of the introduction of new technologies. For example in a drawing office the draughtsmen and women may now have to have computer skills to operate computer aided design programs. Typists may have disappeared in many offices but it is said that the skills required by the operators of word processors are more complex than those needed by typists. So the introduction of new technology can affect the jobs that people do in a variety of ways, both positive and negative.

EXERCISE

Think about the teacher's job. Do you think that new technology, especially information technology, will deskill teaching as a profession or require teachers to gain new skills?

You may want to consider:

- The teacher's choice of how to teach
- Teacher's knowledge of subject
- Ability to put across/explain
- Ability to gain interest
- Video conferencing
- E-mail
- Online text books
- The Internet
- Computer marked assignments
- Distance learning

Workers and technology

Here are two extracts from people writing about work. The first is taken from Karl Marx writing in 1844, the second is from Huw Beynon's book *Working for Ford* which was first published in 1973. When you've read them think about how they are similar, whether they are critical of some kinds of work in the same way, and whether the kinds of ideas expressed in them could be said about some kinds of work today.

> He does not fulfil in his work but denies himself, has a feeling of misery not of well being, does not develop freely a physical and mental energy, but is physically exhausted and mentally debased. The worker therefore feels himself at home only during his leisure. His work is not voluntary but imposed, forced labour. It is not the satisfaction of a need but only a means for satisfying other needs.
>
> (Karl Marx *Economic and Philosophical Manuscripts* 1844 quoted in Bottomore and Rubel K. Marx selected writings 1963 Pelican)

> You don't achieve anything here. A robot could do it. The line here is made for morons. It doesn't need any thought. They tell you that. 'We don't pay you for thinking' they say. Everyone comes to realise that they're not doing a worthwhile job. They're just on the line. For the money. Nobody likes to think that they're a failure. It's bad when you know that you're just a little cog. You just look at your pay packet – you look at what it does for your wife and kids. That's the only answer.
>
> Ford worker quoted in Huw Beynon (1980) *Working for Ford*

What similarities do you notice about these two pieces?

Of course both of these comments were made about different kinds of work and they were written at different times. Do some workers today feel the same about the work that they do? Read the extract below and see what you think.

TROUBLE AT THE 21ST CENTURY MILLS

Employees at BT have criticised call centres, which have been called "the new mills of 21st century Britain". For the first time in their 13 year existence, they have called a one day strike.

Poor training, low wages, demanding targets, long hours without a break, constant monitoring even when visiting the lavatory, and exhortations to work harder flashed up on giant screens are all undesirable conditions quoted by the union as being typical of call centres. What really appears to have annoyed the BT workers is a directive that insists that calls should last no longer than 285 seconds.

The main complaint of the workers is a management instruction that interferes with the way they interact with the public. The workers say that even when lonely elderly people come on the phone and are desperate to chat, they are urged to complete the call within the allotted time. Call centre operators want to talk to the public in a meaningful and personal way, but their management says they should harden their hearts against whingers looking for a free conversation.

The Independent October 2000

Do we like being at work?

For some of us the answer to this is probably no. We go to work to get money to do what we really like doing, so that we can 'have a life.' But there are a large number of people who really enjoy their jobs. For these people work is enjoyable, interesting and stimulating, and for some it becomes their whole lives. Sociologists distinguish between these two attitudes by defining the different kinds of job satisfaction that work can give us.

→ **Intrinsic satisfaction** refers to the kind of satisfaction we get from work that offers interest and fulfillment. There may be elements of skill or creativity in this kind of work.

→ **Extrinsic satisfaction** refers to the kind of satisfaction we get not from doing the job itself but from something outside work which is usually our pay. Jobs which offer extrinsic satisfaction are often boring, repetitive and monotonous. They offer little opportunity to exercise skills or creativity.

Draw up a list of jobs offering intrinsic satisfaction and extrinsic satisfaction. Chances are that you have some creative jobs such as designer, architect, or musician on your list of those offering intrinsic satisfaction alongside others such as doctor, nurse, teacher, and social worker. Those offering extrinsic satisfaction might include production line work, routine office work, shop assistant, call centre operator, or driver.

The boundaries between the two are not always clear cut, however. Think about the following examples:

→ Many professional musicians might gain much intrinsic satisfaction from the creative process involved in their work and get a tremendous 'buzz' from performing in front of a live audience but find that touring is dull and soul destroying.

→ Teachers might still obtain a lot of satisfaction from their actual classroom teaching but find the paperwork associated with their jobs monotonous and pointless.

→ Nurses may find that changes in the way the NHS is run has consequences for how they feel about their work.

As with much in sociology we can rarely divide jobs simply into lists of those offering intrinsic or extrinsic satisfaction. Perhaps there is a potential piece of coursework here.

Alienation and job satisfaction

So far we've looked at the way in which changes in technology can affect the kinds of jobs that we do. This section is about the way in which technology can affect the workers themselves. Go back and look again at the extracts from Marx, Beynon and *The Guardian*. There isn't much in those extracts that is positive, is there? Ever since Marx wrote about alienation in the 19th century sociologists have investigated the ways in which technology can affect workers' attitudes to their work and how different types of technology can influence levels of job satisfaction.

Karl Marx and alienation

Karl Marx realised that modern industry would make many people's working lives very dull and profoundly unsatisfying. However he did not just blame technology for this. He thought that alienation resulted from the way that society was organised. Workers in a capitalist society (see Chapter 6) are alienated because: they do not control what they make, or how they make it; they cannot keep what they make; they only go to work for money because the work they do is boring, repetitive and exhausting and offers very little mental stimulation. In the end, workers suffering the kind of alienation that Marx was describing feel less than human. This is quite a complicated idea but the extract below gives some idea of what Marx was trying to say:

> A mother. . . would feel very alienated indeed if, every time she gave birth, the squealing infant was immediately seized from her by some latter day Herod. This, more or less, was the daily lot of the workers, forever producing what they could not keep. No wonder they felt less than human.'
>
> (Karl Marx, Francis Wheen 1999, Fourth Estate London)

Before reading the next section you might like to think about how the production of goods in society could be organised so that alienation could be avoided. (The same problem that Marx set himself in fact.) You could then compare your ideas to those mentioned later in this section.

Measuring alienation

Marx's ideas on alienation are complex and difficult to grasp at first. Because they are abstract this means that it is difficult for anyone doing research to **measure** exactly how alienated a group of workers is. For example a popular idea for coursework is to find out whether or not men and women are equal in the home. Before you could do this you would need to be able to **measure** equality. Equality, like alienation, is an abstract idea and therefore difficult to measure.

One way of doing this would be to think of the main activities in the home and divide them up into areas such as: housework, childcare, DIY and maintenance, and decision making and finances. Then you could ask questions relating to each area and begin to measure how equal they are. This activity is known as operationalising your concepts. It isn't important that you remember the word, but it is important that you do something like it in your coursework if you want to measure something abstract.

Robert Blauner wanted to find out the relationship between technology and alienation. He thought that the level of alienation would vary according to the level of technology used in a particular industry. To do this he had to be able to define alienation in such a way as to be able to measure it. Blauner thought that alienation could be broken down into four parts:

- Powerlessness: workers having no control over decision making e.g. about their work conditions or about how the job was done.
- Meaninglessness: often workers would only be involved in part of the process and could not see how what they did fitted into the end product.
- Isolation: being cut off from your fellow workers, not being part of a work group.
- Self-estrangement: not being able to develop your potential, to express yourself in your work.

Having broken down alienation into these four parts, Blauner could then collect evidence about each of them in order to measure the levels of alienation in four different industries to test out his theory. The industries were:

i) Printing – a craft with low levels of technology having high status jobs needing high levels of skill.
ii) Textiles – basically 'machine minding' low status jobs needing a low level of skill.
iii) Automobiles – assembly line production, unskilled work.
iv) Chemicals – continuous process production – high technology work teams.

Blauner's findings were as follows:

Type of industry	Printing	Textiles	Automobiles	Chemicals
Type of Technology	Craft	Machine minding Line	Assembly	Continuous
Alienation:				
Powerlessness	Low	High	High	Low
Meaninglessness	Low	High	High	Low
Isolation	Low	Low	High	Low
Self-Estrangement	Low	High	High	Low

Source – J.E.T. Eldridge (1971). *Sociology and Industrial Life* (London: Michael Joseph) quoted in Robin Theobold (1994) *Understanding Industrial Society* (Macmillan: Basingstoke).

Figure 62 Degree of Alienation by Industry.

How do we explain the different levels of alienation? The print workers were highly skilled and had a great deal of autonomy or control over their work and through their unions had a great deal of solidarity. The work in textile mills and car factories was different, not much skill was involved, and the machines determined the speed of work. The work was not intrinsically satisfying, the workers performed only part of the overall process, and perhaps didn't see the end product. However in the chemical industry the high levels of technology required actually encouraged team work. Workers have a variety of tasks to perform and are part of a team. So the overall level of alienation is low.

The difference in levels of alienation between the textile and automobile industries can be explained not so much by the level of technology but by the fact that textile workers tended to live and work close to one another. Car workers in this country have not tended to live near one another in communities like those that existed in the mill towns, but have tended to drive home to family life on an urban housing estate. This meant that levels of isolation were higher in the automobile industry. This shows us that it is difficult to separate work from other aspects of social life.

We have spent some time describing Blauner's work partly because it tells us something about alienation, but also because it shows us how to set about doing a piece of coursework. If we were to treat Blauner's work as like a piece of coursework it might look like this.

➡ General aim: to see if there is a link between alienation and technology.

➡ Hypothesis: the level of alienation experienced by workers will vary according to the level of technology they work with.

➡ Method: because we are testing a hypothesis we need a method that will allow us to do that. We need to be able to ask the same questions to people working in the different industries. Why? So that we can see if their answers are different according to the industry they work in. This way we can test our hypothesis. Some sort of survey seems to be appropriate.

To make our comparisons easy it would make sense if we used closed questions in our survey. Using questionnaires would be a good method. We could either get the workers to fill them in, ask the questions ourselves, or even find out if a survey has already been done asking the questions we want to ask. Of course we also have to define alienation in such a way that we can actually ask questions about it. This is the process of operationalising referred to above. If we follow this kind of plan we can see how our research method links to our aims. We can also make sure that we are only asking questions that are relevant to our aims.

A spanner in the works? Workers, technology and control

From what we have said about technology up to now it might seem that workers are the slaves of machines and that they exercise little control over what they do. There are a number of ways in which workers can gain some control over what happens to them at work.

● They might leave their job and get another. This leads to a high turnover of staff.
● They might take the odd 'sickie' – taking time off sick when you are not, so you still get paid.
● They might not put much effort into their work. This would reduce the quality of the end product: if we have bought a poor quality car or CD player we often say that it must have been made on a Friday afternoon, a time when the worker's attention was on the coming weekend rather than his or her job.
● They might take some sort of industrial action like going on strike or working to rule, or staging a 'go slow'. This can happen in two ways. Workers who are dissatisfied can easily be provoked into taking action if their managers make changes that they don't like. Also groups of workers who are feeling dissatisfied or frustrated may go looking for an excuse to challenge the management, partly to make real changes but also to relieve the monotony.
● They might deliberately sabotage the machinery at work in order to gain a break or to get back at their employers. This is where the phrase "spanner in the works" comes from.

Housework, technology and control

Paid employment is not the only type of work to be affected by changing technology. Housework involves the use of various forms of technology from microwaves to vacuum cleaners. Many of these products are sold to us on the promise that they will remove the drudgery from housework. What is the reality? The classic study of housework was conducted by Ann Oakley in 1974. Look at the following extract.

Oakley studied housework in the framework of the sociology of work. She spoke in depth to 40 mothers in London aged between 20 and 30. The majority of them were full time housewives and half of them had husbands in working class occupations and the rest had husbands in middle class occupations. The women described housework in similar ways to the way in which male assembly line workers have described their work but they reported even more monotony, fragmentation of tasks and excessive speed of work. Seventy per cent of the women were dissatisfied with their role, the most common complaint being loneliness.

Adapted from an *Introduction to Sociology: Feminist Perspectives* Abbott and Wallace (90) London, Routledge.

EXERCISE

Read the extract again then answer the following questions:

i) How is housework like assembly line work?

ii) Why are the tasks involved in housework described as monotonous and fragmented?

iii) Why did housewives in Oakley's study report the need for 'excessive speed'?

iv) Oakley's study was carried out nearly 30 years ago, is it still like that now?

For many women the problem with housework is that it is never done. It is never finished. We have probably heard, or said, something like 'you get the house clean and then they all come home and you have to start all over again'. But housework is different to many kinds of paid employment in one way. The housewives in Oakley's study valued their autonomy, that is to say they valued the control they had over what they did and how quickly they did it. One of the rewards to be had from doing housework was the satisfaction that some housewives got from meeting their own high standards. In this way housework can be seen as different to some kinds of paid work where the standards are set by someone else like a manager or supervisor.

There is another way in which some housewives gain control over the monotony of housework. Many of our access students have told us that they will spend their days meeting friends or otherwise enjoying themselves and then return home and spray some polish in the air and move a few ornaments about to make it look as though they have been really busy. If we think about the strategy of appearing to do housework it tells us quite a bit about the similarities between housework and paid employment.

Housework and paid employment can both be seen as based on contracts. Paid work is often based on a contract of employment; people see housework as being based on the marriage contract, as in the comment 'it starts as you sink into his arms and ends with your arms in his sink'. In other words it is men who benefit from this particular contract because of the inequality between men and women in a patriarchal society. This view of marriage is that of an institution in which women are exploited by providing domestic labour without formally being paid for it. Not only does the man benefit from this unequal relationship but it is also said that women's work in the house provides services that would otherwise have to be paid for by capitalist employers. Paying for the services that housewives provide would reduce the profits made by capitalists. Some kinds of paid employment can help us think about this point. What services do employers have to provide for their workers on oil rigs in the North Sea that might otherwise be performed by housewives?

The unequal distribution of power between men and women within marriage can also be seen as a factor in domestic violence. Some sociologists have suggested that assaults on wives can be triggered by the husband thinking that the wife is not performing her domestic duties adequately. In the same way unequal power between employers and employees can sometimes lead to violence as when strikes are broken up and striking workers attacked.

However it is probably fair to say that the marriage contract is not entered into in exactly the same way as a contract of employment. Doing domestic work is not the same as working for an employer. We do housework for all kinds of reasons: out of love for our partner; out of a sense of obligation; we may feel pressured by our peers to maintain our standards. There are other differences between housework and paid employment: we don't get paid in the same way; there are no fixed hours; and we are not subject to the same kinds of control and supervision when we do housework as we might be in paid employment.

Employers responses to alienation – group production, quality circles and industrial democracy

Alienation or lack of job satisfaction can cost firms a lot of money in time and production lost.

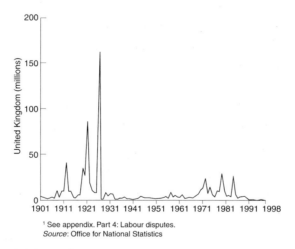

¹ See appendix. Part 4: Labour disputes.
Source: Office for National Statistics

Figure 63 Money lost through labour disputes.

There are various ways in which firms have tried to increase the levels of job satisfaction for their workers.

Group production

In 1974 Volvo built a new factory in Kalmar (Sweden) where assembly line production was abolished altogether. The assembly of each vehicle was broken down into 20 different tasks each performed by teams of 15 to 20 workers. While each team had to meet production targets it was up to the team members to organise their own work. Low levels of noise allowed workers to talk to each other and even listen to music. In 1988 this system was introduced at a new factory in Uddevalla (Sweden). Because the work team members are trained to handle all assembly jobs they work an average of three hours before repeating the same task. On a standard assembly line in Detroit workers work for 1.5 minutes before repeating the same task. At Uddevalla the morale of the employees and the quality of their product has increased. Absenteeism is 8% compared with the industry average of 20%. The turnover of employees is also below average for the industry

(Adapted from Theobald R. (94), *Understanding Industrial Society*, Macmilllan, Basingstoke)

EXERCISE

Read the extract again then answer the following questions:

i)   What evidence is there in this extract that levels of alienation are low?

ii) Why do you think that the workers experience more job satisfaction?

Quality circles

Quality circles are groups of between five and 20 workers which meet regularly to study and resolve production problems. Workers who belong to quality circles receive extra training so that they can make contributions to discussions of technical issues to do with production. Quality circles recognise that workers themselves have the experience to contribute to defining what they do and how they do it.'

(Adapted from Giddens A (89) *Sociology* Polity, Oxford)

Quality circles have been very successful in Japan and they are used in the UK by firms like Ford, Wedgewood, IBM and BT. They are said to improve relations between employer and employees, to increase efficiency and the quality of products and to improve the organisation of production.

EXERCISE

Read the extract again then answer the following questions:

i)   Why might workers feel more involved in their firm if quality circles are used?

ii) Why might efficiency and quality be increased?

Industrial democracy

Industrial democracy tries to give workers more power over the organisations they work in. There are two main types of industrial democracy:

- Works Councils. These are councils on which the employees of a firm have representatives. These councils often have the right to determine certain issues to do with employment such as pay, working hours and holidays. Of course the amount of actual power that the employee representatives have depends upon how many of them are on the council compared to employer and shareholder representatives. Employees tend not to have a majority.
- Cooperatives. In a cooperative the firm is run by the workers themselves so that they perform the tasks normally carried out by the management as well as those involved in production.

EXERCISE

i)   Look at the different examples above and think about which aspects of alienation they address.

ii) Which do you think would be the most successful and why?

Jobs for life? The rise of the flexible worker?

Over the last few years the nature of work has changed. If we are in a job we may have experienced a restructuring of our organisation at least once. We may have had to acquire new skills, especially those related to IT. If we have yet to work for a living we may have been told that the idea of a 'job for life' has disappeared, that we will have to change what we do at least five or six times in our working lives. We may know people who are on temporary contracts; or people who work part-time or have a permanent job for half or a third of the normal working-week. We may know people who work as freelancers or who sub contract work out to others.

Linked to these changes is the way that goods are made and sold to us, and the way that firms and institutions are organised. We may have recently gone to a specialist music shop and bought a limited edition single. We may have travelled to the record shop in a special edition car with features not available on similar models. We may have stopped on our way home to have a cappuccino in a cafe designed to appeal to people like us and we might have noticed others there wearing designer clothes not available in the mass market shops. Having got home we may have listened to a radio station specialising in our kind of music before going to sleep.

Older readers may be aware that the kind of 'niche' selling that we have just described did not exist 40 years ago. In the 1950s and 1960s most of us would buy mass produced goods and wear clothes sold on the mass market. Our cars would have been more or less the same as other models and broadcasting on TV and radio was aimed at the mass of the population.

Fordism and PostFordism

Sociologists distinguish between two types of production which they refer to as Fordist and PostFordist. The table on page 248 illustrates the differences between them.

Read this table carefully and think how it relates to what we have already said about work and technology.

- In a Fordist system of production machines were geared up to one thing, unlike a PostFordist system where they can be reprogrammed quickly to produce a different 'batch' of a particular product.
- If machines are fixed in terms of what they do large numbers of the same thing are produced. Think of Henry Ford's famoussaying: 'You can have any colour you want as long as it's black.' This was because the more of the same car you made the cheaper each one was to produce. But if your machines can be reprogrammed quickly and easily it is then possible to produce batches of slightly different products – special editions or limited editions.

	Fordist	Post Fordist
Technology:	Fixed dedicated machines Mass Production	Micro electronically controlled multi purpose machines, Batch production
Products:	For mass consumer market Relatively cheap	Diverse specialised products High quality
Labour process:	Fragmented few tasks	Many tasks for versatile workers
	Little worker discretion	Some authority
	Hierarchy of authority and technical control	Group control
Contracts	Collectively negotiated rate for the job	Payment by individual performance
	Relatively secure jobs	Secure core workers, highly insecure peripheral workers.

Source: Adapted from adaptation of Alan Warde, Fordism and Post-Fordism, Social Studies Review, Sept. 1989, in Marcus and Ducklin (98) Success in sociology, John Murray London.

Figure 64 The difference between Fordist and Postfordist systems.

Sometimes this kind of operation is contracted out to other firms.

- Products in a Fordist system are pretty much the same. They are produced in their thousands, and are relatively cheap. But in a PostFordist system products will be made to appeal to a particular group of consumers – a 'niche' – and they may vary considerably in price.
- The labour process in a PostFordist system may well have some of the characteristics that we discussed under the heading of employer's responses to alienation – team work, some level of control and so on.
- As far as many workers are concerned the biggest changes have come in terms of their contracts. Work for many people is now insecure. It may be temporary, casual or part-time but for many it is likely to be impermanent. Workers are also expected to be flexible in various ways.

We will look at these last two points – the core and peripheral workers and flexible working.

Core and periphery

Core workers are those with full time and permanent contracts and relatively good conditions of service. They may have perks such as a pension scheme or private health care. Peripheral workers are those on temporary contracts, part time contracts or working for a sub contractor. They may also be self employed.

If you are reading this for a course at a further education college find out whether or not the people who do the cleaning and the catering are employed by the college or whether those services are contracted from another firm. How many of the college's teaching staff are on permanent contracts? How many are part time or temporary?

The advantage for employers is that the core workers can be expected to be more flexible and the peripheral workforce can be increased when necessary. It can also be decreased – workers can be laid off, without having to pay the costs of redundancy payments. For individual workers the major disadvantage of this system is the insecurity arising from short term contracts and the high expectations that employers have of their core workforce. These core workers are often expected to put loyalty to the firm before everything. This might mean giving up weekends to cope with a rush job, or staying late at a moment's notice.

Flexible working

The table below shows what proportion of individuals have some kind of working pattern.

United Kingdom	Percentages		
	Males	Females	All employees
Full-time employees			
Flexible working hours	8.4	13.3	10.2
Annualised working hours	2.9	3.0	2.9
Four and a half day week	2.5	1.9	2.3
Term-time working	1.0	4.6	2.3
Nine day fortnight	0.4	0.2	0.3
Any flexible working pattern[2]	15.5	23.5	18.3
Part-time employees			
Flexible working hours	5.9	8.1	7.7
Annualised working hours	1.4	2.3	2.1
Term-time working	4.8	10.1	9.2
Job sharing	–	2.7	2.3
Any flexible working pattern[2]	15.1	24.2	22.6

1 Percentages are based on totals which exclude people who did not state whether or not they worked a flexible working arrangement.
2 Includes other categories of flexible working not separately identified.
Source: Labour Force Survey, Office for National Statistics

Figure 65 Flexible working patterns.

EXERCISE

Look at the table again and then answer the following questions:

i)   What differences do you notice in the flexible working patterns of males and females?
ii) Why do you suppose these differences exist?

What are the effects of organisational and technological change on workers?

A report from the Joseph Rowntree foundation shows that the drive for ever greater efficiency is putting a mounting burden on workers that is causing insecurity, ill health and unhappiness.

The findings are startling. According to measures used by economists we should be getting happier. The so called Misery Index – which charts unemployment and inflation – has fallen sharply in the 1990s as unemployment has fallen from almost 3 million to well under 1.5 million. Inflation has fallen to its lowest since the 1960s. There is no real evidence that the length of time jobs are held has changed over the last 20 years, but perhaps there is more to job insecurity than how long we spend in each job.

The Rowntree report suggests that there is. It found that job insecurity had become more widespread in the 1990s as more people were forced to work harder. More than 60% said that the pace of work – and the effort they had to put in – had increased over the past five years. More than 40% said that the management could be trusted only a little or not at all. 75% said that management and workers were not on the same side. The report says that the main cause of job insecurity and the greater amount of work demanded from employees is reduced staffing levels implemented in response to market pressures.

It could be that the report merely reflects the fact that workers like to whine, that Britons revel in being gloomy. It could also be argued that we have to sharpen up our act if we are to survive in this age of global competition. America, with its culture of flexibility, is seen as the great role model.

But, in the long run, the American model may be the road to ruin if, as the Rowntree report argues, the result is demotivation, stress and strain on families.

Signs of the pathological, sick nature of the modern labour market are everywhere – the number of people working long hours or taking their work home with them, the way in which new technology (mobile phones, pagers, laptops) have allowed employees to work in what would once have been time to unwind – train journeys, weekends, even holidays – the sense of guilt among women in particular that they are not able to juggle children and a career without something giving.

Adapted from an article by Larry Elliot in *The Guardian,* 23 August 1999.

EXERCISE

Read the article again and answer the following questions:

i)   What are the main effects of job insecurity according to the article above?
ii)   What are the main causes of job insecurity?

Inequality at work

This next section deals with inequalities at work. Probably the main ways in which we can feel ourselves the victims or the beneficiaries of inequalities at work are as follows.

→ What kind of job we can get.
→ How much we get paid.
→ Whether we feel we have an equal chance of promotion.
→ How we are treated by our fellow workers.
→ The risks attached to the job itself.

We can look at how equal work is in terms of four key variables: Gender, Ethnicity, Age and Class.

And we will see that there are areas of inequality associated with each. As we look at the various aspects of inequality associated with paid employment we will be able to answer one of the questions we asked at the beginning of this chapter – who does what jobs?

Gender inequalities at work

Look at the table and chart on page 251

What changes do you notice in the pattern of female employment over the last century? What are the main differences that you notice between the patterns of male and female employment?

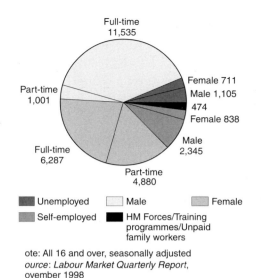

Full-time 11,535

Part-time Male 1,001

Female 711
Male 1,105
474
Female 838

Male 2,345

Full-time 6,287

Part-time 4,880

- Unemployed
- Male
- Female
- Self-employed
- HM Forces/Training programmes/Unpaid family workers

ote: All 16 and over, seasonally adjusted
ource: *Labour Market Quarterly Report*, ovember 1998

Figure 66 Patterns in female employment.

BATTLE OF THE SEXES				
PROFESSION	END OF 19th CENTURY		END OF 20th CENTURY	
	Men	Women	Men	Women
National government	88,894	11,666	143,370	206,120
Police	**44,734**	**0**	**130,030**	**16,580**
Armed forces	134,061	0	176,800	13,090
Barrister, solicitor, advocates	**23,089**	**0**	**57,660**	**22,150**
Medical practitioners	21,519	113	65,890	29,550
Veterinarians	3,752	3	5,090	2,080
Nurses, midwives and related	650	56,829	81,350	899,140
Teaching professional	**57,772**	**157,358**	**325,230**	**530,890**
Domestic housekeepers, cleaners etc	123,098	1,601,656	121,310	688,110
Chartered and certified accountants	**9,129**	**50**	**83,220**	**22,670**
Farming	1,043,780	74,695	356,170	91,530
Milliner, dressmaker, tailors etc	**145,755**	**566,943**	**12,060**	**17,570**
Coal mine labourers	587,452	3,833	20,770	160
General labourers	**659, 124**	**3,022**	**91,660**	**7,740**
Authors, writers, journalists	5,539	689	4,517	3,418
				Source: ONS

Figure 67 Pattern of women in paid employment.

The main patterns in women's paid employment over the last century can be summarised as follows.

→ There are now many more female employees in the workforce. According to the British Economy survey in 1998 72% of working age women were in some form of employment. This compares with 32% in the 1920s. Some sociologists are now talking of the 'feminisation' of the workforce.

→ Although there are now many more women in the workforce they are still concentrated in certain areas as caring, cooking, cleaning and clerical work. Look again at the table above. What are the areas in which women outnumber men? Have any of these altered since the end of the 19th century? Sociologists refer to this concentration of women into certain occupational areas as horizontal segregation.

→ Women also find themselves subject to vertical segregation – within a particular occupation women are likely to find themselves in the lower rather than higher grades which tend to be dominated by men.

→ Women are much more likely than men to be in part time employment. Look again at the pie chart above. Only about 8% of male employees are part time workers compared with almost 44% of female employees.

→ On average women get paid less than men.

What are the reasons for the increasing numbers of women in the workforce?

To explain the increase in the numbers of female employees in the workforce we need to think about a number of factors. Over the last century there have been two world wars which saw large numbers of women brought into the workforce to do the jobs left vacant when the men went to fight. This involvement of women in previously male areas of employment helped to change men's attitudes. As the economy altered, so more 'women's jobs' in the tertiary sector were created. At the same time in the 1960s and 1970s the 'privatised' family emerged and in order to afford the kind of lifestyle that couples wanted for themselves and their children it became an economic necessity for both partners to have some sort of income. With advances in contraception and changes in abortion laws it became possible for women to plan when they were to have children and so plan a working life or career. In the 1970s legislation such as the Equal Pay Act and the Sex Discrimination Act tried to cement and direct a change of attitude to female employment. More recently another kind of economic necessity has drawn women into employment. The decline in traditional forms of male employment – in mining, ship building, the docks, and the steel yards, for example – has meant that many men have been unable to find employment and so in some parts of the country it is increasingly common for women to be the main breadwinners.

Explaining women's position in the labour market

As we saw earlier two of the most significant features of the paid employment that women tend to have are **horizontal segregation** and **vertical segregation**.

> Women are losing out on pay and promotion to men throughout their careers. New figures show women remain under-represented at head and deputy level despite the increasing feminisation of the workforce. A conference of women heads of girls' schools branded the situation a 'disgrace'. Lack of female role models and appropriate professional development plus difficulties with childcare, sexism and long hours were blamed for deterring women from pursuing promotion.
>
> After 10 to 14 years in primary teaching 82.3 % of women have yet to make senior management, with more than a third still on point nine on the salary scale, the maximum without additional responsibility. By the same mid career stage, only 16% of men in primaries are on point nine or under while nearly 45% are heads or deputies, compared with only 17% of women.
>
> Taken from an article by Amanda Kelly and Karen Thornton in the *TES*, 13 October 2000.

Sociologists have used similar explanations for why many women do different jobs to men and why many women experience a glass ceiling when it comes to promotion. (This is quite a powerful image suggesting that while women can see that there are opportunities for advancement at work there is a barrier through which they cannot pass.)

If we think about the kinds of paid employment that women are most likely to find themselves in we can see that most of them are linked in some way to women's stereotypical role in the home. They are jobs involving tasks similar to what women are often expected to do in the household – cooking, cleaning and caring. For some sociologists the fact that women still tend to be seen as those with the caring or domestic role in society means that it is women who will be seen as having the qualities appropriate for certain kinds of work. These sorts of ideas are often referred to as the 'ideology of domesticity'. Women are regarded, in a society dominated by men, as being best suited to tasks which are connected with caring, and providing for, others.

If these ideas are held by parents, teachers, managers, supervisors and employers then we can see how it might be more likely that women are 'directed' into certain occupations. We have seen in Chapter 3 how girls are still in the minority in subjects like physics and maths at A level and above, and how some subjects are seen as masculine or feminine. So because of their lack of suitable qualifications girls' entry into professions like engineering is limited. Likewise their qualifications do prepare them for so called 'women's jobs'. So the ideas about who should do what tasks in society are an important part of any explanation about why women do the jobs they do. It is also important to look at who makes decisions. As we have seen from the table above it is still likely to be men who are in positions of authority in firms and organisations.

Firstly women are accustomed to having men in authority over them, which confirms views that men in authority are 'naturally' suited for authority and women are unfit for top posts. Secondly, decisions are made by men and are likely to reflect male ideas and interests. Thirdly, men are likely to be in positions in which they are able to 'hire and fire' and make recommendations for promotion. Many studies have shown how men will appoint 'in their own image'. Fourthly, it is mainly male managers who are responsible for equal opportunity policies. Though we should be aware of seeing all men as sexist or holding traditional views on gender, some male managers are hostile to some aspects of official policies and in some cases undermine them.

Adapted from Harriet Bradley(1999): *Gender and Power in the Workplace*, MacMillan.

Two of Bradley's respondents put it like this:

A male bank clerk said:

'Women are certainly more organised than men. Jobs like secretary, administration, etc, I think women are better at, but at decision making I think men take things with more thought, rather than just looking at a colourful picture and dithering.'

and a women a working in stock control said:

'When it's put down on paper in "management speak" it's equal, but when it comes down to the nitty gritty you still have to be twice as good, as a woman. . . . We don't seem to be regarded very highly for promotion. What seems to be the trouble is the idea that she's going to get married and have children and run off.'

EXERCISE

i) How far do the ideas in the extracts above reflect what you know about how men and women think?

ii) If you are at school or college how far do the courses that males and females are doing prepare them for different kinds of work?

Why do women get paid less than men?

We saw at the start of this section that women's pay, on average, is less than that of men. How are we to explain this?

➜ The occupations in which women work tend to be lower paid. The lower professions such as teaching, social work and nursing pay less than the higher professions like law, accounting or medicine. Jobs such as cleaning and catering are also subject to low pay.

➜ Within individual occupations we have seen that women tend to be concentrated at the lower end – they are not promoted as often as men are.

➜ Women's domestic responsibilities may mean that they are more likely to be employed as part time workers than men. Domestic responsibilities are also likely to mean that women are less able to take up opportunities for overtime working than men.

→ Women are more likely than men to be employed as homeworkers. This often involves tasks such as addressing envelopes, sewing items of clothing, or packaging cosmetics for example, and is notoriously badly paid.

Question

Do you think that the jobs that women tend to do are low paid because women do them, or do women get to do them because they are low paid?

Being at work – is it the same for women as for men?

An important aspect of paid employment is what it is actually like to be there. We've looked at some of the effects of being at work, or doing housework, in the section on alienation above. However, there may also be many differences in the experience of being at work according to whether we are female or male. Men tend to take home more money in their pay packets, and are more likely to obtain promotion than women. What are the other differences?

Women are more likely to find themselves working with other women than men. Because of both horizontal and vertical segregation it is likely that the people we work with will often be the same sex as ourselves. This often means that particular **gender cultures** are likely to develop and continue in a workplace. The culture of the building site is likely to be different to that of a group of machinists in the textile industry, though each culture can appear quite threatening to a member of the opposite sex. This kind of workplace culture can also have the effect of maintaining gender segregation because it is difficult for women to enter an all male workplace and vice versa.

Women who work in mixed or relatively mixed working environments may also have to contend with sexual harassment over and above the kind of ideological sexism we have discussed above. **Sexual harassment** in the workplace can take many forms, from inappropriate language and looks, and sexual innuendo to displays of 'page 3' calendars, inappropriate touching and holding, to offers of preferential treatment or even promotion in return for sexual favours. While men are also subject to sexual harassment, women are the more likely victims in situations where men still hold power.

As well as actual sexual harassment women might find that they are the objects of sexist language. For example being called 'pet', 'darling' or 'babe', or referred to as 'girls' or 'ladies' rather than women. Women may also find that they are subject to the kinds of assumptions that men make about their roles within an organisation. If a male worker asks a female colleague to 'make us a cup of tea, love' it not only says something about the appropriate roles of men and women, it is also saying that your work is less important than mine and can be interrupted.

Women are also more likely than men to find their working day interrupted by their **domestic responsibilities**. It is probably still usual for women to take care of sick children or relatives. Women are also more likely than men to have their working day interrupted by having to take messages from home. This could be the kids ringing up to see if they can go round to their friend's for tea or to see if their friends can stay the night. Women may experience **role conflict** because of the competing demands of their roles as wife, mother and employee. Many working women feel guilty about leaving their children with a childminder or a nursery and about not being at home when their children get back from school. Because this domestic role is not part of being the 'breadwinner' many men do not experience this guilt. In fact for many men it is probably true to say that they liken being a breadwinner to being a father.

Question

i)   Do you think that men might experience the expectation of being the breadwinner as being somehow oppressive?

The Dual Labour Market

Some sociologists identify the differences in men and women's paid employment by looking at the characteristics of the labour market. They say that we can divide the labour market (that is the kinds of paid employment that are available to all of us) into two: the primary market and the secondary market.

- **The Primary Labour Market** consists of those jobs that offer a career, are relatively secure and well paid. These are usually in large corporations or government agencies.
- **The Secondary Labour Market** consists of the insecure, poorly paid and relatively unskilled jobs, often with poor working conditions.

Women are more likely than men to be employed in the secondary labour market because many of the jobs they do, like cleaning, waitressing, working in shops, or catering are in this category. But it is not only women who find themselves in the secondary labour market. Many members of ethnic minority groups also have jobs which fall into this category.

Ethnic inequalities at work

As with other areas in sociology we cannot generalise about the difference between white workers and members of all minority ethnic groups. There are significant differences between ethnic groups – one particular difference is in relation to unemployment, which is dealt with later in this chapter.

Another significant difference between ethnic groups is in relation to occupation. 13% of Indian men are employed in professional or managerial occupations as compared to 8% of white men. But black, Pakistani and Bangladeshi men are more likely to be employed in semi-skilled or unskilled manual occupations.

However it is true to say that members of minority ethnic groups are particularly likely to be employed in low paid occupations such as retail, transport and nursing.

Class inequalities at work

Figures 68 and 69 illustrate the extent of class, gender and age differences in pay. Pay is obviously a significant aspect of inequality as it has the greatest influence on our life chances.

Distribution of gross hourly earnings
(adults whose pay was not affected by absence)

	Manuals	Non-manuals	All	Part time
£ per hour				
Men				
Bottom 10 per cent	4.85	6.40	5.32	3.75
Bottom 25 per cent	5.88	8.72	6.73	4.22
Median	7.33	12.30	9.25	5.25
Top 25 percent	9.35	17.09	13.42	7.98
Top 10 per cent	11.69	23.80	19.19	15.77
Women				
Bottom 10 per cent	3.94	5.41	4.67	3.89
Bottom 25 per cent	4.48	6.61	5.83	4.40
Median	5.32	8.68	7.74	5.37
Top 25 per cent	6.69	12.30	11.17	7.38
Top 10 per cent	8.52	16.56	15.45	11.35
Men and women				
Bottom 10 per cent	4.46	5.78	5.01	3.86
Bottom 25 per cent	5.41	7.41	6.36	4.38
Median	6.90	10.49	8.65	5.36
Top 25 per cent	8.88	14.97	12.57	7.47
Top 10 per cent	11.29	20.53	17.75	11.80

Dispersion of hourly earnings
(full time)

△ Top 10%
□ Median
○ Bottom 10%

Manual men, Manual women, Non-manual men, Non-manual women

Figure 68 Distribution of earnings table.

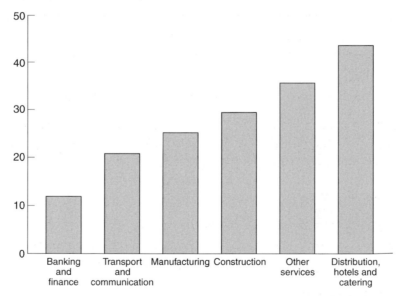

Banking and finance, Transport and communication, Manufacturing, Construction, Other services, Distribution, hotels and catering

Source: Analysis by the Centre for Economic Performance, LSE, based on 1998 Labour Force Survey data

Figure 69 Percentage of employees aged under 25 years who are low paid.

Another significant aspect of class inequality at work is that people who work in many manual occupations are at greater risk of injury or ill health than those who are employed in non manual occupations. Building sites, mines, and factory floors are potentially dangerous working environments. This is not simply because of the risks of explosions, collapsing seams, or dangerous machinery, but also because of the risk of exposure to hazardous substances or polluted atmospheres. Many ex-miners suffer from pneumoconiosis as a result of inhaling coal dust; men who have worked in close contact with asbestos may be at risk of asbestosis, another disease of the lungs, and workers in the chemical industry may find themselves exposed to dangerous chemicals.

Although various governments have introduced health and safety legislation, it is not always adhered to. Sometimes this is the fault of employees, as when construction workers fail to wear knee protectors putting themselves at risk of arthritis when they get older, or when workers using pneumatic drills do not use silencers or ear protectors, endangering their hearing. Sometimes it is the fault of employers, as when the equipment they provide is faulty, safety legislation is not followed, or safety equipment is not provided.

Too old to hire, too young to retire? Age inequalities at work

Ageism refers to systematic stereotyping of people and discrimination against them on the basis of characteristics, abilities and limitations which are imputed to them simply because of their age (Bodily 1994). Thus all older people are seen as less suitable for employment on the grounds that they are physically slow, lacking in dynamism, and not very adaptable to change; all younger people are suspected of being unreliable, reckless, undisciplined and prone to drug taking and promiscuity.

Source Harriet Bradley (96); *Fractured Identities, Changing Patterns of Inequality*, Polity Press.

The first thing to say about ageism is that it is not just a prejudicial view of older people. Ageism can affect all of us. At various stages of our life we can be regarded as too young or too old for a job, or even to take part in a particular leisure activity.

Think about the following:

i) At what age are you told you are too old to out clubbing?
ii) At what age do you think people would take your opinions seriously?
iii) When is someone regarded as 'past it' in terms of employment?

Now read the following extracts:

While age stereotyping acts particularly against the young and the old, middle groupings too may suffer from aspects of it. For example middle aged women applying for jobs as secretaries, receptionists or computer operators may be told they are 'too old for the job'. Where youth and glamour are associated with particular forms of employment, the middle aged find themselves faced with ageist exclusion. Surveys carried out by the Institute of Personnel Management and the Metropolitan Authorities' Recruitment Agency revealed that in many workplaces age discrimination begins for men at 40 and for women at 35.

Source Harriet Bradley (96) as above.

Almost a third of men over 50 but below pension age have no paid work, and most have given up seeking it.

The fast growing trend of early retirement risks creating a group of 2 million men in their 50s and 60s who are doing little with their lives and whose inactivity may put their health at risk, a government study today shows.

Among men aged 50–64, according to a study by the Office for National Statistics, the proportion in paid employment has fallen from 84% in 1979 to 69% in 1998. The 31% not working is made up of 4% who are registered unemployed and 27% who are termed 'economically inactive.' But among women in their 50s the proportion in paid work has increased from 55% in 1968 to 62% in 1998, though almost half work part time.

A main cause of the different employment patterns among men and women is structural change. While many manufacturing jobs have disappeared, particularly in heavy industry, there has been a growth of opportunities in the service sector.

The study also indicates that men who retire early and sit about the house put themselves at greater risk of ill health. The death rates for men aged 50 to 64 are now 60% higher than those for women.

Adapted from an article by David Brindle and Sue Quinn in *The Guardian*, 11 June 1999.

EXERCISE

Read the extracts again then answer the following questions:

i) Why might middle aged women be regarded as 'too old' for a job as a secretary or receptionist?

ii) What kinds of employment are associated with youth and glamour?

iii) Why might age discrimination start earlier for women than for men?

iv) Why might many unemployed men over 50 have given up looking for a job?

v) Why are increasing numbers of women in their 50s in paid work?

vi) What is the link between early retirement and ill health?

The relationship between stereotyping and work is not necessarily a straightforward one. We probably think of ageism as only applying to older people. Thus women of a certain age are considered to be too old to be secretaries or receptionists because they do not fit our stereotypical view of the young, attractive and efficient person we expect to see occupying that position. Likewise both women and men in their 40s and 50s might be regarded as being too set in their ways to undertake training to learn new skills such as computer operating. However, stereotyping can also apply to the young.

Some sociologists and many young working class people feel that training schemes such as YTS and the New Deal were forms of social control based on a particular stereotype of young people as being a potential problem for society and therefore needing to be disciplined and controlled. In some ways then both young people and older people can be said to be victims of ageism.

Sometimes the reason for older people, especially those over 50, taking early retirement or voluntary redundancy may not be specifically to do with their age. The reason may be an economic one. Workers over 50 may decide to take early retirement or voluntary redundancy simply because it is worth their while. They may qualify for an occupational pension once they reach 50, or for a reasonable sum in redundancy payments. Therefore they may decide to leave work and try something new. From the employer's point of view they may prefer to lay off older workers because they have to pay higher salaries and in the long run it will save them money.

Of course if someone over 50 is made redundant it is harder for them to find work because their skills may no longer be in demand and they are regarded as being unsuitable for retraining because of their age. New jobs in the service sector may require skills that older workers do not possess. It is also possible that older men may feel that some jobs are women's jobs and therefore not suitable.

However age is not always a barrier to employment. Look at the extracts from the B+Q document below:

> B & Q understands only too well that the wealth of life experience and knowledge that an older person brings is a huge resource to our company which helps strengthen our diverse workforce.
>
> To answer the Board's concerns about employing an older workforce . . . B & Q decided to open a store staffed entirely by over 50s in Macclesfield.
>
> The results:
> - Profits higher by 18%
> - Staff turnover was six times lower
> - 39% less absenteeism
> - 58% less shrinkage
> - Improved perception of customer service
> - Increase in the base skill of the staff
>
> The results helped lift the barriers to employment.
>
> We have to make the right use of the skills and abilities of everyone – older and younger people, to fulfil the range of job roles that make up our organisation. This means ensuring that our recruitment and development policies do not impose any barriers that might restrict who we recruit, train or promote.

EXERCISE

Look at the extract again and answer the following question:

i) In what ways does the B+Q document challenge our stereotypical view of older workers?

Unemployment

Who are the unemployed?

Although economic changes over recent years have meant that virtually no occupational group is immune to unemployment, there are still certain occupational and social groups who are particularly likely to experience it:

- Young people (aged 18–24) often lack the experience, skills or the qualifications to obtain a job. Many young people experience the 'Catch 22' situation of not being able to get a job because they lack experience, and not being able to gain experience because they can't get a job. Government schemes such as the New Deal are a way of addressing this problem.

- Older people (aged 50 or over). As we have already seen ageism exists to a large extent in our society. Many older women and men find it hard to obtain employment as employers may well regard them as 'past it'. Sometimes employers will not take on older workers because they feel that their investment in training will not be repaid – the older employee will have a fairly short working life before they retire. Older people are also more likely to have skills that are no longer in demand and so are likely to need retraining.

- Unskilled and semi-skilled workers are often the first to be laid off if a firm faces financial difficulties. This is because they are easy to replace – their jobs require little or no training. It is also the case that a skilled worker can do a semi or unskilled job, but this does not work the other way round. When jobs are scarce, unskilled and semi-skilled workers may face extra competition for work.

- Members of minority ethnic groups. Overall an individual belonging to a minority ethnic group is more likely to experience unemployment than a white person. See below.

→ The unemployment rate for white men was 6.9% of the workforce in spring 2000, while the rate for all ethnic minorities was 13%.

→ Black men from countries other than Africa or the Caribbean have the highest rate at 26.6%. Bangladeshi men are next at 20.4%.

→ Indian men have the lowest unemployment rate of any minority ethnic group at 7.2%.

→ The unemployment rate for white women was 4.7%, while the rate for all women from minority ethnic groups was 12.3%

→ Bangladeshi and Pakistani women have the highest unemployment rates among women of minority ethnic groups at 23.9%.

David Blackaby, an expert on the labour market at the University of Swansea, says that legislation designed to combat racial discrimination has failed. In the 30 years since the Race Relations Act was passed the position of black people in the labour market appears to have got worse.

During the recession of the 1990s the unemployment rate for ethnic minority men soared to 25%, nearly 2.5 times the rate for white men, and the gap between the two has remained steady since then, despite the recovery in the economy.

The recession hit black people harder, according to Dr Blackaby, because it gave firms the chance to discriminate. 'When there are lots of people out of work, it's easier for them to pick white workers over black, or men over women.'

Taken (and adapted) from an article by Charlotte Denny in *The Guardian* .

EXERCISE

Read the extract again and answer the following questions:

i) Why should a recession make discriminaton easier?

ii) Why do you think the unemployment rate of Indian men was lower than for other minority ethnic group members?

● Gender is often thought to make a difference to our chances of being unemployed. Men are thought to be more at risk than women. The number of men registering as unemployed is certainly much higher than the official figure for women. This may reflect the fact that many women are ineligible for unemployment benefits in their own right and so do not bother to register. It may also be that many single parents (who are almost all women) may want to work but are unable to do so because they cannot obtain or afford suitable childcare – they see themselves as unemployed but they are not part of the official count.

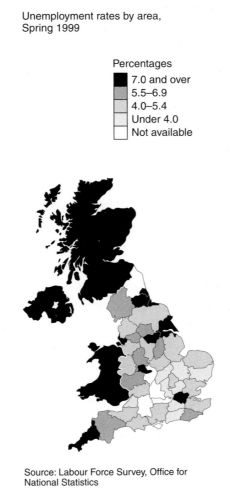

Unemployment rates by area,
Spring 1999

Percentages
■ 7.0 and over
▨ 5.5–6.9
▨ 4.0–5.4
□ Under 4.0
□ Not available

Source: Labour Force Survey, Office for
National Statistics

Figure 70 Unemployment rates in Britain.

● Location. As the map above shows, unemployment rates vary considerably across Britain. Areas with high levels of unemployment tend to be those which had a high proportion of traditional heavy industries, as in the former coalfields of South Yorkshire, South Wales and southern Scotland. In spring 1999 the English counties with the highest rates were the former county of Cleveland at 12.9% and Tyne and Wear at 10.9%. The major industries in these areas included steel, chemicals and ship building, all of which had either reduced the size of their workforce in order to be more efficient or as a result of losing trade to foreign competition. Other areas with high levels of unemployment tend to be those with very little industry, such as Cornwall, where tourism is a major industry, but as a result many jobs tend to be seasonal and temporary.

What are the causes of unemployment?

- People change jobs. Sometimes individuals plan a gap between leaving one job and starting another. During this time they may register as unemployed. This type of unemployment is known as *frictional* unemployment and does not usually last for a long time or have any negative effects on those concerned. Indeed they may see the break as an advantage and use the time to prepare for their new job or do some work around the house.

- The economic structure of countries can change. Industries decline and people lose their jobs. In the 1980s this happened on a large scale in ship building on Tyneside, Wearside and Clydeside and in the coal mining industry. For example in 1955 there were 696 collieries employing 698,700 miners. By 1993 there were 25 collieries employing 23,000 miners. This kind of unemployment, which is known as *structural* unemployment, can affect individuals in that they may well find that there is no longer a demand for their skills. Jobs often disappear permanently.

- Unemployment can also arise when the economy of a country improves or declines. Politicians talk of periods of 'boom' and 'bust'. The British economy went through a recession (went 'bust') from 1980 to 1983, followed by a 'boom' in the mid 1980s. When the economy is doing well more workers are needed; when the economy is in recession firms tend to lay their workers off. The construction industry is a good indicator of the state of the economy. When there is plenty of money about people consider buying new houses, firms think about expanding into bigger premises, and so there is plenty of demand for construction workers. In a recession individuals and organisations have less (or no) money and so there is little demand for building work. This type of unemployment is known as cyclical unemployment. Individuals affected by cyclical unemployment may well find that once the economy picks up their skills are in demand again.

What are the consequences of unemployment?

i) **For individuals** – at first a person who loses his or her job may find they have plenty to do with their time. They may get on with all those jobs around the house and garden that they always meant to do. Wages, savings and maybe holiday pay may help to tide them over while they look for work. If, however, they are unable to find a job quickly they may find that the spare time and the lack of money become a burden. They may become bored and depressed because of their inability to find work. It is also often true that the longer someone is out of work the harder it is for them to find work – this can add to the frustration and depression.

Lack of money is also a problem. Without savings or redundancy pay someone who has only state benefits to rely on will probably find it difficult to adjust to their new circumstances. Nights out with friends may well be avoided because of lack of money or not being able to join in conversations about the day's work. In this way some people can become socially isolated.

For many men in our society being unemployed is a large blow to their self esteem. Many aspects of our identity are bound up with what we do for a living and this is particularly true for men who have been socialised into being the breadwinner. Without a job, many men, and increasing numbers of women, will feel worthless.

Too much spare time, too little money, boredom, lack of status, frustration – for some individuals this can be enough to tempt them into some type of criminal activity. The link between unemployment and crime is complex but individuals who are not at work have more opportunities to become involved in crime – it is not surprising then that some do.

ii) **For households** – many couples find it hard to adjust to unemployment, especially if he has lost his job and she has been a housewife. They may find it difficult to adjust to spending the whole day together. 'Now he's out of work he's under my feet all day' is a familiar refrain for some. Marriages and partnerships can be put under severe strain, especially when money is short. Arguments can start over very little, particularly if everyone is stressed over lack of money – a situation all too likely in households trying to get by on state benefits alone. Divorce or separation are possible results.

iii) **For communities** – high levels of unemployment can have a corrosive effect on communities, especially if unemployment is long term (over 12 months). The main reason for this is lack of money. With a large number of people living off benefits there is not as much money being spent in local shops or pubs, nor is money going to local tradesmen like builders or decorators. As the profits of local businesses fall more people lose their jobs and some shops or businesses close down. As the range of local shops becomes smaller, people may go shopping elsewhere and so even less money is spent in the area. Empty properties may be boarded up, attracting vandalism and graffiti, and some people may well turn to crime – burglary or drugs – to make ends meet or to escape from the depression caused by unemployment. If all of these take place the area can quickly gain a bad reputation, property prices fall and no one wants to move in. However local communities affected by high levels of unemployment do not have to suffer this fate as the article below shows.

GRIMETHORPE TURNS BACK THE TIDE

Thanks to its fictional appearance in the film *Brassed Off*, the village of Grimethorpe, once known for its pit and brass band, has become a national symbol of the devastation that swept through the coalfields in the late 1980s and 1990s. It was left jobless and broken, struggling to contain the rising levels of depression and crime.

But the villagers proved that this image is also out of date when Grimethorpe received an award from the Home Secretary, Jack Straw, for running the best Neighbourhood Watch scheme in Britain. Mr Straw said "the people of Grimethorpe have shown what can be achieved when local people get together to help bring down crime."

The pits closed in 1993 after running for 100 years. But that wasn't all. There was nowhere for the unemployed to turn to because across South Yorkshire 160,000 workers lost jobs in coal, engineering and steel.

By 1995 the unemployment rate was 33%, and half of the population was classed as long term incapacitated through illness. Drugs, burglary and car crime were rife and unlicensed motor cyclists raised merry hell for residents.

The Neighbourhood Watch team first tried to improve relations between the community and the police which had been damaged by the miner's strike. Security lights were installed for every elderly person and money was raised for an ECG machine at the local surgery.

They cleared away derelict land and built a playgroup and youth club. This became a community association to which every household belongs. It tried to tackle social problems. Youngsters have activities to keep them from crime. Money for sports teams has been raised, a drum majorette group has been set up and 50 children have obtained Duke of Edinburgh awards.

Crime has dropped overall by 23% and car crime by 44% compared with 1999. The difference can be seen at the mothers' and toddlers' club set up five years ago. Children who would otherwise be watching TV or, as one person said, "roaming the streets and throwing rocks at one another", are now playing games together.

The Independent on Sunday 29/10/00

EXERCISE

Read the article again and answer the following questions:

i)   What were the consequences of high levels of unemployment in Grimethorpe?

ii) How did the local community tackle their problems?

The consequences of unemployment for society as a whole

Unemployment does not simply affect individuals, households and communities, it can affect society as a whole. High levels of unemployment mean high levels of government expenditure on benefits. This can lead to cuts in other forms of government spending, cuts in benefits or a tightening up of benefit rules as happened with the introduction of Job Seeker's Allowance. High levels of unemployment can also lead to some people finding simple solutions to a complex problem. Scapegoats for the lack of jobs are found, often amongst minority groups, and racist organisations may attract more followers. It is also possible for social unrest to grow with large numbers of disaffected individuals having nothing to do and no apparent hope for the future. During the 1980s there were examples of social unrest – riots – in many of England's major cities. High levels of unemployment can emphasise the divisions that already exist in a society. Those who do not have much to start with are those who are most at risk; those who have most are often least at risk.

Glossary

Alienation	is a complex term in sociology. For Karl Marx it meant, very briefly, that individuals in capitalist societies were prevented from reaching their true potential as human beings. The social organisation of capitalism condemned many people to dull, repetitive work for the bosses. Work was not an expression of human need or creativity, it was similar to forced labour. Some sociologists use a much narrower definition of alienation to refer to the reasons why many workers gain little satisfaction from their work.
Core workers	are those with relatively secure, full time and permanent positions within an organisation. This term is used to distinguish core workers from peripheral workers.
Peripheral workers	are those workers in insecure and non permanent employment, for example those on short term, temporary or part time contracts. Such workers can be brought in by employers when demand for their products or services rises and they can be laid off cheaply when demand falls.
Flexible working	both core and peripheral workers are said to be part of a flexible workforce. Flexible working takes many forms. One of the most common is flexi-time. Workers on flexi-time are able to adjust their working hours to suit their circumstances. Office staff often work **flexi-time**. They have to be at work during core hours (say between 9.30 am and 5.30 pm) but many start from say 10.00 am and finish at 6 pm. Over a period of time flexi workers may accumulate hours or take some time off. This arrangement often suits working mothers.
	Annualised hours is another form of flexible working. In many FE colleges lecturers do not have a fixed weekly timetable but work to an annual total of teaching hours so that they might teach for more hours per week at the start of the academic year and fewer at the end. This is said to benefit the organisation by allowing core workers to teach at busy times (although it is not alway popular with lecturers).
Division of labour	this refers to the way that tasks or jobs are divided up within a society or an organisation. The *domestic division of labour* refers to the way that tasks are divided up within a household.
Dual Labour Market Theory	this is a reference to the way that the market for jobs and careers is divided into two segments. The *primary* labour market is said to consist of relatively secure, well paid and career based opportunities. The *secondary* labour market is said to consist of relatively insecure, relatively low paid jobs with few or no career opportunities. Women and some minority ethnic groups have been said to have their employment opportunities limited to the secondary labour market. However this distinction has become less useful over recent years as many jobs in the primary sector have become subject to redundancy

and are therefore insecure. It is also true that some jobs in the secondary sector offer high rates of pay.

The occupational structure of society refers to the kinds of employment available in a society. Over the last fifty years the number of occupations in the primary sector (mining and fishing, for example) and secondary sectors (manufacturing industry) have decreased while the number of occupations in the tertiary or service sector (for example in banking, insurance, leisure and entertainment) have increased. Changes in the occupational structure of a society may therefore affect the class structure of that society.

Horizontal segregation refers to the way that women tend to be concentrated in certain areas of paid employment and men in others.

Vertical segregation refers to the fact that within a particular occupation women tend to be over-represented in the lower grades and under-represented in the higher grades.

The glass ceiling refers to the difficulty that women have in obtaining promotion in many organisations. They are able to see the opportunities available higher up in the organisation but experience a kind of invisible barrier which prevents them rising up the career ladder. This barrier is most likely caused by men's stereotypical ideas about women – purely emotional rather than rational; focussed primarily on their domestic role and so on.

Politics

8

Introduction

Very few students celebrate the prospect of doing the politics section of a sociology syllabus: 'Politics is boring', teachers and lecturers are told. It is not difficult to feel sympathy with this point of view. Taking an interest in politics – if politics is what politicians do – can so easily appear a waste of time. The individuals and institutions who make the big decisions seem to be remote from ordinary people. Government ministers and top civil servants are not the kind of people who live next door. We can read about politics in the newspapers or watch the news on TV. We can feel ourselves to be on the receiving end of decisions made by politicians. We can even have a good moan when 2p more tax is put on the price of a pint or our local hospital is closed. Very seldom do most people feel, however, that they can play any real part in the making of decisions.

And yet the person in the street does have a part to play in the British political system. British politics, it is commonly accepted, is democratic. We are not governed by generals who seized power by using military violence and who hold on to power by controlling the media, and imprisoning or murdering anyone who opposes them.

> Repression, brutality and terror are watchwords of the Burmese military junta, in which two dozen generals control the minds, if not the hearts, of 48 million people.
>
> Since coming to power in 1962 the generals have sealed the nation off from the rest of the world. They have done it through force. Thousands of people have been slaughtered, tens of thousands more subject to hard labour and democratic movements all but eliminated.
>
> In 1988, the army crushed a prodemocracy uprising and two years later ignored the results of a general election that gave 82% of the vote to the National League for Democracy led by Aung San Sou Kyi. She was put under house arrest. Prodemocracy campaigners are still regularly imprisoned on the flimsiest of pretexts.
>
> One British protester was sentenced to seven years hard labour for singing a prodemocracy song in the street. Another Briton was sentenced to 17 years for distributing anti-government literature.
>
> Adapted from an article by John Anglionby in *The Guardian*, 25 January 2000

In Britain the public have regular opportunities to choose the people who govern them. A general election allows the adult population as a whole to remove the politicians governing the country. Note how easy it is to put a set of politicians out of office in Britain. It does not take brave people to take to the streets to demand an election. Voters walking to a polling station do not have to pluck up courage to risk being beaten up or imprisoned if they vote against those in power. In Britain it is accepted that those who wish to govern must obtain the approval of the people.

Of course it was not always like this. The struggle for democracy has been long and hard and, some would argue, has not yet been won. The elites of birth, land and commercial wealth which at various times in our past have been dominant politically, did not want to share power with the mass of the population. It took much dedication and sacrifice on the part of ordinary men and women in the past to win the political rights and freedoms which citizens enjoy today.

Democracy and elections

Whilst being a vital part of any democracy, elections in themselves do not guarantee that a political system will operate democratically. Many conditions need to be satisfied. All members of the adult population must be entitled to vote. One of the crucial aspects of the struggle for democracy in Britain over the last 200 years was the demand that the vote be given to the working class and to women. There are people alive in Britain today who were born at a time when women did not have the right to vote in parliamentary elections. The principle that all adults whether rich or poor, educated or uneducated are entitled to vote – universal adult suffrage – is now well established.

A closely related principle is expressed by the slogan 'one man or woman one vote'. In a democratic political system all citizens should have an equal political status. The vote of one citizen should be worth no more than that of another. This principle can be seen at work in elections. The ballot papers are impersonal and unsigned. Whether a candidate wins or not depends on how many, not on which, people voted for them. For the electors the privacy of the polling booth and the anonymity of the ballot papers create a situation in which they can cast their votes freely and without fear. Neighbours, employers or state officials do not know for whom an elector voted and, therefore, cannot punish him or her for voting the 'wrong way'. Without such secrecy voters could more easily be pressured, with the result that their votes may not accurately express the wishes of the people.

Political parties

Imagine a general election without political parties. The outcome of such an election would be a House of Commons made up of 651 individual MPs. These MPs themselves would decide who would become prime minister and what policies would be followed. In a general election in which different political parties compete for public support members of the public can influence more directly who becomes the government. Each elector knows that by voting for a particular candidate he or she is voting for a particular political party and voting for the leader of that party to become prime minister. As newspaper headlines make clear the day after, the public – through an election – decide who will govern them. 'Election result – Five more years of Conservative government'.

In this way political parties help the public to make significant choices in elections. The parties can perhaps be likened to businesses. It is as if each party offers a service – governing the country in a particular way – to the public. To be successful a party must win more 'customers' than the other parties. To do this it will try to present itself as offering the public a 'better deal' than the other parties. Those parties not in government – 'the opposition' – have an incentive to 'show up' the government, to expose its wrongdoings and inefficiencies. In this way members of the public become better informed, and the government is given an incentive to govern in a way which suits the public. From the moment it is elected the government is competing with the opposition, knowing that each day brings a general election closer. If by the time that election is held the public no longer have confidence in the government and want a change there is an alternative – the opposition – ready and waiting to take over.

Democratic attitudes

Politics will work like this only if certain conditions are met. Members of the public must have rights and be confident that they can use them without being punished. The right to criticise or make fun of the government or to argue in favour of change is vitally important. Only if individuals and groups within the society feel able to 'speak their mind' can governments be challenged and reminded constantly that they are responsible to the people. Within a democracy the right to 'freedom of expression' extends naturally into 'freedom of association' – the right of individuals to unite and form organisations with others who have similar ideas or interests. Within these organisations groups of individuals can develop opinions on matters of interest to them. These opinions can be expressed publicly through the organisation. In this way the phrase 'public opinion' can come to mean something – particularly to politicians who have to take it into account if they wish to be successful.

A democratic society?

Remember that even such a basic democratic requirement as universal suffrage was introduced relatively recently in Britain. For most of our history our political system has not been democratic. For centuries it was developed and used by elites of one kind or another to run the country. Ordinary people were expected to 'know their place'. Recognise also that introducing democracy into Britain did not involve the abolition of the most obviously non-democratic political institutions: Britain is still a monarchy and only very recently has serious consideration been given to abolishing the largely hereditary House of Lords.

With such a history it becomes sensible to ask how far democratic principles have reached into British society. Major elements of the political system have been democratised. Can other institutions within British society be described as democratic? How democratic are schools and colleges, religious institutions, and the economic institutions within which we work or to which we relate as customers? To what extent is life within modern family types democratic? The answers are important.

Within a non-democratic system the ordinary people are expected to do what they are told. They are not expected to play any part in governing the country. The less questioning, the more obedient the ordinary people are the easier it is for the generals, party bosses or business elites who run things. In principle a democracy is different. It is 'government by the people'. This can be achieved only if the people are willing and able to govern. This does not mean – in a system of representative democracy – that everybody must be willing and able to become a professional politician or even to devote a lot of time to political activities. The citizens of a democracy should, however, feel that they are the masters rather than the servants of those who do govern.

Put simply, democracy is not just about the legal right to participate. It is about people's attitudes, beliefs, values and skills. The right to vote only becomes an instrument of democratic government when people use it. The result of a general election in which only a handful of citizens voted would hardly express the 'wishes of the people!' The right to free speech would contribute very little to democracy if no one could be bothered to say anything controversial or had any ideas. Similarly, what use would be the right to protest if everybody thought that it was up to others to do that sort of thing – so nobody protested about anything? A political system will work democratically only when the ordinary people want to, and know how to, play their part.

Sociologists sometimes refer to the attitudes, beliefs, values and skills which people develop in relation to the politics of their society as forming the 'political culture'. Members of the society will be socialised into this culture as they learn how to live in the society. A child in one family may learn to discuss things and come to believe that even those who lack experience or knowledge are entitled to have a say and to have that say respected. This child is being helped to become an active citizen. In another family, a child may learn not to argue with those who have power and learn that the opinions of those without power do not count. In a similar way, an individual's school life, work life or religious life may or may not encourage a democratic outlook and give the individual opportunities to acquire skills useful to the citizen in a democracy.

Democratic skills and attitudes

Think about your own experiences at school or college, at your work, or as someone with particular religious beliefs and allegiances and/or as a member of a family. Together these experiences are likely to make up a large part of your life and you will be greatly influenced by them.

To what extent do you think that these experiences have prepared and helped you to become a 'good' citizen of a democracy?

Think of the skills you will need as a citizen: to be able to think for yourself, decide what is a strong and weak argument, and argue your point of view.

Think of the attitudes which support the democratic process: being suspicious of those who tell you what you should think, being reluctant to accept the authority of those who are not elected and answerable to the people; being prepared to accept the authority of those properly elected even when you did not vote for them and do not approve of what they are doing; being prepared to listen to and consider seriously points of view with which you do not agree, and believing that it is right for people, including yourself, to become involved in making the decisions which affect you.

Ask yourself how your school/college, work, religious and family experiences have helped or made it difficult for you to develop such skills and attitudes?

The skills and attitudes mentioned above are only examples. Think of others which you would expect the good citizen of a democracy to have.

The question, 'How democratic are the major non-political institutions in Britain?' is signifi-cant for another reason. Those 'at the top' of these institutions make decisions which influence the life of all or most members of our society. The Board of Directors of large banks, for exam-ple, make decisions which affect, amongst other things, the cost of goods in the shops, the fate of small businesses, our mortgage payments, and the rate of unemployment. The decisions made by 'top people' in religious organisations, the universities, the mass media, other big busi-nesses, influence many different aspects of our life. What is more these top people have oppor-tunities not open to ordinary people to influence political decisions.

To the question, 'How democratic are the major non-political institutions in Britain?' the answer is, for the most part, 'Not at all'. Your own experiences provide evidence of this. When were you, your friends or neighbours, ever given the opportunity to vote in an election for the directors of a supermarket or bank, or in a referendum to determine their pricing or interest rate policies? Democratic principles seem to matter only so far as the conduct of politics is con-cerned. The top people in businesses and other major institutions who influence in so many ways the kind of society in which we live are not elected by or responsible to 'the people'. You might wish to say that we have in Britain created a democratic political system within an essen-tially undemocratic society. In such a society it is worth asking whether the democratic princi-ples of the political system are undermined by the non-democratic principles on the basis of which almost all other parts of society work.

Influencing political decisions

A large proportion of the British population say that they do not hold politicians in very high regard and that they do not have much of an interest in politics. Hundreds of thousands of people, however, are active members or supporters of organisations formed to influence the 'powers that be' on particular issues or on behalf of particular sections of the population.

EXERCISE

Pay special attention for two or three weeks to the stories in the mass media relating to groups of people trying to influence the decisions made by the government, local councils or any other public authorities.

- What kind of people appear to be involved in such activities? Are they drawn from all sec-tions of the population?
- By what means are these people trying to influence the decisions?

Of course, the activity to which the media has drawn your attention is only the most visible, perhaps the most obviously newsworthy, part of the process by which people try to influence decisions. Out of view are people writing letters, sitting on committees, having quiet chats.

Individual opportunities

An individual acting alone has opportunities to get his or her views across to the decision makers. He or she is entitled to speak to the constituency MP or local councillor at their surgeries; to stand outside the town hall with a placard. He or she could write to a newspaper, take part in a radio phone-in or TV discussion programme. Increasingly, individuals are expressing views on the Internet. An individual acting alone, however, is likely to have limited success – unless rich, famous or with powerful friends. Picture the following situation. A large company wishes to build an industrial estate on some green fields. Mrs Ordinary Person who lives nearby is worried that if this happens there will be nowhere healthy for local children to play and much wildlife will be made homeless. Who is a government minister or set of local councillors more likely to be in fear of offending? It is easy to imagine the headline, 'Sir Rich Businessman threatens to invest in Portugal if his plans are not approved.' It is less easy to imagine the headline, 'Mrs Ordinary Person is very upset at go ahead for industrial estate.'

There are powerful individuals in our society. People with great wealth or good connections; people who hold a high position in business or the professions, or who are well respected by the public. For the rest of us forming or joining a group can offer the best, or only, chance to have influence. Unity is strength. Numbers multiply the resources available for campaigning. More members more funds, more people to write letters. Crowds can make a greater impact – one person holding a placard might be disregarded as a crank; one hundred people holding placards will be taken more seriously by the public and the media. Additionally, finding that other people feel strongly about the same things or find themselves in a similar situation can help to maintain an individual's commitment to a campaign.

Pressure groups and democracy

Sociologists refer to the organisations which people form to influence political decisions as pressure groups. Some argue that they play an important part in keeping a democracy healthy:

- They help and encourage members of the public to express their opinions to the decision makers and become actively involved in political matters.
- A member of a pressure group can gain knowledge and learn skills which will make him or her a more effective and active citizen. By going to meetings, for example, an individual might develop the confidence to stand up and express an opinion or learn to ask penetrating questions.
- Pressure groups can encourage a government to listen and be responsive to public opinion.
- They constantly challenge the government to explain and justify its policies. Whenever the tax on motorists is increased, for example, the government is immediately criticised in the mass media by the pressure groups representing the car manufacturers, the road hauliers and others. The government is forced to reply. In this way the public get to know what the government is doing and hear the arguments. Voters are therefore more informed when they decide who to vote for at the next general election.

- It is also possible that pressure groups will develop good ideas. One of the beliefs on which democracy is built is that the 'powers that be' are not the only source of good ideas. Every member of society is capable of developing ideas from which we can all benefit. Pressure groups make it at least more likely that the 'powers that be', and the public generally, will be made aware of potentially beneficial ideas.

Identifying some of the functions of pressure groups – that is, the ways in which they can help the society – does not explain why they have come to play such a significant part in our social and political life. Why are there more pressure groups today? Why are more people involved than in the past?

Their increasing significance

The many ways in which our society has changed during the last half century has made it more possible for people to become active in pressure politics:

- Today we have more free time, enough perhaps to devote some of it to pressure group activity.
- People are generally more affluent, allowing money to be spent on membership fees or the expenses of helping a group to campaign.
- The growth of mass communications has given people access to a vast range of information about what is going on in or outside their own neighbourhood. Mass communication – particularly now the Internet – also makes it easier for people to find others with similar beliefs and interests and to act together. People today have an almost unlimited access to issues about which they might be concerned and wish to do something.
- People today have a less deferential attitude to those in authority – they no longer assume that those in authority are bound to be right. People feel that they are entitled to their say. In recent years children have been brought up to think that they have rights, to ask questions and express opinions. Women are less in awe of men. Adults generally have been informed that they have rights as patients, customers, parents. Ordinary people seem 'in the mood' to challenge doctors, solicitors, chief constables, bank managers and government ministers, for example, when they feel that they have been treated unfairly. The Stephen Lawrence case is perhaps the most notable embodiment in recent years of the determination of decent, ordinary people to demand justice from the system.

Not popular with everyone

During the 20th century the role which governments played within British society tended to expand. After 1945, for example, governments were very active in managing economic affairs and in running a comprehensive welfare system. There were therefore more occasions on which citizens might want to put pressure on a government to do more, to do less, or to do whatever it was doing differently.

There were many, particularly in the Conservative Party from the 1970s onwards, who were opposed to this 'big government' and who feared that important features of British democracy were being weakened by the increasing significance of pressure groups. Particularly worrying, it was suggested, was the way in which many pressure groups had established contacts directly with civil servants and government ministers. If more citizens saw this as a good way to influence political decisions key elements in the democratic system such as elections, political parties and parliament might become less important.

Governments in the 1980s were particularly hostile to trade unions and to groups wishing to develop the welfare state at national or local level. Actions were taken to reduce the influence of such groups. At the same time groups representing business and financial interests continued to have good relationships with the government.

Voting is not enough

Although the government made life difficult for some groups during the 1980s, popular support for and involvement in the activities of pressure groups has not diminished. An important reason for this might be that today people are less likely to consider that voting for a political party at a general election gives them sufficient influence on government decisions: 'They're all the same, politicians. They'll tell you anything to get you to vote for them and then forget about you.' Such disillusion with party politicians has led more people to seek other means of furthering their political demands. When upset by what a government is doing or is not doing, people are less prepared to wait until the next election gives them a chance to 'punish' the government by not voting for them. Through pressure groups action can be started immediately.

A further source of disillusion with political parties and elections can arise when they present the electors with no chance to express a preference based on an issue or issues about which they care deeply. Consider the situation of an elector who, by the 1970s, had come to believe that environmental issues were more important than any others. This elector wanted to vote for no more road building or houses on green belt land, massive government investment in renewable energy sources and other green policies. Which party with a chance of winning a general election could this elector have supported? Party politics for a long time during the 20th century had been focussed on class issues. Electors more interested in environmental or women's issues were not really catered for in the politics offered by the main political parties. Pressure group activity seemed to offer an effective way of forcing these issues onto the 'mainstream' political agenda. In recent years the public has seen memorable images of well dressed, well spoken women handing food over wire mesh fences to unemployed young men who have chained themselves to trees to stop a road being built, sitting with women who live on council estates in front of lorries to stop the export of live animals, or living in tents and wilfully trespassing to draw attention to American spy bases in Britain. These images suggest both the frustration of many people with mainstream party politics and a willingness to form alliances which cut across the old class tribalism.

In recent years green and women's issues have, perhaps as a result of pressure group activity, been given places on the mainstream political agenda. All major political parties now claim to be environmentally friendly and in favour of equality for women. Experience has taught electors to be rather suspicious of such claims. Political parties have made many promises in opposition which were not honoured when in power. It is likely, therefore, that many people will continue to see pressure group activity as an important means of pushing their political demands.

Insider groups

Much of the activity which is successful in influencing political decisions takes place out of the public's view. Pressure groups may establish a close relationship with a political party. Trade Unions, for example, have supported the Labour Party and had representatives on its policy making committees. Traditionally, business interests maintained very close contact with and gave money to the Conservative Party. Today, many business interests also maintain contact with New Labour.

Some pressure groups are able to establish close and regular contact with those who actually make the decisions and who are therefore in a position to give a group what it wants. Representatives of pressure groups may, for example, be invited to sit alongside senior civil servants on policy working parties or advisory committees. This arrangement has advantages for the groups. It is as if they have become advisers to the government and as advisers they are in a position to make sure that their interests and point of view are taken into account when policy is being made. Business and industry pressure groups are particularly likely to establish such close working relationships with government.

Having to make a fuss

Those groups unable to achieve insider status are at a disadvantage. Their interests and points of view do not receive automatic consideration when decisions are being made. They are 'outsider' groups. They have to 'make a fuss' to persuade the decision makers to give consideration to their views and interests. This 'fuss' can be made in parliament. Individual MPs or members of the House of Lords who are sympathetic to the group can question ministers, make speeches on the group's behalf or try to make things awkward by voting against any government proposal opposed by the group. In such ways the support of MPs can be useful. For this reason pressure groups sometimes ask their members to write to their MPs or to take part in a lobby of parliament.

Pressure groups may also make a fuss outside parliament, and it is to this kind of activity that the attention of the public is most likely to be drawn. We have all seen reports of protests such as lorries blocking motorways. The aim of this activity has traditionally been to publicise the cause or interest for which the group is fighting. Groups hope that publicity will increase public support and attract the attention of politicians – particularly the government. If the government is impressed by the public support received by the group it might try in some way to meet the group's demands. Such activity is often, however, a sign of weakness – an indication that the group thinks the government has not been listening to it or attached sufficient importance to what it wants.

Whilst publicity has almost always been an aim of this kind of activity, groups have sometimes seen it as a practical, direct way of furthering their cause. A group of homeless people who squat in an empty property not only publicise their plight but give themselves shelter. Digging up genetically modified crops before they seed actually makes it less likely that the countryside will be contaminated. Occupying trees and holes in the ground delays road building schemes and makes them more expensive. These schemes may therefore become less attractive to the government.

Using the courts

Trying to influence politicians through political action remains a vital part of what pressure groups do. Recently, however, some groups have come to see legal action against the government and other authorities as a useful weapon. Today, judges seem more prepared to challenge the decisions and actions of government ministers. Not only this but the British government is under an obligation to uphold the rights listed in the European Convention of Human Rights. Many British citizens, often supported by pressure groups, have over the years, been successful in obtaining a ruling from the European Court of Human Rights that a British government has denied them their rights. Such rulings put great pressure on the government to mend its ways. In 2000 the European Convention of Human Rights became part of British law, allowing British citizens to apply to British courts to uphold the rights it gives them.

What makes for success?

Whether a group is or is not able to get all or some of the decisions it wants depends on many factors. The more resources available to the group the more likely, all else being equal, is the group to be successful. Having more members, more financial resources, more contacts in 'high places', members more strongly committed to the group, leaders with more skill, a more efficient organisation, and more public support may all be significant in enabling one group to be more successful than another. Being in a position to threaten the public with real hardship or to make it difficult for a government to carry out its policies can also help a group to 'persuade' a government.

The political circumstances in which the group is trying to influence the government is also likely to influence the chance of success. A small majority in the House of Commons may put a government in a weak position to resist a group which has the support of some MPs. An approaching general election may increase a group's chances since at that time a government is looking for friends.

Finally, recognise that some demands are satisfied more easily than others. If what a pressure group wants would cost billions of pounds a government may be reluctant to do it. If the group wants merely a small change to a policy already being carried out a government may be happy to oblige.

A changing scene

Some commentators have suggested that direct action is likely to play an increasingly significant part in political life as more and more people begin to suspect that their political representatives, and even national governments, are unwilling and unable to stand up to multinational businesses. What is the point of trying to influence the government if the government is not in a position to do anything to help? Anti-capitalism protests and direct action against multinational businesses in Britain and in other countries reflect the frustration this is causing.

Whilst globalisation may be increasing the power of multinational businesses and diminishing the power of national governments it is also creating new possibilities for ordinary people who wish to challenge what is happening in their own and other societies. Many issues – the environment, for example – are of interest to people all over the world. If something effective is to be done many governments need to be influenced. The Internet offers, for those who wish to know about or to be active on a particular issue, easy contact with others who think the same way. Through the Internet direct action can be arranged without any formal organisation – notice of a protest can simply be posted. There are no protest leaders. The Internet can itself be used as a weapon of protest – Internet activism. With appropriate skills, protesters can disrupt the communications of multinational companies and the governments which support them. Individuals and groups are adapting to changes in the way in which power is held and used in the world today.

Voting behaviour

To sociologists the way people vote – or do not vote – and think about voting can reveal much about what is going on in society. A look at the kind of politics which attract voters, for example, may suggest something about people's priorities and values, about the ways in which they relate to others, about their identities or the way they see themselves, and their aspirations. Changes in a pattern of voting behaviour can suggest that changes have taken place in the social and economic structures or in the culture of society, and perhaps indicate what these changes have been. In particular, many sociologists have focussed on the way in which changes in the pattern of voting behaviour in Britain since 1945 may suggest changes in the class structure and in the importance that social class has as an influence on our lives.

The pattern of voting – 1950s

The pattern of voting in the 1950s had the following significant characteristics:

- All but a small minority of voters voted for either the Labour Party or the Conservative Party. People referred to a two party system, implying that only these two parties had a chance of winning a general election. The Liberal Party was seen as largely irrelevant, attracting in any election some 'protest votes' from disillusioned Labour or Conservative voters but having very few permanent supporters.
- Most Conservative and Labour voters supported their party on a long-term basis. A voter would see him or herself as Labour or Conservative. Occasionally, when offended by something the party or the party's candidate had done a voter might protest in a particular election by abstaining or perhaps voting Liberal. Such a withdrawal of support would usually be temporary.
- The pattern of voting tended to be uniform throughout the country. If in a general election the Conservative Party increased its share of the vote in Yorkshire, it would also increase its share in Somerset or Kent. It was as if the basis on which Yorkshire people voted was the same as the basis on which Somerset and Kentish people voted.

How might it be explained?

On what social basis might a voting pattern with such characteristics have developed? What feature of British society in the 1950s could be seen – to divide people into two camps, or tribes, to provide a basis for long term allegiances, and to cover almost the entire society? The most obvious answer was class. Class was at the centre of any sociological analysis of voting behaviour at this time.

In the 1950s there were significant and obvious differences between working and middle class ways of life. These differences were often visibly linked to inequalities of income and wealth, of social status and authority. A person's accent, his or her clothes or house, were all related to and taken by others as indications of a person's class.

In such a society people might well come to feel part of a class. Men working down the pit, in a steelworks, car factory or engineering works could see hundreds of other manual workers dressed in similar clothes, doing similar jobs, working similar hours under the same sort of supervision, getting a similar sort of wage and living in a similar sort of house. It was relatively easy for these manual workers to feel that they had things in common. At the same time these workers were aware of the non-manual, 'managerial type' people whose position was rather different. These people had offices, did not have to clock in, had a nice dining room rather than the 'works canteen'. They gave the orders, could hire and fire and seemed to have more money. It would be surprising if many miners, foundrymen or dockers felt that they had much in common with this group.

The feeling of having something in common tends to bring people together. Each individual is strengthened by the support he or she can expect from the others. This support can be given informally – neighbours helping each other out – or through formal organisations set up for particular purposes. The cooperative societies, the trade unions and the Labour Party played an important part in working class life during the 20th century. Whilst each organisation had a different focus all were based on the same principle – that when those who do not possess much money, power or status stand together, all benefit. Acting together through cooperative societies – buying in bulk and being able to sell more cheaply – helped individual members of the working class as consumers. Expressed through trade unions, collective action supported demands for decent wages and working conditions. The Labour Party was formed to represent in parliament and in politics generally the interests of the working class and others in society who saw themselves as workers.

Until the 1960s, for many – particularly men – voting Labour was just as much part of being working class as watching a Saturday afternoon soccer or rugby league match. It was a habit passed from generation to generation. Children would learn by overhearing and watching parents, relatives and neighbours that the Labour Party was 'our party'. Society was made up of 'Them' and 'Us'. By voting Labour a member of the working class not only supported policies felt to be in the interest of their class but also expressed solidarity with other members.

Not all members of the working class voted Labour. A substantial minority voted Conservative. These working class conservatives were a much studied group. What they were doing was 'unusual' and therefore demanded an explanation. Working class conservatives were breaking the working class voting norm – they were 'deviant' voters. Recognise that it is appropriate to refer to deviant voters only if there is a voting norm which is being broken. If ever tempted to describe any group of voters today as deviant, consider carefully whether there are still voting norms. If there are not, the phrase deviant voter is inappropriate.

The middle class

Those in white collar, managerial, professional occupations were less likely to see society in Us/Them terms. They saw society as much more open. Individuals were thought to be able to 'better themselves' if they worked hard and had sufficient talent. Despite this more individualistic, less class conscious outlook, the great majority of those in non manual occupations voted as a class for the Conservative Party. Within organisations to which the middle class belonged Conservative sympathies were dominant. It would be assumed by those belonging to a local Chamber of Commerce, for example, that the Conservative Party was the party of business or by those belonging to the Women's Institute that the Conservative Party was the party of respectable people. Membership of such organisations reinforced middle class people in their support for the Conservative Party. Note that at this time the Church of England was said to be the 'Conservative Party at prayer'.

Things have changed, perhaps

The British way of life has changed since the 1950s. It would be rather surprising therefore if the pattern of voting had not changed.

During the last 30 years it has become less realistic to talk about a two party system. The Liberal Democrat, Scottish and Welsh Nationalist parties have won enough votes and gained enough seats in elections to be counted as significant political parties. The Green Party has also been able in local council and European elections to attract public support. The hold which the Conservative and Labour parties had on the allegiance of the British electorate in the 1950s has weakened.

The weakening of this allegiance has also been shown in the way in which voters today seem less prepared to vote for the same party in election after election. A larger proportion of the electorate have become 'floating' or 'swing' voters, prepared to switch their support from one part to another. Nowadays, the commitment of many electors to one particular party is shallow and temporary.

Finally, the behaviour of voters throughout the country is no longer uniform. A party doing well in an election in one part of the country does not necessarily do well in other parts of the country. This weakening of the 1950s pattern of voting might suggest that class is no longer as closely related to voting as it once was.

Why any change?

The boundary between the middle class and the working class is perhaps less clear than in the 1950s. As long ago as the 1960s attention was drawn to the way in which some manual workers appeared to be changing the way they looked at things, such as politics, as they became more affluent. Some sociologists suggested that these workers were becoming a kind of manual middle class, others that they were a new working class. All agreed, however, that these workers could no longer be seen as 'natural' Labour supporters. They were no longer tied by upbringing and community norms to the Labour Party. They had developed an instrumental attitude – that is they voted for whichever party in a particular election seemed to offer policies best suited to their personal and family needs at that time. In one election the Conservative Party might have won their support by offering lower taxes. In the next election a Labour promise to spend more money on education might have been seen as more attractive. More recently this kind of voter has sometimes been referred to in the tabloid press as 'Essex man'. Such an image usefully suggests a different outlook and different values from those who remain loyal to more traditional working class attitudes.

Students who discuss the voting behaviour of the working class often ignore the middle class. This is unfortunate since an increasing proportion of the electorate is middle class. It is as important to consider why many middle class people no longer 'naturally' support the Conservative Party as it is to consider why many working class people no longer 'naturally' support the Labour Party.

Many within the middle class were born in the working class and not likely to have inherited a Conservative voting habit from their parents. Being a non-manual worker today can mean different things. It can mean being paid a lot of money for going to a lot of meetings or it can mean being paid not very well for using a telephone for seven or eight hours a day. Many white collar or desk workers receive no more pay, have no better working conditions and are supervised no less closely than manual workers. Many have responded to their situation as manual workers typically responded – by joining a trade union. These middle class workers might see themselves as having no more reasons for voting Conservative than manual workers in a similar situation.

What a political party stands for can change significantly. A party may become more attractive to some who were unlikely to vote for it previously and less attractive to some who had supported it in the past. Both the Conservative and Labour parties have changed in recent years. A Conservative Party which had supported the public sector became from the mid 1970s onwards a Conservative Party which had a strongly held 'private sector good, public sector bad' attitude. As a result middle class workers in the public sector, such as doctors and teachers, found themselves and the services which they provided 'losing out' under the Conservative governments of the 1980s and 1990s. Many amongst the public sector middle class became alienated from the Conservative Party.

Identity

In the 1950s those who saw themselves as middle class were likely to vote Conservative and those who saw themselves as working class were likely to vote Labour. Voting was related to an individual's sense of his or her class identity. If, for whatever reason, an individual's sense of belonging to a class weakens and other aspects of his or her identity become more significant, the way in which he or she votes may change. During the 1980s being Scottish or Welsh became more significant for those people who resented being governed from London by what they saw as an essentially English Government which lacked a majority in either Scotland or Wales. More people came to think that it was important to vote on behalf of their Scottishness or Welshness.

A longstanding example of a situation in which other aspects of identity have had more influence on voting behaviour than class is that in Northern Ireland. Their religious affiliation and whether or not an individual feels and wants to be British is closely related to how he or she votes.

It may be that during the last 40 years people generally have been able to exercise more choice as regards their identity. The proportion of the working class living the kind of community life in which a Labour voting, working class, identity was cultivated has declined. Many work for small firms in a non-unionised workplace. Many may own or be buying their own home. Remember that one of the Conservative government's motives for encouraging tenants to buy their council houses was to bring about a change in attitude. It was hoped that those who did so would develop a more individualistic outlook. Class would perhaps come to mean less to them. If class has come to mean less, other elements of an individual's experience may have come to mean more. Feminist ideas, for example, have helped during the last 40 years to give women a reason for attaching greater political significance, to being female. 'I'm very pleased we've got a woman Prime Minister,' working class women sometimes said in the 1980s, even though Mrs Thatcher was a Conservative.

Voting today

The occupational structure of British society changed throughout the 20th century. The general trend was for fewer people to be employed in manual and more in non-manual jobs. In the 1950s manual workers and their families still made up a majority of the electorate. It was possible for the Labour Party to win elections on the basis of working class support alone. Today this is not possible.

Recognising this, and concerned that the Conservative Party had won the general elections of 1979, 1982, 1987 and 1992, some Labour Party MPs and members decided that the party must be changed. Its approach to politics, its policies and image must be updated and focussed in such a way as to appeal to 'middle England'. Other MPs and members argued that the Labour Party could remain loyal to its traditional class approach to politics and still be successful. The 'modernisers' won, however, and the party's aims were changed. The Labour Party had defined its aim in terms of the interests of 'workers by hand and brain'. New Labour defines its aims in terms of general principles of social justice. The red rose replaced the red flag.

As recently as the 1980s the Conservative and Labour parties stood for quite different things. General elections offered the British people a significant choice. Today, it is difficult not to sympathise with the person in the street who says, 'I'm sorry I don't really know what the parties stand for. Is there much difference between them?' If the appeal of the parties to voters is not in terms of class or political philosophy, what are elections about?

What are elections about?

Policies seem to be important. All major political parties now use 'focus groups' to help discover what policies would be popular with the public. A focus group is a small number of people who are invited to discuss various issues, such as taxation or the NHS, in some depth. What is said is analysed and the implications for party policy are noted. Some party members have complained that party leaders pay more attention to the results of focus group discussions than they do to the opinions of party members.

Parties try to ensure that their policies are more attractive to voters than those of the other parties fighting the election. Whilst voters take policies into account when deciding who to vote for other factors are important. Psephologists – people who study voting behaviour – sometimes refer to the 'feel-good factor'. This helps them to explain why the party offering the most popular policies does not always win a general election. Voters have a sense of whether things are getting better or worse for themselves and those they care about. If they feel that things have been improving, voters may feel pleased with the government and vote for them. This helps to explain why governments try to push through unpopular policies very soon after being elected. There is then more time before the next election for things to improve. In the two years or 18 months before the election, the government will spend money on popular policies such as tax cuts, better pensions or hospitals – so that the voters feel good.

Image is believed to be very important. Much communication between politicians and voters now takes place through the mass media. Politicians like to look honest and competent, powerful yet caring, in charge yet listening. Political parties like to look united yet full of ideas. Image consultants advise politicians on how they should speak and look, and on the best image for their party. Spin doctors help politicians to write their speeches, advise them on what feelings to show when delivering them, and on what newspapers and organisations to talk to.

It is not difficult to work out, from the significance which politicians, political parties and pressure groups give to their relationships with the media, that it plays an important part in British politics today. The government wants to tell us through the media what it is and will be doing; the opposition what it would do if in government. The government wants to persuade us that things are and will be getting better; the opposition that things are not getting better. All politicians want to show through the media that they are exactly the kind of person for the

GROUP	LABOUR LEAD	GROUP	LABOUR LEAD
All Voters	13	Social Class Groups:	
Women	13	AB	−11
Men	14	C1	21
		C2	28
Age Groups		DE	40
18–29	35		
30–44	23	Those who own their home outright	−6
45–64	10	Mortgage payers	13
65+	−10	Council tenants	53

SOURCE: BBC results analysis BBC/DOP exit poll From *The Observer* Election 97 4 May 1997

Figure 71 How Britain voted in the 1997 general election.

public to 'put into power'. Those who decide what political information is put out by the media and how it is presented are therefore in a position to help political parties of which they approve and to make things difficult for those which they do not like.

In the early 1960s it was commonly believed that the media had a limited influence onpeople's voting behaviour. Their class, upbringing and relationships within the community fixed most people in a voting habit which the media could not really change. If however voting habits become much weaker the influence of the media increases: who owns and runs the various elements within the mass media and what political views they have become significant issues for British Democracy.

EXERCISE

Look again at the table and answer the following questions:

i) From which groups did the Conservative Party receive more voting support than the Labour Party?

ii) Do the figures suggest that a person's sex is related to the way in which he or she votes?

iii) What trends can be seen in the relationships:
   a) between age and voting?
   b) between social group and voting?

iv) How might we explain the Conservative lead amongst the over 65s, and the large Labour lead amongst council tenants?

v) Is it possible to use any of the statistics as evidence that class still has an influence on voting behaviour?

Abstention

The opportunity to vote in an election is one of the most important rights possessed by the citizen of a democracy. There is a variety of occasions on which this opportunity can be taken. Wherever in Britain a citizen lives he or she is entitled to vote in elections for the House of Commons, the European Parliament, and Local Councils. Those living in Northern Ireland, Scotland and Wales elect, additionally, representatives to sit in the Northern Ireland or Welsh Assemblies or the Scottish Parliament. Londoners elect a mayor.

A significant proportion of those entitled to vote in any election do not. Such abstention is of concern to politicians, partly because many of the abstainers may, had they voted, have supported their political party. There is, however, a more general concern. The abstention of large numbers of voters can lower the authority and standing of those elected and of the body to which they have been elected.

Why abstain?

Those who abstain have generally been seen as either negative or positive abstainers:

The former are those who do not have a political reason for abstaining. They cannot be bothered because they are 'not interested in politics' or because they do not know enough about the political process for voting to mean anything to them. This kind of abstainer is more likely to be younger and poorer. Positive abstainers are those who have taken a political decision not to vote. Someone may have strongly held political views which no candidate represents. He or she may be a socialist in a constituency in which only Conservative and New Labour candidates are standing. Someone may be disillusioned with all the parties and may wish to protest by not voting.

Particular acts of abstention may not fit neatly into either category. Someone who is very interested in politics who lives in a 'safe seat' – one in which one party always has a large majority – may decide that he or she does not need to vote.

Whilst a small section of the electorate never vote, most of us vote in some elections and not in others. An elderly person, for example, who has always voted in elections for the House of Commons may abstain in an election for the European Parliament. He or she may not approve of the European Union and does not feel sufficiently European to think it worthwhile to play a part in a European institution. Someone else who has always voted in parliamentary elections may think, perhaps wrongly, that elections for local councillors are a waste of time because they have little influence on anything which matters.

It must not be assumed that everyone who does not vote is necessarily an abstainer. Some voters may be sick or away on business. Other citizens may not get their name entered on the register of electors. Many voters were 'lost' in the 1980s as people tried to avoid paying the poll tax by not registering.

The subject of abstention is often neglected by students – perhaps because, being used to explaining why people do things, they see little need to explain why people do not do something. Abstention is, however, an important part of the pattern of voting behaviour and can suggest what is going on in society. For example, a rise in the proportion of the electorate who abstain may suggest that voters have become increasingly alienated from 'party politics'. Voter abstention, not joining a political party, and all the other ways in which the public do not participate in politics are well worth considering.

REGISTER TO VOTE AND NAFF UP YOUR BALLOTS

Daniel Hooper – better known as the road protestor Swampy – has a vote but he has no intention of using it. He doesn't believe in voting: all politicians are as bad as each other and by voting for any of them he would be endorsing what is, in his view, a bankrupt system.

'I don't feel that any of the parties represent my opinion at all and I don't agree with the political system. If you put people in power they generally get corrupted by power, as is quite clear from seeing the corruption around at the moment.

The best way to deal with politicians is to fight them but at the same time to ignore them. They can't rule our lives if we turn away from them. We're only actively encouraging them by voting. Yeah, register to vote and naff up your voting papers en masse.'

Adapted from an article by Clare Garner in *The Independent,* Monday 17 February 1997

Opinion polls

Today much effort is devoted to measuring the attitudes and opinions of the public – particularly those attitudes and opinions which have significance for the political parties. The results of these polls, whether conducted on behalf of a political party or the media, can have a considerable influence on the way in which politicians think and act. Between elections opinion polls – if properly conducted – provide perhaps the most realistic information about the mood of the general public. They communicate what the public thinks of those in government.

Getting it wrong

Most of the time it is difficult to assess how accurate opinion polls are. There is no more 'real' indicator of public opinion with which to compare the results. At election time, however, it is possible for opinion poll predictions to be tested. Sometimes the polls accurately predict an election result. Occasionally though, as in 1992, the opinion polls have got it wrong – for reasons which should be familiar to a sociology student: the sample selected may not have accurately represented the electorate.

- If quota sampling had been used the pollsters would have had to know what proportion of the population were skilled manual workers or homeowners and so on. If this information had been out of date the sample would not have been representative.
- There may have been interviewer bias, although since trained interviewers are used this is unlikely.
- The voters who had said they would vote Labour may have stayed at home on election day in greater numbers than those who had told pollsters they would vote Conservative.
- Some voters may have changed their mind between the time the poll was taken and election day. A politician may have said something particularly stupid or offensive and put voters off. A bad set of economic statistics might have been published just before election day, causing some to have second thoughts about supporting the government.

Their influence on voters

There are several ways in which the publication of opinion poll results close to an election might influence voters:

- Some undecided voters might be tempted to vote for the party which the opinion polls suggest is the most popular – the bandwagon effect. These people might think that the most popular party is likely to be the best party, or feel more secure voting in a way which would meet the approval of others.
- Some voters may not bother to vote if the opinion polls suggest that one party will win easily. They might reason that their vote would not make a difference to the result. If, on the other hand, the opinion polls suggest that the result might be close more voters may take the trouble to vote because they can make a difference.
- The publication of opinion polls enables tactical voting to take place. Such voting could be seen in the 1997 general election. For a significant number of voters in that election their most important goal was to defeat the Conservative candidate. The opinion polls conducted

285

in particular constituencies helped these anti-Conservative voters to work out whether the New Labour or Liberal Democrat candidate was more likely to defeat the Conservative. If the Liberal Democrat candidate stood the better chance then potential New Labour voters might vote accordingly since this was the best way of achieving their goal.

	GALLUP	HARRIS	ICM	MORI	NOP
Main clients	Telegraph	Independent	Guardian/ Observer	Times, Sunday Mirror	Sunday Times, Reuters
Sampling method	Random	Quota	Mixed	Quota	Quota
Mode of interview	Phone	In person	Phone	In person	In person
Estimate preference of don't knows	Past vote, best PM, economy	Past vote	Past vote	No	Party ID, economy
Weight by past vote	**NO**	**NO**	**YES**	**NO**	**YES**

Figure 72 Methods of polling.

EXERCISE

Look again at the table and answer the following questions:

i) a) What method of interview was used by these polls which took quota samples?

   b) Why was this mode used rather than telephone interviewing?

ii) a) What factor could have caused difficulties if telephone interviewing had been used in the 1950s?

   b) Why should this not have been a problem in 1997?

iii) a) Some people when asked, 'For which party would you vote if an election was held tomorrow?' would answer, 'I don't know'. Even if only 10% answered in this way the votes of these people would have a significant influence on the result of the election. Is it safe for the opinion pollster to assume that the 'Don't knows' will, on election day, support the parties in the same proportions as those who have had their political views recorded?

   b) On what basis might the pollsters try to predict how the 'Don't knows' will vote? (It might be useful to look again at the table.)

Politics of the welfare state

In many ways it is reasonable to see the welfare state as a creation of the Labour Party. The Labour government 1945–1951 introduced many of the most important features of the welfare state such as the National Health Service. It also proclaimed the rights of citizens to free education, to medical help when sick, to financial support when unemployed or old, to accommodation when homeless and so on.

It was accepted by the government that it had a duty to guarantee – if necessary to provide – at least a minimum standard of welfare for all its citizens, 'from cradle to grave'. The welfare state should not be seen, however, as a project of the Labour Party alone. A liberal government had begun the process between 1906 and 1914 and many of the reforms introduced between 1944 and 1950 were supported by both the Conservative and Liberal parties.

It was as if after the Second World War there was general agreement that things should not be left as they were before the conflict. Some commentators have referred to a mood of national unity. During the war all sections of society had stood together and contributed to the victory. To remain a society in which – as before the war – many children of the poor were thin and barefoot and in which able bodied men, unable to find work, had felt the need to go on 'hunger marches' was seen as unacceptable. Welfare reform had been identified as an aim before the war had been won or a Labour government elected.

Other commentators have suggested that the 'establishment' was happy to support the development of a welfare state because it would help to create and maintain an efficient workforce in modern conditions. The better educated a worker, the more skills he or she has to offer an employer; the healthier a worker the less time he or she is away from work; the more the government 'looks after' a worker and his or her family, the more stake the worker and family have in the society and the more loyal they will be to it.

For whatever reasons, the basis upon which the welfare state had been developed was generally supported by the major political parties until the 1970s. From the 1970s both the principle that a government should provide and guarantee the economic and social welfare of its citizens and the manner in which welfare had been provided in Britain have been strongly challenged – initially by the Conservative Party.

The challenge to the welfare state

Underpinning the challenge was, and still is, a particular view of what people are like. It is the rather pessimistic view that people are essentially selfish and lazy. The welfare state allows and encourages people to get and to want 'something for nothing'. If people can 'get by' on government handouts and avoid going to work they will. The welfare state, it was and is argued, undermines important social values and standards. With a welfare state to look after them individuals no longer need such a strong sense of personal responsibility. Why should someone work hard and put a little aside 'for a rainy day' if, because of the benefits system, someone who has neither worked hard nor saved is likely to end up as well, or even better off? Why should a young woman avoid sex until she is in a settled, financially stable situation if, when she becomes pregnant accidentally, she will receive medical care, financial and housing benefits from the government?

The welfare state was accused not only of undermining social values but of being inefficient as an organisation. During the 1970s it had become very fashionable to think that the operation of a free market was the only basis on which a prosperous society could be built and that competition was vital to efficiency. Only the fear of being put out of business by another organisation which did the job better and more cheaply would make employers and workers work hard. Competition created a situation in which organisations always had an incentive to improve the way they did things. Customers would benefit – competition would keep prices down and maintain the pressure on organisations to provide a good service. Those running the successful organisations would be paid lots of money; the employees would keep their jobs.

Enthusiastic advocates of competition and the free market could not believe that the welfare state could deliver services efficiently. Those who provided services within the welfare state were seen as having a monopoly. Hospitals and schools, for example, were not subject to the 'disciplines of the market'. Their patients, and pupils, did not see themselves as having much choice or as being able to take their custom elsewhere.

Since 1979 governments have put much thought and effort into reforming public sector organisations so they operate in circumstances similar to those in the private sector. Hospitals, colleges and schools have been turned, as far as possible, into businesses. This process can be seen clearly in the further education sector. During the 1980s and 1990s the ethos of further education changed as did its structure. Principals of colleges began to call themselves Chief Executives: students became customers; colleges began to establish marketing departments and quality assurance teams; a 'bottom line', 'bums on seats' criterion of success became dominant; everything that went on in a college had to be geared to the 'business plan'. Such developments have been widespread within the public sector. Within the national health service the account-ant and the manager have come to be as important, if not more important, than the consultant and the nurse. The national health service is increasingly paying the private sector to provide services for patients. Through such developments any distinctive character the public sector may once have had is weakened as the values which underpin its operation become increasingly those of business.

Selective and universal benefits

There are two ways in which a government can give financial support to those who need it:

- Through **selective benefits** to which the needy and only the needy are entitled.
- By paying the benefit to everyone in a particular group, all retired people, for example, whether they are needy or not. These are **universal benefits**.

The extent to which the welfare state should use selective or universal benefits has long been a matter of political controversy.

Consider **selective benefits** such as the pensioner's Minimum Income Guarantee. How does the government get the benefit to those entitled to receive it? It publicises the benefit, asking all those who think that they qualify by being sufficiently needy to claim it. Those who do make a claim will be asked about their income and savings. If after scrutinising this very per-sonal information officials find that the claimant is sufficiently needy he or she will receive the benefit.

Not everyone entitled to such benefits receives them:

- Some may not know of their existence. Not every one picks up, or understands, the leaflets in the post office or sees the posters or advertisements in the media.
- Some may know about the benefit but not wish to go through what they think will be a degrading application process. Elderly people may remember their parents undergoing the 'means' or 'needs' test in the 1920s and them being told that they would be helped only if they sold the family's wireless or got rid of their pet dog. Even without such memories an individual may not wish to suffer the indignity of describing to an official how poor he or she is. Benefits for which individuals have to apply in this way can easily be seen as charity rather than as money to which the claimant has a right. Those who identify themselves offi-cially as needy may fear stigmatisation.

Whether not claiming is a problem or an advantage for a government will depend on how the government defines its interests. To any government with a genuine interest in helping the poorest and most vulnerable in society non-claiming is a problem. To any government, on the other hand, which defines its primary interest as keeping taxes low non-claiming is an advantage. Fewer claimants means less money spent and therefore less money needs to be collected through taxation.

Whatever a government's priorities it is faced with the problem that selective benefits may be expensive to administer. Officials must be employed, sorting the valid from the invalid claims; investigating possible fraud; dealing with appeals. At the same time selective benefits may reduce the incentive to earn some, or more, money. An individual receiving benefit may think twice about trying to earn or save more if as a result payments would be reduced or lost. Sociologists refer to this as the 'poverty trap'.

Universal benefits, on the other hand, are relatively cheap to administer, do not create disincentives and have high take-up rates. Money paid out under a universal benefit scheme, however, is not targeted at those who need it. Child benefit is paid at the same rate to rich and poor families, for example. This can be seen as both wasteful and unfair. The money available is spread thinly and those who are poor receive less than if the benefit had been concentrated on them.

Many of those in favour of universal benefits counter this by suggesting that the government could organise the taxation system in such a way that the benefit money paid to those with a high income could be 'clawed back' in tax. The money could thus be targeted without the problems associated with selective benefits.

The issue of selective versus universal benefits is not just about the best way to get money to those who need it. It touches on the wider question of what part the welfare state should play in society. Should it be run as an organisation to which most of us look for our main support when sick, unemployed or retired? Or should it be run only as a safety net for those who cannot, or for whatever reason, do not, arrange private medical and pension schemes?

To those who have challenged the very idea of the welfare state the latter view is more acceptable. The smaller the role played by the welfare state the better. Recently, selectivity has also become attractive to those who are broadly sympathetic towards the welfare state. The arguments about the national insurance retirement pension illustrate this:

It has for a long time been difficult for elderly people to live decently on the money paid to them through their national insurance retirement pension. Many MPs agree with groups campaigning on behalf of the elderly that the basic state pension needs to be raised substantially. Any such rise would go to all pensioners. New Labour ministers have claimed that this is not the most efficient way to help the most needy. They point out that most people in Britain are much better off today. Many who have retired in recent years receive an income from an occupational pension or from a private pension plan. These people, government ministers argue, do not need their state pension to be maintained at a level which by itself would provide a decent standard of living. They have income from these other sources. It is more sensible and fairer to allocate any additional pension money to those who have to rely on what they receive from the government. The Pensioner's Minimum Income Guarantee has thus been introduced. This is a means tested benefit which the poorest pensioners who apply for it will receive.

'Old' Labour opponents point out that this approach risks weakening the welfare state. If its value is not maintained the basic retirement pension will become less and less important to those with occupational and private pensions. There may come a time when these people ask, 'Why should I pay national insurance? Why should my taxes be spent on pensions? The state retirement pension means nothing to me.' If more people come to feel that the state pension is irrelevant to them, fewer people would bother to put pressure on politicians to maintain government spending in this area. The poorer pensioners who had no other income would then lose out if spending on pensions became a lower priority for governments.

Similar concerns can be raised for any welfare state provision when increased affluence enables more and more of the 'better off' to 'go private' and therefore not need the welfare state. More people today have private health insurance, can afford to put their children into the private education system and to buy their own home. The personal stake which such people have in the NHS, state schools, and public housing is reduced. The number of people with an interest in fighting to maintain the quality of welfare services is thus reduced.

When discussing the welfare state students often neglect the issue of funding. Since benefits and services can be provided only when the government has been able to collect sufficient money to pay for them, it is important to include taxation in any consideration of the welfare state. Political attitudes to taxation are linked to how the welfare state is regarded.

Taxation

Those who challenge the welfare state argue that individuals should be taxed as little as possible. They believe that one of the most important rights any individual has is to enjoy his or her property and to decide how to spend his or her income. It is immoral for the government to take from individuals any more than the minimum which is needed to keep the country safe and maintain a stable society. They also believe that the progressive taxation of income penalises success and stifles initiative: 'Why should I work hard to earn more if the tax man takes most if it'?

The Labour Party approached taxation differently. Living in society, an individual is influenced in incalculable ways by the actions of other people, past and present. Millions of people have contributed to making each one of us what he or she is. Squalor, sickness, poverty, unemployment, lack of education make it very difficult for people to fulfil their potential as human beings and as members of society. Every other member of society is thereby deprived of the contribution these individuals could have made had they fulfilled their potential. Taxation which enabled the government to provide benefits and services which helped individuals to fulfil their potential would be in the interest of all and fully justified.

To the Labour Party progressive taxation – that which takes proportionally more from the better off than the poor – was also justified as a means of reducing social inequalities. The degree of inequality within British society, argued Labour politicians, was unjustified. It did not result from the rich working harder than the poor nor from some other attribute of the rich which gave them a moral right to their superior material position. Many were well off because their parents had been well off; others had made great profits by being lucky speculators or by forcing their workers to accept low wages. Such a degree of social inequality could also be seen as damaging society by causing social division. From such a viewpoint taxation could be seen as a means of establishing a better society. The money collected would fund a welfare state from which all citizens would benefit and, by taking more from the rich, taxation could be used to secure greater equality and social justice.

Such an argument is heard very rarely in Britain today. During the last 20 years it has become fashionable to proclaim the virtues of low taxation and governments have reduced the rates of tax which individuals pay on their incomes. This has contributed to an increase in social inequality. Firstly, because those receiving higher incomes have benefited more from tax cuts than those receiving lower incomes. Secondly, because reductions in taxation have limited the funds available to the welfare state. Any cuts in benefits or services are likely to have a greater impact on the poorer than on the better off sections of society since the former depend on them more heavily.

The future of the welfare state is uncertain. The attitude of the public is ambiguous. On the one hand are the results of opinion polls which suggest support for the welfare state and for such levels of taxation as are needed to fund it adequately. On the other hand the public supported governments which reduced taxes rather than funded the welfare state adequately. Today, even politicians who support the welfare state are worried that if the public see them raising taxes they will not win elections. Without an adequate level of taxation the welfare state will decline.

WHEN IT COMES TO TAX AND SPEND, SOCIAL POLICY AND HELP FOR THE POOR, ALL THE POLITICAL PARTIES ARE OUT OF TOUCH WITH THEIR TRADITIONAL VOTERS

Social justice still conditions the response of a lot of people. However, some core attitudes are firmly regressive. Half the population, at least, opposes inheritance tax. A clear majority think income tax is 'too high' and three-quarters say they are paying too much on petrol and in VAT. Confidence in the state is diminishing which implies future support for higher taxes is going to be hard to muster.

Successive British Social Attitudes reports have found a majority of people do favour welfare state solutions to social problems, including extensive redistribution of income to the less well off. But they have distinct views about who they think worthy of any extra state assistance. Those who care for disabled relatives and people with disabilities themselves score highest. The unemployed and single mothers are at the bottom of the list, even among women.

Adapted from an article by David Walker in *The Guardian*, Tuesday 28 November 2000

Questions

Read the article again and answer the following questions:

i)   **a)** Identify one progressive tax mentioned in the article.
      b) Identify one regressive tax mentioned in the article.
ii) Why might the public think that some groups are more worthy of state assistance than others? Consider the examples given in the article.
iii) Why might having less 'confidence in the state' mean that people will be less likely to support higher taxes?

Voluntary organisations

Voluntary organisations are a very important part of society in Britain today. Hundreds of thousands of people are active members of these organisations. Millions of people support them through donations of one kind or another. The fact that a welfare state has been established seems not to have weakened the opinion amongst members of the public that charities and other kinds of voluntary organisation are a good thing. Voluntary organisations can be seen positively from several different viewpoints:

- Those who emphasise that a stable society requires individuals to establish connections with others can point to the opportunities which voluntary organisations offer. People who participate in voluntary organisations show that they care about the communities and society in which they live.
- Those who fear that governments in recent times have begun to do 'too much' for people see voluntary organisations as offering opportunities for individuals to act freely and independently of government. Individuals can choose to join or not to join. They can use their time and/or their money in ways which fit their priorities. They argue that it is better for individuals to support the deprived or particular cultural and social activities personally and by choice rather than through taxation.
- Those who support the welfare state but recognise its limitations see voluntary organisations as supplementing what governments can reasonably be expected to do. Voluntary organisations are able, for example:
→ To approach problems in ways which, because they are controversial, would be difficult for the welfare state to adopt.
→ To offer support above and beyond that offered by the welfare state.
→ To help people who might be reluctant to approach the welfare state for support.
→ To support sections of society or kinds of activity to which governments give a low priority.

Today most voluntary organisations have a role as pressure groups. Many of the issues or problems with which they are concerned are on too large a scale for voluntary organisations to tackle alone. Public and government support is needed and many voluntary organisations see persuading the public or the government to help as a key part of their role.

In recent years the National Lottery has become particularly important. A good way of discovering the vast range of voluntary activity taking place in Britain is to look at the recipients of lottery money. It is almost as if a parallel Welfare State has been established. People pay their 'tax' – on a voluntary basis – each time they buy a ticket. The money collected minus prize money and profit for the lottery company is distributed to organisations to spend on social and cultural activities; improving the environment and the conditions of life for many people.

The government and statistics

Governments have always wanted information about the society which they govern. A nationwide census of the population has been carried out every 10 years – with the exception of 1941. Even when government did very little, basic facts about the population were potentially useful. Knowing how many young men there were, for example, could be significant to a government responsible for maintaining an army and navy.

Changes which have taken place between 1801 and 2001 – most particularly during the last 50 years – have increased the government's demand for information. A government is now expected to develop and administer policies relating to the economy, law and order, education, health, transport, housing, and social welfare, to mention just a few. To be realistic and workable these policies need to be based on full and accurate information about how things are and how things have been changing. It would be very difficult to train an appropriate number of teachers without some information about the birth rate. Estimating the future needs of the services for which it has some responsibility is one use the government makes of information.

Who are you sleeping with? Who is your god? The next census will ask more intrusive questions than ever. Refuse to answer and you could go to prison. But is it a vital social exercise or the beginning of a big brother state?

The census is coming: the once-in-a-decade attempt to hold a mirror up to the face of the nation, will take place in spring 2001.

The face of the nation is changing and so are the nature of the questions. This, some argue, will be the most intrusive census yet. For the first time you will be asked what you believe in and even who you sleep with. For the first time the government will have information not just about who lives where and how long they have been there; but how many gay, mixed race Hindus there are in relationships with Irish, lapsed Catholics. Fill it in and you will be participating in a multi-million pound, statistical project that will help determine the nationwide allocation of everything from birth control to meals on wheels; refuse and you could go to prison.

Adapted from an article by Gary Younge In *The Guardian,* 24 March 1999

Information is also demanded so that the efficiency of those providing the services can be assessed by the government. 'Performance targets' have become a common management tool. Government ministers set targets which services must try to meet. The crime figures, SATS results, numbers of patients on waiting lists become a measure of the competence and commitment of those working for a local police force, a school, a hospital. Of course, it is not only government ministers who are interested in such information. It is important to members of the public. Since the 1980s governments have been saying that they want the education system and the health service to give more choice to parents and patients. Being able to choose becomes an advantage only if the parent or patient has information about the options available. Statistics on pupil numbers, average class sizes, examination results, attendance records, numbers of exclusions and much else become vital to any parent deciding which school they want for their child.

These same statistics become part of the basis on which members of the public judge the performance of government. A trend can go in an unpopular direction – hospital waiting lists can lengthen. To protect and polish its image the government employs 'spin doctors'. Statistics become a weapon in the party political battle. Statistics are reported in the media, often accompanied by a 'human interest' story. An interview with the daughter of a woman who died whilst waiting for an operation can give impact to a set of hospital waiting list figures. Such information can play an important part in giving members of the public an idea of 'how the country is doing' and influence political attitudes and voting intentions. The spin doctors manipulate the statistics to show the party for which they work in the most favourable light.

A huge quantity of statistical information is created by and for the government. This information is very useful to sociologists. It is accessible in publications like Social Trends. It is information which costs the sociologist almost nothing to obtain. It is, in some cases, information which only the government has sufficient resources and authority to collect. Every household in the country, for example, has a legal obligation to fill in the forms for the government's National Census 2001.

The sociologist should approach official statistics with caution. It is important to make sure that we know how the poverty, unemployment, or violent crime the statistics refer to was and is being defined. It is particularly important when considering trends to be aware of any change in the definitions. For example, a government can reduce the unemployment figures in two ways:

(i) By administering policies which lead to the creation of more jobs which the unemployed want to do and are able to do.

(ii) If a government cannot or will not do this it can reduce the unemployment figures by changing the definition of being unemployed and counting the unemployed in a way which leaves some out.

Before 1982 the unemployment statistics issued by the Department of Employment included all those on the unemployed register, whether or not they were entitled to benefits. After 1982 an individual was counted as unemployed only if he or she was entitled to benefits. By reducing the number of groups entitled to benefits the government was able both to save money and reduce their unemployment statistics.

The numbers of people who show up in the figures depend on decisions made by members of the public. An individual can be recorded as unemployed only if he or she comes forward and registers. Individuals may not do this for a variety of reasons:

→ They may anticipate getting a job very quickly and think that registering is not worth the trouble.

→ They may have had a bad experience with a rude or patronising official and be reluctant to face similar treatment.

→ They may be embarrassed or depressed by the lack of a job and not feel like doing anything.

On the other hand, some individuals may claim benefit, saying that they are unemployed, whilst keeping quiet about jobs they are doing for cash in hand.

The unemployment figures published by the government will therefore not include some people who are unemployed and include some people who are not unemployed. Recognise this when considering trends in the figures. Unemployed people may become more or less likely over a period of time to sign on, as may employed people. A well-publicised anti-fraud campaign with tabloid headlines directing public anger towards fraudulent claimants could deter people, whether potential fraudsters or not, from registering. The unemployment figures might fall.

Not all official statistics need to be treated with such great caution. It is difficult to imagine reasons why a government would wish to manipulate the marriage statistics. It is also difficult to imagine how members of the public could act to make these statistics seriously unreliable.

Nonetheless, always remember that all official statistics are the result of a social process. Within this process individuals and organisations will have made decisions which influence the figures. The attitudes and interests of these individuals and organisations thus become significant and should always be taken into account.

JOBLESS TOTAL IN SOME AREAS TWICE OFFICIAL LEVEL

Government claims of a buoyant economy spreading prosperity were dealt a blow yesterday when a new survey claimed that official figures underestimated the real level of unemployment.

A senior research officer at the Unemployment Unit said that the level of 'hidden' unemployment in Britain was much higher than in the rest of the European Union. British counting methods were consistently 'gender biased' excluding hundreds of thousands of women.

Adapted from an article by Peter Hetherington in *The Guardian,* Friday 13 October 2000

EXERCISE

Make a list of official statistics which you have seen or perhaps used. They may relate to family, education, poverty, crime and deviance.

Who was involved in the social process by which these statistics were produced?

Which figures might a government wish to be high and rising or low and falling?

In what ways might a government try to make figures show what it wants them to show?

Glossary

The Establishment
some sociologists believe that Britain is ruled by a small, powerful group of people – the Establishment. This group, made up of 'top people' in politics, business, the military and so on, can, when acting together, pull strings to protect its own interests.

Free market
a free market is said to exist when the government intervenes very little in the way in which companies carry on their business. 'Free' suggests that companies compete with each other for customers and that people are able to choose which companies to give their custom to.

Globalisation
refers to the processes by which what goes on in one country is influenced more and more by what is happening elsewhere in the world. These processes are referred to most commonly in relation to economic activities.

Multinational business/corporation
these are huge businesses/corporations/companies which operate in many different countries. The scope of their operations, their ability to influence greatly the economic situation in any particular country, and their great wealth make such businesses – and more particularly their executives – very powerful indeed.

Political culture
political culture refers to those elements of the culture which have to do with the political way of life in the society. The political culture will contain political values, political beliefs and political skills.

Political socialisation
refers to the ways in which political values, beliefs and skills, for example, are passed on in a society. Political socialisation is part of the general process of socialisation and involves the same 'agents' – family, peer group, school, workmates, mass media and so on.

Pressure- or interest-group
a pressure group is an organisation which tries to influence the decisions made by public bodies such as the government, or local councils. Unlike political parties, pressure groups do not try to become the government.

Voluntary organisations
these are organisations set up by ordinary members of the public who wish to help to tackle what they see as a problem. For example, think of the organisations which run charity shops. Sometimes the phrase **Non Governmental Organisation (N.G.O.)** is used to refer to such groups.

Population, people and place

9

Introduction

Every one of us can give examples of the way in which the population lives and how it has changed in recent years. We can also point to the many consequences – some of which we like, some of which we do not like – of these changes. Here are a few:

'Nobody wants to live here any more. There aren't any jobs, You can buy a house for a couple of thousand pounds. Only the old people and a few squatters live here now.'

'They have just been given planning permission to build 40 houses in the field behind our house. Locals don't need them. More commuters! They'll all have cars. It won't be safe to let the children play out.'

'You never saw black people round here when I was young. I go to a black doctor. Lovely woman but very posh.'

'It was always fish and chips when I was a kid. Now I have curries, Chinese, Italian. It's great.'

We do not only come across population change in our everyday experiences. Some population changes and their consequences are presented to us as serious issues which demand attention. Journalists and politicians tell us, for example, that we must, as a society, think differently in order to cope with being an ageing population; or that we should be concerned with the North – South divide; or that we need tough measures to deter 'bogus' asylum seekers.

An ageing population

Sociologists and demographers are interested in the structure of populations. That is, they are interested in how a population is made up of people of different ages, ethnic backgrounds and sexes, for example. They are interested in how a population has come to have the structure it has and in predicting what will be the structure in the future. Such predictions will be important to those planning future public provision. How many school places will we need? How large will be the demand for pensions?

The population of Britain we are told – sometimes in ways which suggest a crisis – is ageing. An ageing population is one in which the proportion of elderly people is increasing. Note the word 'proportion'. To say that a population is ageing is to say something about the balance between older and younger groups. In an ageing population there are relatively more older and relatively fewer younger people. In an ageing population the average age is increasing.

Population by Gender and age   Percentages United Kingdom

MALES	UNDER 16	16–64	65+	
1901	33.6	62.1	4.3	(100)
1931	25.6	67.7	6.7	(100)
1961	24.8	65.8	9.4	(100)
1998	21.3	65.5	13.2	(100)
FEMALES				
1901	31.4	63.4	5.2	(100)
1931	23.0	68.9	8.1	(100)
1961	22.1	63.9	14.0	(100)
1998	19.6	63.2	18.2	(100)

From Social Trends 2000

Figure 73 Population age table.

EXERCISE

Look again at the table and answer the following questions:

1) What percentage of the male population in 1931 was between 16–64 years old?
2) What was the trend between 1901–1998 in the proportion of the female population who were over 65 years old?
3) Compare the figures for over 65-year-old males with those for over 65-year-old females. What do you notice? What does this mean? How might it be explained?

Why is it ageing?

When asked to explain why a population is ageing, or has aged, many students offer an incomplete explanation. Perhaps because the reference to 'ageing' conjures up images of elderly people, they limit their discussion to what has happened or is happening to the number of elderly people. This is not the whole story. The reasons why there are relatively fewer younger people is an equally important part of the explanation. A complete explanation of why the population of Britain has aged and is ageing must include explanations of both changes in life expectation and changes in the number of babies born each year.

Why do more people live for longer?

Advances in medical understanding, science and technology have enabled doctors and public health authorities to provide successful treatments for and to prevent or limit the occurrence of many illnesses which in the past would have been fatal. A look at your own immunisation/vaccination record card gives a good indication of how many killer or disabling diseases you have been protected from. Medical advances do not, of course, apply themselves. They will contribute to an improvement in people's health, only if the public have access to them. Making health services available – since 1946 through the National Health Service – to all members of society has been a significant development in 20th century Britain.

Advances in medical understanding have also enabled members of the public to take steps in their own lives to lower the risk of becoming ill. From schools and from contact with medical services, individuals receive all kinds of information relating to health matters. The mass media is full of articles and handy hints on how to live longer, healthier lives. The public has developed a widespread interest in dieting, exercising, eating healthy foods and thinking healthy thoughts. Much of the media coverage is used to entertain or to sell things like slimming biscuits or jogging shoes. Public knowledge about the link between tobacco smoking and cancer may, however, be contributing to an increase in expectation of life. The living conditions and standard of living of most of the population have improved during the 20th century. Houses are less likely to be damp and are better equipped. People now take the availability of hot water for baths and washing clothes for granted. Our living conditions have become more hygienic. With family income levels generally having increased the proportion of the population suffering from inadequate diets or unable to afford adequate clothing has decreased.

Working conditions have improved, making it less hazardous. The introduction of health and safety regulations and laws limiting the number of hours employees can work in a week have been important. The growth of trade unions has helped to give workers the confidence to challenge dangerous working conditions. Perhaps more important has been the trend away from work in heavy manufacturing and extractive industry and towards office-type work. It may not be very nice working in a call centre but it threatens the worker neither with the risk of serious accident nor long term physical harm. Working in a foundry or down a pit was rather different.

Conditions in the general environment have also improved during the last 100 years. As a result of laws being passed, standards being set and enforced by local councils and various inspectorates, activities which once threatened people's health have been limited. Factories are no longer entitled to pollute rivers, and air and land as they once did. Food shops and restaurants are permitted to trade only if they meet strict standards of hygiene. Water companies are obliged to supply clean water. Hotels and cinemas must comply with modern safety regulations. Local councils are obliged to keep the streets clean. Our environment has been made safer. In other ways, perhaps most noticeably through pollution and accidents associated with the increased use of motor vehicles, it is becoming more dangerous.

Why fewer children?

The movement of the birth rate during the 20th century was not so straightforward as that of the death rate. There were periods when it went up. However, the generalisation that families are likely to have fewer children today than they did 100 years ago is supported by the statistics. When discussing the reasons for this, recognise that your explanation must answer two questions: how has it become possible for people to avoid having lots of children and why do more people want to avoid having lots of children?

Medical technology has placed at people's disposal a variety of contraceptive methods which are easy to use effectively. People today are also more prepared to use them. Knowledge of contraception is now widespread and few people disapprove of its use. Religious objections have generally weakened over the last 100 years and fewer people, in our more secular society, think that the way they conduct their sexual intercourse is the church's business. People now feel that they are entitled to make choices so far as building a family is concerned. Contraception is the means of implementing that choice.

Why, then, do most people choose to have fewer children today? What sort of reasoning might be involved when a couple or a woman alone consider whether to have a child? Perhaps, as when making decisions about other matters, they would balance the benefits against the costs. Would having a child enhance the life of its parents or parent and outweigh any costs? Or would the fulfilment of having a child be outweighed by the sacrifices which would have to be made?

Of course, in real life the process of deciding would not be as calculating and rational as this. Couples do not discuss whether to have a baby like accountants, making cost-benefit projections for each year until the child is 21. On the other hand people do ask themselves certain questions. Can we, or I, afford a child? Will our career, or my career, suffer? How will having a child influence our relationship? Why do we, or I, want a child? Thinking about having children in these terms might make some potential parents think again.

Over the last 50 years, life has come to offer far more opportunities to have and do things than were open to our grandparents. No longer, for example, does a woman's life focus solely on motherhood and home making. Today, a good education, exciting travel, material comforts, fulfilling leisure, and social, economic or political advancement are possible. Childbearing and rearing has now to compete with these other sources of satisfaction. Of course, having children is still popular. Parenthood can still provide social status and personal fulfilment. At the same time people want and expect other things. A woman might want and expect to be successful in a career, to have an exciting social life, to keep her figure and looks, not to be 'tied down'. Perhaps achieving these wants and satisfying these expectations is compatible with having one or even two children – but four or five?

WE'RE CHILD FREE – AND WE'RE HAPPY

In Britain the child free movement is gaining ground. Nearly 25% of women born in Britain in 1973 will be childless at 45. Just 10% of those born 30 years earlier would reach middle age without bearing children.

The Adamses are 36 and have been married for six years. 'We started out thinking children would just happen one day', said Ed.

'But then one or two subtle things happened that made us wonder why we wanted to do this.

'My parents split up when I was 12. I became aware that as a parent you can just end up replicating your childhood. And, after my father remarried and had another child he once told me, "It's hell". And they had money and nannies and financial support and no problems with school fees or anything like that.

"When it comes to it, Mary didn't want to give up her work. She had worked with children in the past and began to feel that she didn't really want them.

'There's that thing about a natural maternal instinct. But it's just another social pressure. It's rubbish. A lot of women sacrifice their careers and realise they can't pick them up properly again. I could have become a house husband but I didn't want it.

'I've now had a vasectomy. It was very easy. My mum was a bit disappointed: she had expected to be a grandmother one day. With my dad we never discuss it.'

Adapted from an article by Ben Summerskill in *The Observer* Review, Sunday, 30 July 2000

EXERCISE

Read the article again and answer the following questions:

i) What percentage of women born in 1973 are predicted to reach middle age without bearing children?

ii) What seemed to be the most important reason for the Adamses not having children?

iii) What belief of psychologists does Ed challenge – preferring to take a more sociological point of view?

EXERCISE

List the reasons which a woman today might have for:

a) wanting to become a mother

b) not wanting to become a mother.

List the reasons which a man today might have for:

a) wanting to become a father

b) not wanting to become a father.

➡ Do the reasons you have listed suggest that men and women look at the prospect of parenthood in the same way?

➡ Are there any reasons in your lists which would not have been relevant for men and women in 1900?

Why might bringing up a child at the start of the 21st century cost the parents more than bringing up a child at the start of the 20th century?

The consequences

Recognise when considering the consequences of an ageing population that discussions commonly suffer from one or more of the following limitations:

● Firstly, a discussion may be unbalanced. Many students appear to see no positive consequences at all. Elderly people, in a variety of ways, are presented as a burden and a nuisance to their family and to society generally. The larger the proportion they make up of society the heavier the burden, the greater the nuisance. A few students seem unable even to identify positive consequences for the elderly themselves. They are seen as sick, lonely, bored and poor.

Yet there are positive consequences for society, family and the individual. It is important not to approach the consequences with the assumption that they will be negative. Consider the housing needs of the elderly, for example. These are always turned by students into a negative consequence. As the population ages, elderly people occupy houses for longer thereby creating a housing shortage – a negative consequence. A less prejudiced student might recognise that satisfying the housing needs of the elderly offers good opportunities to architects, bricklayers and others – a positive consequence.

- A second limitation is seen when students discuss the ways in which an ageing population influences the distribution of resources in society. These discussions are often unrealistic. Many students appear to believe that the needs of elderly people are always met. More elderly people means more needs to be met, an increased demand on resources and therefore fewer resources available for other sections of the population. A typical suggestion would be that elderly people need home help of various kinds. The more elderly people there are the more money a local council will spend on home help, and the less money there will be left to spend on youth workers and schools. Note the use of the word 'will' in the previous sentence.

  Our society does not work like this! Resources are not devoted to a particular section of society just because it has a need. The extent to which a section of society is able to obtain sufficient resources depends very much on the power it can exercise. Whether money is spent on home helps for the elderly or youth workers is a political decision. In the same way, whether the state retirement pension is set at a level allowing the elderly to live comfortably and with some dignity is a political decision. That such a large number of elderly people have been and are allowed to live in poverty is evidence of the lack of power they have as a section of society. Whether the elderly will be able to exercise more power as the proportion they make up of the population increases becomes a very significant question. So far as the elderly themselves are concerned, there being more of them looks in this respect like a positive consequence. More elderly people means more elderly voters: a greater incentive for politicians and political parties to give a higher priority to their needs.

- Students pay little or no attention to what elderly people actually do. It is as if they think that because elderly people no longer 'work' for money they no longer do anything, or that because they are not paid what they do is not worth anything. The housebound elderly person who sits looking out of his or her window can, however, deter daytime criminals in a street of empty houses – empty because the younger neighbours are 'at work'. Elderly people have the time to volunteer. Many voluntary organisations would find it difficult to survive without them. Most charity shops would have to close, and many churches would be almost empty. An ageing population may increase the burden of dependency but it may also increase the number of those willing and able to sustain religious, political and community activities from which all members of society benefit.

- Students assume that an ageing population is a population which is growing. They discuss overcrowding and lack of food, for example, as consequences of an ageing population. They are not. A population can age without any increase in the population – relatively more elderly people; relatively fewer younger people. In Britain the population did both grow and age during the 20th century. It is misleading, however, to see the latter as the cause of the former.

- Many students fail to recognise that the elderly are a diverse group of people. At the heart of their discussions is a stereotype. This is surprising, particularly when the same students readily take into account class, gender and ethnicity when discussing the situations of children or people of working age. The elderly are discussed as if the inequalities and differences of their younger years have stopped being significant. Perhaps all elderly people look alike – men dressed in beige, women in crimplene – to the younger. The reality is very different. The inequalities experienced and the different decisions made when they were younger have a great impact on the resources and opportunities available to elderly people. Past employment may leave some in ill-health and poor, whilst others are in good health and well off. The elderly who had children may have the opportunity to be active grandparents, others will not. The ageing of a population may result in more people needing medical help but also in more volunteers being available to push the hospital library trolley. It may result in there being more people needing financial support from the welfare state but also more 80- and 90-year-olds paying taxes. Avoid stereotypes.

ELDERLY PEOPLE IN DIFFERENT SITUATIONS – SOME FACTS

Below is a selection of statistics about the situation of 'elderly people' from different ethnic groups in Britain

White and Indian elderly people are least likely to experience multiple deprivation. Pakistani, Bangladeshi, black Caribbean elderly people are the most likely to experience multiple deprivation.

33% of elderly white people receive income support

58% of elderly black Caribbean receive income support

75% of elderly Pakistani, Bangladeshi receive income support

1% of elderly white people live in accommodation with more than one person per room

38% of elderly Bangladeshi people live in accommodation with more than one person per room

Elderly black Caribbean people are nearly twice as likely to live in a household without a car as elderly Indian people.

From *Population Trends*, Autumn 2000 – No.101

EXERCISE

Study the statistics and think how you might explain these differences. It might be useful to consider possible differences in the working lives of people in the different groups.

Recognise that our society is changing in ways which are likely to influence the consequences an ageing population will have. The present age of retirement, for example, could be abolished or raised. Politicians are already considering it. Any such change will have consequences for the burden of dependency. If people retired not at a particular age but when they wanted to or felt that they should, age would become less significant. The point at which someone gave up work would be related more to fitness, economic circumstances, and level of job satisfaction.

Being 70 years old is a physical fact. Being 70 years old also has a social significance. What it means to be 70 years old is influenced very much by the expectations people in the society have about becoming and being elderly. If more 70 year olds climb mountains, run marathons, write books, or make hit records then these expectations might change. Think of the times through which those who became 70 in 1980 had lived. Those who turn 70 in 2010 will have had a rather different collection of experiences, and may well see being elderly rather differently. They may turn out to be a rather different kind of elderly people. What is more, the attitudes of younger people towards the elderly in 2010 may be different to those of younger people in 1980. The relationships between the age groups may change.

The consequences of an ageing population – as alleged by students

Look at the following list. Think of what has been said in the discussion above and ask yourself whether each of the individual items on the list is an appropriately stated consequence, and if the list as a whole gives a realistic impression of the ways in which an ageing population will affect society:

→ the burden of dependency will increase,
→ there will be more young people unemployed because elderly people keep their jobs for longer,
→ the National Health Service will be stretched by an increase in the number of sick elderly people,
→ there will be less money available for schools,
→ there will be more people in poverty,
→ the problems caused by elderly people for families will increase. There will be, for example, more financial hardship, more overcrowding, increased tension between younger and elderly members of the family, greater pressure on women in the family to act as carers for the elderly.

Migration

How many people migrate, who migrates, and where they migrate to and from at any one time depends on a complex set of factors. Any adequate explanation of this pattern will involve answering the following questions: firstly, what makes it possible for this migration to take place? Secondly, what do those who migrate want to achieve by migrating? Students often neglect the first question.

The possibility of migration

The possibility of migrating between two countries depends on the law and government policies. One of the statuses we are ascribed at birth is that of citizen. Children become officially recognised as citizens by the authorities of the country in which they were born – or to which they belong because of their parents. An individual has a nationality which he or she can demonstrate by showing a passport. This nationality generally gives the individual the right to live in his or her country. At the same time governments establish conditions upon which nationals of other countries are allowed to settle on a permanent basis. These rules may be liberal, allowing most people who wish to apply to satisfy the conditions, or designed to keep potential migrants out. During the last 40 years British immigration rules have been restrictive.

Throughout this time immigration has been – and remains – a matter of political controversy. This is because it is believed, realistically or not, to be linked with other issues that concern political parties, pressure groups and members of the general public. Some have expressed concern about the consequences of immigration for the British national identity, for the economic wellbeing of certain groups and for social order. Others have seen immigrants as contributing energy and new ideas to our society. From this perspective hostility to immigration has often seemed to express racism. Many politicians have been, and are, reluctant to offend those who oppose immigration. Other politicians have exploited the racist sentiments found amongst sections of the population. It is therefore unsurprising that the laws regulating immigration which have been passed during the last 50 years have made it difficult for non-white people to enter the country. Restrictive attitudes to immigration are, however, being challenged.

MARKET FORCES TO DETERMINE MIGRATION POLICY LACK OF QUALIFIED STAFF BREAKS DOWN OLD TABOO.

The call by a Home Office Minister for a market-led relaxation of immigration rules to plug Britain's skills gap breaches a taboo that has gripped public life for 40 years.

A combination of growing skilled labour shortages across the economy, an under-trained domestic work force, the accelerating globalisation of the labour market and an ageing population has hammered home the need to open up.

Using foreign labour to fill the gaps in the market is nothing new and a large proportion of post war immigration was organised by the government to meet labour shortages. After a slump in the 1970s and 1980s the numbers have again picked up rapidly.

The annual number of work permits issued, (the main method of entry for non-European Union skilled workers and professionals) rose to nearly 77,000 last year. They cover everyone from senior Japanese and US bankers to agency nurses. Most come from advanced industrial countries outside the EU.

There are suspicions of racial bias in the discretionary decisions left to officials, and anomalies are rampant. Highly paid chefs are allowed in while Indian restaurateurs are unable to bring in staff from the sub-continent to keep their family businesses going.

A spokesperson for the Institute of Public Policy Research hopes the Government will take a lead in arguing the positive case for economic migrants and highlights, for example, the fact that they pay more in taxes than they pay in benefits.

Adapted from an article by Seumas Milne in *The Guardian*, Tuesday 12 September 2000

EXERCISE

Read the article again and answer the following questions:

i)   What is the 'taboo' which has been breached? Why did the taboo exist?

ii) How does the 'fact' mentioned in the final paragraph challenge the stereotype of the economic migrant often presented in the tabloid media?

iii) What evidence is given that the immigration process is administered in a racist way?

iv) What negative consequence might be faced by an underdeveloped country if skilled workers migrate to Britain or other advanced industrial countries?

The possibility of migration also depends on the knowledge people have about the way of life in other countries. Moving to another country to settle is always going to involve risks – 'what if it doesn't work out?' It seems unlikely that, unless desperate, anyone would move to another country without knowing something about its customs, the attitudes of its people, and the chances of being able to earn a living or get a house. With the sort of world-wide communication networks which exist today it is relatively easy for people to feel they know enough about life in other countries.

The development of a world-wide, global economy has created conditions in which people catch glimpses of the ways of life in countries thousands of miles away. Advertisements, the goods on sale in shops, tourism, pop records, making goods to sell abroad, films – all transmit information about what it would be like living somewhere else.

Globalisation and technological advances have made travel around the world easy. Migration no longer involves dangerous voyages, treks across uncharted deserts or mountains to a destination from which there would be no return. For those with sufficient money and the appropriate documentation migration presents few travel problems. Only for those attempting to enter a country illegally is the process of migration likely to be hazardous.

Why people want to migrate

Migration to another country might be more or less possible for an individual. But what might make migration desirable to an individual? What might be his or her motives? An individual may wish to escape from a situation in the country in which he or she lives. Or an individual may be attracted by various features of life in another country. Sometimes sociologists refer to 'push' and 'pull' factors.

Two push factors are suggested by the words 'refugee' and 'asylum seeker'. Civil wars or wars between nations have been common in recent years. Modern wars involve civilian populations and therefore produce refugees. Civilians are forced to flee from their homes.

Natural disasters – droughts or floods – can also produce refugees. Most countries have obligations to refugees under international treaties which they have signed. Some refugees will return to their country when it becomes possible, others may settle permanently in the country which gave them refuge.

Asylum seekers wish to migrate to escape persecution or the threat of persecution by the government or by sections of society in the country in which they live. People have been, and are, persecuted for many reasons – for their political or religious beliefs, because they belong to a particular ethnic or tribal group, or because of their economic situation. In many countries those who are persecuted have few rights and little chance of defending themselves.

Wars, natural disasters and persecution can give people an urgent reason for leaving a country. Differences in the economic conditions of different countries create situations in which millions of individuals might at any time reasonably conclude that they would have a better life abroad. In some cases 'push' factors such as lack of jobs or business opportunities, little chance of earning a decent wage, might be prominent. In other cases 'pull' factors such as skill shortages abroad might be more significant.

Stereotypes of the economic migrant should be avoided. They may be scientists or engineers moving for better prospects. The phrase 'brain drain' has been used to refer to such movement between Britain and the USA. They may be senior executives working for a multi-national corporation. They may, on the other hand, be poor, unskilled people from a developed or underdeveloped country moving in an attempt to better their standard of living or provide better opportunities for their children. Market forces encourage the movement of labour just as they encourage the movement of capital.

For a variety of reasons – to be safe, for the sake of the children, to achieve a better standard of living – many people might feel that they **need** to move. For some, however, migration is not a matter of needing but of **wanting** to move. Individuals who are sufficiently affluent and not tied to a particular country by work have been and are able to migrate in order to achieve a particular lifestyle. The most publicised examples are those who have been successful in the worlds of art and entertainment. In recent years, with the rise in the general standard of living in Britain, this option has become more widely available. Some retired people have, for example, moved to France or Spain because they enjoy the climate or aspects of the culture.

Migration between different countries, whilst more easily accomplished today than in the past, is clearly still a big and often difficult step for anyone. Migration within a country can seem commonplace in comparison. The reasons why people move within a country, however, are no different from those which lead people to migrate from one country to another. People may move to escape war – for example, Catholic families moving out of Protestant neighbourhoods and Protestants out of Catholic neighbourhoods in Northern Ireland. Gays, members of ethnic minorities, and suspected paedophiles have sometimes been forced to flee from neighbourhoods in which they were harassed and abused. People have moved because their factory, mill or pit has shut down or because they have been offered a better job elsewhere. People have moved to achieve a lifestyle they would like – living in a cottage in a quiet, unpolluted rural area, perhaps.

Recognise that whilst many migrate as individuals, others migrate as families. This can mean that, unless the decision to migrate was taken democratically, some members of the family may be reluctant migrants. In some circumstances wives and children may have had little choice when breadwinning husbands and fathers decided to move.

The consequences of migration

Moving, whether between countries or within a country, will have consequences for the individuals and families who move. Some consequences – being safe or having an improved standard of living – were the reasons for moving. Such consequences may not be achieved or may be achieved only partially. Some of those seeking or granted asylum in Britain, for example, have in recent years been harassed and abused by elements within society. Migration has achieved only a partial respite from persecution. Even movement within Britain may not bring the expected gain. Pictures on the television of tearful men and women, just made redundant, telling the interviewer, 'There was no work in the North-East so I came down to this job 18 months ago. Now I'm stuck in the East Midlands without a job,' are not uncommon. Many who move, though, will achieve their aim, thereby encouraging others to migrate.

Even though some aims are achieved, migration can lead to problems. The migrant may be treated coldly or with active hostility by neighbours or colleagues at work. A migrant may face discrimination in various aspects of life. Racism, bigotry, simple dislike of change or suspicion of outsiders may play a part. Cultural differences may create tensions which can be exploited by those with particular political agendas and by employers who believe that they can benefit from disunity amongst their workforce.

Living in an unfamiliar place may cause practical difficulties. Communication may be difficult if the language of the migrant is not that of those amongst whom he or she now lives. Being unfamiliar with the way things are done, the migrant becomes vulnerable to exploitation. He or she may be paid illegally low wages, sometimes by employers who were themselves migrants some years previously. Not being aware of his or her rights the migrant puts up with it.

Some migrants make a success of their move more quickly than others. Those whose migration has been well prepared, who have contacts in the country or area into which they are moving, who are well educated, have skills and capital, and who are committed to getting on in their new situation clearly have an advantage. Success will also depend, however, on many factors beyond the migrant's control. An economic recession can make things difficult for many in society but it may confront the recently settled immigrant with particular problems.

MOVING WITH THE TIMES IN BRITAIN THE NEW GENERATIONS OF MIGRANT FAMILIES ARE BEGINNING TO TAKE CONTROL OF THEIR OWN DESTINIES

In Britain the Chinese are a small and, by their own wish, almost invisible minority – but they are already ahead of the white population in educational achievement, home ownership and professional jobs.

So far among ethnic minorities in Britain, the upward mobility of the Chinese is rivalled only by the Indians many of whose families came via East Africa. The Hindu, like the Chinese, family is very strong, with little divorce. The focus is on getting on. The Ugandan Asians, whose families had been expelled by Idi Amin in 1972, have greatly prospered in Britain. They had no 'myth of return' – which had its advantages. They were twice migrants – from Gujurat to Africa, and from Africa to Britain. They had to start again from scratch. These were the kind of remarks a researcher gathered – 'If I work hard for somebody else, then I get a limited amount. But if I have my own business, I work hard to get more money for myself and my family.' 'I didn't want that charity money, so I decided I must work.' 'It's degrading to accept money from social security.' 'Our children are our hope.'

Adapted from an article by Paul Barker in, *Guardian Society*, Wednesday 4 August 1999

EXERCISE

Read the article again and answer the following questions:

i) What is meant by the 'myth of return'. Why might its absence be an advantage to an immigrant group?

ii) How might the attitude revealed by the remarks help the Ugandan Asians to 'get on'?

iii) What have the Chinese and the Ugandan Asians got in common which might help them to succeed as migrants?

Large scale movements within Britain

An individual may migrate – either between countries or within a country – for personal reasons which are unlikely to apply to many others. A woman may go to live with her sister when her husband dies, for example. However, many pressures to migrate apply generally. High and persistent levels of unemployment or poverty in a particular area put many people, not just a few individuals, in situations which make it sensible for them to migrate.

During the last 200 years there have, at various times, been large-scale population movements in Britain. These have had significant consequences. During the 19th century many of the poorer people were forced to leave rural areas. Losing their rights to use the common land, no longer needed by the big landowners for work, and unable in their homes to produce goods as cheaply as the new mills and factories, they could either starve or move. Many moved towards the towns, hoping to find work. With there being such a plentiful supply of labour in and near the towns businesses were set up there, providing work. Other people were drawn towards these centres of employment, settled there, and the towns grew – some becoming cities. This process sociologists call **urbanisation**.

As the towns and cities grew they developed a structure. Different sections of society tended to live apart. Some parts of the town or city were more pleasant than others. Only those with little money and therefore little choice would live close to smelly, polluting factories or steelworks. Those who could afford it would live away from these industrial neighbourhoods. Towards the outskirts of the town or city it was cleaner and there was more space. Here people could live in larger houses, have gardens and breathe fresh air away from the grime and the poor. From the end of the 19th Century suburbs were thus created for and by the growing middle class. This process sociologists call **suburbanisation**.

Cities had grown with industrialisation. But by the 1970s many of the 'old' industries which had played a major part in that process were in serious decline. Docks, factories, steelworks, for example, no longer needed the large number of workers available. Many cities lost inhabitants. Many towns, particularly those in which new 'high tech' industries had developed, gained inhabitants. The decline in the population of cities was a result, however, not just of changes in the pattern of employment. To many people, cities were becoming unpleasant places to live. The phrase 'inner city' came to conjure up, whether justly or not, all sorts of reasons to be fearful. Those who could afford to began to think in terms of 'quality of life'. Having a home in a village or town away from the city seemed an attractive proposition, particularly if it was possible to commute to a well-paid job. The process by which the proportion of the population living in cities and heavily built up areas declines – deurbanisation – began to be significant.

A population movement which has attracted much attention recently is the 'drift to the South'. During the last 20 years people have been leaving the North of England for the South – particularly the South East. For most of this time the South has seemed to offer better job prospects. Many northerners have become economic migrants. Whilst the greatest part of the pressure to move has been and is the chance of a job or promotion, other factors may be important for particular groups. Women may hope to find more progressive attitudes – more 'new men' – in the south. Gays may perhaps hope to encounter less homophobia.

Consequences

If large numbers of people leave a country there will be consequences. If large numbers of people move into a country there will be consequences. The same is true when relatively large numbers leave or move into a region or neighbourhood. It is important to recognise the significance not only of how many people move but also the kind of people who move. The age, social standing, education and skills, family situation, ethnicity or religion of the migrants may all be significant. It is also important to recognise that consequences may be short or long term. In the short term the movement of people into a country or neighbourhood may lead to tension, hostility and even violence. In the longer term situations change and those who moved in are no longer newcomers but have become part of the country or neighbourhood. There are many kinds of consequence that interest sociologists.

Population structure

MIGRATION AND AGE STRUCTURE

The statistics below suggest how significant the consequences of immigration are for the age structure of a population.

ANNUAL NUMBER OF IMMIGRANTS NEEDED TO MAINTAIN CURRENT BALANCE OF WORKERS TO PENSIONERS	UNITED KINGDOM		
	NUMBERS OF WORKERS TO EACH PENSIONER		
			Projection with zero immigration
	1950	2000	2050
1,194,000	6.24	4.08	2.36

Figure 74 The consequences of immigration.

EXERCISE

Look again at the table and answer the following questions:

i)   According to the table what would happen to the age structure of the UK population if immigration stopped?

ii) Would this matter?

Migration can influence the **age structure** of a population. People entering Britain to settle during the last 40 years have tended to be younger adults – people with sufficient time to build a new life and make the migration worthwhile. This immigration has gone some way to check the ageing of the British population. Migration within a country can affect the age structure of an area or neighbourhood. Those who have moved from the countryside to urban areas have tended to be younger adults seeking to better themselves economically. Those who have moved from urban to countryside areas are often middle aged people using their economic success to improve their lifestyle. In particular areas, therefore, the population in the countryside has aged leading, for example, to the closure of schools.

	UNDER 16	16–64	65 AND OVER	ALL AGES MILLIONS
WHITE	20	64	16 (100)	53.1
BLACK				
Black Caribbean	23	67	9 (100)	0.5
Black African	32	66	2 (100)	0.4
INDIAN	24	70	7 (100)	0.9
PAKISTANI/BANGLADESHI				
Pakistani	35	61	3 (100)	0.6
Bangladeshi	43	54	3 (100)	0.2
CHINESE	15	79	6 (100)	0.2

From Social Trends 2000

Figure 75 Population by ethnic group and age 1998–99, Great Britain.

Migration can also influence the **ethnic structure** of a population. If substantial numbers of those moving into a country to settle are ethnically different from those already there the population will become more ethnically diverse. This does not mean that all or even many areas or neighbourhoods will have populations which are ethnically diverse. Immigrants have tended to settle in cities or large towns, often near others of the same ethnic group. In this way an ethnic group which makes up a very small proportion of the population as a whole can become the largest group within a neighbourhood. If, for whatever reasons, people not belonging to the ethnic group move away from the neighbourhood this process will take place more quickly.

Culture

Migration can influence the culture of a society and the relationships between its members. British society today is generally regarded as multicultural. The different ethnic groups which have settled in Britain over many years have added to the range of cultural experiences available to everyone who lives here. Think of the different foods, music, fashion, for example – a night out in most towns and cities will reflect this.

There are different approaches to ethnic and cultural diversity within our society. Some individuals, sections of society and political groups have responded to the diversity in a negative way, seeing it as threatening British customs, traditions, values and identity: A 'There ain't no black in the Union Jack' approach. Occasionally, during the last 30 years, for example, the media has carried reports of white British parents protesting against morning school assemblies in which Muslim or Hindu festivals were celebrated. These parents wanted their children to be 'brought up in a British, Christian way'. Those who have taken this approach feel that the government should promote Britishness and help those who have settled here to 'become British'. They argue that it is the duty of the immigrant to 'fit in', to conform to the way of life of the majority.

Others have welcomed diversity. In their view society has been strengthened and enriched by the inclusion of people from different cultural traditions: these traditions should be respected and recognised as part of the British way of life. To the extent that this has happened, Britain has become a multicultural society. What it means to be British, Britishness, cannot today be defined in a simple way. This is not just because of cultural diversity resulting from inward migration. It is also because of general changes in the way we live – changes to do with developments in business or the influence of the global media on the way in which groups within society want to see themselves. Many images of Britishness are now only memories.

EXERCISE

i) Consider any conversation in which you or someone else referred to being English or British. What was the context in which the reference was made? What were you or what was the other person trying to convey through the reference?

ii) Write down five things which to you embody or represent Englishness and five which embody or represent Britishness. Ask other people to do the same. Did you or they find it as easy to write the one list as the other. Compare the lists to see how much they have in common. Have you and others referred to attitudes, objects, events, institutions, beliefs or what? Can you draw any conclusions from what you and others have written?

iii) Why might the proportion of people saying that they are English not British have increased?

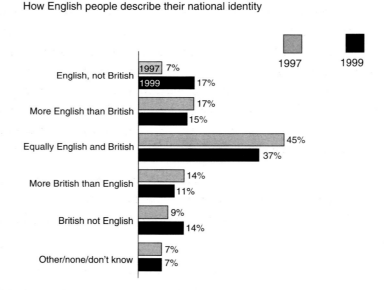

How English people describe their national identity

Figure 76

THE PERCENTAGE OF THOSE WHO DESCRIBED THEMSELVES AS ENGLISH, NOT BRITISH SAYING THAT:

- they were racially prejudiced – 37%

- it was 'bad' that people from ethnic minorities were getting ahead in Britain – 26%

- immigrants take away jobs from people who were born in Britain – 70%

- attempts to give equal opportunities to blacks and Asians in Britain had gone too far – 46%

From information given in an article by John Carvel in *The Guardian* Tuesday 28 November 2000

Politics

Since there are such different – often deeply held – opinions, it is not surprising that immigration and its social and cultural consequences have at times during the last 50 years become big political issues. For much of this time most politicians assumed that support for restrictions on immigration would win them votes. At the same time governments were gradually forced to recognise – partly as a result of pressure group activity – that the discrimination faced by non-white immigrants was unacceptable and socially damaging. Anti-discrimination and race relations acts were passed and governments began to claim that they were committed to ensuring that British citizens, whatever racial or religious group they belonged to, were treated equally.

This has not yet been achieved. Racism in a person to person or neighbourhood context can still lead to violence and harassment. Institutional racism – which those in authority now admit exists – has and continues to put many British citizens at a disadvantage. Immigrants, their children and grandchildren, settled in Britain and committed to making a life here, see evidence that many amongst them are being treated as second class citizens. This they believe to be unacceptable as do many citizens not belonging to an ethnic minority. Issues of race, immigration, and community relations retain a significant place on the British political agenda.

Economics

The movement of people between and within countries often has important economic consequences. The situation, however, is seldom as simple as students like to suggest. That migration into an area inevitably leads to unemployment is perhaps the most common claim. It may be so in some circumstances but not in others. People moving into a country or area can increase the demand for goods and services: more people, more customers, more jobs providing what the customers want. Within a country, an area into which people want to move and do move may come to be seen as an area with a future – an area in which it is worth investing. If facilities are expanded, employment is created.

In other words, inward migration usually creates jobs as well as increasing the number of jobs needed. Whether more jobs are created than the extra jobs needed or vice-versa will depend on many factors – the state of the country's, or area's, economy, the capital and skills possessed by those moving.

Students seldom consider the economic consequences of migration for those countries and areas which the migrants are leaving. Again, the situation should not be seen as simple. Movement of people away from an area of high unemployment may lower the number of jobless in that area – but only if it is the unemployed who move away. Those who move may be people who already have jobs and who are fed up with living in a depressed area. There may be those amongst the unemployed who have more skills and thus more confidence that there will be a job for them somewhere else. In this case the area might lose the very people who might be able to improve things. Such an area can in this way easily become less attractive to potential investors both as a source of customers and as a source of workers.

Housing

Often commented on during the last ten years has been the effect of internal migration on house prices. A large proportion of the British population are owner-occupiers. Internal migration has had an influence on house values. In areas of declining population – in the north of England, for example, house values are low, and houses are difficult to sell. In those areas in the south which have attracted a steady stream of people, house values have risen.

The cost of homes can have significant practical consequences for the way people live. Those on modest incomes – policemen, teachers, nurses, for example – who work in central London are unlikely to be able to afford to live near their work. The houses which they can afford are out from the centre. These workers, along with many others, become commuters which has an influence on their lifestyle. In the same way rural workers, unable to afford the village houses which are being bought by the better off as second homes, are forced to commute to work from their cheaper house in the nearest town.

Planning and politics

The number of houses needed by a population depends on many factors including the pattern of migration, the numbers of children born, life expectation and the percentage of the population which divorces or remains single. Any persistent trend in migration into or within a country increases the demand for houses in the areas into which people are moving. There has been a continuing demand for houses in southern England. Where to build these houses has become a very significant political issue. If they cannot all be built, or those moving do not want to live within existing urban areas, many may have to be built on 'green field' sites. The prospect of having estates built on the edge of villages or of complete towns being built in the middle of the countryside can cause outrage amongst those who live there already and those concerned for wildlife and Britain's shrinking rural heritage. Pressure group activity focussed on environmental issues has thus increased.

Things change

Social change is inevitable in advanced industrial societies and some changes are welcomed by most members of society. These changes people probably call 'progress'. At the same time people may be hostile to or fear change. People want some things to remain the same. Too much change can lead people to feel insecure, or that they are losing control of their life. Migration involves change. The entry of outsiders – some of whom may be of a different colour or religion, who may dress and eat differently – into the society or neighbourhood can be a very visible change. Migration can therefore generate hostility and fear, particularly amongst those – the elderly or the unskilled, for example – whose position in society does not give them the confidence to feel that they can handle whatever changes take place.

The extent to which hostility and fear is likely to influence people's outlook and social behaviour will depend on many factors. If politicians and tabloid headlines suggest that the country is being 'swamped' or 'flooded' by immigrants, fear of immigrants can appear well founded and respectable. If social problems happen to be getting worse at a time when immigration is taking place connections – rightly or wrongly – might be made by members of the public. At various times over the past 40 years some men and women in the street have blamed immigrants for rises in unemployment, crime, benefit fraud, or illness. Immigrants are an easy scapegoat to use. People can believe anything about a group that they know nothing about.

Initially, contact between individual immigrants and members of the host community is likely to be limited, relationships are likely to be shallow and fleeting. Fear, prejudice and practical difficulties, such as language differences, may keep people apart. In such a situation stereotypes can easily be formed and maintained. Being a victim of racist abuse from one or two members of the host community can lead an immigrant to the view that all members of the host community are racist. Such a view might persist until wider and deeper contact with the host community demonstrates that it is not so. Many in the host community in Britain may have thought initially in terms of racial stereotypes built, for example, with images common in old history and geography textbooks, of subjugated African and Asian peoples serving white masters.

Immigrants become, however, part of the society into which they move. Their children and grandchildren, born part of that society, are not immigrants. Inevitably contact between immigrants, their children and members of the host community has increased. Attending school, belonging to trade unions, political parties, business and professional organisations has provided regular opportunities for relationships to develop. Leisure activities such as sport and clubbing have brought people, particularly the young, together. Sometimes open hostility to immigrants and their families by sections of the host society led others to stand with the immigrants. During the late 1970s and early 1980s, the Anti-Nazi League and Rock against Racism united many in opposition to racist propaganda and thuggery.

Through such contacts stereotypes were and are challenged. Immigrants and their children are now encountered by members of the host community in an increasingly wide variety of social contexts. Many immigrants have made a success of their move and many of their children have achieved good qualifications and jobs. Immigrants and their children are now visible as doctors, politicians, accountants, engineers, teachers, top businessmen and so on. Their professional and other achievements have been officially acknowledged through the honours system, appointments to important public bodies and in media coverage.

Any discussion concerning the consequences of there being sections of British society founded on immigration must recognise how complicated the situation is. Racist, anti-immigrant political parties continue to attract recruits and occasionally wider public support. Within some immigrant communities tensions exist between the elderly members, often the original migrants, and their children and grandchildren. The former often wish to maintain the traditions in which they were brought up in the 'old country'. The latter often wish to cast off any parts of these traditions which might make it difficult for them to realise ambitions which have been strongly influenced by modern British culture. Some immigrant communities have maintained their cultural distinctiveness more than others. The situation continues to change.

SIDE BY SIDE

Leicester seems to have become Britain's most ethnically harmonious city. 'The relationship between the communities is wonderful,' says a lecturer at the University of Leicester. 'I'm not just talking between the English and the Asians, I'm talking Hindus and Muslims as well.'

'It's just crept up on us over the past 30 years,' says a 58-year-old woman. The hosiery factory where she works is now Asian owned and most of her colleagues are Asian. 'Everyone is really nice. It doesn't matter does it? They respect our way of life and we respect theirs.'

The explanation, perhaps, lies in the pattern of migration to Leicester in the past 50 years. The first black immigrants arrived from the Caribbean after the war, to be followed in the late 1960s by increasing numbers of people from East Africa. The Asian population quadrupled in a decade and by 1981 of the 200,000 people living in Leicester, 44,000 were ethnic Indians, mostly Hindus and Sikhs. Most of these people were middle class, often bringing capital with them. They were experienced business people and well practised at blending in. Leicester's Gujerati and Punjabi Asian population were on the second leg of their journey from the Indian subcontinent. They had already developed strategies for integrating, as a minority ethnic culture, into an alien society.

A community leader, who had himself arrived in the early 1970s said, 'I think from the very beginning when people started coming to Leicester, there were people who were looking to make the city into one society, not just a city of sections, and they have been working very hard since then.' A politics professor added, 'There have not been many direct clashes on the issues which have been apparent in other areas.'

The result, after 30 years, is a city with ethnic minority representation at the highest level. Leicester has an Asian MP and has had Asians as deputy chief of police, chief executive of the city council, lord mayor and deputy to the Lord Lieutenant. Almost a third of the city's councillors are non-white.

On the still mainly white housing estates to the west and north there is prejudice. 'I'm not racist, but this is a whiteman's country,' says one community leader. A Community College to the southeast of the city presents a more positive image of the new Leicester. The majority of the pupils come from Asian backgrounds, but the intake is mixed with many white children and a few Afro-Caribbeans.

The children here insist they are completely colour-blind. 'Why should it be an issue that we all get along? We have grown up with it. We live with it. To us this is Leicester,' says a 16-year-old Asian girl. 'We don't see each other as Asian or white. Maybe that's a problem in London, but it isn't here,' says a 13-year-old girl.

Adapted from an article by Esther Adley in *The Guardian*, 1 January 2001

EXERCISE

Read the article again and answer the following questions:

i) On what sort of issues might different ethnic communities clash?

ii) What conditions or factors may make such clashes more or less likely?

iii) What suggestions are made in the article as to why Leicester has developed into an ethnically harmonious city?

iv) Why may young people be less aware of or concerned about ethnic differences than their parents or grandparents?

Community

Sociologists have for a long time been interested in the ways in which the social relationships that people establish are related to the kind of place in which they live. Particular attention has been given to the comparison between life in a city with life in a village. Behind much of this discussion is the idea that the city and the village put people who live and work there in such different situations that significantly different kinds of relationship and patterns of life develop. These differences have often been expressed in stereotypes. The city is seen as cold, with isolated individuals rushing about their business, seeing other people as mere faces in a crowd. Relationships are shallow and temporary. Words like 'anonymity', 'impersonal', 'dehumanising' are used to suggest that something important is missing from city life. In contrast, village life is seen as encouraging the warm, deep relationships which are part of real belonging.

The concept of community can be useful in this context. A community exists when a set of people are able to relate to each other as whole people – rather than in terms of particular roles. The individual who delivers the milk is known by his or her customers not just in that role. He or she is there in church on Sunday, in the street shopping, in the pub in the evening, watching the school play. The customers and the milkman or woman find themselves together in a variety of situations. People feel that they know those around them pretty well. A customer would be able to ask the milkman or woman, 'How did your nephew's baptism go?' and not think it a nosy question. Through such relationships a sense of belonging to or being part of something – a community – is likely to develop. People come to feel attached to others in the community. People feel that they should 'look out' for each other and care about the interests of the community as a whole. Customs, ways of treating other members of the community will develop and be upheld out of habit and loyalty. Social control is achieved largely by informal means. In order to keep the respect and be entitled to the support of others in the community members abide by its norms.

In what circumstances might a set of people come to develop a community? When they find that they have sufficiently important things in common on a sufficiently permanent basis: living in a particular place, working with, spending leisure time with, choosing a partner from amongst those with whom a person grew up; living amongst the same families as did the person's parents. In these circumstances, having interests in common, having shared experiences and memories make people part of the lives of those living around them.

Sharing a significant common characteristic can also be the basis for community. Reference, for example, may be made to the gay or Sikh communities without the implication that all gay people or Sikhs live in the same place. Social intolerance or legal discrimination can make sexual orientation, religion or ethnicity a very significant part of an individual's identity. Homophobia, bigotry, racism create risks for anyone with the characteristics targeted. Those with these characteristics are, therefore, likely to find they have similar experiences and common interests which provide a basis for community.

The city

It is possible to focus on elements of life in the city which might seem to make the development of community unlikely. Living in a city brings an individual into contact with large numbers of people – far too many to get to know 'person to person'. The newspaper seller or fellow bus passengers may be greeted with a nod and a smile but they remain strangers. Work colleagues may live in another part of the city. An individual may be part of several sets of people – a set of neighbours, a set of work colleagues, a set of leisure acquaintances. He or she encounters a large number of people in very specific, limited contexts – till operators at the supermarket, traffic wardens. To what might the individual feel that he or she belongs?

The social diversity within the city – people with different cultures and ambitions, living different lifestyles in different circumstances – might seem to stand in the way of community development. Communities depend on those who form them having and recognising that they have things in common. Change might also seem to limit the possibility of community in the city. Neighbours move away up the housing ladder, others move in. Work colleagues are promoted or move to other workplaces. Bar staff, supermarket staff, police officers, and fellow users of the leisure centre come and go.

Emphasis on such features lends support to a picture of the city as a place in which people have only shallow, impersonal, perhaps temporary relationships with those outside family and a few close friends. Individuals share few significant experiences and interests with those they meet and care little for their approval. Formal, official means of social control are thus needed to maintain social order. Police officers, traffic wardens, security guards, store detectives, private investigators and bouncers become essential to the life of the city.

Are cities always like this?

But communities have existed and continue to exist within cities because people in a similar situation and/or with shared interests settle in the same neighbourhood. The phrase '**urban village**' was sometimes used to express the idea that in some parts of some cities people were able to establish the kind of relationships with their neighbours which created a community. During the first half of the 20th century communities developed in some working class city neighbourhoods. In these neighbourhoods people were often employed in the same kind of industry, working and living in the same kind of conditions, facing the same kind of problems, and belonging to the same organisations. Men spent leisure time together in pubs and clubs. Women shared an interest in making family life as comfortable and respectable as possible with limited resources in difficult conditions. People got to know each other person to person. Links between families were passed from generation to generation. Before the expansion of the welfare state after 1945 extended family and community were vital sources of support.

Since the 1950s such urban working class communities have tended to decline. Much of the industry providing jobs closed down. Extended family networks were weakened, both by grown-up children moving away to take up employment elsewhere and by the general tendency for nuclear families to become more inward looking. Home centred families are likely to have less commitment to and time for people in the wider community. In some neighbourhoods communities disappeared very quickly in the 1960s. Bulldozers knocked houses down so that those who lived there could have indoor lavatories, baths, modern kitchens and other amenities. Slum clearance, re-housing schemes were often, however, carried out in ways – putting people in tower blocks, for example – which made it difficult for a community to be recreated.

Characteristics other than class have become, since the 1960s, a basis for further community development. Members of a particular ethnic minority may settle in a neighbourhood. Bangladeshis in parts of East London, Kashmiris in Bradford. Living alongside people with the same culture and traditions can clearly bring advantages. The practical, everyday needs may be more easily met. With a significant number of potential customers, businesses supplying the kinds of clothes or food which are popular or required – halal meat, for example – by a particular group are more easily established. Religious and other valued traditions are more easily maintained when neighbours think and wish to act in the same way. It may also be safer, or feel safer, living amongst people from the same ethnic group. Acting together, members of an ethnic minority are better able to protect themselves from at least some of the manifestations of racism. For similar reasons, gay people may also find advantages in settling near to each other.

GANG WARS FUEL RACE FEARS IN BRADFORD: THE MURDER OF A YOUNG BLACK MAN AMID A SPATE OF SHOOTINGS HEIGHTENS TENSION BETWEEN ASIAN AND AFRO-CARIBBEAN COMMUNITIES

The death is unique in the way it has crystallised a perception among many in Bradford's Afro-Caribbean community, which numbers just 6000, that they are victims of racial persecution – not from the white majority but from some members of the city's 87,000 strong Asian population. 'The Asians have everything,' said a young black man, 'white and black folks were doing all right but the Asians get everything handed down to them. When they talk about having all these things for community – housing schemes, all that stuff – which community do they mean? I remember fighting the NF out here just to keep Asians and blacks here. Now they're fighting us.'

'If this were anywhere else there would be anarchy,' said a local black activist, 'but because this is England, because of the way it is policed, it stops some things happening. But things are boiling underneath.'

The decline of black-run businesses in Manningham – alongside the growth of community centres and mosques catering for the area's diverse Islamic population – is a particularly sore point. Where once around 20 black-owned shops thrived there's now one pub, a community centre, a boarded up cafe, a West Indian mini market. 'Now we have nowhere to go,' a man said.

Asian community workers and older Muslims insist that drugs rather than racism were at the root of the young man's death.

Adapted from an article by Oliver Burkeman in *The Guardian*, Saturday 19 August 2000

Cities have been and are places of change and diversity. Long-established communities decline whilst others develop. Within the same city may be areas of dereliction, caused by industrial decline and population flight, and areas of regeneration. Warehouses alongside canals in the middle of some cities have been converted into highly desirable residences for young managers and professionals who work in the city. Run down neighbourhoods become gentrified as wealthy people move in and 'do up' property. Such neighbourhoods become fashionable and expensive.

Figure 77 Some inner-city areas are developed, while others remain deprived

The neglected neighbourhoods

Alongside images of city prosperity and exciting lifestyles remain images of a life in areas and neighbourhoods which is bleak and often desperate. Few people can hear or read the phrases 'inner city' or 'sink estate' without thinking of problems – high crime levels, illegal drug use, failing schools, anti-social behaviour or high unemployment.

There have always been parts of towns and cities with such problems. Competition for houses pushes those on low or unstable incomes into cheaper houses. To the disadvantages which poor individuals or families already suffer because of their lack of income are then added problems which result from living in a neighbourhood with people similarly disadvantaged. Neighbourhoods become labelled as rough and undesirable. The people who live there may be viewed in terms of negative stereotypes – 'I'm not having you going out with a lad from that estate. They're all idle, thieving druggies up there'. Those who can move away do – to better living conditions and a better environment in which to bring up children. The houses they leave are either boarded up or occupied by people more disadvantaged than those who left.

Businessmen and women have few incentives to set up in such areas and those already there may find that it is not worthwhile staying open. Access to essential services such as banks becomes difficult. Neighbourhood facilities – schools, playgrounds, health centres, sports facilities – may be vandalised. Much can be destroyed if even a small number of people, angry and frustrated by their deprivation, turn on their neighbourhood. As a result life becomes even more difficult for those living or – like teachers, doctors or police officers – working in the neighbourhood. It is not very reassuring to see that the local green grocer has had to protect his or her onions and cabbages with heavy metal shutters and burglar alarms. Unemployment, old age, lack of skills or lone parenthood can disadvantage an individual wherever he or she lives. With the support of a community and well-maintained public provision any disadvantage can, however, be reduced. Not having a garden matters less to an old person if there is a pleasant local park with seats and flowers; or to a young mother and child if the park has safe swings and a slide. But in a neighbourhood in which old people say, 'I don't really feel safe going out' or young mothers are worried about the syringes left near the swings the disadvantage is heightened.

The gap between life in such neighbourhoods and life elsewhere has perhaps widened during the past 20 years. With governments in the 1980s and early 1990s believing that they should not interfere with the operation of market forces – losers must be left to suffer the consequences of losing – the poor in their neighbourhoods became poorer relative to the better off in theirs. Occasionally, the government was forced to take notice of what was happening. Riots in parts of London, Liverpool and other major cities drew attention to the situation and led the government to promise to do something. In general, however, things got worse.

Some people try

It is important not to have an over simple view of life in such neighbourhoods. There may be residents who have given up hope, but there are others active in trying to improve their own situation and that of their neighbours. For some residents selfishness and anti-social behaviour may be a way of life. Others become friends with their neighbours and help each other out by doing the shopping or looking after the children. In many neighbourhoods community may be very weak but not dead. It is not difficult to find examples of projects undertaken by residents acting together – doing up derelict houses, growing food in community gardens, setting up and operating credit unions or Lets schemes.

SALFORD LETS – LOCAL EXCHANGE TRADING SCHEME

Members pay a small joining fee which covers administrative charges, and then they advertise their skills, from painting and decorating to gardening to computer programming. Other members can use their services and the work is paid for in computerised tokens to buy other services with. 'There are many advantages to LETS,' says the co-ordinator of the network. 'Someone might start out as an amateur housepainter, but do a few jobs on LETS and gain the confidence and experience they need to apply for a job.' The group is now setting up a handyman scheme on the troubled Valley Estate in Swinton. 'The idea is that little jobs make a big difference. Hanging curtains, fitting security locks, the kind of things that are easy to do if you are young and have the know how, but which some older people might find difficult. In return, the older members can do whatever is right for them, babysitting, watering plants when people go away, or whatever. Most people would rather do something in return, without having to part with their hard-earned cash.'

'LETS works best when it involves people of all types, all incomes. It is not about poor people isolating themselves, it is about whole communities binding together.'

Adapted from an article by Ally Fogg, in *BIG ISSUE in the NORTH* No.231, 12–18 October 1998

EXERCISE

Read the article again and answer the following questions:

i) In what ways might an individual benefit from belonging to a Lets scheme?

ii) How might a Lets scheme help to bring into the community people who might otherwise be excluded?

iii) Which sociological concept best applies to the activities done by people within a Lets scheme–work or leisure?

The scale of the problem

In spite of the efforts of some residents to improve life in their own neighbourhoods many estates and parts of inner cities have remained desperately deprived. Many of the problems – unemployment, low quality, unpopular housing and poverty – are too big for residents to tackle successfully on their own. That the government needs to be involved has recently been recognised. Neighbourhood renewal and regeneration has become a priority as part of the New Labour government's plan to attack social exclusion. It is easy to see the scale of what needs to be done by considering the following selection of problems:

PROBLEM	MEANS OF TACKLING THE PROBLEM
– UNEMPLOYMENT	More help for individuals who are unemployed to find work and develop their skills
– LACK OF SKILLS	More training centres in the neighbourhood
– LACK OF BUSINESS	A service to help people in the neighbourhood to set up businesses and become self-employed
– HOUSING	Giving people in the neighbourhood more say
– LACK OF COMMUNITY	Encouraging and training people in the neighbourhood to become 'social entrepreneurs'. Encouraging religious organisations to become more involved in regenerating the community. Changing the benefit rules so that they do not discourage voluntary work.
– ANTI-SOCIAL BEHAVIOUR	The authorities should be tougher in using their powers – anti-social tenants should be evicted.

Figure 78 Solving the problem of deprived neighbourhoods.

Rural community?

The idea of community was developed in connection with the way in which people in rural areas lived or appeared to live. It helped sociologists to express the differences between rural life and city life. Today those differences seem less obvious. Stories in the media about the high levels of crime, poverty, and unemployment in rural areas, of the depression and desperation of many who live there challenge the image of the countryside as a cosy place apart. Such stories make rural areas appear like the inner city with grass, trees and cows.

Today many experiences are shared by city dwellers and those living in the countryside. TV is a major source of entertainment and information for both. The National Curriculum is taught to both city and village children who both go to university. Urban and rural areas are no longer remote from each other. Widespread car ownership has enabled those living in towns and cities to spend leisure time in the countryside and those living in the countryside to shop and seek entertainment in cities and towns.

The economic basis of rural life has changed and is changing. Tourists from the towns and cities have become a vital source of income. Fields have become camping sites, farm labourers' cottages have become holiday accommodation. Village shops stock goods aimed at the visitor rather than at locals. Farmers have become business people. Some of the differences between urban and rural life may be disappearing.

Other changes have perhaps made it more difficult for the rural community to survive. Many houses in villages today are owned by newcomers or 'outsiders'. These may be professional or business people who have bought a weekend or holiday home. They may be people who retired to the village in middle age or who commute from the village on a daily basis to a job in a city. Although the newcomers may become attached to the village the basis of their attachment may differ from that of the 'locals'. A farmer or local haulier may want, for example, to erect a building to house livestock or another wagon. The countryside is their place of work. A newcomer might object to the building because it spoils the view. The countryside, for the newcomer, is a place to enjoy. The children of the locals may not be able to buy houses locally because newcomers can offer more money. Such differences, or conflicts of interest, could weaken the spirit of community. On the other hand, opposition to the newcomers might strengthen the relationships between the 'locals':

FEATHERS ARE FLYING: RESIDENTS OF A MID-WALES VALLEY ARE FIGHTING AGAINST THE ANNUAL SLAUGHTER OF PHEASANTS

The social make-up of the countryside has changed dramatically over the last few decades and the acceptance of traditional field sports is being challenged.

The farmers who own the mountain and have sold or leased the shooting rights see it as a way of supplementing their income during troubled times. The majority of people who live around the mountain are against it. They, apart from a dry stone waller, do not work on the land. They are teachers, artists, engineers and business people: quite a few are retired.

Some of the protesters have lived here all their lives, some are recent incomers; they all want good relations with their neighbours but they all share a passion for this place, threatened by what they see as a cruel sport which they fear puts them, their families and wildlife at risk. 'Townie, get back to the city where you come from. You English are all the same,' yell a van load of beaters at an impromptu protest against a recent shoot.

This irony is not lost on the Cwm Mountain residents who are protesting against the shooters coming out from the English cities. A protestor was warned off land she has walked on for many years by a gamekeeper. 'He effed and blinded at me and said I should go back where I came from – but I've been a teacher in my local school for 30 years.'

Adapted from an article by Paul Evans in *Guardian Society*, Wednesday, 4 October 2000

Rural communities have also been threatened by the use of the motor car. Those who own a car become less dependent on the facilities close at hand. They will travel if by so doing they can buy things more cheaply or do more interesting and exciting things in their leisure time. Village shops and pubs lose custom and may be forced to close. The village may also lose its bank and post office. The part that the village is able to play in the lives of local people is reduced. Contact between local residents may decline and as a result the sense of belonging to a particular place and of being part of its community may diminish.

LIVING IN THE COUNTRY TODAY: SOME FACTS

- more than half of all rural parishes now have no school or shop.
- 400 sub-post offices closed in 1999.

- 80% of villages have no General Practitioner.
- 60,000 agricultural jobs have disappeared in the last ten years.

Adapted from *The Guardian*, 2 August, 2000

Villages are losing the heart of their communities as up to 20 rural pubs close down each month, the Campaign for Real Ale warned yesterday.

From an article by Chris Gray in *The Independent*, Monday, 31st July 2000

Use of the motor car has changed policing. A local 'bobby' living in the village is no longer needed. The relationship between the police and those being policed may change. Policing today is more often performed by 'outsiders' who live somewhere else and who relate to the people in the village in terms of their job rather than on the basis of being one of them.

The increased use of cars may also have increased the lifestyle differences between rich and poor, and the young and elderly in rural areas. With more people travelling by car, there has been a reduction during the last 30 years in the number of bus passengers. Since from the 1980s onwards making a profit has become more important than providing a service to the community rural bus services have been reduced drastically. For many who live in the country-side public transport is no longer available. A car has become essential to get to work, to the shops, to school. For those who are poorly paid or on benefits running a car will take a large chunk of their income. Those unable to drive may face a real deprivation. Perhaps the relation-ships between the well off and the poor, the fit and the less fit in rural areas might be a useful indicator of the extent to which community still exists. Do those who have and can, help those who have not and cannot?

There is no simple answer to the question – 'How different is life in the city from life in the countryside?' Today, city and countryside seem less distant from each other. The social and economic problems found in cities are also found in the countryside. There is a continuous flow of people, either as visitors or on a more permanent basis, from one to the other. These are good grounds for expecting life in urban and rural areas to have become quite similar and for doubting whether it is still realistic to think that 'city people' have different attitudes and act differently from 'country people'.

One distinctive aspect of country life has, in recent years, become an important political issue – hunting animals with dogs. For some who live in the countryside chasing and killing animals is a vital part of their life which they believe is under threat. Hostility to hunting is seen by some 'country people' to indicate a lack of understanding by urban dwellers about life in the country. To organise campaigns to defend hunting and other rural interests the Countryside Alliance was established. Many of those living in the countryside see themselves as having dis-tinctive interests which are worth fighting for.

Doing it our way

In this book we have tried to show how sociologists might look at and explain the ways in which people live in modern Britain. Most of us live our lives within the framework of institu-tions which we discover are there as we grow up. We find ourselves in families, in schools; we find ourselves trying to earn a living within an economic system and being citizens within a political system; we find ourselves part of a class structure and, perhaps, a member of a religion. As individuals we play a very limited part in the making of these institutions. For the most part we try to fit in. We go along with what they demand of us. Even when we do make choices, the alternatives are limited. After a few drinks, the man singing 'My Way' in the pub may appear to be saying something significant. Getting up for the early shift, however, we remember: the truth is that most of us do it 'their way'.

At the same time many people have dreams. Often as we live our lives we think that it should not really be like this. Social life becomes a compromise. We 'get by', 'do our best', are 'no worse than the others'. We balance what we believe our lives should be like with what we know or suspect they must be like. Parents, for example, try to raise their children to become good, nice people – but not so good or nice that they will be put upon by others. Motorists will say that they hate the thought that they are damaging the environment but ask – 'What can I do? Public transport is hopeless.'

Dreams and ideals are more important to some than to others. Some people are not prepared to live within society in a conventional way whilst hoping for it to change. A conventional lifestyle may seem to require too many compromises. They would feel themselves hypocrites and lacking integrity if their life involved the wastefulness, competitiveness, materialism, triviality and brutality so prevalent in modern Britain. Joining with others of like heart and mind might make possible the creation of a community or commune within which members could live in harmony with their dreams and ideals.

There are many such communities and communes in Britain today. Some may be formed by a small number of people buying a large house or pair of large houses in a city or town. Others may involve a much larger number of people on a farm or in a large house in the country. Some may be organised to enable the members to live by their religious values. In others, more secular principles – respect for the 'natural' environment, vegetarianism, communism – are the basis on which community life is built. In all, however, sharing, collective decision-making and co-operation are vital elements of community life. Contact and interaction with society outside the community can be considerable or minimal.

The members of some communities have jobs in the wider society. Other communities support themselves by selling what is collectively produced within the community. Some communities 'keep themselves to themselves,' but others are happy and keen to influence the way in which people in the wider society live by setting an example.

These communities perhaps represent a quiet challenge to those of us who live in the wider society. They allow us to glimpse an alternative social life – a social life constructed on the basis of a set of principles with which those who live the life agree. In such societies members can perhaps claim realistically – 'We are doing it our way.'

Glossary

Birth rate   the number of live births in a year per 1000 people in the population.

Death rate, mortality rate the number of deaths in a year per 1000 people in the population.

Dependent, dependency   A population will contain people able to work to support themselves economically and those not. The latter group have to depend therefore on the former group.

Dependent age group – An age group containing people not able to gain an income from work: these below the minimum school leaving age or above the retirement age, for example.

Burden of dependency – This phrase draws attention to the economic support which those who are working must give to those who are not if the latter are to survive. If the proportion of the population which is working goes down and the proportion of the population not working goes up the burden of dependency will increase. Those working might then be required, for example, to pay more tax.

Migration   migration takes place when people move to live, on a permanent basis, somewhere else. This may be in another country – **International migration**. Alternatively, it may be within the country in which the person is already living – Internal migration.
Immigration refers to movement into a new country or area.
emigration refers to movement out of a country or an area.

Rural   rural means to do with the countryside. A rural area is one which is not built up. The largest collection of houses in a rural area is probably a village.

Suburbanisation   this takes place when more and more people live in suburbs – that is, in areas of housing built on the outskirts of cities or large towns.

Urban   urban means to do with towns and cities.
an urban area is a 'built up' area.
an urban lifestyle is a lifestyle of people living in 'built up' areas.

Urbanisation   this takes place when the proportion of the population which lives in large population centres increases. It suggests that more people live in cities and large towns and fewer people live in rural areas.

Deurbanisation suggests a movement in the opposite direction.
Deurbanisation takes place when the proportion of the population living in cities and large towns decreases. Cities and large towns lose population and villages and small towns gain population.

Index